Tax Administration 2021

COMPARATIVE INFORMATION ON OECD AND OTHER ADVANCED AND EMERGING ECONOMIES

OECD
BETTER POLICIES FOR BETTER LIVES

Please cite this publication as:
OECD (2021), *Tax Administration 2021: Comparative Information on OECD and other Advanced and Emerging Economies*, OECD Publishing, Paris, *https://doi.org/10.1787/cef472b9-en*.

ISBN 978-92-64-87076-5 (print)
ISBN 978-92-64-42408-1 (pdf)

Tax Administration
ISSN 2308-7331 (print)
ISSN 2307-7727 (online)

Photo credits: Cover © Bruce Rolff/Shutterstock.com.

Corrigenda to publications may be found on line at: *www.oecd.org/about/publishing/corrigenda.htm*.

Preface

The 2021 edition of the Tax Administration Series, like its predecessors, provides comparative information on the performance of advanced and emerging tax administrations globally and seeks to draw out the main underlying trends and challenges they face. The purpose and value of the Tax Administration Series, first published in 2004, is to assist administrations, governments, taxpayers and other stakeholders in considering how and where improvements might be made in the efficiency and effectiveness of tax administration, including through learning from what others have done.

Looking outwards in this way has never been more important, as the world has changed in unforeseen ways since the publication of Tax Administration 2019, bringing new challenges as well as new solutions. The COVID-19 pandemic has affected the lives of many people around the world, and governments have taken a wide range of actions to support their citizens and businesses during this difficult period. At the same time, due to restrictions on physical contact, the pandemic has accelerated the digital transformation of governments, and tax administrations are at the forefront of this development.

One of the trends identified in this and recent editions of the Tax Administration Series has been the increase in e-administration over recent years, with tax administrations investing significant resources in moving more of their processes online. This has not only enhanced service delivery, reduced burdens and improved compliance, but it has also made us more resilient. Leading a tax administration myself, it became immediately clear to me that digital service delivery would be of significant help in our response to the crisis. Our digital readiness allowed us to quickly take on new roles to assist in the provision of wider government support and ensured that we could continue to deliver effective services to taxpayers during times of social distancing and remote working.

While the data contained within this 2021 edition of the Tax Administration Series relates to fiscal years ending in 2018 and 2019, and the impacts of the pandemic will be seen in the data contained in future editions of the series, the country examples included in this edition illustrate how swiftly tax administrations responded to this new environment. In many cases, administrations had to deal with an increased demand for digital service channels, and introduced enhancements to existing services or developed new services, often at great speed. As Chair of the OECD Forum on Tax Administration and Commissioner of the Canada Revenue Agency, I would like to congratulate my own staff as well as my fellow Commissioners and their staff for their exceptional work during the pandemic.

Finally, I would like to thank tax administration staff involved in producing this engaging and informative report and the OECD Secretariat for its work in preparing and drafting this edition. I would encourage you to make good use of this report as the information within it will assist us as we begin to emerge from the pandemic, helping us all understand our strengths and weaknesses, and the challenges that we face individually and in common. This will not only allow us to consider what we might do in our own jurisdictions but also help us to identify where tax administrations can collaborate to improve our services to taxpayers across the globe.

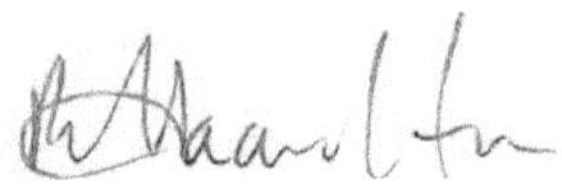

Chair of the OECD Forum on Tax Administration

Commissioner of the Canada Revenue Agency

Foreword

Tax Administration 2021 is the ninth edition of the OECD Centre for Tax Policy and Administration's comparative information series. First published in 2004, the primary purpose of the Tax Administration Series (TAS) is to share information that will facilitate dialogue on the design and administration of tax systems.

This edition of the TAS provides internationally comparative data on aspects of tax systems and their administration in 59 advanced and emerging economies, and includes performance-related data, ratios and trends up to the end of the 2019 fiscal year. While the data does not include impacts of the COVID-19 pandemic, the examples highlight some of the initial responses developed by tax administrations.

The publication also presents the results of the third round of the International Survey on Revenue Administration (ISORA). The ISORA survey is a multi-organisation survey to collect information and data on tax administration. It is governed by four partner organisations: the Inter-American Center of Tax Administrations (CIAT), the International Monetary Fund (IMF), the Intra-European Organisation of Tax Administrations (IOTA) and the OECD. As with the previous survey round, the Asian Development Bank (ADB) also participated in ISORA along with the four partner organisations.

This report was approved by the Committee on Fiscal Affairs on 19 July 2021 and prepared for publication by the OECD Secretariat.

Acknowledgements

The OECD has produced the Tax Administration Series, its comparative information series on tax administration, since 2004. Since that time the publication has grown in terms of its coverage, influence and importance and is now widely recognised as an authoritative source of information on tax administration around the globe.

The 2021 Tax Administration publication presents the results of the third round of the International Survey on Revenue Administration (ISORA), which was launched in September 2020. It would not have been possible without the direct support and help of a large number of people, particularly the staff in the 59 tax administrations that provided data and country examples, reviewed content and responded to feedback and questions on the data and text that form the basis of the publication.

The principal authors of the publication were Oliver Petzold and Paul Marsh both Advisors in the OECD's Forum on Tax Administration (FTA) Secretariat. Management and analysis of the data was undertaken by Oliver Petzold. Authoring support was provided by Peter Green, Head of the FTA Secretariat and Vegard Holmedahl, Advisor in the FTA Secretariat.

The authors are also thankful to Raffaele Articolo, also from the FTA Secretariat, for his assistance in the production of the publication, as well as the work of the Co-ordination team at the OECD Secretariat, in particular Sonia Nicolas and Nicolás Barra, and the OECD Centre for Tax Policy and Administration's Communications team.

Finally, the authors would like to thank the members of the ISORA Technical Working Group for their co-operation and joint efforts on the work of the ISORA survey as well as the IMF for setting up and running the Revenue Administration Fiscal Information Tool (RA-FIT) which is used to collect the ISORA data online.

Table of contents

Figures

Tables

Boxes

Abbreviations and acronyms

ABR	Australian Business Registrar
ACRA	Accounting Compliance and Regulatory Authority
ADAD	Automatic Dialling Announcing Device
ADB	Asian Development Bank
ADI	Integral Digital Administration
ADP3G	Application Development Platform 3rd Generation
AEAT	Agencia Estatal de Administración Tributaria (Spain)
AEOI	Automatic Exchange of Information
AI	Artificial Intelligence
AIAA	Algorithmic Impact and Alignment Assessment
ALEF	Agile Law Execution Factory
APA	Advance Pricing Agreement
API	Application Programming Interface
ATO	Australian Taxation Office
AUD	Australian Dollar
BIM	Building Information Modelling
BPI	Business Presence Indicator
BREEAM	Building Research Establishment Environmental Assessment Method
CAD	Canadian Dollar
CERB	Canada Emergency Response Benefit
CIAT	Inter-American Center of Tax Administrations
CIT	Corporate Income Tax
COTS	Commercial-Off-The-Shelf
CRA	Canada Revenue Agency
CRS	Common Reporting Standard
CSV	Secure Verification Code
DFA	Digital Financial Asset
DGFiP	Directorate Générale des Finances Publique (France)

DMS	Debt Management Services
DN	Demand Note
DSP	Digital Service Provider
eIDAS	Electronic Identification Authentication and Trust Services
EPR	Electronic Payment Receipts
EU	European Union
EUR	Euro
EWSS	Employment Wage Subsidy Scheme
FATCA	Foreign Account Tax Compliance Act
FCInet	Financial Criminal Investigation Network
FTA	Forum on Tax Administration
FTE	Full Time Equivalent
FTS	Federal Tax Service (Russia)
FPS	Federal Public Service (Belgium)
GBP	British Pound
GDP	Gross Domestic Product
GEL	Georgian Lari
GRS	Georgia Revenue Service
GST	Goods and Services Tax
HITS	Hasil Integrated Tax System
HMRC	Her Majesty's Revenue and Customs (United Kingdom)
HNWI	High Net Wealth Individual
HUF	Hungarian Forint
ICAP	International Compliance Assurance Programme
ICT	Information and Communication Technology
IIA	Institute of Internal Auditors
IMF	International Monetary Fund
IOTA	Intra-European Organisation of Tax Administrations
IRAS	Inland Revenue Authority of Singapore
IRBM	Inland Revenue Board of Malaysia
ISORA	International Survey on Revenue Administration
IT	Information Technology
ITA	Israel Tax Authority
JITSIC	Joint International Task Force on Shared Intelligence and Collaboration
LIT	Low-Income Taxpayer

LO	Liaison Officer
LTO/P	Large Taxpayer Office/Programme
MAP	Mutual Agreement Procedure
ML	Machine Learning
MNE	Multinational Enterprise
MSD	Ministry of Social Development (New Zealand)
MSF	Ministry of Social and Family Development (Singapore)
MTD	Making Tax Digital
NDI	National Digital Identity
NLP	Natural Language Processing
NPR	National Population Register
NRICS	National Registry of Identification and Civil Status
NTA	Norwegian Tax Administration
NTA	Netherlands Tax Administration
NTCA	National Tax and Customs Administration (Hungary)
OA	Operational Analytics
OBR	Office for Budget Responsibility
OCR	Optical character Recognition
OECD	Organisation for Economic Co-operation and Development
PAYE	Pay-As-You-Earn
PIT	Personal Income Tax
QTSP	Qualified Trust Service Providers
RA-FIT	Revenue Administration Fiscal Information Tool
RAM	Relationship Authorisation Manager
RETA	Risk Exposure and Tolerances Assessment
SII	Servicio de Impuestos Internos (Chile)
SII	Immediate Supply of Information
SSC	Social Security Contribution
SSO	Single Sign On
SOL	SUNAT Operaciones en Línea
STA	State Taxation Administration (China)
STA	Swedish Tax Administration
START	Simplified Tax and Revenue Technology
SUNAT	Superintendencia Nacional de Aduanas y de Administración Tributaria (Peru)

TAS	Tax Administration Series
TCMM	Tax Compliance Management Model
TNA	Transaction Network Analysis
TWSS	Temporary Wage Subsidy Scheme
UDP	Unified Data Platform
UK	United Kingdom
USD	United States Dollar
VAT	Value Added Tax
VIES	VAT Information Exchange System
VIVI	Virtual Visits for Auditing
WHT	Withholding Tax

Reader's guide

Tax Administrations covered by the report

Tax Administration 2021 is the ninth edition of the OECD Centre for Tax Policy and Administration's comparative Tax Administration Series (TAS). The primary purpose of the series, which commenced in 2004, is to share information that will facilitate dialogue among tax officials on important tax administration issues, and to identify opportunities to improve the design and administration of their systems.

This edition of the series provides internationally comparative data on various aspects of tax systems and their administration in 59 advanced and emerging economies. It covers all 53 jurisdictions that are members of the OECD's Forum on Tax Administration (FTA). In addition, it includes information on the non-FTA jurisdictions that are members of the European Union (i.e. Bulgaria, Croatia, Cyprus, and Malta) as well as Morocco and Thailand (which increases the report's geographical coverage).

Data gathering process and reporting

The publication presents the results of the third round of the International Survey on Revenue Administration (ISORA) which was launched in September 2020. The ISORA survey is a multi-organisation international survey that collects national-level information and data on tax administration. It is governed by four partner organisations: the Inter-American Center of Tax Administrations (CIAT), the International Monetary Fund (IMF), the Intra-European Organisation of Tax Administrations (IOTA) and the OECD. As with the previous survey round, the Asian Development Bank (ADB) also participated in ISORA 2020 along with the four partner organisations.

2018 ISORA survey review and feedback

Following the completion of the 2018 ISORA survey, the ISORA partners reviewed the data produced by the survey, and engaged with participating administrations to gather feedback on the survey process.

The review showed that some questions suffered from a low response rate, and that the quality of the responses was mixed in some areas. Administrations confirmed that the data was useful for international comparison, for preparation of missions to other jurisdictions and for briefing documents. They did note that the survey process was complex and time consuming, and that it was desirable for the data to be timelier.

Changes to the survey structure and process

Considering this, the ISORA partners agreed that there was a need for a major revision before launching ISORA 2020, in order to reduce burdens on tax administrations in completing the survey and to improve the quality of responses. The survey review determined that responses to many questions would remain unchanged between years, thus opening the opportunity for splitting the ISORA survey into two parts:

1. ***Questions to be asked in an annual ISORA survey.*** These questions mainly focus on the operational performance of tax administrations, allowing the annual survey to be significantly reduced in size and easier to complete. This also allows data to be made available more quickly to participating administrations. The 2020 ISORA survey falls in this category.
2. ***Questions to be asked every four-five years.*** These are mainly questions where responses are less likely to change between survey iterations. A significant number of questions included in previous ISORA surveys would fall within this category. Understanding that responses to those questions are more likely to remain stable over a longer period, means they need to be asked less frequently, thus reducing administration's annual burden of completing the survey. The ISORA partners are still in the process of designing this supplementary ISORA survey.

Survey management

The 2020 ISORA survey collected data for fiscal years 2018 and 2019. Survey information was gathered online using the IMF's Revenue Administration Fiscal Information Tool (RA-FIT). Participation was voluntary and more than 150 administrations completed the survey. Each partner organisation, and the ADB, supported participants, by assisting them with the completion of the ISORA survey, based on an upfront agreed allocation key. The 59 administrations included in this publication corresponds to the group of administrations supported by the OECD.

While all data contained in the publication has been subject to a high-level review by the OECD, neither the OECD nor any other partner organisation formally validated the data. As a result, all data included in the publication should be considered as self-reported by the administrations concerned.

Data available to the public

Historically, the OECD makes all ISORA data for TAS participants publicly available through the TAS and its data annex. Similarly, the ADB published jurisdiction-level ISORA data for its members through its publication *A Comparative Analysis of Tax Administration in Asia and the Pacific: 2020 Edition* (Asian Development Bank, 2020[1]). In addition, the other ISORA partners, did the following:

- IMF published in aggregated form. See the IMF publication *ISORA 2016: Understanding Revenue Administration* (Crandall, Gavin and Masters, 2019[2])
- CIAT published selected data points. See, for example, the CIAT publication *Overview of Tax Administrations: structure; income, resources and personnel; operation and digitalization: ISORA* (Díaz de Sarralde, 2019[3]).

Going forward, this will change. Starting with the 2020 survey, all ISORA data will be made available to the public on the RA-FIT data portal (https://data.rafit.org/). It is expected that all data is made available at the jurisdiction-level towards the end of 2021.

Data comparability

TAS 2021 includes performance-related data, ratios and other information for the fiscal years 2018 and 2019. In certain areas, it also uses data from the previous ISORA rounds to show trends for the period 2014 to 2019.

However, as noted above, the changes in the ISORA process meant that the 2020 survey has been reduced significantly in size when compared to the 2018 version. In addition, following the review, a number of changes were made to questions to improve clarity and data quality. Therefore, care needs to be taken when comparing results from ISORA 2020 with ISORA 2016 and 2018, and the wording of survey questions compared whenever relevant. The survey questions can be accessed on https://data.rafit.org/ under "Publication/ Links".

As a result of the changes to the ISORA survey, TAS 2021 may not comment on certain data points that were covered in the 2019 edition of the TAS (OECD, 2019[4]). For those data points, the 2019 edition remains the most recent source.

Also, it should be noted that statistical data is often subject to revisions after publication. As a result, some data may not correspond to what has been published by administrations. For example, it may be that opening balances of a specific year (t) may not correspond to closing balances of the preceding year (t-1) that were published in earlier editions of this publication.

Even more care should be taken when comparing ISORA data with data gathered through pre-ISORA surveys, i.e. data included in the sixth and prior editions of the TAS. When the ISORA survey was initially created and at the request of survey participants, the four partner organisations made considerable effort to agree and document a range of words and terms used in the survey and their meaning. While this has improved data integrity and comparability between administrations, comparisons with pre-ISORA data may be limited as definitions may now exist for terms not previously defined, or in some instances, have changed.

Further, in relation to combined tax and customs administrations, it should be noted that the data in this publication refers to the tax administration activities of such administrations. The data may therefore not be directly comparable with key performance indicators published by them as these indicators may include both tax and customs related data.

Publication structure

The series examines the fundamental elements of modern tax administration systems and uses data analysis and examples supplied by tax administrations to highlight key trends, recent innovations, examples of good practice, and performance measures and indicators.

Structure

The main body of the publication is structured around nine chapters: (i) an introduction followed by chapters on (ii) responsibilities and revenue collections; (iii) registration and identification; (iv) assessment; (v) services; (vi) verification and compliance management; (vii) collection; (viii) disputes; and (ix) budget and workforce.

The publication also contains two annexes:

- Annex A contains the tables with the ISORA 2020 survey responses provided by tax administrations[1] which form the basis of the analysis in this report:
  - The first set of tables contains a number of indicators derived from the data submitted via the ISORA survey (tables starting with "D"). The formulae and data points used for calculating the indicators are shown below each of these tables.
  - The second set of tables contains the raw ISORA 2020 survey data. Those are the tables starting with "A".
  - The last table holds external data points that were used to calculate some of the D-table indicators. This table starts with "E".
- Annex B has the details of the administrations that participated in this publication.

Tables and figures

The tables and figures in the publication are all accompanied by hyperlinks (OECD StatLinks) that direct readers to corresponding MS Excel spreadsheets containing the underlying data. These links are stable and will remain unchanged over time.

Typically, the source notes below the figures in the main body of the publication refers readers to the underlying data that is contained in the Annex A. In some cases, they may refer to previous editions of the TAS.

Symbols and abbreviations that are used in the data tables are explained at the bottom of each table. The reader should note that where no data is shown for a specific jurisdiction in a table this is primarily due to the question not being applicable to a particularly jurisdiction or an opening question to a sub-section of the survey being answered in the negative and, therefore, the jurisdiction did not have to answer the follow-up questions.

Forum on Tax Administration

Readers wishing to find out more about the OECD's work on tax administration should go to www.oecd.org/tax/forum-on-tax-administration/.

Caveat

Tax administrations operate in varied environments, and the way in which they each administer their taxation system differs in respect to their policy and legislative environment and their administrative practice and culture. As such, a standard approach to tax administration may be neither practical nor desirable in a particular instance. Therefore, this report and the observations it makes need to be interpreted with this in mind. Care should be taken when considering a country's practices to fully appreciate the complex factors that have shaped a particular approach. Similarly, regard needs to be had to the distinct challenges and priorities each administration is managing.

Notes

1. For Japan, given that it publishes its currency figures in millions the currency figures included in tables have had added a suffix of "000" in order to fit the survey requirements that currency figures needed to be provided in thousands.

References

Asian Development Bank (2020), *A Comparative Analysis of Tax Administration in Asia and the Pacific: 2020 Edition*, Asian Development Bank, Manila, http://dx.doi.org/10.22617/TCS190240. [1]

Crandall, W., E. Gavin and A. Masters (2019), *ISORA 2016: Understanding Revenue Administration*, International Monetary Fund, Washington, www.imf.org/en/Publications/Departmental-Papers-Policy-Papers/Issues/2019/03/07/ISORA-2016-Understanding-Revenue-Administration-46337 (accessed on 1 September 2021). [2]

Díaz de Sarralde, S. (2019), *Overview of Tax Administrations: structure; income, resources and personnel; operation and digitalization. ISORA*, Inter-American Center of Tax Administrations (CIAT), Panama City, www.ciat.org/overview-of-tax-administrations-structure-income-resources-and-personnel-operation-and-digitalization-isora-santiago-diaz-de-sarralde-miguez-spanish-only/?lang=en (accessed on 1 September 2021). [3]

OECD (2019), *Tax Administration 2019: Comparative Information on OECD and other Advanced and Emerging Economies*, OECD Publishing, Paris, https://dx.doi.org/10.1787/74d162b6-en. [4]

Executive summary

Together the 59 tax administrations participating in the ninth edition of the OECD's Tax Administration Series (TAS 2021) collect net revenues of EUR 12.3 trillion (2019). They are large and complex organisations employing around 1.8 million staff. They deal with the tax affairs of around 860 million personal income tax and corporate taxpayers who contact tax administration in excess of 500 million times via telephone, in-person, e-mail or paper and generate more than 1.1 billion contacts through online taxpayer accounts. The tax administrations do this on a combined operating budget amounting to around EUR 79 billion, equivalent to less than 1% of total revenues collected.

Figure 0.1. **Key figures related to the administrations covered in this publication**

Jurisdictions covered by this publication	59
Staff employed	1 840 000
Audits/verifications conducted	23 000 000
In-person enquiries	110 000 000
Telephone calls received	330 000 000
Number of active PIT and CIT taxpayers	860 000 000
Contacts via online taxpayer account	1 160 000 000
Number of tax returns (PIT, CIT and VAT) received	1 350 000 000
Operational budget (in EUR)	79 000 000 000
Collectable arrears debt at year-end (in EUR)	750 000 000 000
Total arrears at year-end (in EUR)	2 100 000 000 000
Net revenue collected (in EUR)	12 300 000 000 000

Note: The figures are based on data obtained through the 2020 ISORA survey. They are minimum figures as not all administrations were able to provide information for all data points. Figures typically relate to the fiscal year 2019. Data for fiscal year 2018 was used where 2019 data was not available.

Source: OECD Secretariat calculations based on data included in this publication.

The TAS, which provides comparative information in 75 tables covering tax administration performance and profile data, is intended to assist tax administrations in consideration of where further improvements might be made, as well to enhance wider public understanding as to the scale and nature of global tax administration. This edition of the TAS also attempts to draw out, from both the data provided through the International Survey of Revenue Administrations (ISORA) and the more than 100 examples received from tax administrations, the most significant changes that tax administrations are dealing with. It focuses in particular on how tax administrations are increasingly looking at the opportunities to take more proactive approaches to influencing and managing compliance as well as the challenges they face in adapting to the changing resource requirements.

Accelerating digital transformation

Previous editions of the TAS have shown a significant trend towards e-administration with increasing uptake of online filing of tax returns as well as online payments and the full or partial prefilling of tax returns. This edition of the TAS shows how that trend has continued and digital contact channels now dominate interactions with taxpayers and the number of administrations using or developing mobile applications continues to grow. For example, tax administration reported more than 1.1 billion contacts via online taxpayer accounts.

Many tax administrations have also reported that their services are now starting to integrate machine learning and artificial intelligence into their contacts with taxpayers. This is allowing services to run closer to 24/7, often driven by the use of digital assistants such as "chatbots", tools already used by around 50% of the administrations covered in this publication.

This transformation is also helping to bring important improvements in taxpayer compliance, and there are growing signs that the pace of digital transformation is accelerating even more. This edition of the TAS highlights three broad themes within digital transformation relating to engaging with taxpayers, compliance risk management and the impact of the COVID-19 pandemic.

Engaging with taxpayers

The core of tax administration's work to manage voluntary compliance remains the supporting of positive compliance attitudes of taxpayers to reporting their taxable income and paying tax. This report highlights the different ways that administrations are looking to influence such attitudes, including through:

- **Initiatives to improve the accessibility of the tax administration**: Tax administrations are continually looking to improve their reactive processes, be they online, in-person or by telephone, to make it easier for taxpayers to contact the tax administration. In turn, this helps taxpayers understand their obligations and how to meet them. This is increasingly being supplemented by proactive outreach through education campaigns.
- **The growing importance of digital identity and verification**: As tax administrations deliver more and more of their services digitally, the importance of digital verification and digital identity is growing. Tax administrations are leveraging their expertise and data sets to not only give taxpayers access to tax administration services, but also wider government systems.
- **Collaboration with third party service providers**: Embedding services and processes in the natural systems used by taxpayers in their daily lives and businesses is a growing trend among tax administrations. While this helps to improve tax compliance, it also reduces administrative burdens and frees up time that owners can use to grow their businesses. As these forms of collaboration become more common and sophisticated, tax administrations are starting to take strategic approaches to managing and providing support to service providers, including allowing access to tax administration internal systems through application programming interfaces (APIs).

Compliance risk management

Compliance-by-design approaches have been in place for many years for salaried personal income taxpayers through pay-as-you-earn withholding and reporting by employers. These systemic arrangements, adopted by almost all tax administrations, have helped maximise compliance for this significant part of the tax base. The increasing availability and sharing of data is now allowing such approaches to expand to cover other sources of income and other classes of taxpayers, including through the prefilling of corporate income tax and value-added tax returns.

Digital techniques are also allowing tax administrations to take a more preventative approach to risk management. By seeking to intervene at earlier stages in taxpayer processes, they can prevent non-compliance happening rather than having to uncover it after tax returns have been filed. This can be seen in:

- **The increasing use of large and integrated data sets**: This has fuelled a significant increase in the use of analytics tools and techniques to improve risk management and help design-in compliance. More than 80% of tax administrations report using data science and analytical tools to manipulate electronic data from third parties, including other tax administrations, as well as internally generated electronic data to guide their compliance work.
- **The increasing use of artificial intelligence and machine learning**: Close to 75% of tax administrations report that they are using or that they are in the implementation phase for the future use of cutting-edge techniques to exploit data in ways that reduces the need for human intervention. Although still at an early stage in general, this is already creating efficiencies which is freeing up resources to be deployed into other areas.
- **A continuing emphasis on segmenting taxpayers to create personalised interactions**: The power of data analysis is allowing tax administrations to create more tailored approaches to their interactions with taxpayers. This may be through one-to-many channels or for managing specific groups of taxpayers such as large business taxpayers, or High Net Wealth Individuals (HNWIs). Examples provided by tax administrations now show increasing segmentation in other areas, helping to guide more focused compliance and service actions and interventions, including at the individual level.

Impact of the COVID-19 pandemic

Whilst the data contained within this edition of the TAS relates to fiscal years ending in 2018 and 2019, and is thus pre-pandemic, the country examples highlight some of the swift changes that tax administrations have made in their operating model in response to the new environment. These examples show how the trend towards digital transformation has been accelerated by the COVID-19 pandemic as restrictions on movement and interaction forced core tax administration services to be delivered digitally.

Tax administration's close connections to citizens and businesses, their long experience of operating at scale and skills in handling extensive data sets have led many governments to turn towards tax administrations to assist in the provision of wider government support measures. Administrations' experience of constantly adapting to the digitalisation of the economy, be it to meet taxpayer expectations or managing emerging compliance risks, has helped the in responding rapidly to the pressures of the COVID-19 pandemic.

Many tax administrations report that the pandemic forced them to implement these digital solutions at great spped, often accelerating pre-existing implementation timelines. It is a sign of the resilience of tax administrations that these solutions were delivered without significant impacts on their core services and, as shown by anecdotal evidence, has led to high satisfaction rates among taxpayers and other stakeholders. Future editions of the TAS will examine these impacts in more detail.

Tax administration resources

Budgetary constraints continue to impact tax administrations. While the majority of them report increasing operational expenditures in absolute terms, this may not show the whole picture as administrations are dealing with increased responsibilities, the pressures of technology change and the changing structure of their workforce. There is also significant variation in the amount of operational and capital expenditure on information and communication technology. While this may often be due to different sourcing and business approaches, it also raises the question as to whether expenditure levels in some cases may be somewhat low to support the demands for more sophisticated services and the ongoing digital transformation. The importance of preparing existing staff for the challenges ahead continues to be recognised with many administrations creating new approaches for staff training and development, including moving training programmes into a virtual environment allowing staff to upskill at any time and from anywhere.

International cooperation

Underpinning much of the work of tax administrations is the continuing growth in the scale and scope of international co-operation. This report highlights how international co-operation and the sharing of knowledge between tax administrations has never been more important as countries undergo significant change at significant cost and as the digitalisation of the economy increasingly transcends national borders.

Tax administrations are working together to effectively implement key OECD/G20 BEPS actions and in the development of the OECD's multilateral International Compliance Assurance Programme, where taxpayers and tax administrations work co-operatively and multilaterally in close to real-time to undertake risk assessment and assurance of key international tax risks.

The growth in the use of big data, which allows for increasingly sophisticated analysis, is enhanced by the international exchange of information which has also increased markedly. The adoption of automatic exchange of information through Country-by-Country reporting, the exchange of rulings and through the OECD/G20 Common Reporting Standard has made large volumes of data on cross border activities available to tax administrations, which is increasing the effectiveness of existing domestic activities.

Chapter 1

Introduction

This chapter provides an overview of the content of the 2021 edition of the OECD's Tax Administration Series.

Previous editions of the OECD's Tax Administration Series (TAS) have set out how, over time, tax administrations have evolved to respond to the changing environment in which they operate. This 2021 edition continues to set out that evolution, and provides further insight into how tax administrations are:

- enhancing their technological capabilities to deliver new ways of serving their customers
- becoming more collaborative and integrated with wider government
- building their skills in exploiting the large data pools they hold
- creating new compliance management techniques
- enhancing their collection capabilities.

The rapid pace of the wider technological changes taking place across the economy, including the expansion of social media, mobile platforms, cloud computing, big data technologies and advanced analytics techniques are all creating new opportunities and expectations for citizens and businesses.

Tax administrations around the globe are implementing new digital technologies to enhance taxpayer service quality, reduce operational and compliance burdens and increase revenues. In addition to the ongoing incremental improvement of the core tax administration functions, there are also increasing signs of transformation towards a more fundamental change in the nature of tax administration. This concerns a more system-wide compliance management approach in which tax administrations try to closely engage with the natural systems that taxpayers use to manage their business, engage in transactions and communicate in order to reduce errors, minimise burdens and increasingly build-in tax compliance.

Box 1.1. **Country examples: Digital transformation**

Malaysia – The Digital Transformation of Inland Revenue Board of Malaysia (Hasil Transformation)

The Inland Revenue Board of Malaysia (IRBM) has launched a new digital transformation initiative known as Hasil Transformation. A major component of this project is the development of the "Hasil Integrated Tax System" (HITS), which enables IRBM to better manage its data resources and implement end-to-end processes using real-time information. Other parts of this project are increasing data analytics capabilities to deliver more effective compliance risk management, using behavioural insights to improve compliance (for example, pre-filled returns) and provide a better customer service experience.

The main characteristic of HITS is a simplified, seamless, real-time information flow, based on a secure platform. Using HITS, IRBM has re-engineered its workflow processes to deliver improved automation and greater productivity throughout the system. The development is based on the latest innovations and user-friendly web technologies and is fully integrated with various end-to-end processes in IRBM.

IRBM is integrating its tax system to reduce 70% of batch job processing and at the same time fully utilise resources. The advantages of the digital transformation initiatives in IRBM are:

- providing a better customer experience, effectively reducing administration costs by making it easier for taxpayers to fulfil their obligations
- transformation of processes and capability to tackle the highest tax risks
- development of an interactive platform as a One Stop Centre that supports interactive two-way communication between tax administration and taxpayers
- improving compliance activities by identifying areas where resources should be directed by undertaking real-time risking.

Box 1.1. Country examples: Digital transformation *(continued)*

Netherlands – Agile Law Execution Factory (ALEF)

Adapting existing IT systems to a change in tax legislation is extremely difficult and requires significant amounts of time and money. To tackle this, the Netherlands Tax Administration (NTA) has been working on a new method of software development, combining the need to be agile, with the ability to clearly track the legislative basis for any change.

The core element for this new way of working at NTA is ALEF. ALEF is a management environment for the creation, testing and management of decision rules. ALEF was developed using an open source language workbench.

In ALEF, rules can be specified in a controlled natural language, called RegelSpraak, and the logic of these RegelSpraak specifications can immediately be tested using the pre-existing examples cases in ALEF. Using ALEF these rules can then be automatically transformed into a decision service for automated decision making. An example of a calculation rule in RegelSpraak is shown in Figure 1.1.

Figure 1.1. **Netherlands: Example of a calculation rule in RegelSpraak**

Rule result tax amount first bracket 01
valid from 2014
legal source: https://wetten.overheid.nl/jci1.3:c:BWBR0011353&hoofdstuk=2&afdeling=2.3&artikel=2.10a&z=2021-01-01&g=2021-01-01

The result tax amount of the first bracket of a taxpayer must be set at the maximum value of A and B
If he meets all of the following conditions:
- applying table 2.10a is equal to 'no'
- the taxable income Box-1 minus the applied different rate is smaller or equal to the MAXIMUM AMOUNT TO WHICH THE FIRST DISC IS APPLIED

The following applies:
A is rounded down to whole euros (the taxable income Box-1 minus the applied different rate times the PERCENTAGE OF THE FIRST DISC)
B is 0.

Source: Netherlands Tax Administration (2021).

The use of ALEF and RegelSpraak has resulted in the following benefits:

- Since each RegelSpraak rule is traceable to its legal source, it is easy for a legal expert to validate the rule against the legislation it is based on.
- The effort to analyse the impact of legislative changes is reduced. When legislation is changed, the impacted rules are easily traceable.
- RegelSpraak rules are readable by all. This makes it possible eventually to explain the logic that is used to process tax applications to tax payers.
- RegelSpraak rules are technology independent. In the future these rules can be used to generate code for other platforms, without a need to change the specifications.
- The quality of specifications improves, reducing risks of misunderstanding or misinterpretation.

See Annex 1.A. for a link to supporting material.

Sources: Inland Revenue Board of Malaysia (2021) and Netherlands Tax Administration (2021).

These developments also mean that there are new opportunities to administer taxes, support taxpayers and enhance compliance, enabled by the new technologies and tools. In particular, many tax administrations are starting to explore the benefits that machine learning and artificial intelligence can bring to their work. Tax administrations are also starting to explore how technology can "embed" a tax administration into the support that third parties, such as software suppliers, provide to taxpayers. Partnerships and collaborations in this way can help both the service provided to taxpayers and ensure that compliance is embedded upstream.

Box 1.2. **Canada: Embedding artificial intelligence into a tax projects**

To support its experimentation with and responsible deployment of artificial intelligence (AI) solutions, the Canada Revenue Agency (CRA) continues to strengthen AI governance and oversight. As part of the governance suite, the CRA put in place the Directive on Artificial Intelligence in January 2021.

This Directive sets out the roles and responsibilities within the CRA and is supported by the mandatory use of the Algorithmic Impact and Alignment Assessment (AIAA) Tool. The AIAA has a three-fold purpose. The AIAA is open by design, it serves as a central repository of AI projects at the CRA that all users can view to enhance horizontality. To assess alignment and to potentially focus our resources, the AIAA categorises AI projects based on CRA's core business priorities.

Finally, the AIAA tool evaluates and calculates an associated risk score to AI projects in the development and production phases, including mitigations and ethical considerations. Through the metric collected, the AIAA allows for the CRA to report on what is happening where. As AI governance continues to mature and respond to the rapidly evolving AI context, so will the AIAA tool evolve to support informed oversight and promote transparency.

Source: Canada Revenue Agency (2021).

These changes can be seen in the data collected through the 2020 version of the International Survey on Revenue Administration (ISORA). Alongside this, the tax administrations covered in the TAS were invited to provide examples of innovative practices that they are undertaking to help achieve their objectives. They have provided a rich source of over 100 examples, covering a wide range of topics. While these examples do not form a basis for comparison across tax administrations in the same way as the data points can, they do add more colour to the data, and tell a forward-looking story of the strategic direction of travel of tax administration.

It goes without saying that the COVID-19 pandemic provided a shock to that direction of travel. The pandemic has catalysed a lot of change within tax administrations, and they have had to adapt to new ways of working both within the administration and with taxpayers. Some have also taken on roles that may not traditionally been part of a tax administration as they leverage their core skills and data sets to provide economic support. Throughout this edition of the TAS, there are statistics and examples that show some of the rapid innovation that the pandemic has forced tax administrations to adopt. Future editions of the TAS will inevitably highlight more of this change as the world moves to the post pandemic phase, and tax administrations consider the longer-term changes the pandemic has brought about.

Regardless of the pandemic, the core tasks of a tax administration remain, namely the timely and accurate collection of tax owed, to fund public services. ***Chapter 2*** explores this topic in more detail, and provides statistics on the range and value of taxes that administrations are responsible for. Central to effective collection is the work of tax administrations to ensure that all relevant taxpayers are registered. ***Chapter 3*** sets out the work of tax administrations in this field, and also shows how this expertise is being leveraged to support wider governmental objectives on digital identity.

Chapter 4 looks at the tax assessment function, which includes all activities related to processing tax returns and payments. This chapter examines the use of e-channels for filing and paying, and outlines administrations' efforts to provide pre-filled returns, and levels of on-time return filing and payment.

A common theme in this edition of the TAS is how tax administrations are becoming increasingly proactive in their management of the compliance environment, using the data generated by digital transformation to get insight into compliance work, and use it as the basis for innovative approaches.

Box 1.3. **Chile: Using data to strengthen compliance approaches**

In Chile, the Tax Compliance Management Model (TCMM) aim to provide structured, reliable and timely data to the entire tax administration (the Servicio de Impuestos Internos, SII), which can then be used to improve risk analysis, leading to better decisions. The main tools are:

- ***Risk Catalogue***: This takes the tax heads managed by the SII, splits them into different components and then uses the existing management information to categorise and identify various risks, which is then visualised it in a simple and interactive way.
- ***Prioritisation and Consolidation Process Dashboard***: This process is at the heart of the TCMM, where the input are the analyses related to the tax system, and the output are treatment actions for the taxpayers considered most at risk. Given the complexity and volume of the information available, the simplicity of the tool to display the information stands out, accounting for anomalous situations, that are new or of institutional interest.
- ***Gap Map***: Shows the measurement of the levels of compliance with the main tax heads. It visualises the taxpayer's risk classification, segments of institutional interest, size of the taxpayer, geographic location, and many other indicators.

Source: Chile – Servicio de Impuestos Internos (2021).

Chapter 5 highlights how tax administrations are using sophisticated technological approaches to encourage "self-service" by taxpayers. This is part of a more fundamental change whereby tax administration becomes a seamless process, with non-compliance increasingly "designed out" which helps reduce burdens. ***Chapter 6*** explores this further and picks out how compliance approaches are changing to tackle those who fail to meet their obligations.

Chapter 7 explores how tax administrations manage the collection of outstanding debt, and examines the features of a modern tax debt collection function. These functions are essential to maintaining high levels of voluntary compliance and citizen's confidence in the overall tax system. This chapter also provides examples of approaches applied by administrations to prevent debt being incurred. However, inevitably, disputes between taxpayers and tax administrations do arise, and ***Chapter 8*** considers those processes that safeguard taxpayer rights and ensure appropriate checks and balances exist on the exercising of tax powers by administrations.

Underpinning all this work, is the resources that are devoted to tax administrations, and the dedicated workforce that delivers this work. ***Chapter 9*** provides information on the resources that tax administrations have at their disposal, and the trends in that. It also sets out the challenges administrations are managing in increasing their capability while managing a workforce that in general terms is reducing in size and on average is getting older. These challenges have been compounded by the pressures of the pandemic, and this chapter begins to consider the longer term impact of those pressures. Again technology has a role to play in delivering efficiencies for the workforce.

Annex 1.A

Links to supporting material (accessed on 1 September 2021)

- Box 1.1 – Netherlands: Link to a video explaining the Agile Law Execution Factory: https://youtu.be/yo_tCMYT0H0

Chapter 2

Responsibilities and collection

This chapter looks at the performance of tax administrations in discharging their primary role of collecting taxes as well as the responsibilities given to them during the COVID-19 crisis. In this respect, it provides information on the aggregate net tax revenues collected as well as other key figures related to the activities of the administrations covered in this publication.

Introduction

The primary purpose of a tax administration is the collection of tax revenue on behalf of citizens to fund public services. Over time, many tax administrations have also been tasked with other responsibilities. Confidence in the proven ability of tax administrations to deliver complex administrative processes on a large scale undoubtedly plays a significant part in such decisions and was probably also a key driver behind many governments giving their tax administrations additional responsibilities to assist in the provision of wider support measures during the COVID-19 crisis. This chapter provides an overview of the net tax revenues collected as well as some other key figures related to tax administration performance, and looks at the wider role tax administrations are playing.

Responsibilities of tax administrations

With few exceptions, jurisdictions have unified the collection of direct and (most) indirect taxes within a single body for tax administration; see Table 2.1. for the revenue types for which the tax administrations participating in this publication have responsibility.

Table 2.1. **Revenue types for which the tax administration has responsibility, 2019**

Percent of jurisdictions that have responsibility for the following revenue types

Personal income tax	Corporate income tax	Value added tax	Excises - domestic	Motor vehicle taxes	Real property taxes	Wealth taxes	Estate, inheritance, gift and other taxes	Other taxes on good and services	Social security contributions	Customs
98	100	93	59	53	42	20	53	47	41	42

Source: Table A.1 Revenue types for which the administration has responsibility and employer withholding.

However, as found in previous editions of the Tax Administration Series (TAS), governments have given tax administrations other areas of responsibility (including shared responsibility in some areas) in addition to their traditional tax roles.

Typically these may be to provide financial benefits to taxpayers (for example, welfare-type benefits) or to collect loans or debts owing to government (for example, student loans or child support). In other situations, the role/function is less directly related to the tax system, for example oversight of certain gambling activities or population registries.

Box 2.1. Norway: The modernised National Population Register is faster, simpler and open 24/7

The modernised National Population Register offers more digital services

Over the last couple of years, the Norwegian Tax Administration (NTA) has developed a new, modernised National Population Register (NPR). The new register, which was ready in the autumn of 2020, offers more information, easier access and new digital services. Citizens can now handle many important tasks online, for example they can send notifications of birth, provide change of address notifications with the Norwegian postal service, obtain "Certificates of no impediment" for marriages, and give notifications of death.

Box 2.1. **Norway: The modernised National Population Register is faster, simpler and open 24/7** *(continued)*

Over 2 000 public and private sector organisations use information from the NPR. Now enterprises can receive a notification every time something changes in the NPR, and they can look up or extract various information. The modernisation allows these enterprises, in turn, to offer inhabitants of Norway new and user-friendly digital services.

Better ID management

The NPR has also been prepared to improve ID management. All people that stay in Norway, whether they were born in Norway, or moved permanently or temporarily to Norway, are issued with either a permanent national identity number or a temporary identification number called a D number. In the new register, third country nationals moving to Norway can also provide their personal information once, in one place.

Access to own information

In March 2021, the NTA opened up digital access to the NPR for citizens. Anyone over 18 years old may now log in and view their own information and report back to the NTA if there are any errors. This is critical as an accurate NPR protects the rights of all inhabitants of Norway by ensuring they receive the correct services from public authorities.

Source: Norwegian Tax Administration (2021).

While the 2020 version of the International Survey on Revenue Administration (ISORA) did not have detailed questions on additional responsibilities, interested readers may wish to consult Chapter 2 of the previous edition of this series *Tax Administration 2019* (OECD, $2019_{[1]}$) for a more detailed overview of the wider roles of tax administrations.

With the emergence of the COVID-19 crisis, the wider responsibilities of tax administrations were taken to new levels, as many governments turned towards tax administrations to assist in the provision of support to citizens and businesses. Many of these new responsibilities often go beyond the functions normally provided by tax administrations and, typically, involved:

- **financial assistance**, providing support to citizens and businesses, whether closely targeted or on a more universal basis
- **providing services**, using tax administration staff or services to support wider government COVID-19 responses
- **information assistance**, supporting government by sharing information or using the administration's data analytics capabilities.

The reasons for turning towards tax administrations during the COVID-19 response included that tax administrations have:

- pre-existing close connections with citizens and businesses
- long experience of operating at scale
- skilled and specialised staff that interact with citizens on a daily basis
- extensive data sets along with the analytical resources and experience in handling and sharing data.

Box 2.2. Country examples: Assisting citizens and businesses during the COVID-19 pandemic

Canada Emergency Response Benefit (CERB)

The Government of Canada introduced the Canada Emergency Response Benefit (CERB) to provide temporary financial support to employed and self-employed Canadians who were directly impacted by the COVID-19 pandemic.

It was important to make the CERB application process simple, quick and convenient for Canadians, and to provide the financial support needed as quickly as possible. The Canada Revenue Agency (CRA), as the administrator of the benefit, used agile programme management to manage risk and accelerate the delivery of the support payments. Applications to the CRA were received through the secure online portal, by automated phone lines, or through call centre agents as, for the first time, the CRA did not have a paper option. During the first week, there were 3.5 million applicants alone, and those who chose the direct deposit option received payments within 5 business days. Those who were eligible received CAD 2 000 every 4 weeks (equivalent to CAD 500 weekly) between 15 March 2020 and 26 September 2020. After 27 September 2020, the Government of Canada transitioned most Canadians who still needed income support, to a simplified Employment Insurance programme.

The CRA designed, developed, and delivered the CERB application in a virtual environment in a purely agile and iterative manner from end-to-end. The programme had a strong communications strategy, and leveraged partnerships within the CRA as well as with external partners within the Government of Canada and financial institutions. The result was the successful delivery of billions of dollars in emergency response payments to Canadians.

Ireland: Wage subsidy scheme

In Ireland, the Temporary Wage Subsidy Scheme (TWSS) was an emergency measure to deal with the impact of the pandemic on the economy. It met the urgent Government objective of getting much needed assistance to employers and employees, while retaining the link between them in anticipation of economic recovery. Additionally, the scheme reduced the burden on the Department of Social Protection as it dealt with other COVID-19 related payments.

The introduction of real-time reporting under the Pay-As-You-Earn (PAYE) system in January 2019 meant that when the pandemic escalated in March 2020, Revenue could quickly re-engineer the PAYE system, in conjunction with the Payroll Software sector, to rapidly support impacted employers and employees. Employers claimed the wage subsidy scheme through their payroll reporting and Revenue made payment to the employer within a day of receiving their payroll submission. This process ensured there was no additional administrative burden on employers and the subsidy could be processed and paid to employers before they made payments to employees, thus providing much needed cash flow to businesses and retaining the link between employers and employees.

Revenue's headline result for 2020 outlines the level of support provided to business and employees through the wage subsidy scheme:

Temporary Wage Subsidy Scheme
EUR 2.8 billion in subsidies
664 500 employees
66 600 employers

Box 2.2. Country examples: Assisting citizens and businesses during the COVID-19 pandemic *(continued)*

The use of the real time reporting regime for the wage subsidy scheme also ensures that Revenue can partake in real time compliance activities to ensure any non-compliance is identified and tackled quickly.

TWSS was paid as a non-taxable amount to employees and these amounts were incorporated into the employees preliminary end of year tax calculation, which was made available to all employees on the 15 January 2021. Any under-payments arising are collected, interest free, by reducing an employee's future tax credits from 2022 over a maximum period of 4 years.

Revenue operated the TWSS from 26 March 2020 to 31 August 2020 when it was replaced by a new scheme called the Employment Wage Subsidy Scheme (EWSS).

Singapore: Proactively assisting taxpayers in financial difficulties

The Inland Revenue Authority of Singapore (IRAS) reviewed the frameworks for assisting taxpayers in financial difficulties so as to proactively render assistance, in particular to those individuals who are receiving financial assistance from the Ministry of Social and Family Development (MSF).

The review focused on two key areas:

- ***Inter-agency collaboration with MSF***: IRAS obtained data on taxpayers receiving financial assistance from MSF. Using this data, IRAS' enforcement division could:
  - calibrate actions such as proactively reaching out to taxpayers and offering assistance in tax payment or suspending enforcement actions
  - exercise more care and empathy when officers engage with these taxpayers.

Apart from identifying relevant taxpayers through data from MSF, IRAS also developed an internal classification of "Low-Income Taxpayer (LIT)" for more empathetic handling.

- ***Instil greater empathy in interactions with taxpayers***: For taxpayers receiving financial assistance from MSF or who meet the LIT classification, IRAS can provide greater payment flexibility, including longer instalment plans, deferring payment or even remission of tax. The framework is applied across all types of tax owed by the individual on the basis that if an individual does not have the ability to pay for one tax, they are unlikely to have the ability to pay other taxes.

Sources: Canada Revenue Agency (2021), Ireland – Office of the Revenue Commissioners (2021) and Inland Revenue Authority of Singapore (2021).

Figure 2.1 summarises the additional responsibilities for the 32 administrations covered by the 2021 OECD note *Tax Administration: Digital resilience in the COVID-19 environment* (OECD, 2021[2]). It shows that supporting other government agencies in providing financial assistance and providing information to other government agencies are the most common new responsibilities, followed by providing financial assistance.

The 2020 OECD note *Tax Administration Responses to COVID-19: Assisting Wider Government* (OECD, 2020[3]) also captures some of the new responsibilities taken on by tax administrations and describes a number of implementation challenges and potential mitigation strategies. It also briefly describes the opportunities that may arise from taking on these new responsibilities including the use of agile development and implementation processes for new digital services and tools.

Close to half of the administrations covered by that 2020 note indicated that they had changed their IT development methods to be able to deliver IT solutions at speed, with the vast majority referring to agile project development practices when developing or enhancing existing IT solutions during the COVID-19 crisis. Generally, all administrations that changed their project management practices considered this to be a success and plan to use these new practices in the future (OECD, 2021[2]).

Figure 2.1. **Additional responsibilities for tax administrations as a result of COVID-19 and the related economic recovery and/or stimulus measures**

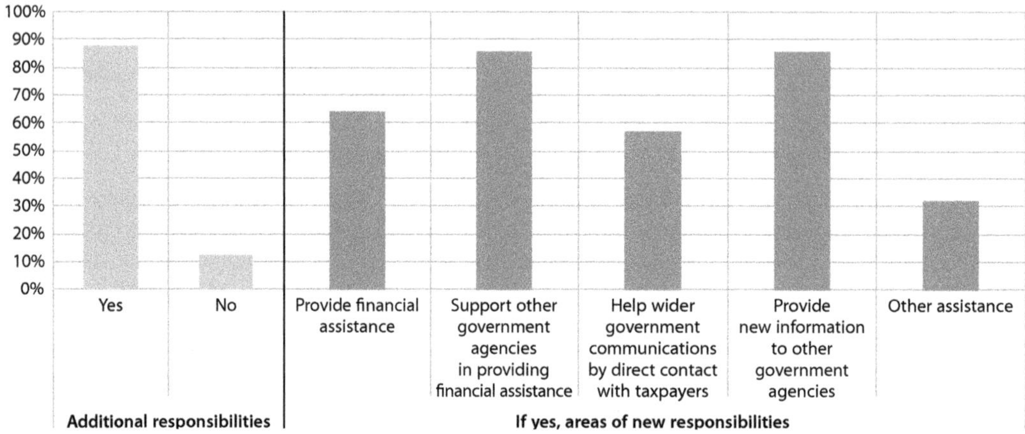

StatLink http://dx.doi.org/10.1787/888934271131

Source: OECD (2021), "Tax Administration: Digital Resilience in the COVID-19 Environment", *OECD Policy Responses to Coronavirus (COVID-19)*, https://doi.org/10.1787/2f3cf2fb-en.

Box 2.3. Country examples: Assisting other parts of government

Australia: Sharing Business Data to support disaster recovery and economic recovery efforts

Throughout 2020, the Australian Taxation Office (ATO), through the Australian Business Registrar (ABR) provided core business data to Local, State and Federal Government Agencies to help them to connect with businesses in their community:

- During the Australian Bushfires in 2019/20, ABR data was used by 55 government agencies to plan, prioritise and respond to the crisis. In the aftermath of the disaster the business data was used to identify affected businesses in and around the fire scars which urgently needed government funding and support.
- For COVID-19 response, ABR and taxation data was supplied to Australian State government departments to assist with pandemic modelling through cross matching of job type and/or location for those workers and businesses with the highest risk factors for contraction, transmission and movement of COVID-19.

ABR data is available to eligible government agencies through multiple channels and is mainly accessed through the ABR Explorer, a free reporting and analytical tool. This tool allows government users to self-serve data and create custom queries, visualise and overlay

Box 2.3. **Country examples: Assisting other parts of government** *(continued)*

business locations using satellite maps, convert business data into graphs and charts to observe historical trends, either by postcodes or business type. By allowing the downloading of pre-defined ABR data sets it allows users to incorporate the data within their own various systems. This means that smaller agencies without mature data and IT capabilities are able to conduct simple but effective queries using common office computer programmes to discover and detect shifts and understand trends in communities and business activities.

New Zealand: Portal for information sharing with the Ministry of Social Development

In New Zealand, Inland Revenue supported the Ministry of Social Development (MSD) to deliver the Wage Subsidy as part of the New Zealand Government's response to COVID-19. While the Wage Subsidy is administered by MSD, it relies on data held by Inland Revenue to verify applications.

Initially, supporting Wage Subsidy applications was very labour-intensive. Inland Revenue shared information with MSD which meant many applications were automatically approved. For those that could not be, Inland Revenue set up a toll-free number and answered more than 350 000 calls from MSD staff in the period to 30 June 2020.

To support the extension of the Wage Subsidy, in early June 2020 Inland Revenue made a portal available enabling MSD staff to access the information they needed themselves directly from Inland Revenue's systems, with appropriate security permissions.

The portal benefits customers as their applications can be processed more quickly, benefits MSD through an improved ability to administer the subsidy, and benefits Inland Revenue as it receives far fewer calls from MSD to validate information.

Sources: Australia Taxation Office (2021) and New Zealand Inland Revenue (2021).

Revenue collections

This section looks at the net revenue collection of tax administrations as well as a number of other key figures related to their activities. It is worth noting that this is based on 2018 and 2019 fiscal year data. The COVID-19 related impact on revenue collections is not reflected but will be seen in next year's publication.

Net collections by tax administrations averages 20% of jurisdiction GDP

Through its Global Revenue Statistics Database (see www.oecd.org/tax/tax-policy/global-revenue-statistics-database.htm) the OECD generally seeks to publish internationally comparable data on the tax revenues of its members as well as a number of other jurisdictions for all levels of government. As the information contained in the Global Revenue Statistics Database reports data at a jurisdiction and not an administration level, tax administrations were asked in the ISORA survey to provide a range of information on their revenue collection activity. This information aptly demonstrates the importance of tax administrations to the economies of their jurisdictions.

Net revenue collected by tax administrations participating in this report as a percentage of gross domestic product (GDP) in 2019 ranges from less than 10% to reach more than 30% in the case of Croatia, Denmark, Estonia, Hungary, Latvia, the Netherlands, Norway, Slovenia and Sweden. Average net revenue collected by administrations in this report is 20% of GDP (see Figure 2.2).

Figure 2.2. **Net revenue collected as a percent of gross domestic product, 2019**

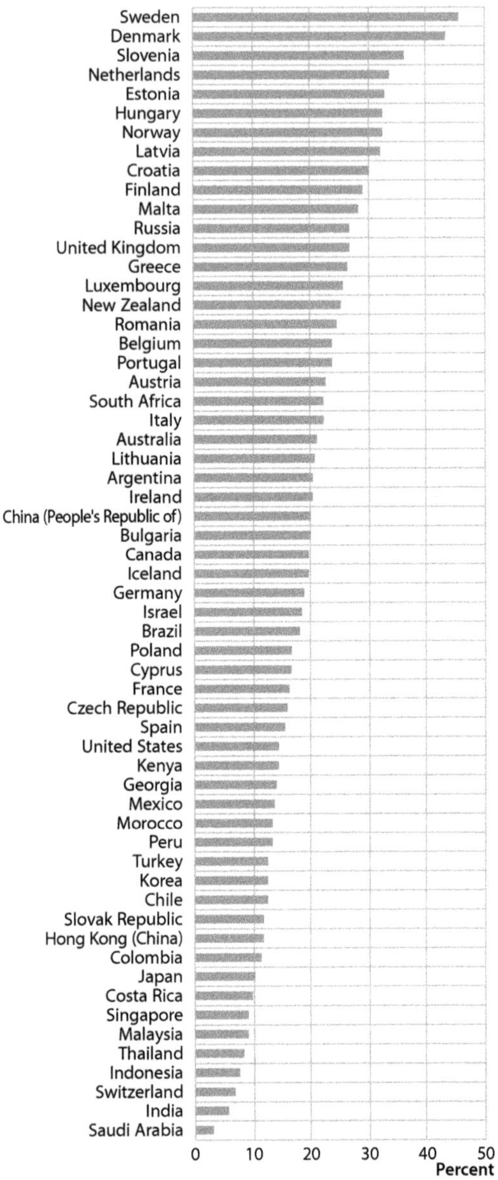

StatLink http://dx.doi.org/10.1787/888934271150

Source: Table D.1 Revenue related ratios.

Figure 2.3. **Net revenue collected as a percent of total government revenue, 2019**

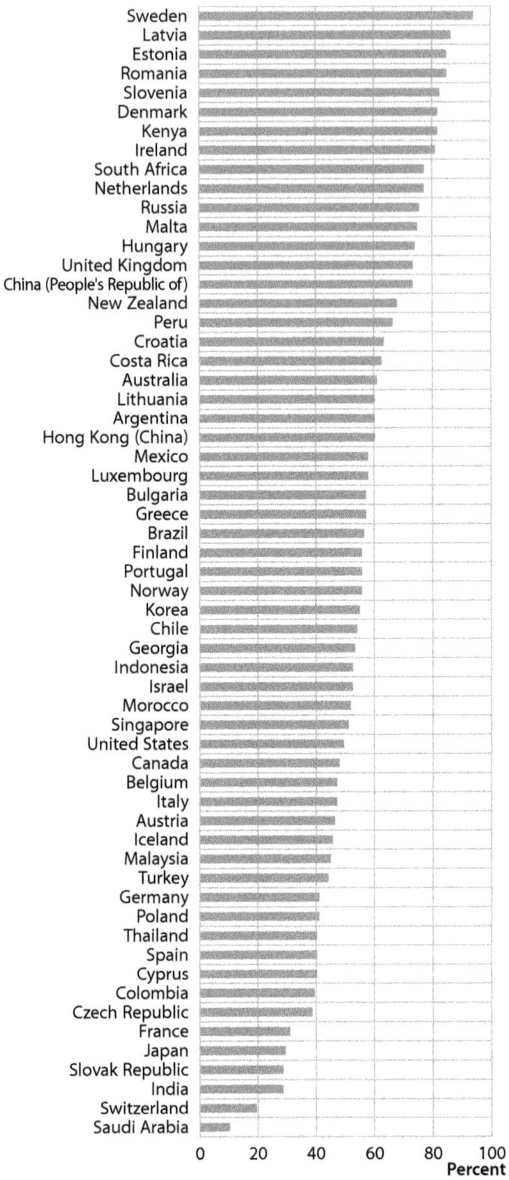

StatLink http://dx.doi.org/10.1787/888934271169

Source: Table D.1 Revenue related ratios.

Net collections by tax administrations averages 56% total jurisdiction revenue

Thirty-eight tax administrations report net revenue collections exceeding more than 50% of total government revenue in 2019, making tax administrations the principle government revenue collection agency in close to two-thirds of jurisdictions covered in this report. Average net revenue collected by administrations in this report is 56% of total jurisdiction revenue (see Figure 2.3.)

Personal income tax accounts for 28% of net revenue collections and is the major tax type collected by around 45% of the tax administrations covered in this report. Value added tax (23%), corporate income tax (20%) and social security contributions (11%) comprise the other major revenue types as reflected in Figure 2.4. In many jurisdictions, social security contributions are not collected by tax administrations and are therefore underrepresented when looking at average net revenue collections for all jurisdictions covered in this publication. Where collected, they are often the predominant source of tax revenue (see Table D.2.)

Figure 2.4. **Average net revenue collections (in percent) by major revenue type, 2019**

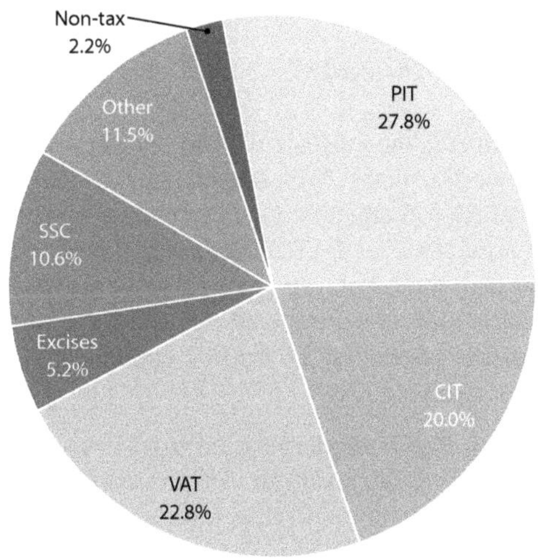

StatLink http://dx.doi.org/10.1787/888934271188

Sources: Tables D.1 Revenue related ratios and D.2 Tax structure and SSC proportions.

Streamlining collections: Withholding at source

Withholding regimes can form part of compliance-by-design approaches which support overall compliance while significantly reducing burdens for large numbers of taxpayers depending on the extent of taxpayer involvement in any post-payment adjustments that might be needed (i.e. where withholding results in under-payment or over-payment of tax). In place of self-reporting and paying, withholding taxes are taxes paid directly to the tax administration, usually by a principal who pays the net income to the recipient (for example withholding by an employer on salary paid to an employee), or by an intermediary between the payer and customer. The most common withholding tax in operation globally is income tax on employment income (so called Pay-As-You-Earn (PAYE) approaches). Other examples include withholding taxes on interest, dividends or royalties. Depending on the underlying tax regime and nature of the payments, withholding can vary from a simple system, at a universal set rate, to a more complex system that is responsive to the customer's wider circumstances.[1]

In addition to minimising burdens, withholding regimes can also reduce misreporting and underpayment as principals or intermediaries responsible for forwarding taxes to the administration have no right over the respective amounts. Of course, there remains scope for failures in such approaches by misapplication of rules or errors by principals or intermediaries where the system relies on them providing information. However, increased automation, greater cross-checking of data and whole of government approaches have the potential to reduce such issues.

To understand the importance of withholding at source for personal income taxes, the survey underlying this publication asked participating administrations to estimate the percentage of total personal income tax withheld by third parties and subsequently paid to the administration. Forty-six administrations that were able to provide this information estimate that 78% of total personal income tax collections were withheld at source (see Table D.18).

Box 2.4. **Ireland: PAYE Modernisation**

PAYE Modernisation delivered the most significant reform of the PAYE system since it was first introduced in 1960. Since 1 January 2019, employers and pension providers are reporting details of employees' and pension recipients' pay and statutory deductions to Revenue every time they are paid. The cornerstone of PAYE Modernisation is the seamless integration of the reporting requirements with the employer's payroll software. These changes have brought about significant efficiencies and improvements in accuracy and transparency for some 180 000 employers and pension providers, 2.6 million employees and pension recipients, and for Revenue.

Employer satisfaction with PAYE Modernisation is reflected in the results of a survey of employers carried out during 2019. For example, 78% of employers agreed that payroll now takes less time, while 80% agreed that payroll runs more smoothly because of the new system.

Employees, through the myAccount portal, have a real time view of their pay and tax details providing transparency that the deductions made by their employers have been reported to Revenue as well as their social insurance contributions for the Department Social Protection. At the end of year, a preliminary end-of-year calculation is made available to every employee to show if they have paid the correct amount of tax for the year. Income tax and social insurance deductions for 2019 reported in real time totalled EUR 31.6 billion for the year, which represented a EUR 178 million surplus on the 2019 target. Revenue actions following the implementation of PAYE Modernisation (from 1 January 2019) directly delivered additional income tax collection of an estimated EUR 52 million from employers in 2019.

Source: Ireland – Office of the Revenue Commissioners (2021).

Outlook: The impact of COVID-19 on revenue collections

As noted in the introduction, the information in this chapter relates to the pre-COVID-19 situation. While information for fiscal year 2020 (the first year where a COVID-19 impact will be visible) will be collected through the ISORA 2021 survey, it can be expected that COVID-19 has had a significant impact on revenue collections in 2020. Reasons for this include:

- **Decrease in economic activity**: COVID-19 related lockdown measures have been introduced by many governments and the forced closure of many businesses will negatively affect the taxable income and sales of many businesses and may cause a temporary increase in business insolvencies and bankruptcies.

- **Increases in unemployment**: the decrease in economic activity may also impact on employment levels as businesses lay-off staff or pause recruitment.
- **Policy support measures**: To support consumption and the health system, many countries introduced temporary reductions in standard and reduced VAT rates. (OECD, 2020[4])
- **Administrative support measures**: Many tax administrations have taken measures to ease the burdens on taxpayers and to support businesses and individuals with cash flow problems or with difficulties in meeting tax payment obligations. Measures introduced include extension of payment deadlines, deferral of tax payments and easier access to debt payment plans and extension of plan duration.[2] While in many cases this may lead to timing differences in the receipt of tax payments due, in some cases the additional debt built up may become unrecoverable.

The report *Revenue Statistics in Latin America and the Caribbean 2021* confirms this (OECD et al., 2021[5]). As part of a special feature, the report looked at the fiscal policy responses to the COVID-19 crisis in Latin America and in this context noted:

> Tax revenues fell precipitously in the first half of the year, while showing some signs of recovery by year's end. Tax receipts for the region's two principal taxes, the VAT and the income tax, contracted sharply in the first half of the year as a result of the fall in economic activity and the extension of tax relief as part of COVID-19 policy packages. In the second half of the year the fall in tax revenues began to gradually revert as countries eased public health measures and taxpayers liquidated liabilities that had been deferred earlier in the year.

Further, an April 2021 report published by the Inter-American Center of Tax Administrations (CIAT) analysed the impact of COVID-19 on revenue collected in twenty-three CIAT member jurisdictions. Based on data provide by its members, CIAT calculates that revenue collection has fallen on average during 2020 by -9.3% (Díaz de Sarralde Miguez et al., 2021[6]).

Notes

1. For further information on the withholding regimes put in place in jurisdictions, please see Tax Administration 2019 (OECD, 2019[1]), Tables A.73 and A.74.
2. For a detailed description of support measures taken by tax administration, please see the 2020 note Tax administration responses to COVID-19: Measures taken to support taxpayers (CIAT/IOTA/OECD, 2020[7]).

References

CIAT/IOTA/OECD (2020), *"Tax administration responses to COVID-19: Measures taken to support taxpayers", OECD Policy Responses to Coronavirus (COVID-19)*, OECD Publishing, Paris, http://dx.doi.org/10.1787/adc84188-en. [7]

Díaz de Sarralde Miguez, S. et al. (2021), *Revenue Report COVID-19 (RRC) Year 2020*, CIAT, www.ciat.org/Biblioteca/Estudios/2021_Revenue_Report_Covid-19_CIAT.pdf (accessed on 1 September 2021). [6]

OECD (2021), *"Tax Administration: Digital Resilience in the COVID-19 Environment", OECD Policy Responses to Coronavirus (COVID-19)*, OECD Publishing, Paris, http://dx.doi.org/10.1787/2f3cf2fb-en. [2]

OECD (2020), *"Tax administration responses to COVID-19: Assisting wider government", OECD Policy Responses to Coronavirus (COVID-19)*, OECD Publishing, Paris, http://dx.doi.org/10.1787/0dc51664-en. [3]

OECD (2020), *Tax policy responses to COVID-19; table with measures takes by countries*, www.oecd.org/tax/covid-19-tax-policy-and-other-measures.xlsm (accessed on 1 September 2021). [4]

OECD (2019), *Tax Administration 2019: Comparative Information on OECD and other Advanced and Emerging Economies*, OECD Publishing, Paris, https://dx.doi.org/10.1787/74d162b6-en. [1]

OECD et al. (2021), *Revenue Statistics in Latin America and the Caribbean 2021*, OECD Publishing, Paris, https://dx.doi.org/10.1787/96ce5287-en-es. [5]

Chapter 3

Registration and identification

A comprehensive system of taxpayer registration and identification is critical for the effective operation of a tax system. This chapter comments on some of the issues that are of significance for registration and identification processes.

Introduction

A comprehensive system of taxpayer registration and identification is critical for the effective operation of a tax system. It is the basis for supporting self-assessment, value-added tax and withholding tax regimes, as well as third party reporting and matching. This chapter comments on five issues of significance in taxpayer registration and identification: levels of registration, registration channels, integration with other parts of government, identity management, and identity across borders.

Levels of registration

The fundamental importance of an effective tax registration system cannot be underestimated. Tax administrations need strong processes to both manage those taxpayers that are "part of the system" and to help them identify those yet to register. Further, they need to be able to monitor and determine actions and interventions to establish any liability to tax for both individuals and corporate bodies, even in systems where filing is not mandatory.

Figure 3.1 provides information on the rate of registered personal taxpayers as a percentage of the total population. The rate would seem highest among those jurisdictions that report using the tax system for purposes other than just tax collection, which includes the management of social programmes.

Figure 3.1. **Registration of active personal income taxpayers as percentage of population, 2019**

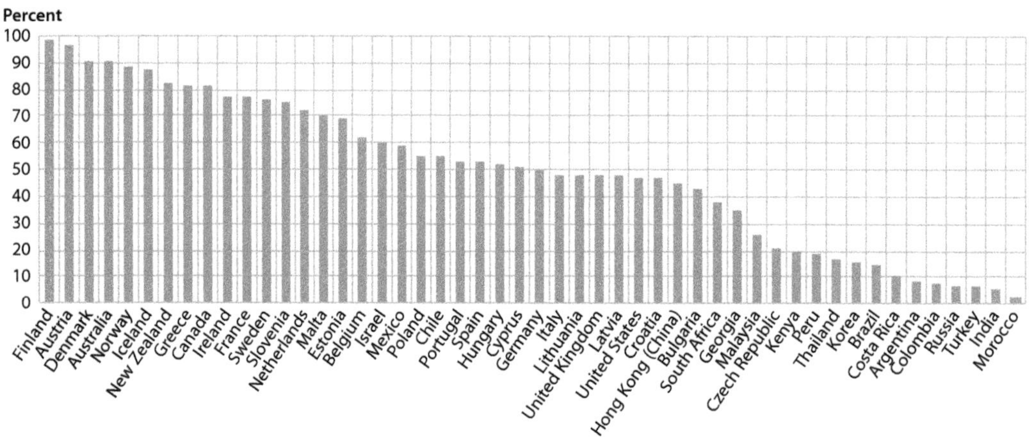

StatLink http://dx.doi.org/10.1787/888934271207

Source: Table D.10 Registration of personal income taxpayers.

Box 3.1. **Georgia: The Employees Registry**

In 2020, the Georgia Revenue Service (GRS) initiated a new programme called "Employees Registry". The programme aims to detect those employers who provide incomplete/misleading information on the number of employees they have. In 2020, the programme was tested on a voluntary basis, and in 2021 it will become mandatory for the employers to fill in Employees Registry.

Under the programme, at the start, termination or suspension of any employment relationship, employers must fill in the Employees Registry, and provide an employee's personal information (ID number, first name/last name, sex, nationality, date of birth and so on) to the GRS. This is done through a personalised, secure webpage. Employers are also obliged to update the registry when an employee's personal information changes.

Through this database, the GRS can provide valuable information to other government institutions as well, such as those eligible for social security payments, data on unemployment rates, and those eligible for COVID-19 related payments.

Source: Georgia Revenue Service (2021).

Registration channels

While the majority of administrations are solely responsible for the system of registration for tax purposes within their jurisdictions, previous editions of this series have shown that in many jurisdictions the registration processes can also be initiated outside of the tax administration through other government agencies (OECD, 2019[1]).

Figure 3.2. **Availability of registration channels for taxpayers, 2019**

Percent of administrations that provide the respective registration channel

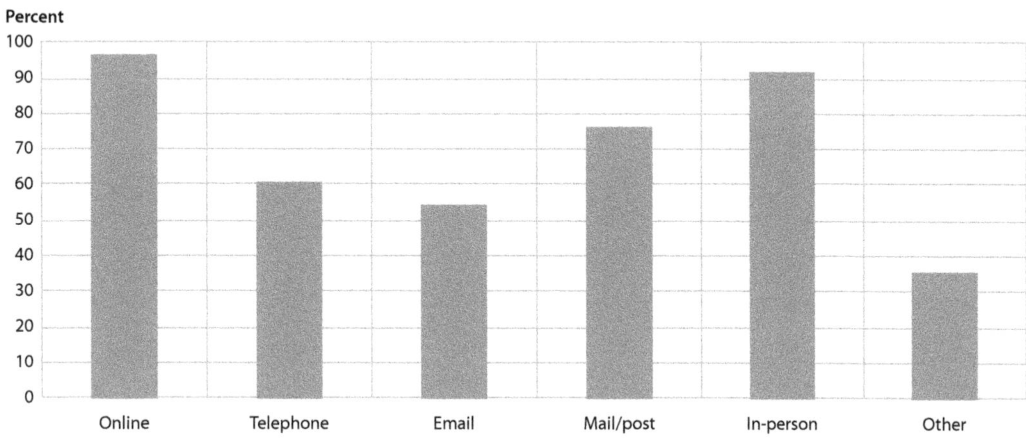

StatLink http://dx.doi.org/10.1787/888934271226

Note: The registration channels may not always be available for all tax types or taxpayer segments.

Source: Table A.39 Registration channels.

In looking at how taxpayers can register, almost all administrations reported they provide more than one channel for taxpayers to use and all but two administrations (i.e. 97%) report that it is possible to register online. Compared to data from the 2017 edition of this series (OECD, 2017[2]) this is a 25 percentage point increase. In fact, online has become the most widely offered registration channel (see Figure 3.2.) and in one jurisdiction, Saudi Arabia, taxpayers can only register online (see Table A.39).

While the underlying survey does not allow identification of whether the online registration channel is available for all tax types or taxpayer segments, it still illustrates the ongoing impact of digitalisation in tax administration processes. Online registration also allows non-residents to register from abroad as shown in the Chilean example included in Box 3.2.

Box 3.2. **Country examples: Use of technology to facilitate taxpayer registration**

Chile: Platform for Registration and Payment of VAT for Digital Services

As of 1 July 2020, remunerated remote services provided by either those not resident in Chile or those non-domiciled in Chile are liable for value added tax (VAT). Accordingly, the Chilean tax administration (Servicio de Impuestos Internos, SII) implemented a Digital Services VAT Platform aimed at foreign taxpayers without residence or domicile in Chile who provide remote services in Chile to individuals or legal entities, and those individuals or entities are not already registered for VAT.

This platform, available in both Spanish and English, was designed to simplify the process of declaration and payment of VAT on digital services by foreign taxpayers. It also gathered all the information related to this new tax in one place.

To access the platform, foreign taxpayers must register through an online process, and subsequently, taxpayers can:

- Declare the number of transactions carried out in a tax period (monthly or quarterly, at the choice of the taxpayer), and the value of the transactions. The tax due is calculated automatically by the system.
- Check their declaration status for the current and previous periods.
- Check their overdue debts, to review whether there are differences between their declaration and payment.
- Review and modify their record.
- Access updated regulations related to the digital tax.
- Access guidance on using the digital service.
- Report activity with those Chilean entities and individuals who have self-identified as VAT registered, and is therefore excluded from this measure.

See Annex 3.A. for links to supporting material.

Sweden: The TAIS project

In 2021, Sweden introduced new legislation extending Swedish tax liabilities to temporary staff having no permanent residency for tax purposes. The registration process already in place for non-Swedish customers was manual, paper-form based, and spikes in volumes created delays, sometimes for several weeks. The process did not compare favourably to the tax registration of Swedish customers, which is digital, fast and seamless. At the same time, there was increased

Box 3.2. **Country examples: Use of technology to facilitate taxpayer registration** *(continued)*

a risk of fraud and error because of the use of temporary non-Swedish staff in labour intensive sectors and the complexity of international tax and treaty rules which might be difficult to understand.

To tackle this, the Swedish Tax Administration (STA) created the TAIS project using artificial intelligence (AI) and machine learning to improve the tax registration process for non-Swedish people. Through this project Sweden aimed to deliver better customer service, respond to spikes in volume more effectively and to better manage the complex legal landscape.

To start, in 2019, STA identified different customer segments, and designed a new digital automated service based around those segments Separate customers profiles of those aiming to defraud were identified (from the experiences of internal tax auditing staff), which was the first time STA had tried to build fraudulent customer segments into a normal service design. This helped STA avoid an over optimistic solution that did not account for fraud and avoidance.

Then, in June 2020, STA launched three e-services based on these segments to help train the new machine learning based (AI) model for risk management. In parallel, capability to manually handle all incoming matters were retained and used to help with the training of the new model, and, and STA implemented AI/algorithm-based support services to help manage non-standardised information (for example: appended foreign government documents and ID documents).

Following this process, the intention is to use the results of the AI-based risk management to allow more customers to register in a completely automated process, in near real time, even though the information required is partly un-structured documentation. STA expect the AI to reach good levels of accuracy in early 2022.

Sources: Chile – Servicio de Impuestos Internos (2021) and Swedish Tax Agency (2021).

Integration with other parts of government

Given the pivotal role that registration and taxpayer identification play in underpinning the tax system and thus the collection of revenues needed to finance government programmes and services, it is a priority for tax administrations to have up-to-date tax registers. As past editions have shown, the large majority of administrations have formal programmes in place to improve the quality of the tax register (OECD, 2019[1]).

Box 3.3. **Brazil: Using blockchain to exchange registry information with other parts of government**

The Brazilian taxpayer registry is the most reliable registry in Brazil. As such, its data is required to be shared with other government agencies, in a secure and cost-effective way. The use of blockchain as a data exchange tool was identified as a way to fulfil these requirements, and it has already been used as a tool for data exchange with customs.

Source: Federal Revenue Service of Brazil (2021).

Therefore, it is unsurprising that other government bodies may wish to use the tax administration register for their own purposes to provide services to citizens or ensure compliance with laws and regulations.

This became even more relevant during the COVID-19 crisis, when a number of governments saw the potential in using information maintained by tax administrations on large parts of the population and economy, such as taxpayer address and bank information, to contact citizens and businesses or to make direct benefit or support payments (OECD, 2020[3]).

Many administrations are also integrating their IT systems with other government agencies to make tax registration part of other actions taxpayers undertake, such as registering for tax at the same time as registering a company or registering the birth of a child; and/or to use the same identifier to allow taxpayers to access other government services.

In this context, many governments are now using, implementing or considering a unique and secure identification system for citizens and businesses to allow for a greater joining-up of systems and services.

Box 3.4. **Australia: Digital identity**

The Australian Taxation Office (ATO) is a contributor to the Australian Government's Digital Identity Programme which aims to make it easier for Australians to securely access government online services. The ATO was responsible for delivering two key components that make up part of the digital identity ecosystem:

- myGovID – the Government's digital identity provider which enablies individuals to prove who they are, via a mobile app, and to log into a range of government online services
- Relationship Authorisation Manager (RAM) – the Government's authorisation service that enables users to be authorised to act on behalf of a business.

myGovID & RAM has been developed and accredited against the Government's Trusted Digital Identity Framework, which sets out the standards, rules and accreditation criteria that govern the identity ecosystem.

Together myGovID & RAM currently provides access to over 70 online services across 30 government agencies. The flexibility and ease-of-use offered by myGovID was key for businesses and tax professionals being able to access COVID-19 economic stimulus payments and adopt flexible or remote working arrangements during the pandemic.

Enhancements to be delivered to myGovID include the ability to leverage biometrics (e.g. face verification and tests to ensure the biometric data is from a living personsolution), which will provide a greater level of confidence in the identity of individuals accessing online services. Other benefits include reduction in the occurrence of fraud and to the burden on our contact centre operations.

This improvement in Digital identity will enable individuals to apply for and automatically receive a Tax File Number online. Until now, this had to be done in person with notification received via mail in 28 days.

Further opportunities to use myGovID are currently underway to make it easier for users to interact with the ATO digitally.

See Annex 3.A. for links to supporting material.

Source: Australian Taxation Office (2021).

Identity management

All tax administrations, whether required to by law or as a matter of sound business practice, put considerable effort into ensuring the security of taxpayer information. In addition to internal processes to prevent unlawful attempts to obtain information and to ensure taxpayers' rights are protected, all administrations have processes to ensure the person they are dealing with is in fact the taxpayer. Increasingly these approaches, which in many instances have now been extended to multi-step authentication, are making use of biometric information, unique to the taxpayer.

Tax administrations face similar challenges to other organisations in dealing with individuals or organisations that may misuse personal information to impersonate taxpayers in order to commit fraud. The on-going and, in many cases, organised nature of this activity is requiring administrations to devote considerable effort to dealing with tax-related identity theft. Details stolen in this way can be used to fraudulently obtain tax or VAT refunds or to access tax credits.

Box 3.5. **Peru: Usage of biometry to identify citizens and get a digital single register of taxpayer numbers**

The Peruvian Tax Administration, SUNAT, wanted to establish a digital single register of taxpayers (SRT) so they could provide remote delivery of the SUNAT Operaciones en Línea (SOL) Key, which is a private electronic signature that allows access to virtual services offered by SUNAT.

Previously, registration was an offline process, because it needed to identify the citizen in person. To improve the service to citizens and to increase efficiency, SUNAT sought a digital verification process to identify the citizen using any online device (such as a cell phone).

That solution was found in remote fingerprint biometric verification, a service provided by the National Registry of Identification and Civil Status (NRICS). In this service, a photograph is taken of the fingerprints, which are uploaded and examined by the NRICS. On validation of the fingerprint, citizens complete their registration, by providing information on their economic activity, contact details and other information necessary to register on the SRT and generate the SOL key.

This service has been implemented first for individuals, so now citizens can obtain their SRT number and their SOL Key in just a few steps.

The implementation was in August 2020, as a 24/7 service, and currently 105 thousand citizens have registered, representing almost 31.6% of individuals registered in the STR. This has generated significant savings for citizens in time and money, and provided an alternative solution when COVID-19 prevented attending SUNAT offices.

See Annex 3.A. for links to supporting material.

Source: Peru – Superintendencia Nacional de Administración Tributaria (2021).

Identity across borders

Once the domain of multi-national businesses and those involved in international trade, increasingly small and medium-sized enterprises and individual taxpayers are now earning income sourced outside their country of residence. The proliferation of online market places and the sharing economy compounds this issue, as it is now easier than ever, for example, to rent out holiday homes or sell goods abroad through online platforms.

Tax administrations are facing a raft of issues in supporting and responding to this growth in cross border activity, including how they manage taxpayer information flows across borders. Previous editions of the tax administration series (OECD, 2019[1]) highlighted two international measures aimed at helping administrations to address these issues:

- The European Union's Electronic Identification Authentication and Trust Services (eIDAS) approach, which was introduced in 2014 and aims at increasing the confidence taxpayers and tax administrations can have in dealing with information flows and being able to manage identity and registration issues across borders.
- The global standard on Automatic Exchange of Information (AEOI) – the Common Reporting Standard (CRS) which together with the United States Foreign Account Tax Compliance Act (FATCA) provides for the exchange of non-resident financial account information with the tax authorities in the account holders' country of tax residence.

Following the 2019 OECD report *The Sharing and Gig Economy: Effective Taxation of Platform Sellers* (OECD, 2019[4]), in 2020 the OECD published a set of Model Rules that when used in legislation require digital platforms to collect information on the income realised by those offering accommodation, transport and personal services through platforms and to report the information to tax authorities. A key objective for the Model Rules is to help taxpayers be compliant with their tax obligations, and to provide a consistent framework to help business provide information to tax authorities. This supports the Model Rules goal of streamlining reporting regimes for tax administrations and platform operators alike. (OECD, 2020[5])

The Model Rules are complemented by a Code of Conduct, published by the OECD Forum on Tax Administration, to facilitate a possible standard approach to co-operation between administrations and platforms on providing information and support to platform sellers on their tax obligations while minimising compliance burdens. (OECD, 2020[6])

Box 3.6. **Spain: Electronic certificates of tax residence**

The current Spanish certificates of tax residency were introduced in 2010 with the possibility to be requested electronically. With this system, the taxpayer gets a pdf document issued by the Spanish Tax Agency (Agencia Estatal de Administración Tributaria, AEAT) that contains a Secure Verification Code (CSV) that guarantees the integrity of the document. The CSV can be verified through the AEAT´s electronic office.

In March 2020, the lock-down caused by the COVID-19 crisis meant it was not possible to process paper forms from other countries that required a physical signature and stamp. In order to find a quick solution to this, AEAT decided to extend the use of the electronic tax residence forms to these purposes. AEAT informed other countries of the solution adopted and added to the certificates an explanatory document in Spanish and English explaining the guarantee offered by the CSV, as well as how to check the validity of the tax certificates issued by the AEAT and presented by taxpayers to other tax administrations.

In summary:

1. The taxpayer requests and obtains the certificate of tax residence through a website on the AEAT's e-Office.
2. When completing the foreign certificate of tax residence the taxpayer includes a notice that the Spanish certification is attached in a separate document (i.e. the Spanish certificate with the CSV).
3. The foreign tax administration can verify the document through a website created for that purpose.

Box 3.6. **Spain: Electronic certificates of tax residence** *(continued)*

The satisfactory results of this approach together with the need to minimise paper handling as a prevention measure against COVID-19 prompted AEAT to maintain the system.

See Annex 3.A. for links to supporting material.

Source: Spanish Tax Agency (2021).

References

OECD (2020), *"Tax administration responses to COVID-19: Assisting wider government", OECD Policy Responses to Coronavirus (COVID-19)*, OECD Publishing, Paris, http://dx.doi.org/10.1787/0dc51664-en. [3]

OECD (2020), *Code of Conduct: Co-operation between tax administrations and sharing and gig economy platforms*, OECD, Paris, www.oecd.org/tax/forum-on-tax-administration/publications-and-products/code-of-conduct-co-operation-between-tax-administrations-and-sharing-and-gig-economy-platforms.pdf (accessed on 1 September 2021). [6]

OECD (2020), *Model Rules for Reporting by Platform Operators with respect to Sellers in the Sharing and Gig Economy*, OECD, Paris, www.oecd.org/tax/exchange-of-tax-information/model-rules-for-reporting-by-platform-operators-with-respect-to-sellers-in-the-sharing-and-gig-economy.htm (accessed on 1 September 2021). [5]

OECD (2019), *Tax Administration 2019: Comparative Information on OECD and other Advanced and Emerging Economies*, OECD Publishing, Paris, https://dx.doi.org/10.1787/74d162b6-en. [1]

OECD (2019), *The Sharing and Gig Economy: Effective Taxation of Platform Sellers : Forum on Tax Administration*, OECD Publishing, Paris, https://dx.doi.org/10.1787/574b61f8-en. [4]

OECD (2017), *Tax Administration 2017: Comparative Information on OECD and Other Advanced and Emerging Economies*, OECD Publishing, Paris, https://dx.doi.org/10.1787/tax_admin-2017-en. [2]

Annex 3.A

Links to supporting material (accessed on 1 September 2021)

- Box 3.2 – Chile:
  - Link to a video on the platform for registration and payment of VAT for digital services: https://youtu.be/MZ60ijG6S4U
  - Link to the Digital Services VAT Platform: www.sii.cl/vat/index.html
- Box 3.4 – Australia: Link to supporting illustrations for the digital identity example: www.oecd.org/tax/forum-on-tax-administration/publications-and-products/australia-digital-identity.pdf
- Box 3.5 – Peru: Link to a video on the usage of biometry to identify citizens: https://youtu.be/1XyjzScWUhM
- Box 3.6 – Spain:
  - Link to a sample of an electronic certificates of tax residence issued with a CSV, including explanatory notes: www.oecd.org/tax/forum-on-tax-administration/publications-and-products/spain-example-document-issued-with-CSV-and-explanatory-notes.pdf
  - Link to the website where taxpayers can request and obtain the certificate of tax residence through the AEAT's e-Office: https://www.agenciatributaria.gob.es/AEAT.sede/en_gb/procedimientoini/G305.shtml
  - Link to website where foreign tax administrations can check the veracity of Spanish certificates of tax residency: www.agenciatributaria.gob.es/AEAT.sede/tramitacion/ZZ05.shtml

Chapter 4

Assessment

This chapter looks at the tax assessment function, which includes all activities related to processing tax returns and payments. It comments on the use of e-channels for filing and paying, outlines administrations' efforts to provide pre-filled returns, and discusses the level of on-time return filing and payment. It also provides examples of the impact of technology and data sciences techniques on refund processes.

Introduction

The tax assessment function includes all activities related to processing tax returns, including issuing assessments, refunds, notices and statements. It also includes the processing and banking of payments. These "processing" activities, as they are referred to in many administrations, continue to be an area of significant change and focus as administrations look to take costs out of high volume processes.

Higher levels of electronic filing and payment by taxpayers helps administrations reduce their costs and improve the services they provide to taxpayers. This function is also heavily involved in managing an expanding range of data that administrations are collecting electronically from a growing number of third party organisations. As well as updating information on the use of e-channels for filing and paying, this chapter will:

- outline administrations' efforts to provide pre-filled returns for individual and corporate taxpayers, including the expansion of this approach by some into "no-return regimes"
- discuss the levels of on-time return filing and payment
- provide examples of how technology and the application of data sciences have improved refund processes.

Box 4.1. **Chile: Providing taxpayers with an overview of their information, declaration and payment obligations**

The Chilean tax administration (Servicio de Impuestos Internos, SII) provides taxpayers with an overview of their tax obligations on their personal SII site. The "Tax Responsibilities" is a customised viewer for taxpayers where information on three of the four groups of tax obligations defined by the SII is displayed. These are:

1. information obligations (requirements to present income tax sworn statements)
2. declaration obligations
3. payment obligations (pending tax payments and property tax obligations).

The primary goal is to alert the taxpayer, in a simple way, to tax obligations in advance of the compliance deadline date.

"Tax Responsibilities" presents pending responsibilities, in different colours according to their status: "completed" in grey, "within the term" in green, "limited non-compliance" in yellow and "total non-compliance" in red.

The data is collected from different systems to form a single view that allows the reviewing of obligations, the submitting of forms or paying the pending tax debt. This information is available for tax officials too, and the operational systems are updated when transactions are carried out.

Source: Chile – Servicio de Impuestos Internos (2021).

Use of e-channels for filing and paying

With digitalisation continuing to transform everyday life, it is unsurprising that the uptake in the use of e-filing and payment channels keeps growing.

Table 4.1 provides average e-filing rates from jurisdictions that provided details of channels used by taxpayers to file. In 2018 and 2019, more than nine-out-of-ten business taxpayers filed their returns electronically. For personal income tax return filers this figure is now above 80%. Also, it should be noted that for a significant number of administrations a 100% e-filing rate has already become reality (see Table D.13).

Table 4.1. **Average e-filing rates (in percent) by tax type**

Tax type	2018	2019
Personal income tax (51 jurisdictions)	82.1	84.4
Corporate income tax (53 jurisdictions)	92.1	92.7
Value added tax (46 jurisdictions)	95.9	96.7

Note: The table shows the average e-filing rates for those jurisdictions that were able to provide the information for the years 2018 and 2019. The number of jurisdictions for which data was available is shown in parenthesis.

Source: Table D.13 Electronic filing.

Looking at the evolution of e-filing rates over the period 2014 to 2019 shown in Table 4.2, it becomes clear that e-filing rates increased significantly – between 13 and 18 percentage points – across the three main tax types. It should be noted that the table only takes into account information from jurisdictions that were able to provide data for both years 2014 and 2019, which explains the differences in 2019 averages shown in Tables 4.1. and 4.2.

Table 4.2. **Evolution of e-filing rates (in percent) between 2014 and 2019 by tax type**

Tax type	2014	2019	Difference in percentage points
Personal income tax (31 jurisdictions)	66.1	82.8	+16.7
Corporate income tax (34 jurisdictions)	76.7	94.2	+17.5
Value added tax (30 jurisdictions)	84.7	98.6	+13.9

Note: The table shows the average e-filing rates for those jurisdictions that were able to provide the information for the years 2014 and 2019. The number of jurisdictions for which data was available is shown in parenthesis.

Sources: Table D.13 Electronic filing and OECD (2017), *Tax Administration 2017: Comparative Information on OECD and Other Advanced and Emerging Economies*, Table A.8, https://doi.org/10.1787/tax_admin-2017-en.

When looking at the proportions of electronic payments in Table 4.3, around 80% of payments, measured by number and value, are made electronically. The percentage of e-payments by value is slightly higher than the percentage of e-payments made by number, suggesting that particularly larger taxpayers make use of this payment channel. Due to a change in the definition of the underlying survey question, it is not possible to look at the evolution of e-payment rates.

Table 4.3. **Average e-payment rates (in percent) by number and value of payments**

Measurement type	2018	2019
Percentage by number of payments (49 jurisdictions)	79.6	81.9
Percentage by value of payments (48 jurisdictions)	84.8	86.1

Note: The table shows the average e-payment rates for those jurisdictions that were able to provide the information for the years 2018 and 2019. The number of jurisdictions for which data was available is shown in parenthesis.

Source: Table D.18 Electronic payment proportions and third party withholding.

There remains a number of jurisdictions where the volume of returns filed using paper as well as payments through non-electronic means remains high. Among those jurisdictions that provided data, more than 75 million returns were still filed on paper (see Tables A.44 to A.46). It is to be expected that this figure will further decline over time as more administrations take steps to encourage more taxpayers to use electronic platforms where possible. This will not only lower administration costs but could also reduce the administrative burden on taxpayers.

Pre-filled returns

One of the significant innovations in tax return process design over the last two decades has been the development of pre-filled tax returns, primarily for personal income taxpayers. The pre-filled approach involves administrations "pre-populating" the taxpayer's return or on-line account with information from third parties. The pre-filled return can be reviewed by the taxpayer and either filed electronically or in paper form. As the extent of pre-population is generally determined by the range of electronic data sources available to the administration, it is critical to this approach that the legislative framework provides extensive and timely third party reporting covering all relevant taxpayer information.

Advocates of pre-filling initially encouraged its use with individual tax regimes that allowed relatively few deductions and credits, and where they could be verified with third party data sources. Advances in rules based technologies, information-reporting requirements and the application of data science techniques mean that the approach can now be considered more widely. For example, survey responses show that in many jurisdictions personal income tax (PIT) returns are now pre-filled with different income information as well as deductible expenses like donations, school and university fees and insurance premiums (see Figures 4.1. and 4.2). The latest developments in some jurisdictions are described in Box 4.2.

In a growing number of jurisdictions, this concept now goes as far as totally pre-filling PIT returns, which the taxpayer then has to either agree (which may be by deemed agreement after a certain period of elapsed time) or provide further information which may lead to an upwards or downwards adjustment (see Table A.45). In their most advanced form, complete pre-filled returns are being generated for large proportions of the individual tax base.

In addition, the availability of electronic invoicing systems allows tax administrations to start to go beyond PIT returns and (fully) pre-fill corporate income tax (CIT) and value-added tax (VAT) returns (see Tables A.44 and A.46). See also the examples from Peru and Spain included in Box 4.2.

Figure 4.1. **Categories of third party information used to pre-fill PIT returns, 2019**

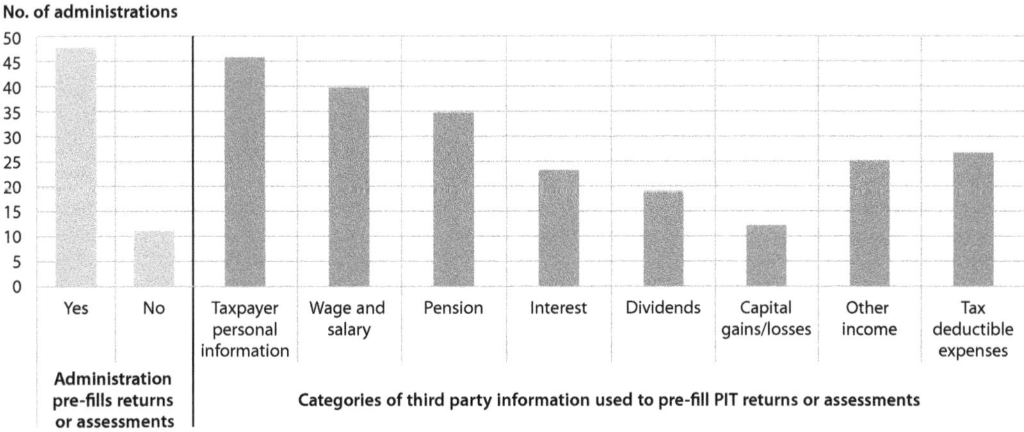

StatLink http://dx.doi.org/10.1787/888934271245

Source: Table A.42 Pre-fill of tax returns.

Figure 4.2. **Categories of tax deductible expenses used to pre-fill PIT returns, 2019**

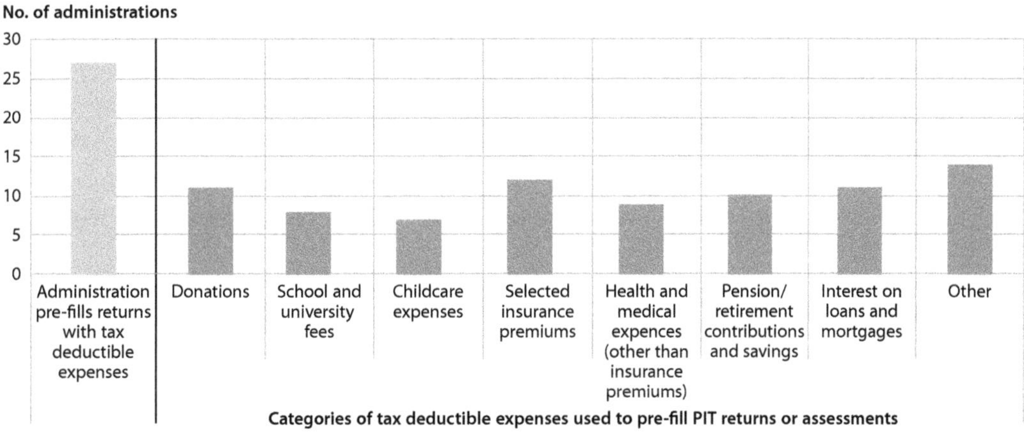

StatLink http://dx.doi.org/10.1787/888934271264

Source: Table A.42 ADD Categories of tax deductible expenses used to pre-fill PIT returns or assessments.

Box 4.2. **Country examples: Pre-filling and no return regimes**

China (People's Republic of): IT utilisation on China's groundbreaking annual reconciliation

From 1 March to 30 June 2020, China conducted the first ever annual reconciliation of individual income tax. With around 100 million individual taxpayers, who lack detailed tax-related knowledge, the Chinese tax authority leveraged cloud computing, big data, the Internet and other advanced technical means to facilitate the successful implementation of the first annual reconciliation of individual income tax.

By building the largest transaction cloud in China's e-government, the Chinese tax authority could support more than 120 000 simultaneous transactions per second, ensuring the smooth operation of the Electronic Taxation Bureau for individual taxpayers during the annual reconciliation period.

Box 4.2. **Country examples: Pre-filling and no return regimes** *(continued)*

In terms of design, the Chinese tax authority has built a "one-person tax-related data file" for hundreds of millions of individual taxpayers across the country, based on real-time real-name authentication of identity information and data sharing with other government departments. Supported by big data, it has provided taxpayers with pre-filing services for the annual reconciliation of individual income tax and a tailored reminder service, to address the issue of lack of knowledge on the part of taxpayers.

With artificial intelligence as the starting point, the "machine pre-examination and manual review" tax refunds review model was put into practice, cutting 90% of the workload for tax officials. Using digital technology, the individual income tax app was launched, facilitating all key operations digitally, as well as the electronic transfer of tax refund payments and supplemental payments.

New Zealand: Automatically issued income tax assessments

In 2019, as part of its business transformation, Inland Revenue introduced a new, automatic year-end process so that people who only earn income which is reported to Inland Revenue no longer need to do anything at the end of the tax year.

Legislative changes to the collection of employment and investment income information mean that from the 2018-19 tax year, people who earned salary and wages, or income from a financial institution, were able to see it in their myIR account, Inland Revenue's secure online service. From 2020-21, customers are able to see a full year of pre-populated information for all their relevant income.

The changes mean people whose incomes are from salary, wages, dividends, or interest do not need to do anything at the end of the year to work out whether they have a refund or a bill to pay. Inland Revenue will do it for them.

As Inland Revenue is receiving information more frequently, inconsistencies and errors can be more quickly identified. Helping customers get it right during the year also means fewer errors for employers and payers of investment income to deal with.

The second year of automatic income tax assessments included a number of improvements, based on customer feedback. The things Inland Revenue did differently in 2020 included sending the assessments out over a shorter time period so that customers had certainty earlier, and using analytical capability so that refunds were made early to the customer groups who were likely to need it the most.

Norway: A solution for reporting third party data from property rental

In 2020, the Norwegian Tax Administration (NTA) established a technical solution enabling them to receive key data and information from companies who provide marketplaces for property rental, including an overview of payments from third parties. This solution was driven by a new regulation requiring disclosure information from property rental.

The received data is used for pre-filling tax returns, which, together with dedicated guidance for taxpayers, helps the taxpayer fill in the tax return correctly. The data received from third parties can also be used for analysis and control purposes.

The NTA succeeded in getting all known companies to report to them but, because a large part of the reported data lacked the correct tax identification number or the correct addresses, the data cannot yet fully be used. To address this, the NTA is now collaborating with the reporting companies in order for them to provide correct tax identification numbers and addresses.

Box 4.2. **Country examples: Pre-filling and no return regimes** *(continued)*

Most of the reported data will be used for pre-filling tax returns in the future, and the NTA expects long-term benefits that will increase compliance and revenue, such as making it simpler for taxpayers to complete their tax returns. For businesses, they expect this solution to create a more level playing field.

Peru: Proposal for filing VAT returns by using electronic records from taxpayers

Transactions subject to VAT go through a three-step-process: (i) the issuance of receipts; (ii) recording the transaction; and (iii) creation of the tax return. Technology has allowed these processes to become digital. Using electronic invoicing, taxpayers prepare electronic sales reports and the tax administration simplifies the tax filling process with virtual tax returns. Such simplification helps to reduce compliance cost and improves the quality of information included on tax returns.

As the Peruvian Tax Administration (SUNAT) aims to improve the taxpayer experience and simplify procedures, SUNAT links information from electronic records such as sales reports with information from VAT withholding schemes and monthly online tax returns. On average, 87.28% of the taxpayer supplied information is accepted.

SUNAT continues working on further improvements with the aim of creating partially prefilled tax returns using issued electronic invoices, which could lead to the elimination of electronic sales reports. SUNAT expects to implement this measure from 2022.

See Annex 4.A. for links to supporting material.

Russia: Zero filing for transport and land tax

Starting from the 2020 tax year, businesses in Russia are no longer required to submit tax returns for transport tax and land tax.

The Federal Tax Service of Russia is using data provided by other government agencies (including the Ministry of the Interior, the Aviation agency, the Ministry of Trade, the land registry, and the register of ships etc.) to automatically calculate the amount of taxes due by corporate taxpayers and notify them. As this exercise might disregard certain applicable tax reliefs (deduction, amortisation, etc.), in cases where the amount actually paid by the taxpayer does not match the amount produced by the system, the taxpayer is asked to provide, within 10 days from the date of receipt of the notification, explanations and/or documents confirming that: (i) the taxpayer's calculation is correct; (ii) the tax payment has been made in full and in time; and (iii) the application of reduced tax rates and tax benefits was valid.

The technology of centralised processing and storage of information on taxable vehicles, land and its owners allows the tax authorities to eliminate the need to annually request and process over 1 million tax returns for these taxes, optimising their work and making it more efficient. Moreover, it alleviates the burden for taxpayers as it minimises compliance costs.

Spain: Pre-filled VAT return

In order to explore the extension of the pre-filled return to VAT, in 2020 the Spanish tax administration (AEAT) ran a pilot with taxpayers enrolled in the Immediate Supply of Information (SII) system who have to keep their VAT books within the electronic office of the AEAT. The service was named "Pre-303" after the form 303 in which the VAT self-assessment return is submitted, and is a service offered through the AEAT electronic office via a web form.

In summary, the service makes available to SII taxpayers the aggregated VAT records, made by grouping the amounts held by AEAT in the SII records. These aggregated amounts are

Box 4.2. **Country examples: Pre-filling and no return regimes** *(continued)*

the ones to be declared in the VAT return. Taxpayers are then able to transfer the information from the aggregated records to the corresponding box of the VAT return and, if required, to modify them before the electronic submission. In addition, a table of equivalence between the aggregate records and the VAT return is created to facilitate the data transfer.

In February 2021, the service has been extended to all VAT taxpayers and renamed "Pre303. Un servicio para todos" (Pre-303. A service for all). The information pre-filled varies depending on the type of taxpayer and the data that AEAT gets from several sources: previous self-assessments, census, third party information, etc. As a result, 3.5 million taxpayers will receive a pre-filled return including census data and some economic data. From them, 41 000 SII taxpayers and 600 000 real estate lessors will get a fully pre-populated return.

This new service will enhance certainty and reduce the administrative burden on taxpayers by reducing the time they need for the completion of the return.

See Annex 4.A. for links to supporting material.

Sources: China – State Taxation Administration (2021), New Zealand – Inland Revenue Department – Te Tari Taake (2021), Norwegian Tax Administration (2021), Peru – Superintendencia Nacional de Administración Tributaria (2021), Federal Tax Service of Russia (2021), and Spanish Tax Agency (2021).

On-time return filing

Even allowing for changes occurring because of pre-filled or no-return regimes, the filing of a tax return is still the principal means by which a tax liability is established and becomes payable. As a result, the on-time filing rate is seen as an effective measure of the health of the tax system as well as the performance of the tax administration itself.

Table 4.4 summarises on-time return filing for those administrations able to supply information by tax type. Apart from CIT, the rates are between 85 – 90%. The lower rates for CIT may be explained through more complexity in the corporate income tax system and the preparation of financial statements and year-end reports.

Table 4.4. **Average on-time filing rates (in percent) by tax type**

Tax type	2018	2019
Personal income tax (43 jurisdictions)	86.8	86.2
Corporate income tax (44 jurisdictions)	78.7	79.9
Value added tax (44 jurisdictions)	86.8	86.6
Employer withholding (32 jurisdictions)	88.5	88.0

Note: The table shows the average on-time filing rates for those jurisdictions that were able to provide the information for the years 2018 and 2019. The number of jurisdictions for which data was available is shown in parenthesis.

Source: Table D.12 On-time filing rates.

Table 4.5 shows the evolution of on-time filing rates. This has remained broadly static between 2014 and 2019 but may be expected to improve further as electronic filing and taxpayer services, such as pre-filling, continue to grow. It should be noted that the table only takes into account information from jurisdictions that were able to provide data for both years 2014 and 2019, which explains the differences in 2019 averages shown in Tables 4.4. and 4.5.

Table 4.5. **Evolution of on-time filing rates (in percent) between 2014 and 2019 by tax type**

Tax type	2014	2019	Difference in percentage points
Personal income tax (34 jurisdictions)	86.1	87.7	+1.6
Corporate income tax (34 jurisdictions)	80.2	82.4	+2.2
Value added tax (38 jurisdictions)	86.0	86.0	±0.0
Employer withholding (26 jurisdictions)	87.7	85.8	-1.9

Note: The table shows the average on-time filing rates for those jurisdictions that were able to provide the information for the years 2014 and 2019. The number of jurisdictions for which data was available is shown in parenthesis.

Sources: Table D.12 On-time filing rates and OECD (2017), *Tax Administration 2017: Comparative Information on OECD and Other Advanced and Emerging Economies*, Table A.6, https://doi.org/10.1787/tax_admin-2017-en.

A broader examination of the on-time return filing data reveals two issues of note:

- Firstly, the range of on-time filing performances shown in Figure 4.3. illustrates a significant gap in on-time filing across the main tax types for a number of jurisdictions, in some cases above 50 percentage points.
- Secondly, overall on-time filing rates that averaged between 80% and 88% in 2019 (see Table 4.4.) may be lower than desirable and an area of concern given that most respondents operate tax systems that rely on voluntary compliance by taxpayers. Looking at the underlying data, approximately 100 million returns were not filed on time.

Figure 4.3. **Range in on-time filing performance across major tax types, 2019**

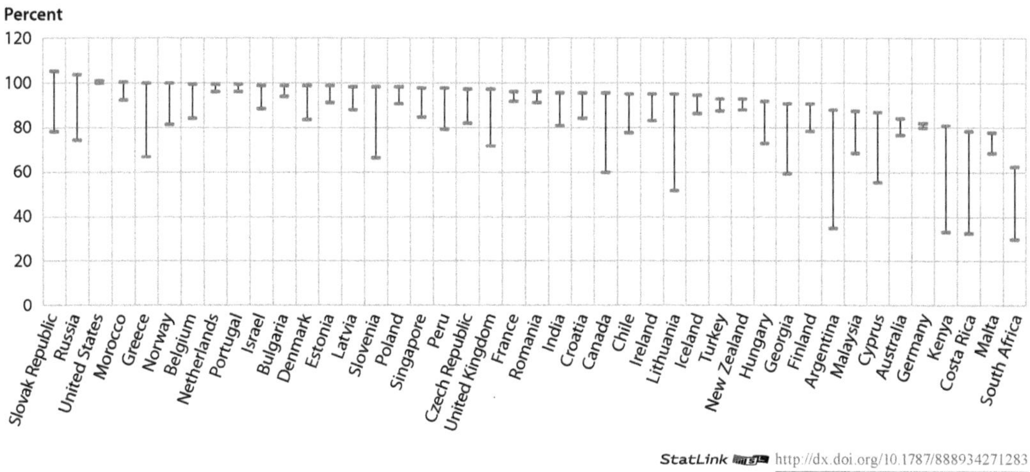

StatLink http://dx.doi.org/10.1787/888934271283

Note: On-time filing performance is expressed as a percentage of returns expected and can therefore be above 100%. The figure shows for each jurisdiction the range in on-time filing performances in 2019 across the four tax types: PIT, CIT, Employer WHT and VAT (where applicable). It only includes jurisdictions for which information was available for at least three tax types. Data for Malta relates to the year 2018.

Source: Table D.12 On-time filing rates.

Figure 4.4. **PIT and CIT on-time filing rates, 2019**

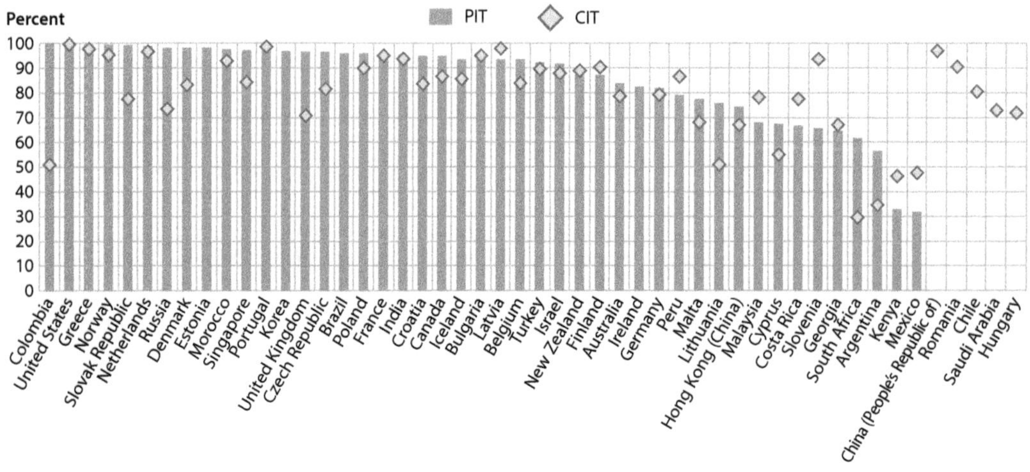

StatLink http://dx.doi.org/10.1787/888934271302

Note: Rates for Malta relate to the year 2018.

Source: Table D.12 On-time filing rates.

On-time payment

Payment of tax constitutes one of the most common interactions between taxpayers and tax administrations, especially for businesses that are typically required to regularly remit a variety of payments covering both their own tax liabilities and those of their employees. Administrations continue to make progress in increasing the range of e-payment options available to taxpayers and to increase their use. This progress not only lowers the cost to the administration, it can increase on-time payments and reduce the number of payment arrears cases by providing improved access and a better payment experience.

Table 4.6. **Average on-time payment rates (in percent) by tax type**

Tax type	2018	2019
Personal income tax (34 jurisdictions)	83.8	82.5
Corporate income tax (35 jurisdictions)	85.6	85.8
Value added tax (36 jurisdictions)	88.7	88.9
Employer withholding (30 jurisdictions)	91.5	91.3

Note: The table shows the average on-time payment rates for those jurisdictions that were able to provide the information for the years 2018 and 2019. The number of jurisdictions for which data was available is shown in parenthesis.

Source: Table D.17 On-time payment performance.

The on-time payment rates for those administrations able to supply information by tax type are summarised in Tables 4.6. and 4.7. The tables show that:

- On average, the on-time payments rates for CIT, VAT and employer withholding tax are higher than the on-time filing rates, whereas for PIT the on-time payment rates are lower than the on-time filing rates. This means businesses are more likely to pay on time than file on time; while individuals are more likely to file on time than they are to pay on time.

- While average on-time payments rates in 2019 of between 82% and 92% appear high, lifting these rates should continue to be an area of focus for administrations given the amounts of revenue involved.
- Similar to on-time filing, the evolution of on-time payments between 2014 and 2019 shows consistent outcomes.

Table 4.7. **Evolution of on-time payment rates (in percent) between 2014 and 2019 by tax type**

Tax type	2014	2019	Difference in percentage points
Personal income tax (16 jurisdictions)	80.4	80.4	±0.0
Corporate income tax (16 jurisdictions)	90.4	88.5	-1.9
Value added tax (19 jurisdictions)	93.0	94.1	+1.1
Employer withholding (14 jurisdictions)	89.1	90.9	+1.8

Note: The table shows the average on-time filing rates for those jurisdictions that were able to provide the information for the years 2014 and 2019. The number of jurisdictions for which data was available is shown in parenthesis. Data for Costa Rica has been excluded from the calculation as it would distort the average ratios.

Sources: Table D.12 On-time filing rates and OECD (2017), *Tax Administration 2017: Comparative Information on OECD and Other Advanced and Emerging Economies*, Table A.9, https://doi.org/10.1787/tax_admin-2017-en.

The range of on-time payment depicted in Figure 4.5. shows a significant gap in on-time payment across the main tax types for a number of jurisdictions, in some cases above 50 percentage points. This is similar to what has been observed in relation to on-time filing.

Figure 4.5. **Range in on-time payment performance, 2019**

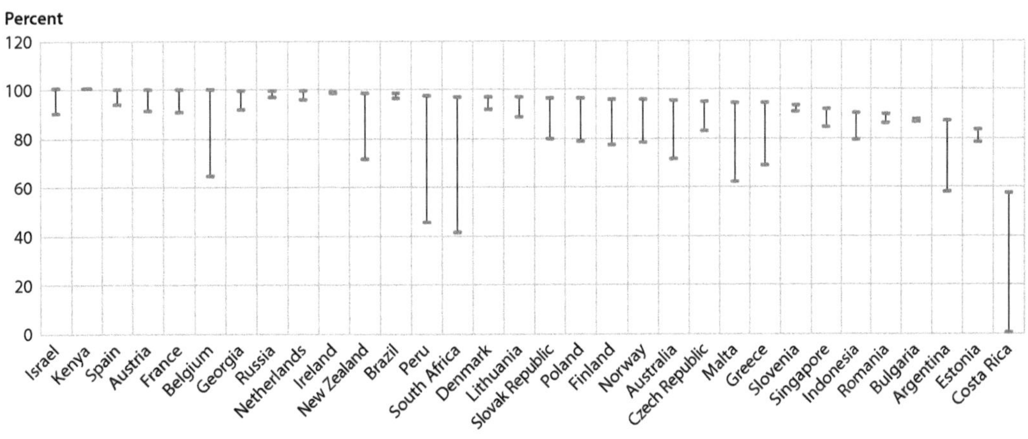

StatLink http://dx.doi.org/10.1787/888934271321

Note: On-time payments are expressed as a percentage of estimated payments expected by due date and can therefore be above 100%. The figure shows for each jurisdiction the range in on-time payment performances in 2019 across the four tax types: PIT, CIT, Employer WHT and VAT (where applicable). It only includes jurisdictions for which information was available for at least three tax types.

Source: D.17 On-time payment performance.

Refunds

Given the underlying design of the major taxes administered (i.e. PIT, CIT and VAT), some element of over-payment by a proportion of taxpayers is unavoidable. Excess tax payments represent a cost to taxpayers in terms of "the time value of money", which is particularly critical to businesses that are operating with tight margins where cash flow is paramount. Any delays in refunding legitimately overpaid taxes may therefore result in significant "costs" to taxpayers.

During the COVID-19 crisis, the importance of paying out refunds quickly was a key issue for many governments, as a significant number of taxpayers were (or still are) facing severe cash-flow problems. Tax administrations responded to this by prioritising refund applications or adapting refund processes, in some cases fully automating them (CIAT/IOTA/OECD, 2020[1]).

Table 4.8. **Treatment of VAT refunds, 2019**

Percent of jurisdictions were ...			
VAT refunds are automatically paid out immediately	VAT refunds are paid out immediately subject to the availability of funds	VAT refund are established as a "credit" in the taxpayer's account, until such time as the taxpayer may legally request the refund	VAT refund are established as a "credit" in the taxpayer's account, until such time as the taxpayer may legally request the refund, subject to the availability of funds
57%	2%	37%	4%

Source: Table A.30 VAT refunds.

Relaxing the risk checks done before making some refunds is another option, but tax administrations need to continue being cognisant of fraud risks. Tax regimes with a high incidence of tax refunds are particularly attractive to fraudsters (especially via organised criminal attacks) and for this reason can present a significant risk to administrations, necessitating effective risk-based approaches for identifying potentially fraudulent refund claims.

Advancements in technology and the application of data science provide tax administrations with new options to address risks and simplify processes, thus reducing administrative and compliance burdens (see Box 4.3).

Box 4.3. **Country examples: Using technology to advance the refund process**

Georgia: Risk module of VAT refund validation

In February 2019, the Georgian Revenue Service (GRS) introduced an Automatic VAT Refund System. Initially, the system checked VAT returns through an automated risk-based verification process, where VAT returns with a credit were identified. Those identified as low-risk returns, more than 90% of all tax returns, would be allocated a "Green Card", which is an account allowing taxpayers to manage their credits as required, either by requesting a repayment through the system or allowing them to be offset against tax arrears. The high-risk returns would be subjected to manual processing.

Since being introduced, the system has been modified and improved, and from November 2020 it was made fully automatic, and VAT amounts were automatically credited to the taxpayer's bank account without a need for a request.

Box 4.3. **Country examples: Using technology to advance the refund process** *(continued)*

For the automatic refund, taxpayers and tax returns are subjected to the wide variety of types of assessments and verification processes, one of which is a validation process. The process checks tax return data provided by the taxpayers against that available on the unified electronic database of the GRS to identify mismatches.

The aim of the validation process is, on the one hand, to identify errors/mistakes provided in the tax return forms in the early stage of declaration and on the other hand, to promote tax compliance. While examining the risk returns identified through the validation module, taxpayers are contacted by Revenue Service staff and given the opportunity to correct mistakes/ errors made in the tax returns. As a result, only 3% of above tax returns end up being audited.

The automatic VAT refund system, gained even greater importance in the event of COVID-19 pandemic. It is expected to support business and therefore the national economy by increasing cash flow. According to the statistics for 2020, more than 30 000 VAT refund claims have been approved and paid with a total value above GEL 900 million (see Table 4.9).

Table 4.9. **Georgia: VAT refund trends 2019-20**

	2019	2020
Number of claims	5 307	34 153
Value of VAT refunded	320 047 876	928 327 011

Source: Georgia Revenue Service (2021).

Israel: VAT refund system for tourists

The previous refund process for tourists required manual filling of forms at the business and additional checks performed at the departure stage (including filling and entering data of all purchase data manually) which sometimes caused congestion at the airport and denial of refunds due to errors.

Under the new system, when a tourist makes a purchase at an approved business, real-time verification of the transaction data is performed. The smart cash register at the business connects to the tax administration's web service and sends the transaction details. The system performs various checks, such as verification of the business, tourist visa validity and more, and prints out confirmation of the transaction.

This means the new system offers verification checks and eligibility for a refund conducted automatically at the time of purchase. The tourist receives full certainty about their eligibility for a refund.

Additionally, inspection time and payment of the refund has been reduced from an average waiting time of approximately 9 minutes to less than a minute, and the process can be done by self-service. There was also a decrease of 99% in errors. As more businesses offer this service, it will be possible to reduce the staffing levels required to handle tax refunds, and the service to tourists will be more efficient.

New Zealand: The donations tax credit process

As part of New Zealand's ongoing plans to leverage technology and analytical tools, two new tools made a significant difference to the process for paying donation tax credits in 2020. These were optical character recognition (OCR), which is used to scan documents, and Decision Manager, a tool within the START system that uses analytical capabilities to support and recommend the most appropriate actions.

Box 4.3. **Country examples: Using technology to advance the refund process** *(continued)*

Inland Revenue used OCR to read donation receipts and Decision Manager to verify receipts in straightforward cases. The two tools, working together, process and pay donation tax credit claims with no human intervention. For customers who submitted their claims online and where there were no issues with the information provided, refund payments went out in a matter of days. Approximately 60% to 70% of claims were received online in 2020.

These changes are estimated to have saved around 2 000 hours of processing time. In 2019, it was a paper process and required around 80 people at any one time to key tax donation credits receipts into Inland Revenue's systems, meaning refund payments took weeks to be made.

Singapore: Analytics models to score GST returns

Inland Revenue Authority of Singapore (IRAS) conducts both pre-refund and post-refund goods and services tax (GST) audits. In addition to business rules at the pre-refund stage, analytics were deployed at the post-refund stage.

With the positive results from use of analytics to strengthen the risk analysis process, IRAS has since 2018 embedded analytics into its refunds processing. Both business rules and analytics are therefore fully integrated and now deployed at the pre-refund stage and on a near real-time basis. This new process has sharpened the identification of erroneous or high-risk claims upfront, including the capturing of new risk areas. At the same time, it has reduced the number of low risk refunds that require manual review by about 30%, allowing the GST Division to prioritise the review of riskier cases.

In addition, IRAS has enhanced its GST registration process for businesses by embedding a network analytics model to score GST registration applications as they are received. Under this new approach, applications of lower compliance risk are automatically processed while those with high compliance and fraud risks are flagged out for scrutiny. More businesses now enjoy faster registration for GST. With a reduction in cases for manual review, more time can be spent on applications that truly require attention. Since implementation in end December 2020, the percentage of applications processed automatically by the system has increased from 10% to 40%. The model is being fine-tuned to enhance the number of cases processed automatically.

Sources: Georgia Revenue Service (2021), Israel Tax Authority (2021), New Zealand – Inland Revenue Department – Te Tari Taake (2021) and Inland Revenue Authority of Singapore (2021).

References

CIAT/IOTA/OECD (2020), *"Tax administration responses to COVID-19: Measures taken to support taxpayers", OECD Policy Responses to Coronavirus (COVID-19)*, OECD Publishing, Paris, http://dx.doi.org/10.1787/adc84188-en. [1]

OECD (2017), *Tax Administration 2017: Comparative Information on OECD and Other Advanced and Emerging Economies*, OECD Publishing, Paris, https://dx.doi.org/10.1787/tax_admin-2017-en. [2]

Annex 4.A

Links to supporting material (accessed on 1 September 2021)

- Box 4.2 – Peru: Link to a presentation explaining the proposal for filing VAT returns by using electronic records from taxpayers: www.oecd.org/tax/forum-on-tax-administration/publications-and-products/peru-proposal-for-filing-VAT-return.pdf
- Box 4.2 – Spain:
  - Link to the Spanish Tax Agency's website under which all the information on the Pre-303 service is available, including FAQs and other services: www.agenciatributaria.es/AEAT.internet/Inicio/La_Agencia_Tributaria/Campanas/IVA/_SERVICIOS_DE_AYUDA/PRE303_Ayuda_modelo_303_SII/PRE303_Ayuda_modelo_303_SII.shtml
  - Link to videos (in Spanish) regarding assistance for filling form 303 for self-employed: https://youtu.be/JvfNjEftqf8 and real estate lessors: https://youtu.be/Ey8j7ko9xAs.

Chapter 5

Services

This chapter considers how tax administrations' compliance goals are enhanced by providing effective and efficient services to taxpayers, often through digital services. This is helping increase voluntary compliance amongst taxpayers by making it easier to understand tax obligations, report taxable income and make payments.

Introduction

Voluntary compliance is by far the most efficient way of achieving a tax administration's compliance goals, and central to this is the provision of a wide range effective and easy to use taxpayer communication channels, both on a reactive and proactive basis. Often, these communications have been delivered on a one-to-many basis, such as the provision of guidance or reminders as well as calculation and reporting tools. However, tax administrations report that their use of innovative tools is growing, and those tools are also allowing communications to become more personalised to the taxpayer's individual circumstances, to be delivered via an increasing range of communication channels and to facilitate the drive towards self-service, on a real-time and 24/7 basis.

There are perhaps three emerging trends from the examples provided by tax administrations:

- a clear shift to seeking greater understanding of taxpayer preferences in the design of services (including services for tax intermediaries)
- increasing the options for self-service to allow taxpayers more control as and when they want it
- increasingly taking a more joined-up approach to providing services both internally within the tax administration and across government.

Much of this has been driven by the move to digital services, which has been catalysed by the COVID-19 pandemic. Most administrations now report offering an expanding range of self-services, including the ability to register, file and pay on-line, along with a range of interactive tools. Some report exploring with third party providers how they can support embedded software or other arrangements that allow taxpayers a greater array of in-system support or other self-service options.

Box 5.1. Country examples: Moving procedures online

Chile: 100% Online Procedures

The Chilean tax administration (Servicio de Impuestos Internos, SII) implemented a new IT system that allows a completely digital journey throughout a taxpayer's lifecycle, including business related procedures from starting a business through to closing it. This system facilitates taxpayers providing supporting information through their individual Electronic Tax Folder for each procedure, and this is accessible by tax officials.

As a result, SII enabled a platform that allows the taxpayer to initiate a procedure, attach the required documentation and interact remotely with an official, if necessary, to complete the application online. This makes things easier for taxpayers as it reduces their time and money costs, as they will not have to go to the SII offices to submit supporting documents.

The statistics for 2019 and 2020 show that for business start-ups, their online requests increased from 92% to 97%, Taxpayer Identification Number applications increased from 80.7% to 93.1% and the online requests for the modification of partners increased from 16.2% to 56.2% in the last year. This advance in the line of digital transformation has benefited all taxpayers, and particularly those living in extreme or more isolated areas.

See Annex 5.A. for links to supporting material.

Box 5.1. Country examples: Moving procedures online *(continued)*

Costa Rica: The Virtual Procedures Portal (TRAVI, by its Spanish acronym) review

Due to the closure of the regional tax offices as a result of the COVID-19 pandemic, in March 2020, the Costa Rican tax administration had to rapidly expand their virtual channels to facilitate requests for procedures, consultations and appointments.

After 4 months of hard work the tax administration in conjunction with the technology department, launched The Virtual Procedures Portal (TRAVI). The portal allows users to send, check and receive the results of 45 different types of procedures, and validates the user's identification against the tax administration database, which contains the identifications of nationals and foreigners accredited in Costa Rica. Before the launch, there was significant work to study the different scenarios and system configurations to ensure the system was effective.

The system includes 5 service queues which match how the tax administrations offices are subdivided: taxpayer services, collection, audit and verification, and tax assessments. In addition, a chatbot was launched, with 237 frequently asked questions on 6 high-demand topics, which led to a decrease in emails sent to the contact centre of approximately 30%.

India: Scheme for Faceless Assessment, Penalty and Appeal Proceedings

The Indian Income Tax Department has implemented a scheme to facilitate faceless Assessment, Penalty and Appeal Proceedings by enabling team-based working delivering greater efficiency, transparency and accountability. The organisational hierarchy consists of a National Centre, Regional Centres consisting of various functional units (assessment, verification, penalty, appeal, technical, review units etc.) to achieve economies of scale and allow functional specialisation.

For the optimal utilisation of resources, the notion of a "fixed" jurisdiction has been replaced with a "dynamic" jurisdiction, enabling the National Centre to assign cases to a specific unit in any Regional Centre through an automated allocation system. This system is being further enhanced to consider the competence and experience of the units during the allocation process.

All communications with taxpayers and amongst the functional units, are through the National Centre and exclusively digital. The scheme aims to minimise the interface with taxpayer and Department to the maximum extent and there is no requirement to physically appear, and video conferencing facilities can be used, if required.

The assessment unit prepares draft assessments which are examined in accordance with the risk management strategy using an automated examination tool. The tool decides to (a) finalise the assessment, (b) provide an opportunity to the taxpayer to comment, in case a modification is proposed or (c) assign the draft assessment to a review unit through an automated allocation system. Machine learning models have been developed to enhance effectiveness of the automated examination tool. The review unit reviews the draft assessments and provides agreement or suggests a modification. When a modification is suggested, the case is assigned to another unit for finalisation.

All assessments are passed under the signature of the National Centre which transfers all the electronic records of the case to the jurisdictional Officer.

India: e-portal for filing complaints

In January 2021, the Central Board of Direct Taxes, the Indian direct tax administrator, launched a dedicated e-portal on the website of the Income Tax Department to receive and process complaints of tax evasion, undisclosed foreign assets and certain property transactions.

Box 5.1. **Country examples: Moving procedures online** *(continued)*

As a result, both Indian residents and non-residents can now file a "tax evasion petition" electronically. After a validation process (mobile and/or email), the complainant can file, using three specially designed forms, violations in respect of income-tax, undisclosed foreign income and assets, and certain property transactions.

Upon successful filing of the complaint, a unique number is allotted to each complaint, and the complainant can use this to view the status of the complaint. This e-portal is part of the wider drive to make it easier to interact with the tax administration through digital channels.

See Annex 5.A. for links to supporting material.

Spain: Integral Digital Assistance (ADI)

The Spanish Tax Agency's (AEAT) Strategic Plan 2020-23 targets the development of a new model of customer service based on digital assistance and information services. To achieve this, AEAT aims to deliver the Integral Digital Administration (ADI, by its Spanish acronym) to allow the completion of formalities and procedures without unnecessary visits to AEAT tax offices.

The ADI has been configured to serve as AEAT's virtual regional tax offices, to provide personalised digital information and assistance on a 24/7 basis, that compliments the traditional desk services in the regional offices. The COVID-19 crisis outbreak made ADI become a crucial means of service delivery as access to regional offices was restricted.

ADI is a multichannel service incorporating the different tools that modern technology offers (e.g. virtual assistants, instant chats, video-calls, and a click-to-call button of the website) to optimise and streamline assistance to taxpayers. A holistic approach has been followed when setting up this new assistance model, since the services provided by ADI are integrated into the rest of AEAT's functionalities and procedures.

The model has been designed to provide the highest standard of service, and is delivered by skilled officials which helps provide a consistency of application which reinforces legal certainty.

The project is being deployed progressively, starting with the creation of the first ADI's in Valencia in October 2020 for assistance in VAT, lump sum schemes, census procedures and some customs procedures as well as in Madrid for some PIT control procedures. In 2021, the ADI of Galicia will be set up and in 2022 the one of Andalusia. All of them will have a nationwide competence and a workforce of 300 tax officials will deliver assistance services through the ADIs.

Up until 22 March 2021, the ADI answered 7 332 incoming calls which resulted in 2 619 returns being submitted.

See Annex 5.A. for links to supporting material.

Sources: Chile – Servicio de Impuestos Internos (2021); Costa Rica – Directorate of Taxation, Ministry of Finance (2021); India – Income Tax Department (2021) and Spanish Tax Agency (2021).

Managing service demand

An important aspect of meeting taxpayer preferences is getting the mix of channels right. While there is an increasing shift to the use of electronic services for both convenience and cost-efficiency purposes, a proportion of taxpayers will not have access to, or be comfortable with such services. This calls for considered strategies as to how to influence channel shift for those for whom it would offer better outcomes without adversely affecting the service offering to other taxpayers.

Such strategies of course need to be based on good measurement and understanding of demands and constraints. However, it is clear from Table 5.1. that the use of digital communication channels (online, email, digital assistance) is increasing, while traditional channels (telephone, in-person and paper) continue to decrease.

Table 5.1. **Service demand by channel**

Channel type	No. of jurisdictions providing data	2018	2019	Change
Online via taxpayer account	31	943 968 722	1 140 362 160	+20.8%
Telephone call	54	339 045 062	327 330 943	-3.5%
In-person	35	109 579 208	109 041 549	-0.5%
Mail/post	21	50 372 394	49 137 284	-2.5%
E-mail	30	12 568 291	13 959 880	+11.1%
Digital assistance	29	10 942 071	21 783 351	+99.1%

Note: The table only includes jurisdictions for which data was available for 2018 and 2019.

Sources: Table A.40 Incoming service contacts: Monitoring and number of contacts by channel (online, digital assistance, telephone) and Table A.41 Incoming service contacts: Number of contacts by channel (e-mail, mail/post, in-person).

As noted above, the COVID-19 pandemic has further accelerated this move to digital communication. This is well documented in the 2021 OECD report *Tax Administration: Digital Resilience in the COVID-19 Environment* which, based on a survey of 32 tax administrations, noted that during the crisis administrations were able to shift a significant percentage of communications from paper to digital, with many administrations estimating that they shifted 75% or more (see Figure 5.1). (OECD, 2021[1])

Figure 5.1. **Broad estimates of the percentage of paper communication shifted to digital communication during the COVID-19 pandemic**

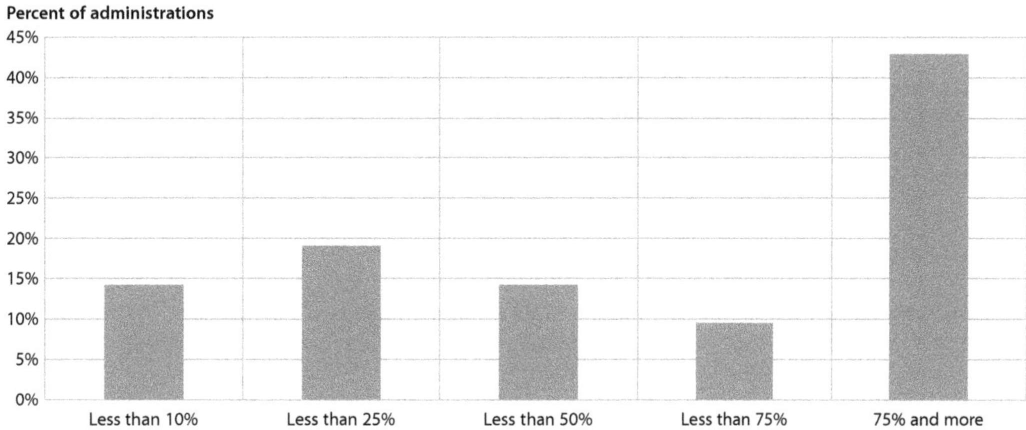

StatLink http://dx.doi.org/10.1787/888934271340

Source: OECD (2021), "Tax Administration: Digital Resilience in the COVID-19 Environment", *OECD Policy Responses to Coronavirus (COVID-19)*, https://doi.org/10.1787/2f3cf2fb-en.

The channels that tax administrations consider taxpayers have used to substitute in-person communication were taxpayer portals, email, telephone, applications and web services (social media, live chat, etc.). (OECD, 2021[1]). It will be therefore be interesting to see how the figures in Table 5.1. evolve when fiscal year 2020 data is available. A first glimpse of this can be seen by looking at the examples in Box 5.4. where Australia and Canada report that their chatbots had conversations in the millions.

Supporting self-service

The self-service offering from tax administrations is growing, and there is an expanding range of self-services being provided. Common examples of this include the ability to register, file and pay on-line, along with a range of interactive tools. This is leading to efficiency gains in tax administrations, as well as being able to provide a more 24/7-style service to taxpayers. As seen above, these services have proved to be invaluable during the COVID-19 pandemic, and tax administrations are applying artificial intelligence techniques to the large amounts of data that is collected through these services to develop them further.

Box 5.2. **Country examples: Support self-service**

Australia: Supporting Agents to Self-Serve Online

The Australia Tax Office (ATO) conducted an extensive review of call drivers and key trends from Tax Time 2019. Tax Time is the period when most people need to lodge a tax return and engage with the ATO. The ATO found there were several topics where tax professionals could have self-served using Online Services for Agents instead of calling an ATO contact centre. The ATO, through a Top 10 Call Drivers project, analysed 76 000 calls received from tax professionals in 2019 and found that 43% of these calls could have been self-served in some manner.

The ATO undertook a variety of activities including communications (internally and externally) and strengthen the support given to staff to promote the use of online services. Through this project, the ATO had a 28% decrease in calls received from tax professionals within the Top 10 Call Drivers group. Additional savings were recorded as tax professionals were able to save time by dealing with the ATO via online channels.

China (People's Republic of): Guiding taxpayers to "non-contact" channels

As part of their response to COVID-19, the Chinese State Taxation Administration (STA) actively expanded the "non-contact" taxpayer service channels so that 214 tax-related matters could be resolved online, and guided taxpayers to use mobile apps, official accounts on social media, self-service machines and other channels to handle tax-related matters. As a result, tens of millions of legal entities and hundreds of millions of individuals conducted tax-related businesses online during the pandemic.

Further, using emerging technologies such as artificial intelligence, cloud computing and deep learning, STA can accurately respond to taxpayer questions, deliver policies on tax and fee reduction, and provide intelligent consulting services for taxpayers. During the COVID-19 pandemic, STA applied this learning to provide 24/7 self-service for taxpayers, which ensured taxpayers had a range of tailored services at their fingertips to help them understand tax policies. This new self-service channel now accounts for more than 25% of consultations, meaning it has become an important channel for serving and helping taxpayers.

Box 5.2. **Country examples: Support self-service** *(continued)*

Georgia: Redesign of administration's website

Totally redesigned and equipped with additional functionality, the new website of Georgia Revenue Service has been tailored to meet the requirements of taxpayers and other users of the website. As the result of the redesign:

- The visual design of the website has been entirely changed and adjusted to modern needs.
- The website content has been updated and reorganised into 3 clear sections, general information, taxpayers – natural persons, and taxpayers – legal persons.
- Around 200 definitions on tax and customs matters have been translated into English.
- Internal guidance on managing the website has been enhanced.
- A user feedback page has been added.
- A new communication channel has been added: the "Revenue Service Chat".

Since the changes, 0.01% of all users left their feedback on the website, with 54% of all feedback being positive, and the vast majority of user recommendations with regards to the website have been incorporated.

Sources: Australian Taxation Office (2021), China (People's Republic of) – State Taxation Administration (2021) and Georgia Revenue Service (2021).

E-services

As part of the of the ongoing shift to digital services, a growing number of tax administrations are investing in new digital tools that can support their wider goals of helping taxpayers get their tax right first time. These tools provide new ways for taxpayers to interact with tax administrations, and are helping drive efficiencies through increased self-service and reduced use of more labour intensive channels such as call centres. This section provides examples of the infrastructure tax administrations are putting in place to support these new services, along with examples of the services themselves such as chatbots and mobile apps. A growing trend is that tax administrations are starting to embed services with third parties such as advisors and agents, to help improve the quality of advice they provide.

Box 5.3. **Country examples: Developing new e-services**

Australia: The Digital Partnership Office

The ATO is progressively enabling a digital ecosystem that facilitates the exchange of event based, real time data. This data can be used by multiple partners and shared with other authorised government agencies in order for individuals and businesses to meet their obligations, including tax and superannuation. The ATO is achieving this by working in partnership with a variety of digital providers to design, test and build new products and services that can be integrated into existing natural business systems (e.g. business or accounting software).

The ATO Digital Partnership Office was formed to manage and provide support to the rapidly growing number of Digital Service Providers (DSPs), all with varied demands, complexities and challenges.

Box 5.3. **Country examples: Developing new e-services** *(continued)*

These DSPs are software developers or digital intermediaries that contribute to the delivery of digital services which support individuals, tax professionals, businesses and super funds to meet their tax and superannuation obligations.

The ATO Digital Partnership Office guides and supports DSPs throughout the process of building ATO web services and Application Programming Interfaces (APIs) into their software products. This is mainly achieved through the ATO's:

- Online Services Platform for DSPs: An online single point of entry for DSPs to access services and request support 24/7 (for example, log and track requests, share data, access reports and tailored information, etc.). This service enables the ATO to manage the growing number of DSPs and demand for API based services effectively.
- DSP Operational Framework: A set of security requirements applied using a risk-based model, which all DSPs must meet in order to consume the ATO's digital services. This ensures appropriate controls are in place within the DSP environment to protect the integrity of the ATO's digital ecosystem and client data.
- DSP Engagement model: This provides a consistent approach to engaging, communicating and collaborating with DPS to deliver mutually beneficial outcomes.

See Annex 5.A. for links to supporting material.

Canada: Implementation of the ADP3G (Application Development Platform 3rd Generation) platform

In Canada, the Canada Revenue Agency (CRA) is in the process of implementing the ADP3G (Application Development Platform 3rd Generation) platform by bridging consumer-focused digital IT-services, API management, interoperability capabilities, automation/DevOps and cloud.

- Automation/DevOps: The automation of software development tools and processes to develop, deploy and sustain applications in a more agile and automated environment required to quickly and efficiently build better secure digital solutions. DevOps is an organisational concept serving to bridge the gap between development and operations, in terms of skills, mind-set, practices and silo-mentality.
- Consumer-focused digital IT-services: Working to evolve CRA IT-service offerings to better support digital solutions that are designed with Canadians, not just for them, and therefore meet their needs. There is also a focus on services that are more business use-case driven, so they can be reused across different endpoints while still leveraging traditional services.
- Cloud: Adopting cloud computing for the 3rd Generation platform, i.e. the technologies, tools, supporting processes, frameworks and governance needed to run workloads and host services on public cloud infrastructure.
- Interoperability capabilities (beyond APIs): While APIs will become more prevalent in CRA solutions, there are other methods of integration that will be required to support interoperability.

Netherlands : Developing trusted online ecosystems

The Netherlands Tax Administration (NTA) aims to help taxpayers reduce the overall amount of paperwork. To that end, the NTA participated in a public-private partnership online service trial. This system allows different parties to submit and exchange various datasets in a secure digital environment. It relies on a central hub where information is collected through

Box 5.3. **Country examples: Developing new e-services** *(continued)*

a Standard Business Reporting Process; this is information typically required for prefilling tax returns. What is new is that this system allows taxpayers to opt into peer-to-peer sharing of datasets among various different bodies and for many different purposes. These datasets might, for example, be shared and used in mortgage or insurance applications, or in public service claims. The benefit of this system, compared to regular systems, is enhanced confidence in the authenticity of the data provided.

To deliver this, new architecture and technology were developed for which it was essential that taxpayers had easy and affordable access to a high level of assurance of electronic identity, as well as the certainty that personal data was being managed within relevant legal frameworks. To achieve this, a network of qualified trust service providers (QTSPs) was established. These QTSPs enable their users to register a validated identity, supply information, and take part in information exchanges.

The trial made clear that the most important part in this system is clear governance between the public and private sectors. All organisations involved must specify the information exchanges in which they participate and their exact responsibilities regarding data. This governance is also crucial in formulating requirements and ensuring the public interest is protected.

See Annex 5.A. for links to supporting material. The NTA has also highlighted that there is more detail on this topic in an article published in 2018 (Dijkhuis et al., 2018[2]).

Sources: Australian Taxation Office (2021), Canada Revenue Agency (2021) and Netherlands Tax Administration (2021).

Digital assistants

A growing number of administrations also report using virtual or digital assistants to help respond to taxpayer enquiries and support self-service (see Table 5.2). Early reports suggest that these services have been invaluable in helping tax administrations respond to the service challenges of the pandemic (see the examples included in Box 5.4).

Advances in artificial intelligence (AI) are also being used in some tax administrations, and use of AI may increase rapidly in services supporting taxpayers and tax officials, although perhaps more gradually in decision making given public concerns raised in some countries (see Table 5.2).

Table 5.2. **Use of virtual assistants, artificial intelligence and APIs, 2019**

Percent of administrations that use this technology

Status of implementation and use	Virtual assistants (e.g. chatbots)	Artificial intelligence, including machine learning	Application programming interfaces (APIs)
Technology is implemented and used	46%	38%	86%
Technology is in the implementation phase for future use	17%	34%	9%
Technology is not used, incl. situations where the implementation has not started	37%	28%	5%

Source: Tables A.50 Innovative technologies: Implementation and usage (Part 1) and A.51 Innovative technologies: Implementation and usage (Part 2)

Box 5.4. Country examples: Digital assistants

Australia: Improvements to the online digital assistant – Alex

Alex is the persona and face of the ATO's virtual assistant service and was launched in February 2016. Alex understands conversational language and the service allows taxpayers to ask tax-related questions via the website as if they were talking to a person.

Since the launch, Alex has performed consistently in her core role of answering high volume general tax and superannuation related enquiries. Alex can be found on the ATO's website and can be accessed by computer or smartphone. A conversation with Alex can be started by clicking on one of the most commonly asked topics, or by simply typing a question into the text box.

During 2020, the pandemic and the related Australian government stimulus measures saw client enquiry volumes skyrocket. This provided the ATO with the opportunity to improve Alex's capabilities. Alex's entire knowledge base was revised, and new content added. In addition, Alex's comprehension ability was significantly uplifted and Alex's performance metrics were also refined to improve her reporting capabilities.

Alex has had 1.4 million conversations between 1 July 2020 and 23 March 2021. This is an increase of 79% from the same period for the previous financial year. Alex's metric for "Final Answer – Provided" for this period is averaging 94%. This means that Alex was able to provide a final business answer to the client's enquiry.

Considerations for the future of Alex include the use of emerging technologies to provide clients with a more immersive and responsive experience.

See Annex 5.A. for links to supporting material.

Canada: Live agent chatbot

Current research and client feedback indicates that Canadians want access to new technologies such as chatbots and live agent chat services as part of a full suite of online services offered by their government. The CRA undertook several pilots to explore how artificial intelligence and natural language processing technologies, such as chatbot and live chat, could be used to meet the needs of Canadians. The first pilot was launched in 2019 and focused on a single topic. A subsequent chatbot service was launched just prior to the COVID-19 crisis, which expanded the number of topics to include commonly received enquiries from taxpayers on the phone lines, as well as information related to emergency benefits administered by the CRA. Within the first year, the chatbot responded to just over 5 million questions.

In addition, in response to the COVID-19 pandemic, the CRA experimented with a live chat agent service by leveraging redeployed employee call centre agents already trained in COVID enquiries to respond to Canadians' questions online. The live agent chat experiments offered Canadians empathetic assistance during a time of uncertainty on a communication channel that was easy and accessible to them, and feedback indicated a high level of satisfaction and interest in expanding this service to include more topics. Information gathered from these experiments will be used to refine both the chatbot and live agent chat services.

Costa Rica: TRAVI chatbot and online chat review

In Costa Rica, the tax administration has several communication channels with users, including a portal for filing returns, online taxpayer registration and electronic billing. However, in March 2020 as a result of the COVID-19 pandemic, the Costa Rican Technology Department supported the opening of new channels.

Box 5.4. **Country examples: Digital assistants** *(continued)*

In conjunction with the existing Virtual Procedures Platform (TRAVI, see Box 5.1.) and using specialist software, a new chatbot was developed. This was trained in record time by tax officials and 237 questions were included on the most asked 6 topics such as electronic billing, self-management of keys, cryptographic keys, etc. Additionally, an online chat function was added, which was supported by two chatbot agents from the Costa Rican Services Call Centre.

In its first 4 months, the chatbot answered 50 240 enquiries, and 6 993 enquiries were attended by the chatbot agents. This was a successful launch for Costa Rica as it meant taxpayers had alternative channels to the existing telephone and written routes which are under great pressure, especially when new tax reforms are implemented by the tax administration.

See Annex 5.A. for links to supporting material.

Peru: Virtual assistant – SOFIA

In early 2018, the Peruvian tax administration (SUNAT) decided to introduce a chatbot, SOFIA, to answer a range of the most straightforward and frequent taxpayer queries, with the aim of reducing call volumes.

SUNAT created a multi-disciplinary team which was responsible for both the technical build of the chatbot, and designing the content. The service launched with two topics: the tax receipt lottery and income tax refunds, with other topics related to employment income added during 2019.

During 2020, the tool continued to evolve, and improved both the accuracy and speed of response. Now it handles queries related to taxes on capital and income and some tax procedures, and this year SOFIA has responded to 248 125 messages with 97% effectiveness (see Table 5.3). SUNAT expects to improve SOFIA further and to incorporate new topics related to customs enquiries.

Table 5.3. **Peru: Evolution of the effectiveness rate of chatbot SOFIA**

	2018	2019	2020	2021 (until March)
Percentage of messages understood	74%	69%	93%	97%
Percentage of messages not understood	26%	31%	7%	3%

Source: Peru – Superintendencia Nacional de Administración Tributaria (2021).

See Annex 5.A. for links to supporting material.

Russia: Virtual assistant (chatbot) – TAXIK

The "Intelligent Web Chat" (TAXIK) of the Federal Tax Service of Russia (FTS) provides taxpayers with quick answers, 24/7, to standard enquiries. TAXIK is integrated with the following online services: (i) appointments with the inspectorate; (ii) transport tax calculator; (iii) insurance premium calculator; and (iv) land tax and property tax calculator.

Users can ask questions in the TAXIK widget on the website of the FTS. The answers are provided using a specialised information resource containing standardised answers on tax matters. The information resource – the "Knowledge Database of the Intelligent Web Chat of the FTS" – is based on the existing database of the central call centre of the FTS. The quality of answers provided by TAXIK is monitored daily by IT staff, and the analysis is used to update and supplement the answer database.

Box 5.4. **Country examples: Digital assistants** *(continued)*

TAXIK has proved itself to be an efficient and useful service with 75% of the total answers provided answering the taxpayer query. Furthermore, this 24/7 online service has strengthened trust between FTS and taxpayers.

See Annex 5.A. for links to supporting material.

Singapore: Filing chatbot

In partnership with Government Technology Agency (Govtech), the Inland Revenue Authority of Singapore (IRAS) launched the filing chat bot to help taxi and private-hire car drivers file their income tax easily through conversational-styled filing. The bot leverages on AI technology and Natural Language Processing (NLP) to understand users' inputs and provide intuitive, humanised responses. This enables the provision of seamless, and personalised digital taxpayer experiences.

The filing chat bot is also the first-ever experimentation of simplifying the statutory tax return submission or e-filing processes through a personalised, simple-to-understand conversational style interface with taxpayers – mirroring conversational dialogues with tax officers during the tax filing process. 70% of the taxpayers surveyed found chat filing more intuitive and spent 60% less time filing their income tax returns. The use of layman industry terms also helped the less tax-savvy taxpayers understand the filing requirements better and reduced their need to seek IRAS officers' assistance to file.

For the year of assessment 2021, IRAS has extended the chat filing bot to include hawkers, benefiting approximately 10 000 taxpayers. IRAS is also building more transactional bot services and broadening its informational database with a conversational design approach.

Spain: Virtual assistants – Personal income tax and personal information

In 2021, the Spanish Tax Agency (AEAT) launched two additional virtual assistance services: one for the 2020 personal income tax (PIT) campaign and another for personal information purposes.

In March 2021, the PIT portal opened with a wide range of assistance services: pre-filled returns, explanatory videos, leaflets, "we call you" options, FAQs and so on. For the first time, the PIT assistant was incorporated into the portal.

This tool offers information on the most relevant issues for successful completion of the PIT return. It has been designed using decision trees and consists of eleven different topics (for example, assistance services, identification issues, liability, taxation options, benefits, immovable property, deductions, modification of a submitted return). For each topic the tool asks further questions in consecutive levels of drop-down menus until it reaches the answer, which can include links to other pages for additional information. Then it asks the customer to rate the service and allows a download of the answer in pdf for further certainty.

Furthermore, in March 2021, a new assistant was been added to the personal information section. It works in the same way as the PIT assistant (drop-down menus, printable final answer), but offers information on ten different topics related to the personal information of the taxpayer (for example, TIN, declarations, tax certificates, identification and electronic signature, agent/advisors).

See Annex 5.A. for links to supporting material.

Box 5.4. **Country examples: Digital assistants** *(continued)*

United Kingdom: Webchat and other digital services

In the United Kingdom, Her Majesty's Revenue and Customs (HMRC) encouraged more customers to use its digital services during the pandemic.

HMRC improved its existing online service and acted on customer feedback to enhance its Business Tax Account features and increase the visibility of the service. HMRC also introduced better webchat services and an enhanced digital assistant, as well as the ability for customers to communicate with HMRC electronically where authorisation is required. All this helped to ensure customers have the support they need to meet their obligations and claim benefits and has also reduced the need for colleagues to travel into offices and manually handle requests.

HMRC trained more than 1 000 new colleagues in its webchat service, all of whom could work from home. Webchat was also expanded into new areas. This led to the number of webchats increasing from 4 000 a day before the pandemic to a peak of over 33 000 on 21 April 2020.

Following changes that allowed individuals who were now working from home to claim GBP 6 per week to cover additional household costs, HMRC was expecting a large increase in working from home expense claims. It developed and introduced a new online service which went live on 1 October; by March 2021 over 2.3 million users had successfully made claims using the new service.

HMRC continued to record high levels of customer satisfaction with its digital services with it being consistently above 85% during 2020/21.

Sources: Australian Taxation Office (2021); Canada Revenue Agency (2021); Costa Rica – Directorate of Taxation, Ministry of Finance (2021); Peru – Superintendencia Nacional de Administración Tributaria (2021); Federal Tax Service of Russia (2021); Inland Revenue Authority of Singapore (2021); Spanish Tax Agency (2021) and United Kingdom – Her Majesty's Revenue and Customs (2021).

Mobile apps

The recent trend for the increasing use of mobile applications by tax administrations seen in other editions of this series has continued. While the main use often remains the provision of information and guidance, mobile apps are becoming increasingly transactional, allowing taxpayers to access relevant records and personal tax accounts, communicate with the tax administration, supply information and tax returns and make payments.

Box 5.5. **Country examples: Mobile apps**

Brazil: Mobile app tax and customs

The mobile application for monitoring tax and customs regulations ("Normas") was launched in November 2020. The new version of the "Normas" application allows users to keep up to date on tax and customs publications, by being notified whenever their favourite regulations are modified or new regulations on preferred themes are published.

Russia: Special tax regime "Professional income tax"

The new online service solution "My Tax" allows freelancers to register in just a few minutes for this new tax regime remotely with a mobile device, and keep income records, issue payment invoices and pay professional income tax via the platform. All the recordkeeping, tax payments and accounting are done "on the go" by the system, and the software solution also includes an API that allows banks and digital platforms to integrate taxes into their environment.

Box 5.5. **Country examples: Mobile apps** *(continued)*

There is no need to submit any reporting or returns. The taxes are deducted automatically on a transaction-by-transaction basis. Thus, the software solution provides an end-to-end seamless experience for this new category of taxpayers.

This is the first time that FTS has used such a technologically enabled solution and it is changing the way it views compliance policy and service delivery.

See Annex 5.A. for links to supporting material.

Sources: Federal Revenue Service of Brazil (2021) and Federal Tax Service of Russia (2021).

Application programming interfaces (APIs)

While many tax administrations develop their own apps internally, a large number is also creating APIs and makes those available to third party developers. APIs allow connectivity between systems, people and things without providing direct access. This limits the risk of compromise to the system as opposed to if someone was allowed direct access to the system and the underpinning data stores. Previous editions of this series have highlighted solutions that have given third party developers direct access to a suite of API services that can be integrated into their systems, and this trend has continued to grow (see Table 5.2. for the percentage of administrations using APIs).

The OECD report *Unlocking the digital economy – a guide to unlocking application programming interfaces in government* (OECD, 2019[3]) provides an overview of the practices, techniques and standards used to deliver contemporary and effective digital services for taxpayers.

Box 5.6. **Country examples: How APIs can help providing better services**

Israel: Zero VAT on hotel accommodation services

Tourists pay zero rate VAT on various services consumed in Israel, such as hotel accommodation services, car rental and more.

The Israeli Tax Authority (ITA) has access to entry and exit data of residents and foreigners, through the border controls database and the ITA allows access to the tax authority's API service for permitted software, for the purpose of checking the accuracy of tourists' visa. For example, hotels can enter the details of the transaction (including passport number, country of origin), and receive an indication of whether the tourist is entitled to a zero rate VAT.

As the system verifies that it is indeed a tourist entitled to zero rate VAT, it prevents forgeries and mistakes, and reduces the administrative burden on the hotel. It also reduces hotels' exposure to audit and charges due to guests not being eligible to zero rate VAT.

Norway: The modernisation of the Norwegian VAT system

The Norwegian Tax Administration (NTA) is developing a new IT system for VAT in order to meet the needs of an increasingly digital business community. The goals are to increase compliance rates among businesses, and to provide simplifications for the business community that are also efficient for the NTA.

Box 5.6. **Country examples: How APIs can help providing better services** *(continued)*

For many businesses, the rules relating to VAT seem complicated. Audits are one of the tax authorities' most important instruments for securing compliance, but with limited resources, the number of audits the NTA can carry out is restricted. By offering online guidance directly embedded in the new VAT form, the NTA's ambition is to help businesses become VAT compliant while saving time and resources. Furthermore, the rules for filling the VAT forms are accessible directly from a business's accounting systems, meaning that validation checks are performed in the VAT forms before they are even submitted.

The guidance and validation processes are available through the use of an API in the business's accounting systems. This ensures that the services that are developed are accessible via all digital channels. It is also a way to make information accessible for system-to-system communication. Additionally, it also supports advisors and agents such as accountants and banks providing guidance to their customers based on NTA information.

Russia: Tax Monitoring

Since 2016, the FTS has enacted a new tax compliance regime called "Tax Monitoring". Tax Monitoring is not mandatory; it is an optional system that taxpayers can use, and which runs in parallel to the existing tax system.

Robust and secure authentication are the core principles of Tax Monitoring. These are required to grant the tax authority remote access to the taxpayer's accounting and tax reporting system(s) through APIs. Direct access to the taxpayer ecosystems based on a risk-based approach, embedded at a transaction-level, provides for ongoing due diligence and monitoring to determine whether transactions may contain emerging risks or early warning signs.

Those taxpayers who volunteered to participate in a pilot testing of the system were the most digitally advanced largest taxpayers with the highest level of process automation. This allowed them to have more time to adapt their systems, staff and business processes prior to the new tax compliance regime becoming mandatory.

The Tax Monitoring system makes it possible to embed tax controls within taxpayers' natural ecosystems. This, in turn, facilitates compliance by design creating a seamless customer experience carried out due on time in an effective and efficient manner.

See Annex 5.A. for links to supporting material.

Singapore: Collaboration with software developers

The Inland Revenue Agency of Singapore (IRAS) has long advocated partnerships with third parties to allow a seamless tax-filing experience from taxpayers' natural systems. This has led to the following initiatives:

- The corporate tax seamless filing solution leverages on the API by extracting financial data from within accounting software, converting it into tax data based on predefined tax rules and mapping it from the software to a prescribed list of data elements. The end-user authenticates themselves via Singapore's National Digital Identity (CorpPass), reviews the automatically computed corporate tax return and other supporting documents before filing to IRAS seamlessly.

  This solution addresses key challenges faced by Singapore's SMEs such as rising costs and the complexities posed by accounting and tax rules to in-house staff. An alternative would have been to outsource the accounting and compliance function to external service providers, but the cost might be high. With seamless filing managed in-house, an SME can reduce the overall preparation and filing time for submissions to

Box 5.6. **Country examples: How APIs can help providing better services** *(continued)*

both IRAS and the Accounting and Regulatory Authority (ACRA) from approximately nine hours to 35 minutes.

- Similar in concept to the seamless filing for Corporate Tax returns, seamless filing for Goods and Services Tax (GST) returns enables transmission of GST returns and their accompanying transaction listings directly from taxpayers' accounting software to IRAS via API services.

  Other than time-savings and reduced compliance cost for taxpayers, the collection of transaction listings also has the benefit of enhancing IRAS' compliance capabilities. The submission of such listings together with GST returns improves audit efficiency and reduces audit turn-around time for both IRAS and its taxpayers.

  The pilot for seamless GST submission was successfully completed in Feb 2019. 75% of the users who responded to IRAS' feedback survey agreed that the new mode of submission via API was easy to use and 63% responded that it resulted in higher accuracy in their tax declarations. IRAS has enhanced the API services in October 2020 to include the submissions used to correct errors made in the GST returns as well as the final GST return.

See Annex 5.A. for links to supporting material.

United Kingdom: Making Tax Digital

The United Kingdom (UK) is implementing a new system for tax management as part of its 5-10 year tax strategy. Making Tax Digital (MTD) will help facilitate the wider digitalisation of the UK economy, reduce errors in tax returns and help close the tax gap. It will provide benefits to businesses by improving the ease of use and resilience of the tax system.

Through improved data gathering, MTD will enhance the government's ability to provide direct and targeted support, aiding our national resilience and capability for crisis response. MTD requires taxpayers to keep digital records through software and to file their tax information directly from those records using secure digital links, increasing the accuracy and availability of data. Application programming interfaces (APIs) are used to enable software to supply business tax information directly to HMRC.

HMRC introduced MTD for VAT registered businesses with taxable turnover above the VAT threshold (GBP 85 000) in April 2019. Since then, over a million businesses have used the MTD service, submitting over 9 million returns. Customers have reported a number of benefits, particularly through the replacement of paper-based and manual methods, including reductions in input errors and time spent on tax. HMRC is extending MTD for VAT to apply to all VAT registered businesses from April 2022 and from April 2023 MTD will apply to income tax for taxpayers with business and/or property income over GBP 10 000 per year.

The UK's Office for Budget Responsibility (OBR) has certified that MTD will generate over GBP 2 billion in cumulative additional tax revenue by 2025-26 from these VAT and income tax self-assessment groups. HMRC are exploring options for introducing MTD to corporation tax in future years.

Sources: Israel Tax Authority (2021); Norwegian Tax Administration (2021); Federal Tax Service of Russia (2021); Inland Revenue Authority of Singapore (2021); and United Kingdom – Her Majesty's Revenue and Customs (2021).

As these services become more sophisticated, and play a greater role in delivering a quality service to taxpayers, tax administrations are having to invest more in careful management of these APIs. Box 5.7. sets out some of the work that is being done in this area.

Box 5.7. **Country examples: API management**

Australia: The ATO Strategic direction for APIs

The ATO is experiencing a rapid increase in demand for digital services, namely real-time, event-based APIs. This is evidenced in the growth in volume of digital service providers requesting to access the ATO's APIs and the significant increase in associated message volumes and transactions across a variety of tax services.

The Australian whole of government vision is to deliver services around a citizen's life events which are seamless across agencies. The ATO strives to deliver its APIs seamlessly through user's natural systems (e.g. business or accounting software).

The ATO is expanding its range of digital channels to suit the different types of APIs and complexities and has recently invested in the implementation of a Digital Service Gateway which will cater for simple, lightweight API delivery.

The new gateway will complement existing digital channels to provide the right technical fit to interact with clients' and service provider's natural systems.

Key outcomes:

- delivery of a modern digital platform that is lightweight, event driven, contemporary, accessible and trusted
- provide APIs that are delivered to industry standard and are easy to consume
- enables real-time information sharing and life event driven services through user's natural systems
- modernising existing platforms to ensure scalability and high availability
- delivering platforms that continue to provide confidence and trust in the system
- focus on improving efficiency in API development process and capabilities.

See Annex 5.A. for links to supporting material.

Canada: API Centre of Excellence

The role of the CRA's API Centre of Excellence (CoE) is to support effective API management to improve the sustainability of selected existing and future CRA services by increasing their integration and interoperability capabilities now and into the future. This is achieved by promoting responsible API adoption, establishing standards, foundational principles for API development, and providing support to API development teams. This includes APIs to be consumed by other CRA systems, other Government of Canada departments, other levels of governments, third party vendors or the general public.

Sources: Australian Taxation Office (2021) and Canada Revenue Agency (2021).

Non-digital services

Digital transformation has been critical to tax administrations delivering enhanced services to customers, and whilst digital can deliver a lot, an important aspect of meeting taxpayer preferences is getting the mix of channels right. This calls for considered strategies as to how to serve taxpayers in the most appropriate way, that delivers the best outcomes without adversely impacting the service offering to other taxpayers.

Box 5.8. **Country examples: Supporting taxpayers through non digital channels**

Canada: Digital Mailroom Project

The CRA initiated the Digital Mailroom Project (DMP) to help it convert documents received through a variety of channels into a digital format. These digital documents are managed through a horizontal CRA-wide digital content delivery solution that is also part of the project. Using a gradual on-boarding approach, various business areas will either transition from a paper-based process or enhance existing digital processes. The solution, developed in partnership with a service provider, offers the following standardised capabilities: Receive, Digitise, Extract, Store, and Internal Notification. It also provides for better analytics, and allows multiple areas to simultaneously access information, reducing paper correspondence and processing timelines.

The project successfully launched in October 2020 for use across the CRA. With the onset of the COVID-19 pandemic, the project pivoted and focused on accelerating the digitisation capability for the initial business areas. Accordingly, in October 2020, additional business areas were identified for acceleration into the on-boarding process, with deployment targeted for the summer of 2021.

In addition, the project has demonstrated full data extraction capabilities and is looking to expand this functionality to other business areas in the CRA.

Canada: Liaison Officer service

The CRA continues its transformation toward a culture of service ensuring the CRA is fairer, more helpful, and client-focused. The CRA is committed to adapting their services to better meet the needs of their clients.

One example is the CRA's Liaison Officer (LO) service. The LO service is designed to help small businesses and self-employed individuals by providing them with free, personalised support, information, and guidance about their tax obligations and responsibilities. The objective is to reduce their compliance burden by making it easier for them to comply and to avoid costly intervention in the future. The LO service has had success in supporting this population in their interactions with the CRA to promote and ensure voluntary compliance from the start. Since the launch of the programme in 2014, more than 57 000 small businesses and self-employed individuals have benefited from this service.

Traditionally, the LO service was offered through in-person, one-on-one visits and group seminars at a time and place that was convenient for the client(s). Now, the CRA is taking an innovative approach to the new work environment by shifting to offer the LO service virtually through telephone and secure videoconference platforms, and expanding to include information about COVID-19 relief programme funds. This approach aims to remove geographical barriers, increase flexibility, accessibility and convenience, and provide better service, while ensuring that clients' safety and privacy are respected. The service is voluntary and is readily available by request to any small business or self-employed individual in Canada.

Box 5.8. **Country examples: Supporting taxpayers through non digital channels** *(continued)*

Georgia: Modernised call centre

In recent years, the number of call centre users has increased significantly. During the pandemic the heavy workload in the call centre made it necessary to extend ordinary working hours. Furthermore, to respond to the strong rise in demand for assistance by taxpayers, the Georgia Revenue Service, as a part of its distance service strategy, fully updated the call centre's infrastructure and moved it into a modernised building. As a result:

- The management of the calls received and processed by staff was carried out entirely through special system software, which provides information on quantitative and qualitative performance indicators. The system can generate a total of 35 performance reports and also has the ability to display 10 "live" reports on-screen in real-time.
- The call centre staffing structure now includes a small team of supervisors, responsible for permanently taking care of the information provided to staff, adapting information to customer needs, preparing bespoke answers, updating the knowledge base, and staff training.

Sources: Canada Revenue Agency (2021) and Georgia Revenue Service (2021).

Joined-up services

The report *Tax Administration 2019* highlighted how tax administrations have become increasingly joined-up with other functions of government, often sharing data or platforms to provide better services for citizens (OECD, 2019[4]).

These efforts to join-up with other government agencies often includes a "collect once, use many times" approach. Tax administrations (together with social security agencies) have a special place within government in this respect since they will often hold up-to-date verified information on identity, will be involved in both receiving and making payments and will receive and send information to third parties (such as financial institutions and employers).

Box 5.9. **Country examples: Joined-up services**

China (People's Republic of): One-stop services on real estate transaction taxation and ownership registration

Currently the registration of real estate ownership also involves tax-related matters such as tax declarations and payments. Since 2020, the Chinese State Taxation Administration and the real estate registration agencies have strengthened their collaboration, reformed their business processes and delivered one-stop services to optimise customer service.

Before the reforms, there were separate service windows for real estate transaction taxation and ownership registration. Enterprises and individuals had to queue up and submit two sets of documents respectively, for both the tax declaration and the payment, before they could apply for ownership registration. This led to repeated submissions that were inefficient and burdensome for taxpayers.

Box 5.9. **Country examples: Joined-up services** *(continued)*

After the reforms, a "one-stop shop service" for the two departments was set up in the real estate registration department that collected all the requested materials at one time. The back offices of the two departments now deal with the business concurrently with the relevant data transmitted internally and real-time sharing of data realised in some areas. As a result, the final outcomes can be issued by the same "one-stop shop". This means that taxpayers only need to visit the department once, and submit one set of documents to complete tax related matters and registrations of ownership.

By the end of 2020, one-stop services have been implemented in all cities at prefecture level and above, and the satisfaction rate of taxpayers has significantly improved. The processing time of real estate registration has been reduced to less than 5 working days, and the processing time of general tax related matters has been reduced to less than 1 hour.

France: Company portal

In 2018, France launched a wide-ranging reform of the collection of social contributions and taxes.

The first goal of the reform is to streamline tax collection within the central government's Directorate General for Public Finances (DGFiP), and social contributions within the social contribution collection offices (URSSAF).

The second goal of the reform is to simplify tax and social contribution processes, through a common online portal owned by the DGFIP, French customs and URSSAF.

This common online portal will be opened to companies at the beginning of 2022. It will mostly support small business owners, self-employed workers and new entrepreneurs, who face challenges with time and resource allocation to fulfil administrative activities. The first version of the portal includes:

- a Single Sign On (SSO) system to:
  - enable businesses to use the existing websites with one password (instead of 3)
  - perform tasks more quickly (e.g. VAT declarations, payment of social contributions)
- a dashboard enabling users to have an overview of all their upcoming statements and payments for taxes and social contributions, on a single page (this information is currently dispersed on 3 existing portals)
- a secure mail system to contact the three organisations.

The features of the portal were designed following consultation with user groups. Permanent user groups will be created to improve the portal's content in the future.

Singapore: National digital identity

The National Digital Identity (NDI) is the cornerstone of Singapore's Smart Nation Vision. Building upon the SingPass (an individual digital identity for all residents) and CorpPass (a corporate digital identity for businesses and other entities) authentication systems, the NDI is a unified platform that enables citizens and businesses to transact with both the public and private sectors in a secure and convenient manner using a single digital identity. It also includes MyInfo (a personal data management service akin to a digital profile that enables citizens and residents to simplify online transactions).

The NDI and collaboration with government and private partners also enables personalised services for individual taxpayers in Singapore. Data from IRAS and other agencies and

Box 5.9. **Country examples: Joined-up services** *(continued)*

partners contribute to MyInfo tied to each unique NDI which facilitates seamless form-filling for tax and access to other personalised services across digital channels, reducing or even eliminating the need for submitting supporting documents. Leveraging NDI, 98% of individual taxpayers e-filed in Singapore.

NDI and APIs help to integrate taxes (income tax, GST/VAT) into businesses' natural systems. Companies can harness various NDI features via CorpPass to interact with customers and transact with government agencies and other entities securely and easily with the requisite consent and authorisation. For instance, companies can seamlessly file returns using their accounting software to both IRAS and the national company registry via CorpPass and APIs, resulting in about a 75% reduction in time spent on preparing tax returns, schedules and financial statements.

See Annex 5.A. for links to supporting material.

Sweden: Moving to Sweden to work – one entrance

In this project, four Swedish governmental agencies have developed a digital solution that simplifies and streamlines the process for those who want to move to Sweden to work. The project is a collaboration between the Swedish Tax Agency, the Swedish Migration Agency, the Swedish Social Insurance Agency and the Swedish Public Employment Service.

Sweden offers the applicant a government-wide digital mobile service, which visualises an overall picture of the process for those who move to Sweden to work with personal guidance and the opportunity for personalised feedback. The solution contains information and services, starting from when the individual is seeking information about moving to Sweden to work, until the individual has obtained a work permit, and been registered and established in Sweden. The service also contains information about the Swedish labour market and the Swedish social system.

The product is available in Swedish and English, meets the accessibility requirements according to current legislation, and it is the first step to comply with the requirements of the European Union (EU) regulation Single Digital Gateway.

By creating an account, users can identify themselves and save their answers. They can also choose to continue on their personalised guide later.

In its first phase, the product is aimed at citizens outside the EU who apply for a work permit in Sweden (applicants and accompanying persons). Work is ongoing to develop the technical platform with additional functionality and to include more target groups and life events.

Further development of the product's functionality takes place on existing applications such as graph database, content management/editorial support and container technology for load balancing. Participating authorities can add, edit and delete content through the product's content management system, for example, text, translation, formatting and display order.

The purpose of the solution is to offer people a simpler, safer and faster establishment in Sweden and gives an opportunity to provide a single gateway to the authorities in Sweden. Sweden also expects this project to deliver increased internal efficiency and reduced costs, with a larger analysis of saved costs and other benefits to be carried out soon.

Sources: China (People's Republic of) – State Taxation Administration (2021); France – Direction Générale des Finances Publiques (2021); Inland Revenue Authority of Singapore (2021) and Swedish Tax Agency (2021).

Behavioural insights

Behavioural insights is an interdisciplinary field of research using principles from the behavioural sciences such as psychology, neuroscience, and behavioural economics to understand how individuals absorb, process, and react to information. These principles can be used to design practical policies and interventions based on human behaviour. This can be particularly powerful when combined with insights gathered from the analysis of the increasingly large volumes of data available to tax administration, both internally and externally generated.

Previous editions of this series have seen more and more tax administrations report employing behavioural researchers and using behavioural insights in specific areas to influence voluntary compliance. Chapter 10 of the 2019 edition of this report contains further insight into these developments. This trend has continued, with behavioural insights being increasingly mainstreamed into wider tax administration strategies and interventions. In 2019, two-thirds of the administrations covered by this report used behavioural insight methodologies or techniques (see Table A.48).

Two examples of how tax administrations are using behavioural insights are included in Box 5.10. Further examples are included in other chapters of this report, for example, in Box 7.2.

Box 5.10. **Country examples: Behavioural insights**

Canada: Nudge initiatives

The CRA has a number of nudge initiatives that have been undertaken:

- ***Using nudge to manage unusually high network traffic*** – In the early days of the COVID-19 pandemic, the Canadian Government launched the Canada Emergency Response Benefit which provided financial support to employed and self-employed individuals who were directly affected by COVID-19. Announced in March, application intake opened on 6 April 2020. Prior to the launch, there was a serious concern about the ability of the CRA's network to handle what was expected to be unusually high traffic. To mitigate potential risks, the CRA employed one of the most powerful tools in behavioural sciences – setting a behavioural default, to design and manage the Canadian Emergency Response Benefit applications initial intake volumes. The successful nudge distributed the applicant population to each of the first four days of the week (Monday – Thursday) based on the applicant's month of birth. Through the first 3 periods of applications, over 60% of applicants chose to follow the behavioural default. Easy and simple, the behavioural default was extremely effective.
- ***Nudging using an Automated Telephone Call for Individual and Corporate Filing Compliance*** – Since 2016, the CRA has initiated four nudge pilot campaigns that focus on improving individual income tax filing compliance using an Automatic Dialling Announcing Device (ADAD) to contact and remind individual taxpayers of their tax obligations. These campaigns prove that a nudge delivered in a successful ADAD call had a positive impact on personal income tax filing compliance. In January 2020, the CRA undertook a similar campaign but this time for corporate income tax filers. A randomised controlled trial was designed to test the effect of a reminder nudge. Results show that the nudge message had a positive impact on the filing rate of corporations that were contacted by ADAD.

Box 5.10. **Country examples: Behavioural insights** *(continued)*

- ***Benefits Letter Campaign*** – This initiative uses business intelligence and data analytics to identity and send letters to those who typically do not file income tax returns and may be eligible for benefits. As a result of letter mail-outs in 2019, a total of 28 665 returns were filed resulting in over CAD 15.17 million in tax refund payments and CAD 22.46 million in credits or benefits paid. Five phases of the campaign have been conducted so far, the latest being in November 2020.

Hungary: Behavioural science based campaign

Since 2017, the Hungarian Ministry of Finance and the National Tax and Customs Administration (NTCA) have run joint annual campaigns to promote the alternative, simplified taxation method, the small business tax (KIVA) to the small and medium-sized business sector. After analysing tax returns, Hungary targets those businesses which would benefit from converting to KIVA. Some of the selected businesses receive a traditional letter highlighting the benefits of KIVA, while others – where the data enables accurate calculations – receive a letter containing the estimated value of available tax savings. In 2020, the campaign scope was extended to introduce intermediaries (accountants, tax advisors) meaning for some businesses it was the manager who was contacted but in other cases the information was sent directly to the accountant or tax advisor.

The KIVA campaigns have been carried out as a random controlled experiment, making it possible to assess the effectiveness of each type of letter. The analyses clearly show the success of the campaigns, with the proportion of enterprises opting into KIVA being significantly higher among those who were part of the campaign.

See Annex 5.A. for links to supporting material.

Sources: Canada Revenue Agency (2021) and Hungary – National Tax and Customs Administration (2021).

References

Dijkhuis, S. et al. (2018), *When Willeke can get rid of paperwork: a lean infrastructure for qualified information exchange based on trusted identities*, Association for Computing Machinery, New York, NY, United States, http://dx.doi.org/10.1145/3209281.3209324. [2]

OECD (2021), *"Tax Administration: Digital Resilience in the COVID-19 Environment", OECD Policy Responses to Coronavirus (COVID-19)*, OECD Publishing, Paris, http://dx.doi.org/10.1787/2f3cf2fb-en. [1]

OECD (2019), *Tax Administration 2019: Comparative Information on OECD and other Advanced and Emerging Economies*, OECD Publishing, Paris, https://dx.doi.org/10.1787/74d162b6-en. [4]

OECD (2019), *Unlocking the Digital Economy – A guide to implementing application programming interfaces in Government*, OECD, Paris, www.oecd.org/tax/forum-on-tax-administration/publications-and-products/unlocking-the-digital-economy-guide-to-implementing-application-programming-interfaces-in-government.htm (accessed on 1 September 2021). [3]

Annex 5.A

Links to supporting material (accessed on 1 September 2021)

- Box 5.1 – Chile: Link to a video on the new IT system that allows a completely digital journey throughout a taxpayer's lifecycle: https://youtu.be/GoEpNiSk1Wg
- Box 5.1 – India:
  - Link to the process flowchart for faceless assessment, penalty and appeal proceedings: www.oecd.org/tax/forum-on-tax-administration/publications-and-products/india-process-flowchart-for-remote-proceedings.pdf
  - Link to the e-filing website of the Income Tax Department: www.incometaxindiaefiling.gov.in/
- Box 5.1 – Spain:
  - Link to a presentation on the Integral Digital Administration (ADI) the Spanish Tax Agency's virtual counter: www.oecd.org/tax/forum-on-tax-administration/publications-and-products/spain-integral-digital-assistance-adi.pdf
  - Link to videos explaining the ADI: www.youtube.com/embed/sYa-e8-iR-E (Spanish), and www.youtube.com/watch?v=4LJlGb9hnBQ (English)
- Box 5.3 – Australia: Link to a presentation on the digital partnership office: www.oecd.org/tax/forum-on-tax-administration/publications-and-products/australia-digital-partnership-office.pdf
- Box 5.3 – Netherlands: Link to a poster showing the added value of the Trusted Online Ecosystem for standard business reporting: www.oecd.org/tax/forum-on-tax-administration/publications-and-products/netherlands-trusted-online-ecosystems-poster.pdf
- Box 5.4 – Australia: Link to a presentation on the virtual assistant Alex: www.oecd.org/tax/forum-on-tax-administration/publications-and-products/australia-virtual-assistant-alex.pdf
- Box 5.4 – Costa Rica: Link to a presentation on the TRAVI chatbot and online chat: www.oecd.org/tax/forum-on-tax-administration/publications-and-products/costa-rica-travi-chatbot-and-online-chat.pdf
- Box 5.4 – Peru: Link to a presentation on the virtual assistant SOFIA: www.oecd.org/tax/forum-on-tax-administration/publications-and-products/peru-virtual-assistant-sofia.pdf
- Box 5.4 – Russia: Link to a presentation on the virtual assistant TAXIK: www.oecd.org/tax/forum-on-tax-administration/publications-and-products/russia-virtual-assistant-taxik.pdf

- Box 5.4 – Spain:
  - Link to the virtual assistant for personal income tax: https://www2.agenciatributaria.gob.es/wlpl/AVAC-CALC/InformadorRenta2020
  - Link to the virtual assistant for personal information: https://www2.agenciatributaria.gob.es/wlpl/AVAC-CALC/InformadorCensal
- Box 5.5 – Russia: Link to a presentation providing an overivew of the special tax regime "Professional income tax": www.oecd.org/tax/forum-on-tax-administration/publications-and-products/russia-special-tax-regime-professional-income-tax.pdf
- Box 5.6 – Russia: Link to a presentation providing an overview of the new "Tax Monitoring" compliance regime: www.oecd.org/tax/forum-on-tax-administration/publications-and-products/russia-tax-monitoring.pdf
- Box 5.6 – Singapore: Link to a graphic illustrating the use of an API to allow a seamless tax-filing experience: www.oecd.org/tax/forum-on-tax-administration/publications-and-products/singapore-collaboration-with-software-providers.pdf
- Box 5.7 – Australia: Link to an illustration on the ATO's strategic direction for APIs: www.oecd.org/tax/forum-on-tax-administration/publications-and-products/australia-strategic-direction-for-apis.pdf
- Box 5.9 – Singapore:
  - Link to a graphic illustrating how NDI and collaboration with government and private partners enable seamless and personalised services for taxpayers: www.oecd.org/tax/forum-on-tax-administration/publications-and-products/singapore-national-digital-identity-individuals.pdf
  - Link to a graphic illustrating how NDI and APIs facilitate the integration of taxes into businesses' natural systems: www.oecd.org/tax/forum-on-tax-administration/publications-and-products/singapore-national-digital-identity-businesses.pdf
- Box 5.10 – Hungary: Link to a video on the use of behavioural insights to promote a simplified taxation method for the small and medium-sized business sector: https://youtu.be/ZZg_w0T-SKw

Chapter 6

Verification and compliance management

Assessing the accuracy and completeness of taxpayer reported information is one of the key functions of tax administrations and critical for supporting voluntary compliance. This chapter takes a closer look at tax administrations' work in this area, including how they manage compliance. It also briefly comments on tax administrations' work on moving audit tasks into a virtual environment, including during the COVID-19 pandemic.

Introduction

The audit, verification and investigation function assesses the accuracy and completeness of taxpayer reported information. This function employs on average thirty percent of tax administration staff and verifies that tax obligations have been met. While this mainly happens through conducting desk or field based "tax audits," there is an increased use of automated electronic checks, validations and matching of taxpayer information. The undertaking and visibility of these and other compliance actions is critical in supporting voluntary compliance, including through their impacts on perceptions of fairness in the tax system.

In this respect, this chapter looks at:

- how tax administrations manage compliance risks, including the use of large and integrated data sets
- the coverage and results of compliance actions undertaken by tax administrations
- the work on tax and crime.

It also briefly comments on tax administrations' progress in moving field audit work into a virtual environment, something that received more traction during the course of the COVID-19 pandemic.

Compliance risk management

The OECD report *The Changing Tax Compliance Environment and the Role of Audit* (OECD, 2017[1]) looked at the range of incremental changes occurring across tax administrations which, taken together, were changing the nature of the tax compliance environment, allowing for more facilitated and managed compliance.

A significant part of this is driven by the hugely increased availability of data which allows for a sharpened targeting of risks, future trend analysis, and an increased automation of compliance checks. With increasing digitalisation, even more tax related data from taxpayers and third parties will become available (for example data from e-invoicing, online cash registers and financial account information). This data has to be processed

Figure 6.1. **Use of techniques and methodologies to improve compliance, 2019**

Percent of administrations that use those techniques and methodologies

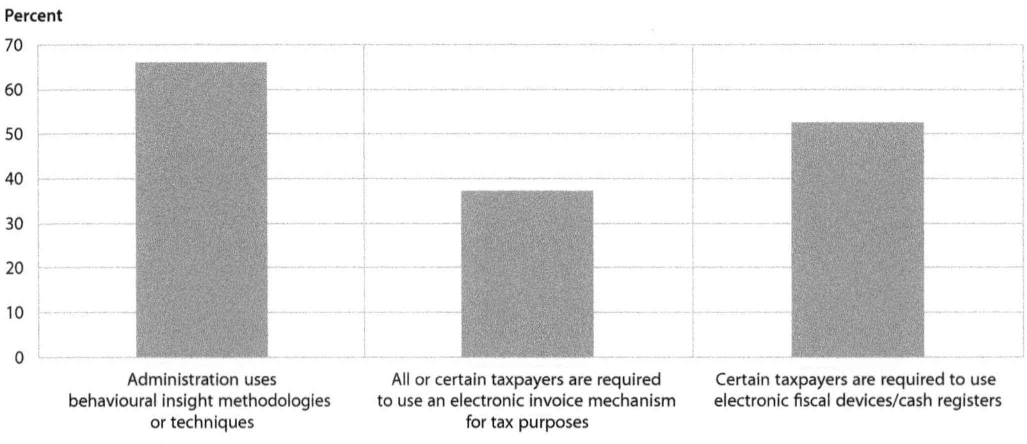

StatLink http://dx.doi.org/10.1787/888934271359

Source: Table A.48 Techniques and methodologies to improve compliance.

and managed by tax administrations, many of whom apply data sciences techniques and use analytical tools as part of this process. This sophisticated analysis is being combined with behavioural analysis to build a more complete picture of compliance risks. Figure 6.1, shows the percent of tax administrations who are using these types of approaches.

Box 6.1. Country examples: Data exploration

Canada: Data Mining Pipeline

The Canada Revenue Agency (CRA) is leveraging machine learning techniques to facilitate data exploration and data understanding for situations where there are overwhelming amounts of data, and little to no prior knowledge of the databases or systems. Even in cases where good documentation and metadata exists, thorough knowledge of a database could take years to acquire. To support business understanding, data mining approaches were developed to shed light on how variables within the databases are related. Harnessing enormous datasets with voluminous numbers of variables, these approaches provide straightforward results, that are easily comprehensible and consumable for analysts. These techniques have been utilised by various areas within the CRA to help fast track the data exploration phase, providing rapid preliminary insights, and allowing more targeted areas of focus for subsequent analysis, in addition to uncovering undiscovered trends and insights within their data.

France: Data lake project

At the core of the French tax administration's (Direction Générale des Finances Publiques, DGFiP) digital strategy lies their data lake, a Big Data infrastructure tailor-made to address the issue of processing an incredible amount of data regardless of its original source. It does this in a robust and secure way, and pays special care as regards the use and storage of personal data.

It is also the playground for data scientists to devise a DGFiP-compatible workflow in order to explore, and assess the viability of an AI project, and to explore and deliver automation projects. DGFiP aim to ensure that their data lake supports their wider vision of AI projects that are consistent with their goals of automation, supervision, ethics and data protection.

Their first use of this infrastructure has effectively reduced by a factor of 20 the time needed to perform one of the statistical aggregates needed for annual tax management. This was critical as demands for statistical aggregates were barely being met due to the amount of data involved in the process.

Since then, data from several applications has flowed into the data lake, providing a solid ground for AI projects that rely on data previously stored in different segments of the IT system which has prompted a wider consideration of data governance.

See Annex 6.A for links to supporting material.

Singapore: Unified Data Platform

As part of the Inland Revenue Authority of Singapore's (IRAS) journey to be data-centric, IRAS implemented the Unified Data Platform ("UDP") to consolidate data from various sources into a single flexible and scalable data repository. The platform facilitates timelier movement of data across systems and the use of timely data in decision-making, which is particularly beneficial as processes and digital interactions with taxpayers become closer to real time. The base technology of the UDP supports the storing and processing of larger and more complex data formats. This significantly improves IRAS' ability to handle a larger variety of data, beyond structured data.

Box 6.1. **Country examples: Data exploration** *(continued)*

The UDP's capability to handle more complex data formats has opened up new frontiers in IRAS' exploitation of data. For example, the Email Recommender tool, built on unstructured text search capability, has enabled officers to retrieve relevant past responses as references to handle email queries faster. Advanced machine learning and natural language processing techniques are applied to enhance the relevance of the search results, as well as to improve its accuracy over time.

Utilising Change Data Capture technology, the UDP is able to ingest data from source systems much faster. This resolved a key pain point of the previous analytics system, where there could be a delay of up to several weeks for data ingestion to be completed. With the consolidation of data from various sources into a single data platform, coupled with the use of contemporary data visualisation tools, IRAS is able to perform more timely and more holistic analyses using up-to-date data to enhance insights and decision-making.

Sources: Canada Revenue Agency (2021), France – Direction Générale des Finances Publiques (2021) and Inland Revenue Authority of Singapore (2021).

Increasing availability of data

As more and more data is stored electronically, and the transfer, storage and integration of data has become easier through the application of new techniques and processes, there has been a huge increase in the amount of data available to tax administrations for compliance purposes.

Data sources include:

- ***Data from devices***: Data can be collected from devices that register transactions such as online cash registers and trip computers for taxis and trucks, and also gate registrations from barriers and weigh bridges.
- ***Data from banks, merchants or payment intermediaries and service providers***: This allows direct verification of income or assets reported by the taxpayer. Some countries already receive transaction details or transaction totals for taxpayers on a regular basis.
- ***Data from suppliers***: Collecting data from suppliers, either directly or through the taxpayer, allows a more complete picture to be drawn about the activities and income of the taxpayer. This is seen in the increasing use of e-invoicing systems which, as noted in Chapter 4, even allow some tax administrations to prefill tax returns.
- ***Data from the customer***: This is easiest in cases where the number of customers is limited and known, but increasingly mechanisms to leverage customers in compliance are being used, for example in the verification of cash receipts. Another example is included in Box 6.2, where Chilean citizens can use a mobile app created by the tax administration to verify the validity of the tax certificate of cigarette packs and report any inconsistencies.
- ***Unstructured data concerning the taxpayer***: Increasingly electronic traces relevant to business activities and transactions can be found on the internet and in social media. Also the analysis of unstructured data in emails can improve response times and accuracy as set out in the example from Singapore in Box 6.1.

- ***Data from other government agencies***: Data held by other government agencies for example for licensing, regulatory or social security purposes can be relevant in verifying tax returns or in risk assessments. For example, the Costa Rican tax administration uses information from local property maps, municipalities, the real estate registry and aerial photographs available on the web to identify real estate that, due to its use and value, is subject to special tax (see Box 6.2).
- ***Data from international partners***: New international exchanges of data commencing under the Common Reporting Standard and Country-by-Country Reporting is massively increasing the quantity of data available on international activity and providing useful information for audit and case selection processes and in some cases for prefilling of tax returns.

Box 6.2. **Country examples: Using the increased availability of data**

Canada: Data Analytics, Machine Learning, and Natural Language Processing for Assurance and Advisory Intelligence

As data analysis tools advance, so do the organisation's expectations for timely, relevant, and holistic data in order to inform strategic, fact-based decision-making. To address these evolving needs, the CRA is using innovative tools to change how the organisation effectively and efficiently analyses data to deliver evidence-based assurance and advisory services.

Leveraging Artificial Intelligence (AI) techniques, such as Machine Learning (ML) and Natural Language Processing (NLP), to reduce analysis time and augment the ability to understand a large amount of information is leading to an increase in the scope and breadth of the CRA's internal audit and evaluation engagements. For example, in 2021, full populations were analysed using ML models rather than a random sample when searching for potential risks of internal fraud, allowing senior management to make more informed decisions on how to mitigate the risk of fraud. Through NLP, many types of documents were analysed to generate topics, sentiment summaries, and network diagrams, allowing the CRA to analyse more pieces of information in detail, which provides employees with more time to interpret results. These AI techniques are applied to all stages of the internal audit, evaluation, and risk management processes, and the CRA encourages their development and use across the agency to promote innovation.

The CRA has seen first-hand how these tools can be used more broadly across the agency and is demonstrating how understanding and applying them can add value by saving employees' time and leading to better decisions.

Chile: Cigarettes tracking system

As of March 2019, cigarette packs sold in Chile must have a marking system that allows for the distinguishing of counterfeit products from genuine ones. This allows the online monitoring of the national production of cigarettes by brand and variety (SKU), the amount of wastage, as well as the correct payment of specific sector taxes. This implementation was carried out in conjunction with market agents. During 2019, 487 044 855 packs were marked for the domestic market and 10 800 000 for exports, while between January and December 2020, 514 639 534 packs were marked for the national market and 20 412 000 for exports.

To help with compliance, a portable tool can verify the product markings, validate the ink used and the characteristics of the product. It also allows the centralised registration of the results obtained from the on-site inspection.

Box 6.2. **Country examples: Using the increased availability of data** *(continued)*

Additionally, the tax administration also enabled a mobile app, called e-Verifica, through which citizens can verify the validity of a pack. Specifically, the app reads the code, verifies its validity, and displays the information about the product. The same tool allows the user to report any inconsistency, incorporating information regarding the place of purchase, the reason for the inconsistency, and so on.

All of this gives the Chilean tax administration access to timely information, allowing a sharper focus to compliance work.

See Annex 6.A. for links to supporting material.

Costa Rica: Use of geographic information system to locate real estate, that is subject to tax

The Costa Rican Central Tax Administration has worked to improve their knowledge of the geographical location of real estate in seven municipalities of the country, to ensure that the real estate is taxed appropriately. This was needed because of inconsistencies in the owners' address and the real estate identification plates (property or estate identification number) which were obstacles for proper tax management.

With inputs such as local property maps, records from the municipalities, aerial photographs, and the data held by the Costa Rican real estate registry and tax administration, a central geographic tax information system was created. Through this the owners of properties who had not complied with their tax obligation were identified.

Following the detection, location and identification of non-compliant property owners, a tax control process has begun, that also gives taxpayers the chance to rectify their omission voluntarily.

The results of this work include:

- detection of 75% more taxpayers that were previously hidden (not registered in the real estate registry as having paid their property taxes)
- a 5% increase in new tax filers
- savings in field work time and expenses
- creation of a resource that can support other compliance work.

See Annex 6.A. for links to supporting material.

Hungary: Tracing invoicing chains

As a result of the introduction of the mandatory online invoice data reporting in Hungary, the National Tax and Customs Administration benefits from a considerable amount of real-time data. This is also a breakthrough in detecting those hiding behind fraudulent invoicing chains, allowing the administration to take more targeted and faster action against intentional offenders. It also allows for a clear distinction between fraudulent and compliant taxpayers.

Milestones for mandatory reporting

1 July 2018 – Introduction of mandatory data reporting on invoices between domestic taxpayers with VAT amounting to HUF 100 thousand or more.

1 July 2020 – Regardless of the VAT amount, reporting on invoices between domestic taxable persons is mandatory.

1 January 2021 – All invoices must be reported, if the place of supply is in Hungary including those where the buyer is a natural person.

Box 6.2. **Country examples: Using the increased availability of data** *(continued)*

Risk analysis based on online invoice data

The system compares the incoming invoice data with the VAT returns data, filters out the anomalies, and cross matches data to make the invoicing chains visible on a network-visualisation tool.

The data generated is used for risk analysis, and allows for rapid identification of risk based on profiles, as well as more targeted selections for pre-allocation checks. An example of risk profile might be that an issuer of the invoice is under tax enforcement procedure and the payment deadline has not expired yet.

Results

In the year of the introduction of the mandatory online invoice data reporting (2018), the VAT payment balance was HUF 3928.7 billion, which increased by 11.44 % compared to the previous year and showed a further increase of 15.35 % in 2019. In 2020, the indicator showed a decrease of 9.65 % due to the pandemic situation.

See Annex 6.A. for links to supporting material.

Peru: E-commerce

The sustained increase in e-commerce in Peru has grown since the second quarter of 2020 due to the pandemic scenario, creating new business ventures where goods and services are sold through on-line platforms. However, the risk of undeclared activity has also expanded, leading to unfair competition and decreasing tax revenues.

In this context, the aim of the initiative is encouraging voluntary compliance amongst citizens, and to make it easier to formalise their business activities. For this purpose, SUNAT used a web scraping technique that, through programming algorithms, and obtained information from different sources such as social networks and e-commerce websites. Subsequently, a categorisation of goods and services is applied by text-mining. Once non-compliant sellers on on-line platforms have been identified, information is provided to them on their compliance obligations.

As a result of the initiative, 14 562 new sellers through on-line platforms were detected in one year. This was higher than achieved through other actions, and there is evidence of an impact on the detection costs incurred by SUNAT, which were reduced from 19 to 0.12 Soles per citizen detected.

See Annex 6.A. for links to supporting material.

Russia: Analytical system "Financial accounts (CRS)"

After the Common Reporting Standard (CRS) data is received from peers it is loaded into a data lake that also includes data sets from other internal data bases. Then the system uses 16 pre-set algorithms to connect the CRS information with data in the other systems and to ensure there are no mistakes. The algorithms are hard tuned i.e. unless at least two data elements simultaneously match, the data is sent for semi-manual verification by an operator. At this point the operator is assisted by the system to show where the error might come from and what might be the best solution. The results of this work are copied by the system for further verification exercises.

When the data is successfully matched, it is taken to another data lake containing further internal information for risk-profiling. The purpose of these exercises is to find out if the matched taxpayer has any undeclared income from sources outside Russia, if they own a foreign company or if they have assets that can be used to pay tax arrears. The algorithms are largely pre-set, however when the resulting risks are verified by territorial tax officers, the system takes this into account.

Box 6.2. **Country examples: Using the increased availability of data** *(continued)*

After the two matching processes are complete, the results are provided to the tax officers responsible for compliance actions as regards the particular taxpayer for further investigation and feedback.

Currently 83% of data is matched successfully by the system.

See Annex 6.A. for links to supporting material.

Sources: Canada Revenue Agency (2021), Chile – Servicio de Impuestos Internos (2021), Costa Rica – Directorate of Taxation (2021), Hungary – National Tax and Customs Administration (2021), Peru – Superintendencia Nacional de Administración Tributaria (2021) and Federal Tax Service of Russia (2021).

There are, though, some emerging risks to the availability of large data sets. In particular, it is increasingly possible for data relevant to the tax administration in one jurisdiction to be held within the territory of another jurisdiction. In these circumstances, it can be difficult to obtain the data on an automatic basis from the data holder located in another jurisdiction. This could make it more difficult to risk assess in some circumstances, as well as prefilling of tax returns or the development of compliance by design processes.

An example of this comes from the growth of the sharing and gig economy facilitated through online platforms which can operate across border. This may become an increasing risk as the online economy grows, particularly if it is accompanied by a shift from salaried employment (and the reporting of incomes by employers) to self-employment. This issue was considered in the OECD report *The Sharing and Gig Economy: Effective Taxation of Platform Sellers* (OECD, 2019[2]). That report looked at a number of strategies currently being adopted by tax administrations as well as their limitations and recommended the development of standardised reporting requirements to facilitate possible future automatic exchange of information between tax administrations. It also led to the development of:

- a set of Model Rules that when used in legislation require digital platforms to collect information on the income realised by those offering accommodation, transport and personal services through platforms and to report the information to tax authorities (OECD, 2020[3])
- a Code of Conduct to facilitate a possible standard approach to co-operation between administrations and platforms on providing information and support to platform sellers on their tax obligations while minimising compliance burdens (OECD, 2020[4]).

Another risk that has been identified is that posed by digital financial assets (DFAs), such as cryptocurrencies. The owners of DFAs can be very difficult to trace even though they may be linked to the creation of a specific digital wallet (which is somewhat similar to a bank account). Tracking down the individuals or entities behind particular wallet addresses is at best very difficult and resource intensive.

While not a risk as such, it should also be noted that data protection requirements could limit the circumstances in which data can be kept, processed or shared.

Sharpened targeting of risks

Data science

Over recent years, there has been a significant increase in the application of advanced analytics to risk management. The OECD report *Advanced Analytics for Tax Administration: Putting data to work* (OECD, 2016[5]) provides practical guidance on how tax administrations can use analytics to support compliance and service delivery.

Currently, 49 tax administrations report using data science/analytical tools and many others are in the process of preparing the use of such tools going forward. Similarly, the use of artificial intelligence, including machine learning, is already undertaken or in the process of being implemented by the majority of administrations covered in this publication (see Table 6.1).

Table 6.1. **Application of data science, 2019**

Percent of administrations

Status of implementation and use	Data science/ analytical tools	Artificial intelligence, including machine learning	Robotic process automation
Technology implemented and used	84%	38%	27%
Technology in the implementation phase for future use	14%	34%	14%
Technology not used, incl. situations where implementation has not started	2%	28%	59%

Source: Tables A.50 Innovative technologies: Implementation and usage (Part 1) and A.51 Innovative technologies: Implementation and usage (Part 2)

Increasingly sophisticated use of analytics on expanding data sets is leading to a sharpening of risk management and the selection of a range of intervention actions, including through automated processes. A selection of examples is included in Box 6.3.

Box 6.3. **Country examples: Using analytics to sharpen the targeting of risks**

Australia: Automated bank statement analysis

Many tax audits and most investigations require a time-consuming analysis of bank statements.

The Australian Taxation Office (ATO) has automated this process using purpose-built spreadsheet based templates (the Templates), resulting in:

- bank statement analysis speed increasing by 10 times or more (i.e. a 90% time saving).
- an increased ability to react in "real time" to current/ongoing offending.
- improved insights into large data sets.

The Templates were developed in-house at no additional cost and they present an example of a determined organisation deriving efficiencies from existing resources.

How do they work?

Spreadsheet compatible bank statement data is copied into the Templates, which apply formulae to "read" the bank statement description fields for each transaction. Banking "jargon" is ignored and transactions are classified in seconds based on the remaining bespoke words/

Box 6.3. **Country examples: Using analytics to sharpen the targeting of risks** *(continued)*

phrases (e.g. if the bank statement description read "Internet banking transfer 1010 Jane Smith loan", then the Template classifies it as "Jane Smith loan".

The Templates:

- suggest potential related party transactions
- automatically generate a variety of dashboard reports from the data
- are easily "taught" to "read" new bank statements
- readily incorporate new data as it is received.

See Annex 6.A. for links to supporting material.

Belgium: Transaction Network Analysis (TNA)

Transaction Network Analysis (TNA) is the new system established at the European level that allows Member States (MS) to rapidly deal and jointly process VAT data, leading to earlier detection of suspicious networks in order to combat VAT fraud.

This tool is inspired by the approach applied since 2002 by the Belgian FPS Finance's Special Tax Inspectorate (ISI) which was responsible for the development of the TNA and currently chairs the expert group. The tool is made available to anti-fraud units in all member states in the now well-known network called Eurofisc.

TNA is a data mining tool for information exchange and common processing of data for Eurofisc officials that uses VIES (VAT Information Exchange System) and Eurofisc data to build networks around known risky traders. Once the networks are built, they are prioritised in accordance to business rules agreed upon by Member States. TNA allows Eurofisc Liaison Officials to provide feedback on signals they have received, in an effective way. The TNA tool is complementary to national risk analysis tools and methods and does not replace the latter.

The TNA system consists of two parts: the core TNA application and the business rules and algorithms that will be applied to the data.

The main functionalities of TNA makes it possible to:

- automate the collection of targeted information over VIES
- visualise suspicious networks without manual interventions
- improve MS ability to send early warnings and provide feedback
- improve the quality, reliability and security of information shared.

TNA has been put at the disposal of Eurofisc for production use in April 2019. Currently all Member States actively participate in TNA with the systemmanaged by a team of experts from tax administrations.

Brazil: Wolf in sheep's clothing – Artificial intelligence to identify possible frauds

People who live in the same neighbourhoods usually have similar earnings, assets and expenses. With geoprocessing and artificial intelligence, the Brazilian Tax Administration is able to map the "wolf in sheep's clothing". These are taxpayers in a given neighbourhood who have earnings, assets or expenses beyond what is considered normal for this locale, indicating a high probability of fraud.

Box 6.3. **Country examples: Using analytics to sharpen the targeting of risks** *(continued)*

Chile: Aggressive taxpayer predictive model

The Servicio de Impuestos Internos (SII) has detected the existence of people or companies that issue fraudulent invoices to simulate real transactions, which they deliver to their clients, who use them to reduce their Value Added Tax (VAT) liability.

Through the use of technological tools and the expertise of SII officials, SII have been able to generate mathematical models that

- allow the detection of taxpayers using fraudulent electronic documents
- verify that taxpayers receiving fraudulent tax documents cannot use the tax credit
- apply all the powers of the tax administration to catch those who facilitate the fraud.

Using specialist software, which allows access to various sources of information, SII have used techniques such as data mining, big data, and clustering, to map a taxpayer's life cycle in order to identify a special group classified as "aggressive issuers", and also uses the false positives to recalibrate the models and the behaviour patterns.

This has helped SII deal in a timely manner with actions that cheat the tax system, preventing those actions from impacting the reputation of SII, and the confidence of taxpayers in the tax system.

China (People's Republic of): Innovating supervision methods

Using tax big data, the Chinese tax administration (STA) built a dynamic system of credit and risk management, which implemented differentiated alerts to taxpayers to encourage voluntary compliance. In addition, by using this sophisticated new technology, law enforcement can identify high-risk taxpayers allowing them to crack down on tax evasion and avoidance. This means that taxpayers who are voluntarily compliant can see fairness and justice in the tax system.

For example, a new VAT invoice management system was created using this approach. Building on the previous system, this new system has now integrated every piece of information on an invoice, and is used to prevent fake invoices, and upgrade the service to taxpayers as well as informing future policy making. In 2020, with this system, the Chinese tax authorities were able to monitor invoice risks in real time, and could respond promptly and precisely to VAT fraud; with over 94% of the risk correctly identified. Furthermore, to reinforce the supervision and regulation of tax credits, data on credit risks is combined with sophisticated algorithms to enable the dynamic monitoring of taxpayer credit scores. Such scores are updated in real time through the model to produce an overall credit risk profile of taxpayers. For those with low credit scores, STA follow the strictest rules in the existing laws and regulations; while for those with high credit scores, a "fast pass" with reduced formalities and swifter processing is granted.

New Zealand: Data and analytics tools built into our new START system

Data and analytics are helping Inland Revenue to improve its services, act early to help people pay and receive the right amounts, target its activities more effectively and make better informed decisions.

Within Inland Revenue's new tax and revenue technology system START (Simplified Tax and Revenue Technology), the Discovery Manager tool looks at returns received and other information held to "discover" errors and issues requiring action. START's Integrity Manager tool stops assessments and refunds from being issued if there is a high likelihood they are wrong or fraudulent, based on risk indicators built into the system.

Box 6.3. **Country examples: Using analytics to sharpen the targeting of risks** *(continued)*

Inland Revenue also implemented a data and intelligence platform that complements START's analytical capabilities. It brings together multiple data sets, both Inland Revenue's and those of external parties, to identify patterns, understand more about customers and prioritise areas where they may need help or guidance.

The end-to-end capabilities that will maximise the value from these tools are still maturing. However, Inland Revenue has made big advances in integrating tools and systems to trial interventions and develop insights.

For example, the capabilities were used to help the 2020 process for automatically issuing income tax assessments, allowing the process to run faster and with less customer contact. The process took three months in 2019 and two months in 2020.

Peru: Atypical situations in electronic receipts

The Peruvian Tax Administration, in recent years, has been promoting the extensive use of electronic payment receipts (EPR), and by 2020 91% of the declared sales by taxpayers are based on this type of receipt. Considering the significant progress and the need to show that the huge amounts of information generated is successfully incorporated into risk management, the use of this source of information is extremely important. Therefore a preventive strategy for controlling the issuance of EPR was implemented, identifying patterns of atypical behaviour in taxpayers through a risk assessment approach. Continuous monitoring of these transactions allows the administration to analyse emerging risks or early warning signals.

The tax administration uses automatic learning that detects atypical transactions in these datasets and goes on to interpret and explain predictions to decision makers. This whole process is done in a big data environment because of the sheer volume and speed of data processing.

Not only has this work uncovered new risks, but it has also reduced by 21% the specialised working hours, prevented errors in the handling of information, and reduced operating costs by 15%.

See Annex 6.A. for links to supporting material.

Sources: Australian Taxation Office (2021), Belgium – Federal Public Service Finance (2021), Federal Revenue Service of Brazil (2021), Chile – Servicio de Impuestos Internos (2021), China (People's Republic of) – State Taxation Administration (2021), New Zealand – Inland Revenue Department – Te Tari Taake (2021) and Peru – Superintendencia Nacional de Administración Tributaria (2021).

Taxpayer programmes

Another approach for targeted risk management is the creation of units looking into the tax affairs of specific taxpayer segments. Two specific areas where tax administrations have found it advantageous to manage specific groups of taxpayers on a segmented basis are large business taxpayers, and High Net Wealth Individuals (HNWIs). The rationale for focusing administration resources on managing these groups revolves around the:

- ***significance of tax compliance risks***: due to the nature and type of transactions, offshore activities, opportunity and strategies to minimise tax liabilities; and in the case of large business, the differences between financial accounting profits and the profits computed for tax purposes

- ***complexity of business and tax dealings***: particularly the breadth of their business interests and in the case of HNWI, the mix of private and tax affairs
- ***integrity of the tax system***: the importance of being able to assure stakeholders about the work undertaken with these groups of taxpayers.

Additionally, in the case of large taxpayers, a small number of taxpayers are typically responsible for a disproportionate share of tax revenue collected. Data collected as part of the 2020 ISORA survey indicates that for most jurisdictions between 30% and 60% of their total net revenue, including withholding payments on behalf of employees, was received from taxpayers covered by their large taxpayer programmes (see Figure 6.2). On average, around 2% of corporate taxpayers covered by those programmes account for 43% of all revenue collected (see Table 6.2).

Figure 6.2. **Percentage of revenue administered through large taxpayer offices/programmes, 2019**

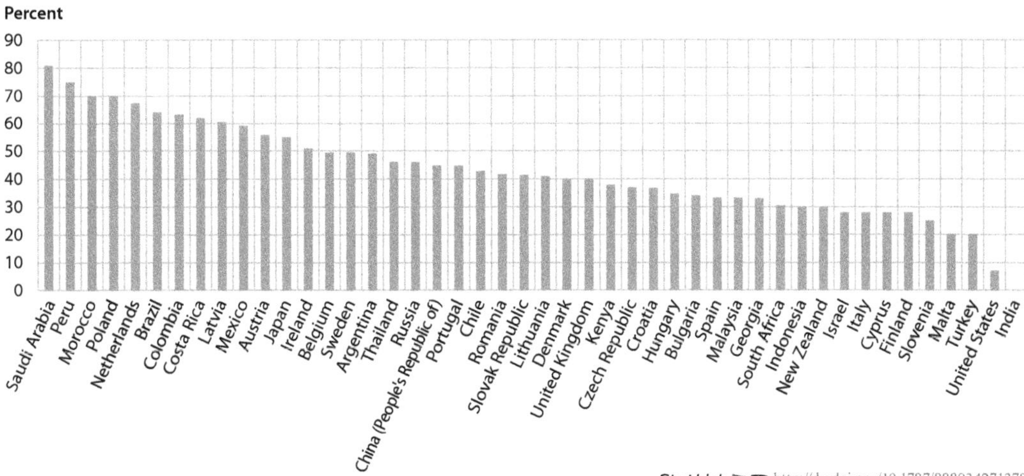

StatLink http://dx.doi.org/10.1787/888934271378

Source: Table D.9 Segmentation ratios: LTO/Ps.

Table 6.2. **Importance of large taxpayer offices/programmes (LTO/P), 2019**

FTEs in LTO/P as percentage of total FTEs	Corporate taxpayers managed through LTO/P as percentage of active corporate income taxpayers	Percentage of net revenue administered under LTO/P in relation to total net revenue collected by the tax administration	FTEs on audit, investigation and other verification function in the LTO/P as percentage of total FTEs in LTO/P	Total value of additional assessments raised through LTO/P as percentage of total value of additional assessments raised from audits
4.1	1.7	42.7	65.8	33.9

Note: The table shows the average percentages across the jurisdictions that where able to provide the information. The ratio of "Corporate taxpayers managed through LTO/P as percentage of active corporate income taxpayers" does not include Saudi Arabia as it would distort the overall average since the figures reported by Saudi Arabia for their LTO/P also include Zakat payers as well as CIT payers, which results in the ratio being over 100%.

Source: Table D.9 Segmentation ratios: LTO/Ps.

While the management of these groups of taxpayers is often undertaken as a programme, in a large number of jurisdictions these programmes are also structural involving a Large Taxpayer Office or HNWI unit. The scope of the work of these units varies considerably, ranging from undertaking traditional audit activity, through to "full service" approaches (see Figure 6.3). However, on average two-thirds of tax administration staff in large taxpayer offices or programmes are working on audit, investigation and other verification related issues (see Table 6.2).

Figure 6.3. **Large taxpayer offices/programmes: Existence and functions carried out, 2019**

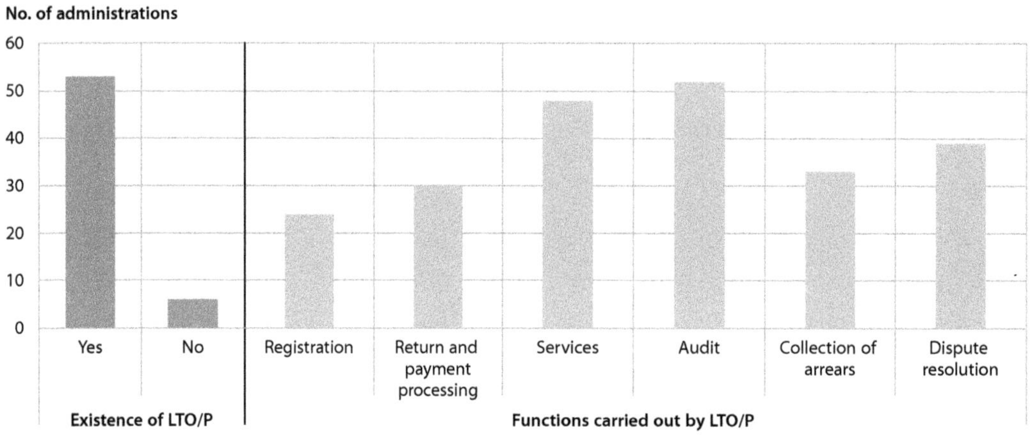

StatLink http://dx.doi.org/10.1787/888934271397

Source: Table A.15 Large taxpayer office/program: Existence and functions.

Figure 6.4. **HNWI programmes, 2019**

Number of administrations

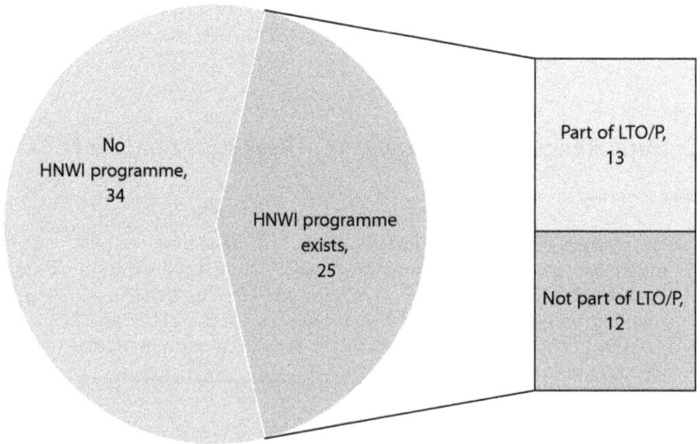

StatLink http://dx.doi.org/10.1787/888934271416

Source: Table A.18 High net wealth individuals (HNWIs) program.

Understanding future risks

While it is key for tax administrations to understand current compliance risks and prepare appropriate response strategies, it is equally important to understand which risks may arise in the future. The availability of vast amounts of data and tax administration's capacity to handle and analyse this puts them in a position to assess where new compliance risks may arise and develop in time the necessary mitigation strategies.

This is particularly important during times of crisis, such as the COVID-19 pandemic, which may influence taxpayer's compliance behaviour. Government lockdowns and related measures have affected income streams of many taxpayers, resulting in reduced profits or even losses. Coupled with most administrations reducing or suspending compliance activities, some may be tempted to change their future compliance behaviour.

Crisis situations may exacerbate non-compliance behaviour but there are many factors that need to be considered, including the rise of the digital economy, cryptocurrencies, perceptions of unfairness, new ways of working, etc. Many tax administrations are looking at this and Box 6.4. contains one example.

Understanding that administrations are together in this and face similar issues, the Forum on Tax Administration (FTA) has undertaken a pilot data-driven horizon scan, led by the Australian Taxation Office and the FTA Joint International Task Force on Shared Intelligence and Collaboration (JITSIC). This analysis may result in further collaborative work on understanding and mitigating the main emerging risks. (OECD, 2020[6])

Box 6.4. **Canada: Applied Futures Lab at the Working-Level**

The Futures Lab supports Canada Revenue Agency (CRA) compliance programmes to explore how the trends shaping the digital landscape may impact tax compliance, both now and into the future. The Lab's mission is to support the CRA's progress in the digital economy by introducing foresight techniques, tools and mindsets with CRA staff, on a voluntary basis. The following initiatives formed part of the Futures Lab:

- The Compliance 2050 project explored the futures of income, pay and taxation, and identified change drivers that will impact the future of tax compliance. This project introduced foresight to over 300+ CRA employees through the Compliance 2050 open house.
- Applied foresight at the working level for an e-invoicing initiative which contributed to an e-invoicing business case to ensure alignment with emergent futures. The future of supply chain and procurement were explored to inform the discovery process and a set of taxpayer personas were developed to understand the Small and Medium Enterprise's digital adoption tendencies.
- Post-COVID-19 Futures Scan Club was created to break down silos across the CRA while discussing emerging changes. This inter-branch scan club is an informal discussion on signals of change and their implications for the CRA. Collaborations with other sections created themed scans to support respective business objectives.
- Foresight outreach to build foresight literacy within the CRA. A collaboration with diverse sections within the Agency was done to provide strategic foresight support. Futures workshops helped participants understand the application of foresight for risk management and innovation.

Source: Canada Revenue Agency (2021).

Coverage and results

The type of "compliance actions" undertaken by tax administrations to determine whether taxpayers have properly reported their tax liability is changing. As set out above, the increasing availability of data and the introduction of sophisticated analytical models are allowing administrations to better identify returns, claims or transactions which might require further review or be fraudulent. Furthermore, these models, many of which can operate in real-time, are allowing administrations to conduct automated electronic checks on all returns or on transactions of a particular type.

Electronic compliance checks

While traditional audits (including comprehensive, issue or desk audits) are still the primary verification activities, the use of automated electronic checks using rules-based approaches to treat some defined risks (e.g. automatically denying a claim, issuing a letter or matching a transaction) is providing administrations with more effective and efficient ways to undertake some verification work.

These approaches do, however raise the question of how to reflect those automated electronic checks in the performance information that administrations report. To include all checking may distort coverage, adjustment and yield rates. However where it replaces previously undertaken manual actions it would seem appropriate to reflect what administrations are now doing in this area.

In this respect, the 2020 version of the International Survey on Revenue Administration (ISORA) invited participants to break down the total value of additional assessments raised from audit and verification actions into (i) audits and (ii) electronic compliance checks (defined as electronic checks, validation and matching of taxpayer information).

Only a few administrations were able to provide information on electronic compliance checks (see Table A.34). However, for some of those administrations (e.g. Austria, Chile, Estonia, Greece, Morocco, Malta and South Africa) electronic compliance checks make-up an important part (around 20% and more) of the additional assessments raised through all audits and verification actions.

Box 6.5. **Country examples: Automated checks**

Australia: Pre-issue Automated Operational Analytics

To support the community in getting their individual income tax return right the first time, the ATO uses automated solutions to rectify taxpayer errors or omissions.

The ATO has developed a number of operational analytics (OA) solutions and by using high-quality, third-party data as well as other information the ATO will identify and automatically adjust the tax return within two (2) days of receiving the return.

Once an income tax return has been automatically corrected by the OA solution, a tailored script is generated providing taxpayer specific details about the adjustment made. The tailored script is used by ATO telephony staff if an individual calls querying the treatment. A short description of the adjustment made is also included in the assessment notice provided to the taxpayer.

If the taxpayer disagrees with the adjustment made or response provided by the telephony staff when they contact the ATO, then the ATO operative will escalate the call to a specialist area for a further review.

Box 6.5. **Country examples: Automated checks** *(continued)*

If the individual disputes the ATO's pre-issue adjustment to the return with evidence of their claim then the automated treatment will be fully or partially reversed.

Since commencing the automated pre-issue compliance programme in July 2017, the ATO has adjusted 1.4 million individual income tax returns, protecting approximately AUD 684 million in revenue. Around 17% have called the ATO for an explanation of the reasons for the adjustment with less than 2% of treated returns escalated for a further review.

Getting the tax return right in the first instance avoids post-issue compliance work which generally involves amending the assessment and raising a tax shortfall amount with penalties and debit interest that the taxpayer would have to repay.

Netherlands: Error recovery request in return process

Since 2015, the Netherlands Tax Administration (NTA) sends a so-called "pro-memoria" letter to personal income tax payers who have most likely provided wrong information in their tax returns. These tax returns are selected by the risk based verification system for personal income taxation. The letters draw the attention of the taxpayers to potential errors or mistakes in their tax returns and request them to verify their tax returns and to adjust them if needed.

If a supplementary tax return is submitted, the latter one is added to the initial one and the compound tax return is subsequently checked again by the risk based verification system. The tax returns that are selected after this process – just as the tax returns of the taxpayers who did not respond to the letters – are manually processed for verification and assessment. The pro-memoria letters can be sent on various topics, such as study and training expenses, revision interest or pension contributions.

The impact of the letters has so far been above expectations. In the past years, approximately 70% to 75% of the taxpayers who received the letters responded by adjusting their tax returns. This means that the letters on each topic saved around 16 800 to 18 000 working hours in the verification and assessment process.

See Annex 6.A. for links to supporting material.

Sources: Australian Taxation Office (2021) and Netherlands Tax Administration (2021).

Audits

While previous ISORA surveys distinguished between audit adjustment rates by audit type, this has changed with the 2020 ISORA survey which invited administrations to provide information for all audits combined. A comparison with data from previous surveys is therefore not possible.

Looking at the ISORA 2020 data, there are some general observations that can be made:

- ***Audit adjustment rates*** vary significantly across the administrations covered by this report ranging from as low as 5% in Norway to as high as 95% and more in Brazil, Morocco, Russia and the United States (see Figure 6.5). (High adjustment rates can of course result from highly targeted audits.)
- The importance of audits can also be seen when looking at the ***additional assessments raised*** (see Figure 6.6). In many jurisdictions, the additional assessments raised from audits correspond to more than 5% of total revenue collections. The 50 administrations that were able to provide data report on average 5.5% of additional assessments raised through audit as percentage of tax collections.

- Breaking this down by tax type, it shows that the ratio of additional assessments raised to tax collected is the greatest for corporate income tax (CIT). On average, CIT additional assessment raised as a percentage of CIT collected is 11.3%, around three times the percentage for value added tax (3.7%) and more than four times the percentage for personal income tax (2.6%). (See Figure 6.7.)
- In many jurisdictions, the ***additional assessments raised through large taxpayer offices or programmes*** (LTO/P) make-up a significant share of the total additional assessments raised from audits (see Figure 6.8). On average, LTO/Ps contribute around one-third of the total additional assessments raised from audits (see Table 6.2).

Figure 6.5. **Audit hit rate, 2019**

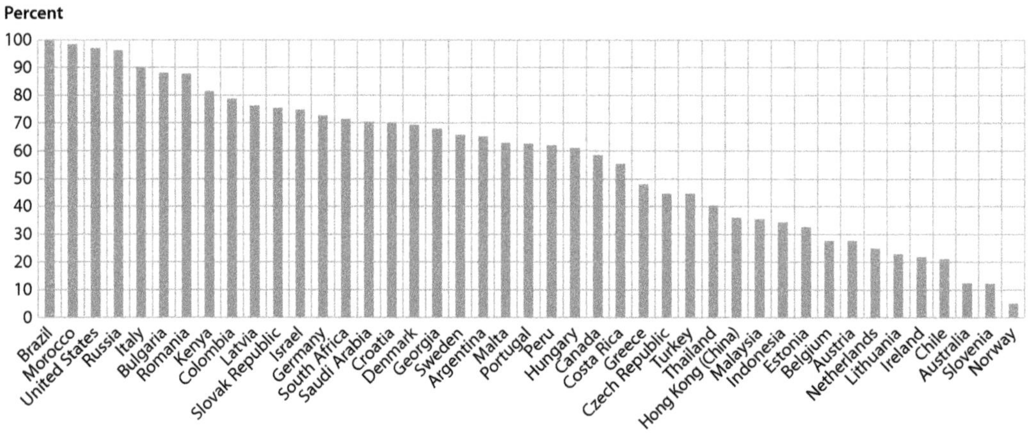

StatLink http://dx.doi.org/10.1787/888934271435

Source: Table D.22 Audits: Hit rate and additional assessments raised.

Figure 6.6. **Additional assessments raised through audit as percentage of tax collections, 2019**

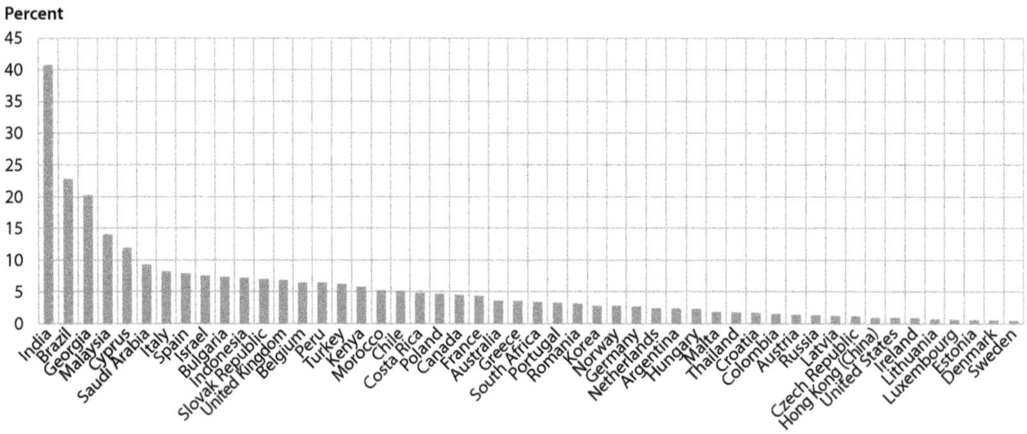

StatLink http://dx.doi.org/10.1787/888934271454

Source: Table D.22 Audits: Hit rate and additional assessments raised.

Figure 6.7. **Additional assessments raised through audit as percentage of tax collected by tax type, 2019**

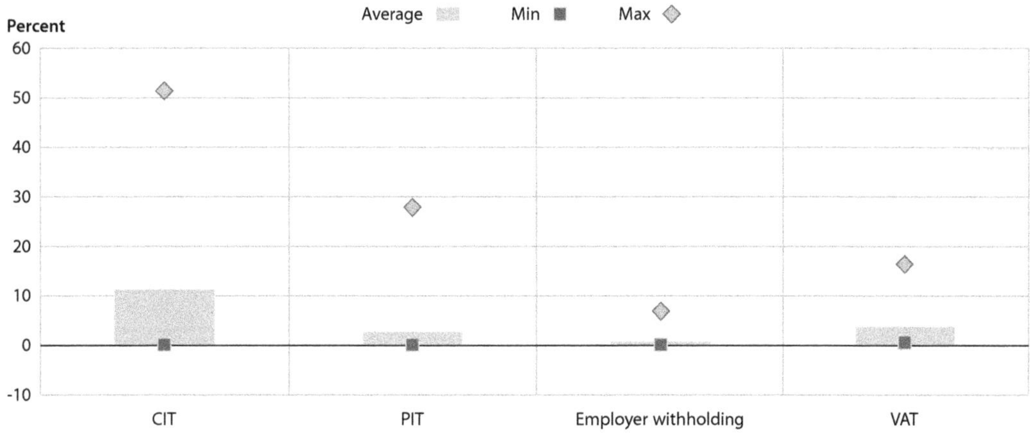

StatLink http://dx.doi.org/10.1787/888934271473

Source: D.23 Audits: Additional assessments raised by tax type.

Figure 6.8. **Additional assessments raised from audits undertaken by LTO/P as a percentage of additional assessments raised from all audits, 2019**

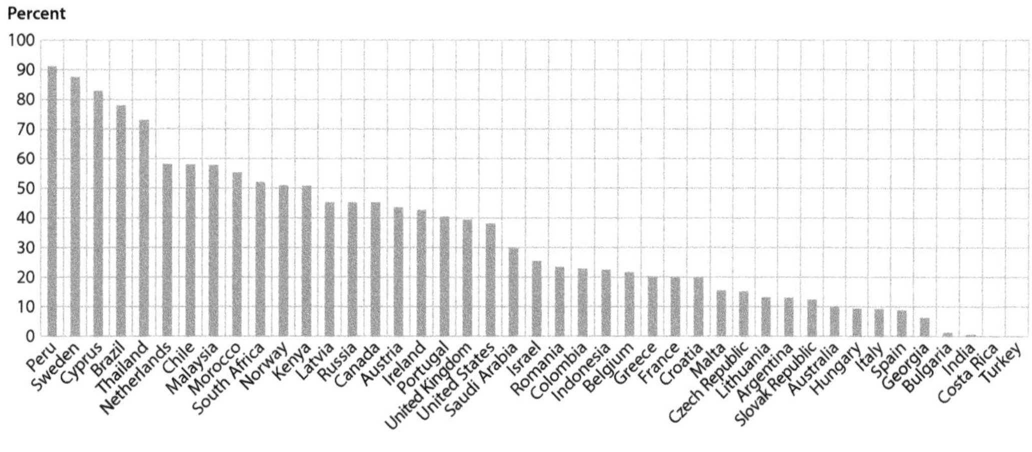

StatLink http://dx.doi.org/10.1787/888934271492

Source: Table D.9 Segmentation ratios: LTO/Ps.

Moving audit work to a virtual environment

Traditionally, administrations apply a variety of different audit types including comprehensive audits, issue-oriented audits, inspections of books and records, and in-depth investigations of suspected tax fraud. Often those audits require the administration to visit the taxpayer's premises (so called field audits).

Advancements in technology have led administrations to consider new ways of engaging with taxpayers during the audit process including the electronic submission of audit related documentation. This trend has accelerated significantly since the beginning of the COVID-19 crisis as the closure of tax offices and the move to remote working for large numbers of tax officials has significantly affected compliance interventions and how they are conducted.

The 2021 OECD report *Tax Administration: Digital Resilience in the COVID-19 Environment* (OECD, 2021[7]) noted that three-quarters of the 32 administrations covered by that report suspended or drastically reduced regular field audit work. However, of those, close to ninety percent shifted parts of their field audit work to a virtual/digital environment accessing electronically the documents that are relevant for the audit process and/or conducting remote interviews (see Table 6.3).

Table 6.3. **Shifting field audit work to a virtual/digital environment**

Percent of administrations

Field audits (leaving aside fraud/evasion cases) were ceased or drastically reduced	Parts of the field audit work were shifted to a virtual/digital environment	Experience of administrations that shifted field audits to a virtual/digital environment			
		Relevant documents could be accessed electronically	Remote interviews could be conducted satisfactorily	Taxpayers (or other stakeholders) considered this a positive experience	Plan to continue moving field audit work to a virtual/digital environment
75%	88%	90%	86%	90%	76%

Source: OECD (2021), "Tax Administration: Digital Resilience in the COVID-19 Environment", *OECD Policy Responses to Coronavirus (COVID-19)*, https://doi.org/10.1787/2f3cf2fb-en.

The fact that 90% of the administrations covered in the digital resilience note reported that they and the taxpayers involved considered the use of virtual/digital tools for audit purposes a positive experience is very encouraging for future developments in this area. Moreover, 76% of those administrations plan to continue moving field audit work to a virtual/digital environment going forward (see Table 6.3). Box 6.6. contains some examples of what administrations have been doing in this area.

Box 6.6. **Country examples: Remote audits**

Chile: Remote Inspection

One of the key strategic goals of the SII is the establishment of an improved relationship with citizens undergoing audit procedures. For this purpose, communication tools were strengthened, creating a system that facilitates interaction between tax officials and taxpayers, and that tracks the impact of those interactions.

The objectives of this programme are:

- to facilitate tax compliance through smooth and swift attention, by using communication channels such as email, telephone contact or video call, that provide personalised actions
- to improve information quality supplied to SII by reducing errors in taxpayer submissions
- to encourage correction of errors or tax discrepancies through remote contact with an examiner, during the analysis or review process
- to simplify compliance by eliminating the times associated with trips to the tax administration office and giving the possibility that the taxpayer can present or supplement their information using their electronic file.

Box 6.6. **Country examples: Remote audits** *(continued)*

Hungary: E-audit – a safe solution without limitation

The Hungarian tax authority (NTCA) started preparing for e-audits already in 2015, when it sent audit information and the credentials of its auditors electronically to taxpayers. The mandatory e-administration launched in Hungary in 2018 led not only the NTCA but taxpayers as well to using more electronic communication. This meant the NTCA had to develop innovative IT solutions, and it was a legal requirement that any new tool had to be made available to taxpayers without data size limits and free of charge.

The platform finalised by the end of 2018 allowed the transmitting of digitised documents without size limits, which made e-communication very popular in audits, and in 2019 e-audit could be launched in Hungary which was unique even in the EU. This whole process takes place in the digital space, the relationship between the taxpayer and the NTCA is free of paper communication. In 2019 and 2020, the audited taxpayers sent in total 2.7 million megabytes of e-documents and the NTCA sent out nearly 1 million e-documents.

As a result of e-audit, even restrictions implemented because of the coronavirus pandemic do not hinder these activities. Using IT tools, taxpayers are able to co-operate with the authority from anywhere. E-audit is not only safe, but also a highly cost-effective and environmentally friendly process, replacing more than 5 million sheets of paper means saving considerable printing capacity and postal charges.

An additional advantage of e-audit is that it can be carried out in a much shorter time compared to the traditional procedure. While the average length of a traditional tax audit was 128 days, it was reduced to 86 days in the case of e-audits.

E-audit is beneficial for all: both taxpayers and the NCTA can save resources, which can be put to more productive use.

See Annex 6.A. for links to supporting material.

Peru: The GIE System (Electronic Inductive Management)

GIE is a platform that facilitates interaction between taxpayers and the Tax Administration (SUNAT), through the management of a large number of tax audits.

The main advantage of this application is that it avoids face-to-face meetings between tax auditors and taxpayers, during the tax audit process. In this virtual interaction, SUNAT communicates to the taxpayer the inconsistencies detected in his or her tax returns, including a report revealing those inconsistencies. Later, the taxpayer submits the documentation requested by SUNAT with the appropriate notes, if necessary.

The main benefit for SUNAT is the increase in the number of tax audits to 80 000 a year. In the case of the taxpayers, the benefit is the reduction in tax compliance costs, since the face-to-face attention in the offices during the audit process is eliminated. In this way, those services provided by the administration are modernised and simplified.

Furthermore, this remote monitoring application allows:

- a responsive case selection process at the national level by using automatic electronic notifications
- online rescheduling of the submission date for taxpayers to deliver the documentation requested by SUNAT
- online consultations on the electronic files related to the tax audit between the taxpayer and the tax auditors

Box 6.6. **Country examples: Remote audits** *(continued)*

- automatic feedback to the case selection programmes based on the tax audit results in terms of those inconsistencies previously communicated to the taxpayer.

See Annex 6.A. for links to supporting material.

Spain: Virtual Visits for Auditing (VIVIs)

In 2019 a project was started by the Tax Auditing and the IT Directorates for the implementation of "virtual visits for auditing" (VIVI). The COVID-19 crisis boosted the need for videoconferencing systems to ensure the business continuity and the safety of taxpayers and tax officials. Therefore, the AEAT has taken this opportunity to speed up its effective implementation and extend it to the rest of the tax application procedures. For this purpose, a modification to legislation was needed in order to grant legal coverage to this new method of interaction with taxpayers.

Under the law, tax application procedures with taxpayers now may be performed through digital systems that, via videoconference or other systems, allow bidirectional and simultaneous image and sound communication, visual, auditory and verbal interaction and guarantee a secure transmission and reception of documents ensuring their authorship, authenticity and integrity. For the utilisation of this system the taxpayer's consent is required.

The rationale behind this new tool is avoiding unnecessary trips to the tax offices while complying with the requirements of data protection, authenticity and integrity of documents and the identification of taxpayers and tax officials just as if a face-to-face meeting was taking place. As additional advantages, it enables a full digitalisation of the file and is sustainable and ecologically responsible since the use of paper is limited and the carbon footprint is reduced by avoiding trips.

The system integrates all the necessary tools to resemble a face-to-face meeting:

- a videoconferencing system
- an electronic registry to load documentation submitted by the taxpayer
- the electronic signature of both the tax official and the taxpayer
- the electronic file of the taxpayer, so that the tax official can access all the information.

In the second half of 2020, 1 490 documents were signed using the VIVI system and in February 2021 the first assessment through VIVI took place, showing a positive trend in the use of the system.

See Annex 6.A. for links to supporting material.

Sources: Chile – Servicio de Impuestos Internos (2021), Hungary – National Tax and Customs Administration (2021), Peru – Superintendencia Nacional de Administración Tributaria (2021) and Spanish Tax Agency (2021).

Tax crime investigations

Tax crime occurs when people intentionally avoid paying tax or claim money they are not entitled to. Figure 6.9., which summarises the role of tax administrations in tax crime investigations, shows that around half of the administrations covered in this publication have responsibility for conducting those investigations:

- 39% of tax administrations have the responsibility for directing and conducting tax crime investigations.
- 15% of tax administrations have the responsibility for conducting investigations but under the direction or authority of another agency, such as the police or public prosecutor.

The remaining administrations do not have any responsibility for conducting tax crime investigations. In those cases, this is done by another agency, such as the police or public prosecutor. This could also be a specialist tax agency, established outside the tax administration.

Figure 6.9. **Role of administrations in tax criminal investigations, 2019**

Percent of administrations

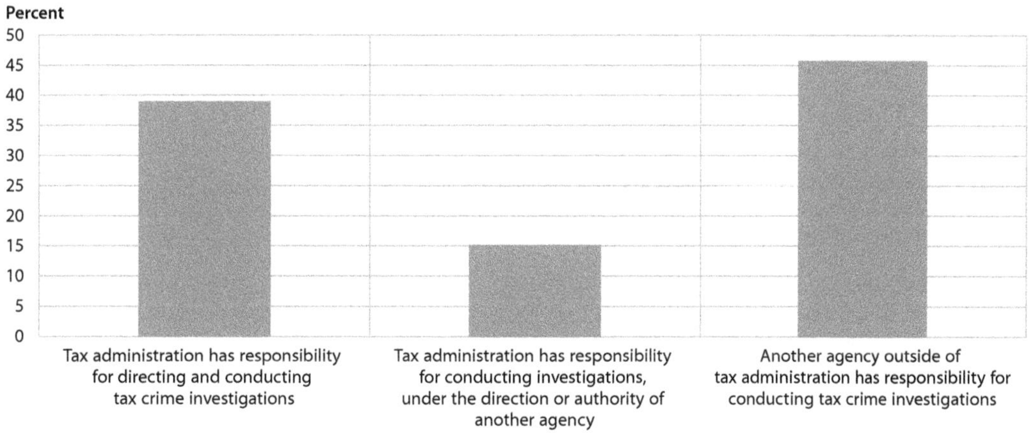

StatLink http://dx.doi.org/10.1787/888934271511

Source: Table A.36 Tax crime investigations: Role of the administration and number of cases.

Table 6.4 shows the total number of cases referred for prosecution during the fiscal year for the 32 administrations that have responsibility for conducting tax crime investigations. A comparison with previous year data is not possible due to the changes between ISORA survey iterations.

Table 6.4. **Tax crime investigation cases referred for prosecution, 2018 and 2019**

Year	No. of cases referred for prosecution during the fiscal year
2018	48 555
2019	49 285
Change in percent	+1.5%

Note: Only includes administrations that have responsibility.

Source: Table A.36 Tax crime investigations: Role of the administration and number of cases.

Criminal activities are dynamic and adapt to take advantage of new opportunities for financial gain, frequently outpacing the legislative changes designed to combat them. Finding better ways to fight tax crime is a high priority. Money laundering, corruption, terrorist financing, and other financial crimes can threaten the strategic, political and economic interests of jurisdictions. Countering these activities requires improved transparency and greater efforts to harness the capacity of different government agencies, including across borders, to collectively deter, detect and prosecute these crimes through a whole of government approach and international co-operation. Box 6.7. provides an example of such co-operation.

Box 6.7. **Netherlands: FCInet, the game changer – connect, don't collect**

An important consideration in tax crime investigations is finding information on a target, without exposing the name of that target to third parties. The Financial Criminal Investigation Network (FCInet), the government developed decentralised computer network with privacy-friendly technologies, provides just that. Originally an initiative from the OECD's Forum of Heads of Tax Crime Investigation, it has grown into a cooperation instrument in several governmental domains worldwide.

FCInet started in 2016 under the leadership of the Dutch Fiscal Intelligence and Investigation Service (FIOD) and the United Kingdom's HM Revenue and Customs (HMRC). Since then, the network has been further developed internationally and domestically to take a big step forward in the fight against financial-economic crime. (OECD and The World Bank, 2018, p. 61[8])

With the FCInet and ma³tch technology, members can identify which targets they have in common without disclosing information (see movie: https://www.fcinet.org/). Source data is cryptographically pseudonymised and aggregated in ma³tch filters, so source data can no longer be traced. Subsequently, members can use received filters locally to match their targets, and only hits on targets that are known to both members are revealed.

In the Netherlands the use of ma³tch technology already uncovered various links to financial-economic crime and resulted in a major criminal investigation into money-laundering. While undetected relationships are being discovered, the risk of unnecessary exposure of information is also minimised. This is also one of the reasons why FCInet won the Dutch Privacy Award 2021 for government services. According to the jury: "a good investment in privacy by the government".

See Annex 6.A. for links to supporting material.

Source: Netherlands Tax Administration (2021).

References

OECD (2021), *"Tax Administration: Digital Resilience in the COVID-19 Environment", OECD Policy Responses to Coronavirus (COVID-19)*, OECD Publishing, Paris, http://dx.doi.org/10.1787/2f3cf2fb-en. [7]

OECD (2020), *2020 FTA "Amsterdam" Plenary Communique*, www.oecd.org/tax/forum-on-tax-administration/events/2020/forum-on-tax-administration-communique-2020.pdf (accessed on 1 September 2021). [6]

OECD (2020), *Code of Conduct: Co-operation between tax administrations and sharing and gig economy platforms*, OECD, Paris, www.oecd.org/tax/forum-on-tax-administration/publications-and-products/code-of-conduct-co-operation-between-tax-administrations-and-sharing-and-gig-economy-platforms.pdf (accessed on 1 September 2021). [4]

OECD (2020), *Model Rules for Reporting by Platform Operators with respect to Sellers in the Sharing and Gig Economy*, OECD, Paris, www.oecd.org/tax/exchange-of-tax-information/model-rules-for-reporting-by-platform-operators-with-respect-to-sellers-in-the-sharing-and-gig-economy.htm (accessed on 1 September 2021). [3]

OECD (2019), *The Sharing and Gig Economy: Effective Taxation of Platform Sellers : Forum on Tax Administration*, OECD Publishing, Paris, https://dx.doi.org/10.1787/574b61f8-en. [2]

OECD (2017), *The Changing Tax Compliance Environment and the Role of Audit*, OECD Publishing, Paris, https://dx.doi.org/10.1787/9789264282186-en. [1]

OECD (2016), *Advanced Analytics for Better Tax Administration: Putting Data to Work*, OECD Publishing, Paris, https://dx.doi.org/10.1787/9789264256453-en. [5]

OECD and The World Bank (2018), *Improving Co-operation between Tax Authorities and Anti-Corruption Authorities in Combating Tax Crime and Corruption*, https://www.oecd.org/tax/crime/improving-co-operation-between-tax-authorities-and-anti-corruption-authorities-in-combating-tax-crime-and-corruption.pdf (accessed on 1 September 2021). [8]

Annex 6.A

Links to supporting material (accessed on 1 September 2021)

- Box 6.1 – France: Link to a video on the Data Lake project, the engine of DGFiP's digital transformation: https://youtu.be/0uZVBAZrTIo
- Box 6.2 – Chile: Link to the mobile app "e-Verifica" which allows citizens to verify the tax code validity of the cigarette pack acquired: www.sii.cl/ayudas/apps/everifica/index.html
- Box 6.2 – Costa Rica: Link to a presentation on the use of geographic information to locate real estate that is subject to tax: www.oecd.org/tax/forum-on-tax-administration/publications-and-products/costa-rica-use-of-geographic-information-system.pdf
- Box 6.2 – Hungary: Link to a video explaining the tracing of invoicing chains: https://youtu.be/Z88he9N2XZw
- Box 6.2 – Peru: Link to a video on the use of web scraping techniques to non-compliant sellers on on-line platforms: https://youtu.be/jQUMKJyOWOE
- Box 6.2 – Russia: Link to a presentation regarding the experience in automation of matching and risk analysis of CRS data: www.oecd.org/tax/forum-on-tax-administration/publications-and-products/russia-analytical-system-financial-accounts.pdf
- Box 6.3 – Australia:
  - Link to an example of the classification of bank statement transactions: www.oecd.org/tax/forum-on-tax-administration/publications-and-products/australia-template-example-of-the-classification-of-bank-statement-transactions.pdf
  - Link to examples of the dashboard report:
    - Data demographics: www.oecd.org/tax/forum-on-tax-administration/publications-and-products/australia-template-example-a-dashboard-report-data-demographics.pdf
    - Entity receipts: www.oecd.org/tax/forum-on-tax-administration/publications-and-products/australia-template-example-a-dashboard-report-entity-receipts.pdf
    - Transaction values per month: www.oecd.org/tax/forum-on-tax-administration/publications-and-products/australia-template-example-a-dashboard-report-transaction-values-per-month.pdf
- Box 6.3 – Peru: Link to a presentation on the identification of atypical aspects in electronic receipts: www.oecd.org/tax/forum-on-tax-administration/publications-and-products/peru-atypical-situations-in-electronic-receipts.pdf

- Box 6.5 – Netherlands – Link to a pro-memoria letter infographic: www.oecd.org/tax/forum-on-tax-administration/publications-and-products/netherlands-pro-memoria-letter.pdf
- Box 6.6 – Hungary: Link to a video explaining the e-audit process: https://youtu.be/uO6G2iUKSZM
- Box 6.6 – Peru: Link to a video explaining the GIE platform: https://youtu.be/hsc74aNryhc
- Box 6.6 – Spain: Link to a video explaining the Virtual Visits for Auditing: https://youtu.be/40elZUcJUKM
- Box 6.7 – Netherlands: Link to the FCInet process chart: www.oecd.org/tax/forum-on-tax-administration/publications-and-products/netherlands-fcinet-process-chart.pdf and a video on the FCInet: www.fcinet.org/

Chapter 7

Collection

The collection of outstanding returns and payments is important for maintaining high levels of voluntary compliance and citizen's confidence in the overall tax system. This chapter comments on tax administration performance in managing the collection of outstanding debt, and describes the features of a modern tax debt collection function. It goes on to provide examples of approaches applied by administrations to prevent debt being incurred.

Introduction

The collections function involves taking action against those who do not file a return on time, and/or do not make a payment when it is due. Even with the growth in "pre-filled or no return" approaches over past years (see Chapter 4), the filing of a tax return or declaration still remains the principal means by which a taxpayer's liability is established in the majority of jurisdictions participating in this publication. Although 2019 on-time filing rates averaged between 79% and 88%, around 100 million returns were not filed on time that year (see Chapter 4). It is important therefore that administrations continue to focus efforts on improving the timely collection of late and outstanding returns.

Looking at the collection of late payments, all but one administration participating in the survey report staff resources being devoted to taking action to secure the payment of overdue tax payments.[1] Information provided in 2019 by 52 of these administrations, attributes around 11% of total tax staff numbers to the collection function (see Table D.4).

The legislative framework provides tax officials with powers that enable them to undertake certain actions in relation to the management of debt, the collection of amounts overdue and the enforcement actions that can be taken against delinquent debtors. The 2019 edition in this series had a section summarising the availability of such management, collection and enforcement powers and their usage by tax administrations (OECD, 2019[1]). While the survey underlying this year's edition did not take a closer look at this topic, it is fair to assume that the availability and usage of such powers has not significantly changed.

This chapter:

- takes a brief look at the features of a modern tax debt collection function and the elements of a successful tax debt management strategy
- comments on tax administration performance in managing the collection of outstanding debt
- provides examples of preventive approaches to debt being incurred.

Although the data covered by this report is pre-pandemic, it also briefly comments on the impact of the COVID-19 pandemic on the debt collection function, and this will be assessed more fully in a future edition of this series.

Features of a debt collection function

To maintain high levels of voluntary compliance and confidence in the tax system, administrations must ensure that their debt collection approaches are both "fit for purpose" and meet taxpayer's expectations of how the system will be administered. This means not only taking firm action against taxpayers that knowingly do not comply, but also using more customer service style approaches where taxpayers want to meet their obligations but for understandable reasons, such as short term cash-flow issues, are not able to do so. Increasingly, tax administrations are taking an end-to-end or systems view of their processes and researching the reasons why returns may not been filed or payments made. They are also using information about the taxpayer's previous history, to identify patterns and/or anomalies.

The 2014 report *Working Smarter in Tax Debt Management* (OECD, 2014[2]) provided an overview of the modern tax debt collection function, describing the essential features as:

- ***Advanced analytics*** – that make it possible to use all the information tax administrations have about taxpayers to accurately target debtors with the right intervention at the right time.

- ***Treatment strategies*** – the collection function needs a range of interventions, from those designed to prevent people becoming indebted, to measures to support taxpayers make payments and to tough enforcement measures where appropriate.
- ***Outbound call centres*** – which make it possible to efficiently pursue a large number of debts.
- ***Organisation*** – debt collection is a specialist function and is usually organised as such. The right performance measures and a continuous improvement approach help drive desired outcomes.
- ***Cross border debts*** – the proper and timely use of international assistance is crucial, particularly the "Assistance in Collection Articles" in agreements between jurisdictions.

The 2019 report *Successful Tax Debt Management: Measuring Maturity and Supporting Change* (OECD, 2019[3]) provides further insights into the elements of a successful tax debt management strategy, setting out four strategic principles that tax administrations may wish to consider when setting their strategy for tax debt management. These principles focus on the timing of interventions in the tax debt cycle, from consideration of measures to prevent tax debt arising in the first place, via early and continuous engagement with taxpayers before enforcement measures, to effective and proportionate enforcement and realistic write-off strategies. The underlying premise for these principles is that focusing on tackling debt early, and ideally before it has arisen, is the best means to minimise outstanding tax debt. The report also contains an overview of a *Tax Debt Management Maturity Model* and a compendium of successful tax debt management initiatives.

Box 7.1. **Country examples: Programmes and tools to advance debt management**

Ireland: The Debt Management Services application

In March 2019, the Irish tax administration (Revenue) introduced the new Debt Management Services application (DMS) to provide advanced profiling of cases and deliver significantly increased capacity for compliance and enforcement activities. This development has fundamentally reshaped and enhanced debt management capacity such that Revenue can now continuously monitor all businesses registered with them.

A new systemised compliance process notifies customers of late returns and payments eliminating the vast majority of routine case administration. The increased capacity, in tandem with a more agile and responsive case management structure, allows Revenue to speedily adapt its response to customer behaviour. This enables earlier engagement with non-compliant taxpayers. For those who fail to respond, Revenue can move swiftly to take the appropriate enforcement action. The substantial increase in enforcement activities leads to an increase in successful compliance and collection outcomes.

To support viable businesses seeking to be voluntarily compliant but having tax payment difficulties, a new online Phased Payment Arrangement facility was introduced which significantly improves the application and approval process and allows the customer to self-manage certain aspects of the arrangement.

Recently, the flexibility of DMS was clearly demonstrated in the manner in which it was quickly adapted to implement critical government support for business with tax payment difficulties due to the COVID-19 pandemic. This allowed businesses to warehouse or "park" certain tax debts for periods of time, tailored according to the needs of the individual businesses. DMS will also manage customised programmes for repayment of the debts at a future date.

Box 7.1. **Country examples: Programmes and tools to advance debt management** *(continued)*

Russia: Integrated debt management and administration system

In order to improve debt management and streamline the procedure for property seizure, the Federal Tax Service of Russia began to digitalise behavioural information about taxpayers. There are in total 10 risk factors (digital markers) that may trigger enforcement. The digital markers represent certain features of taxpayers' actions that indicate potential fraud and may serve as a trigger to activate the property forfeiture decision. The markers include information on whether the taxpayer is selling their property or is attempting to flee the country to avoid enforcement.

The decision of property forfeiture is processed automatically, based on the analysis of information received about the taxpayer's behaviour. Whenever the system identifies a risk factor, it automatically launches the process of property seizure, with the communications using different wording depending on the triggered marker. Implementation of this new system has allowed for a six-fold reduction in labour costs.

In 2020, taking into account the temporary moratorium on the application of penalties and interim measures due to COVID-19, the budget of the Russian Federation received USD 73.5 million due to the implementation of this new system.

Spain: New services in the field of tax collection

During 2020, the Spanish Tax Agency (AEAT) launched two new initiatives dedicated exclusively to tax collection and assisted by specialised operators in that matter.

The first was REC@T: a national telephone helpline for assistance and processing in tax collection. Using a system of secure identification (Cl@ve Pin) this help line offers the following services in 2021, which will be progressively increased over time:

- information on tax debt demands and seizures
- processing deferrals to the enforcement period
- direct debits for applications and deferral agreements
- telephone payment
- frequently asked questions regarding the impact of the COVID-19 pandemic.

Table 7.1. **Spain: Usage of national telephone hotline for assistance and processing in tax collection**

Year	Number of calls handled
2019	304 581
2020	486 881
2021	658 730

Note: The 2019 figure corresponds to the previous assistance service and the 2021 figure is estimated based on a linear projection of the actual data for the period January-March 2021.

The system allows for "proof of transaction" documents for all the procedures possible in REC@T. Taxpayers have expressed their satisfaction with the service in the phone survey conducted after the call.

Box 7.1. **Country examples: Programmes and tools to advance debt management** *(continued)*

The second initiative was the launch of two new calculators to assist taxpayers in the field of tax collection:

- The ***calculator of payment deadlines*** provides personalised answers on the deadline to pay taxes and other debts managed by AEAT, and also allows for the verification of the debt status and gives information on possible actions by AEAT.
- The ***calculator of interests and deferrals*** gives detail on interest accrued by tax debts and other debts managed by AEAT. This service is divided into three blocks: calculation of interest on deferrals and instalments; calculation of interest on late payment of tax debts; and calculation of interests on non-tax debts managed by AEAT. It also informs the taxpayer about the interest rate and its breakdown in days.

Table 7.2. **Spain: Usage of the calculators in the field of debt collection, 2020**

Calculator	Number of users in 2020
Payment deadlines	14 720
Interests and deferrals	44 062

See Annex 7.A. for links to supporting material.

Sources: Ireland – Office of the Revenue Commissioners (2021), Netherlands Tax Administration (2021), Federal Tax Service of Russia (2021) and Spanish Tax Agency (2021).

Performance in collecting outstanding debt

The total amount of outstanding arrears remains very large, in the region of EUR 2.1 trillion. For survey and comparative analysis purposes, "total arrears at year-end" is defined as the total amount of tax debt and debt on other revenue for which the tax administration is responsible, that is overdue for payment at the end of the fiscal year. This includes any interest and penalties. The term also includes arrears whose collection has been deferred (for example, as a result of payment arrangements). "Collectable arrears" is the total arrears figure less any disputed amounts, amounts that are not legally recoverable, or arrears which for other reasons are unable to be collected, but where write-off action has not yet occurred. Despite those efforts to make data comparable, care needs to be taken when comparing specific data points as the administration of taxation systems and administrative practices differ between countries.

In 2019, the average arrears to net revenue ratio was 32%. However, as in past years, it remains heavily influenced by the very large ratios of a small number of jurisdictions (Brazil, Chile, Greece, India, Italy, Malta and Peru) that show ratios above 100%. If these jurisdictions are removed, the average reduces to around 15% of net revenue (see Figures 7.1. and 7.2. as well as Table D.19).

Looking at collectable tax arrears, the 2019 data for 43 jurisdictions shows that on average 55% of the total arrears are considered collectable (see Table D.19). However, Figure 7.3. illustrates well the differences between jurisdictions: in some jurisdictions almost all arrears are considered collectable, while in others almost all arrears are considered not collectable.

Figure 7.1. **Total year-end arrears as a percent of total net revenue, 2019 – Administrations with a ratio above 100%**

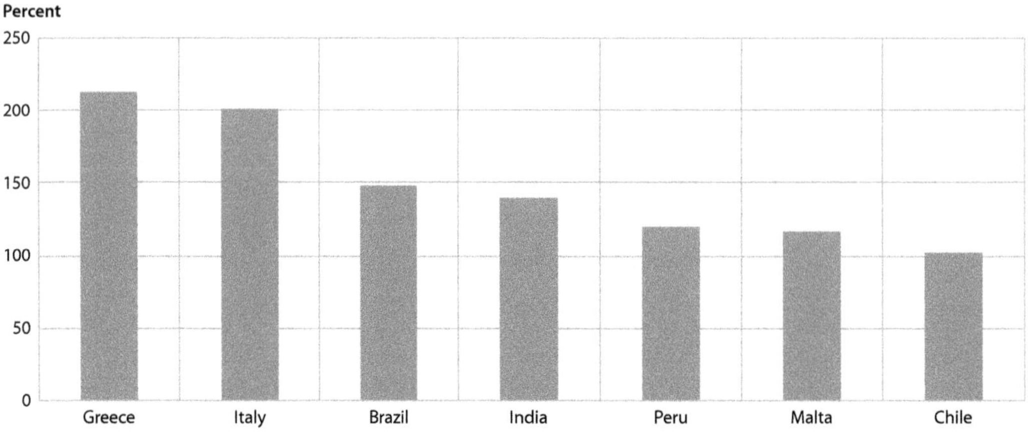

StatLink http://dx.doi.org/10.1787/888934271530

Source: Table D.19 Arrears: Closing stock, collectable arrears, and arrears relating to state owned enterprises.

Figure 7.2. **Total year-end arrears as a percent of total net revenue, 2019 – Administrations with a ratio below 100%**

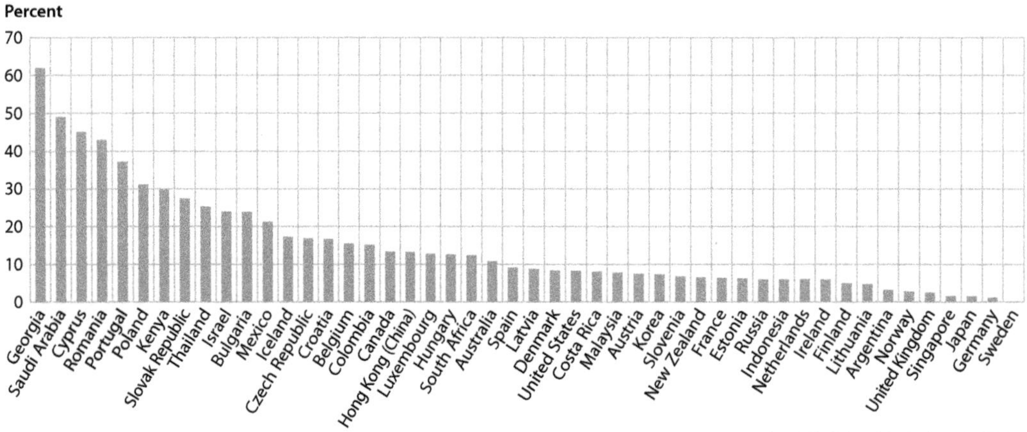

StatLink http://dx.doi.org/10.1787/888934271549

Note: Data for Indonesia relates to 2018.

Source: Table D.19 Arrears: Closing stock, collectable arrears, and arrears relating to state owned enterprises.

Figure 7.3. **Total year-end collectable arrears as percentage of total year-end arrears, 2019**

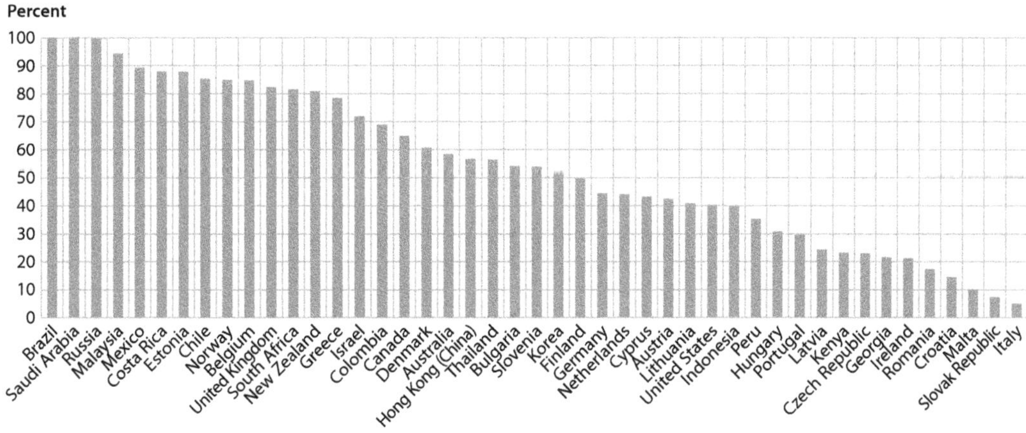

StatLink http://dx.doi.org/10.1787/888934271568

Note: Data for Germany and Indonesia relate to year 2018.

Source: Table D.19 Arrears: Closing stock, collectable arrears, and arrears relating to state owned enterprises.

Figures 7.4 and 7.5. show the change of arrears (total and collectable) between 2018 and 2019. While in most jurisdictions the amounts of arrears remained relatively steady, there are some exceptions in both directions.

In looking at the amount of arrears for the main tax types (see Table 7.3.), it seems that individuals are more likely to pay on time than businesses. The average ratio of corporate income tax (CIT) arrears to CIT net revenue collected is around 38% and the ratio for value added taxes (VAT) is around 30%. At the same time, the ratio for personal income tax (PIT) is much lower at around 17%.

At around 7%, the ratio is the lowest for employer withholding taxes (WHT). However, this is expected, as employers are responsible for forwarding those taxes to the administration on behalf of their employees and have no right over the amounts.

Figure 7.4. **Movement of total arrears between 2018 and 2019**

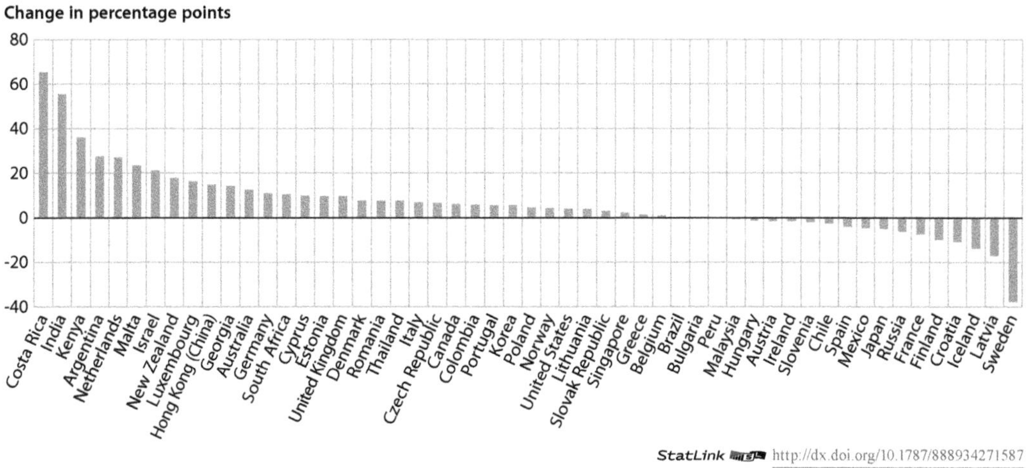

StatLink http://dx.doi.org/10.1787/888934271587

Source: Table D.21 Arrears: Movement between 2018 and 2019.

Figure 7.5. **Movement of collectable arrears between 2018 and 2019**

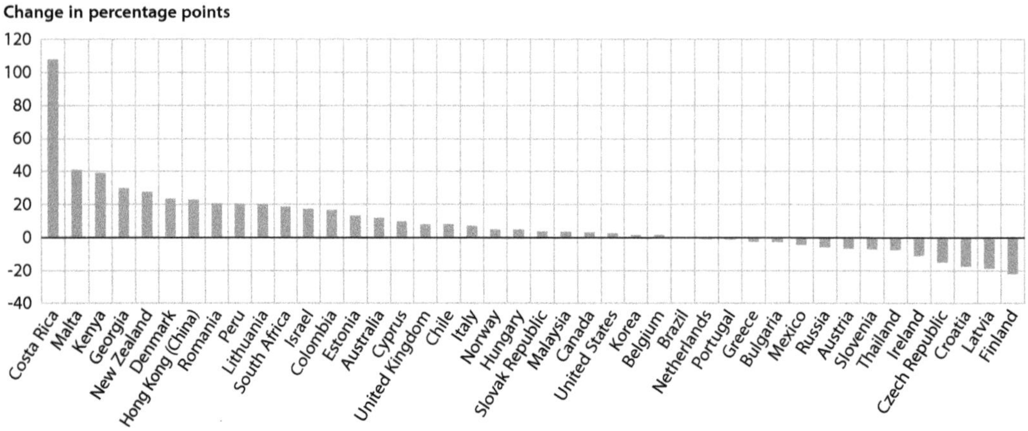

StatLink http://dx.doi.org/10.1787/888934271606

Source: Table D.21 Arrears: Movement between 2018 and 2019.

Similar to what has been observed above in relation to the ratio of total arrears to total net revenue, the average ratios by tax type are considerably lower when excluding outliers, i.e. administrations that show ratios above 100% for a tax type (see Table 7.3).

Table 7.3. **Average ratio of year-end arrears to net revenue collected by tax type, 2019**

Tax type	Average ratio	Average ratio for administrations with ratio below 100%
CIT arrears as percentage of CIT collected (45 jurisdictions)	37.5	22.6
PIT arrears as percentage of PIT collected (46 jurisdictions)	17.3	11.3
Employer WHT arrears as percentage of PIT collected (35 jurisdictions)	6.5	6.5
VAT arrears as percentage of VAT collected (43 jurisdictions)	30.2	16.8

Note: The table shows the average ratios for jurisdictions that were able to provide the information for the year 2019. The number of jurisdictions for which data was available is shown in parentheses.

Source: Table D.20 Arrears in relation to collection by tax type.

Preventive approaches

The range of actions undertaken by tax administrations to prevent debt from arising and to collect outstanding arrears continues to evolve. Advances in predictive modelling and experimental techniques as reported in the OECD report *Advanced Analytics for Better Tax Administration* (OECD, 2016[4]) and in the compendium of successful tax debt management practices contained in the OECD report *Successful Tax Debt Management: Measuring Maturity and Supporting Change* (OECD, 2019[3]) are helping many administrations better match interventions with taxpayer specific risk. The approaches used fall into one of the following categories:

- Predictive analytics, which tries to understand the likelihood of certain outcomes and, as regards debt collection, includes modelling the risk that an individual or company will fail to pay as well as models that attempt to assess the likelihood of insolvency or other payment problems.

- Prescriptive analytics, which is about predicting the likely impact of actions on taxpayer behaviour, so that tax administrations can select the right course of action for any chosen taxpayer or group of taxpayers. (OECD, 2016[4])

Many administrations are blending both practices and have trialled a variety of approaches aimed at changing "taxpayer behaviour." As pointed out in Chapter 5, two-thirds of administrations are using behavioural insight methodologies or techniques. These practices have the potential to transform the approach to tax debt as administrations move away from the "one-size-fits-all" approaches (where it is cost-effective to do so) and instead try to identify:

- which cases should be subject to an intervention
- when to intervene (for example, even before a return or payment might be due)
- which type of action would achieve the best cost-benefit outcome.

Box 7.2 illustrates the approaches taken by some administrations.

Box 7.2. Country examples: Preventing debt from arising

Belgium: Studying the impact of behavioural techniques on tax compliance

The General Administration for Collection and Recovery under the Belgian Federal Public Service (FPS) Finance has been running a series of behavioural experiments, studying the impact of behavioural techniques such as simplification, deterrence and promoting a moral duty to be tax compliant. Several randomised controlled trials on paper letters were set up with scientifically based effect measurements.

A consistent picture emerged across these experiments: simplifying communication substantially increases compliance, deterrence messages have an additional positive effect but promoting the moral duty to be tax compliant seems to be generally ineffective, and often backfires in this context. The set-up of these trials and their results are published (De Neve et al., 2021[5]).

From an operational point of view, these findings were and are still being used to fine-tune communication towards taxpayers. They helped to raise payment compliance by 9 percentage points in the debt collection area, leading to EUR 22 million of advanced payments, which is a high return on the investment.

In another project using behavioural insights, tax assessments of taxpayers facing financial hardship were altered using behavioural insights in order to nudge them to apply for supporting measures such as instalment arrangements as soon as possible in the tax collection process. These targeted messages resulted in a 15% increase in instalment arrangements, which is beneficial for both taxpayers (debt prevention) and the tax administration (workload reduction).

See Annex 7.A. for links to supporting material.

Hungary: Behavioural insights elements in tax debt management

A pilot project launched in Hungary by the Ministry of Finance and the National Tax and Customs Administration (NTCA) aimed, amongst other things, to test the impact of new types of payment notifications. It was based on behavioural science methods, and took into account international best practice and the specificities of the Hungarian tax system.

Box 7.2. **Country examples: Preventing debt from arising** *(continued)*

It examined whether it was possible to increase the volume of voluntary payments by modifying the content or form of payment notifications. At the time of sending out the notifications, 21 000 individual entrepreneurs with a tax debt of between HUF 10 thousand and HUF 1 million were selected. Half of the randomly selected taxpayers received a traditional payment notice while the other half received the newly designed notice.

When designing the new letters, the main guiding principle was to prioritise the tasks of the taxpayers. Greater emphasis was placed on clear wording and using personalised content, and detailed legal references were removed with further information made available through direct links instead.

The form was also redesigned, and NCTA followed the principles of behavioural science to create clear and easy to follow instructions that were also clear about the consequence of non-compliance. Additionally, NCTA used colour highlighted text boxes to help improve this further.

The new-type notification increased the payment ratio by 1.4% on average, but the increase was even higher, 2.9%, for those with a debt of at least HUF 100 thousand. The results of the project showed that by making NTCA communication clearer, the payment of arrears, compliance with tax payment deadlines and voluntary compliance can be encouraged in a very cost-effective manner. The NTCA is now looking to incorporate this learning into general practice.

See Annex 7.A. for links to supporting material.

Singapore: Use of data tools and analytics models

Inland Revenue Authority of Singapore (IRAS) has leveraged data tools and analytics models to identify/prioritise cases with high risk factors for earlier interventions to improve tax collection rates. Three such tools are elaborated on below:

- **A Business Presence Indicator Dashboard to help identify inactive entities**: In the past, IRAS would learn about companies having ceased business after the commencement of enforcement actions. Using a more data-led approach to help IRAS take more targeted and effective actions, IRAS developed Business Presence Indicators (BPIs), which made use of 30-plus data items (e.g. reported revenue, owned assets, contributions to employee provident funds), to help gauge whether a company was likely to have business operations in the relevant year. IRAS have been able to use the BPIs to better customise enforcement actions and has streamlined the process for officers to access the BPI information.

  As a result of the use of BPI information and the BPI Dashboard, IRAS achieved the following:

  - Customised enforcement actions: IRAS made use of BPI to customise the pre-filing reminders and nudged ex-directors of companies with no BPIs to submit a Waiver to File form instead of sending them a generic enforcement reminder.
  - Reduction in futile work and prevention of further non-compliance: IRAS also made use of BPI to take targeted enforcement action against non-filer companies, including waiving the requirements to file tax returns if specific conditions were met. These targeted measures allowed more efficient allocation of enforcement resources.

- **Behavioural insights and digital tools to prevent debt from arising**: To leverage taxpayers' natural systems, IRAS conducted a pilot of including calendar notes on payment due dates into the SMS reminders for the IRAS Demand Note (DN) for late tax payments. This allowed individual taxpayers to synchronise due dates indicated on their SMS reminders into their mobile smartphones or calendars.

Box 7.2. **Country examples: Preventing debt from arising** *(continued)*

The pilot was conducted from June to October 2019 on a sample size of about 6 700 taxpayers and IRAS observed an uplift in compliance with DN for taxpayers who received the enhanced SMS with a calendar synchronisation feature. Following the successful pilot, IRAS scaled up deployment to all DN SMS reminders sent to individual taxpayers from 2020.

- **Digital tools to prevent debt from arising**: An e-service for individuals and corporate taxpayers to apply for tax instalments and manage their GIRO payment plans has been introduced. (GIRO is an automated electronic payment service which allows payments to be made directly from bank accounts to billing organisations, following the bank account holder's authorisation.)

  IRAS receives about 85 000 contacts a year on instalment payment matters. Now, instead of calling IRAS, taxpayers can self-help using the new digital service if they wish to shorten the number of instalments, appeal for extended instalments, re-active their GIRO arrangements, or cancel them. Taxpayers can also apply for instalments for multiple tax types within a single transaction.

  99% of these request were automatically processed by the digital service, relieving officers' time in handling the contacts and the manual processing of the instalment plan requests. Since implementation in September 2019, the take-up rate was 43% in Year 1 and it has increased to 65% in Year 2.

Sources: Belgium – Federal Public Service Finance (2021), Hungary – National Tax and Customs Administration (2021) and Inland Revenue Authority of Singapore (2021).

Debt collection in light of the COVID-19 pandemic

Understanding the impact of the COVID-19 pandemic on citizens and businesses, many tax administrations reacted swiftly and suspended debt recovery actions, such as taking money directly from wages or bank accounts and asset seizures and sales. Instead, tax administrations offered taxpayers easier access to payment plans or extensions to existing plan durations. (CIAT/IOTA/OECD, 2020[6])

These measures aimed to prevent hardship or significant cash-flow concerns, to help stabilise the wider economy. However, it is likely that those actions have further increased the debt ratios described in the previous sections.

While it will be possible to analyse this in the 2021 edition of this series (which will comment on fiscal year 2020 data), it is important to underline the importance of considering the economic impact of restarting debt recovery actions and less generous payment plan terms when planning for the post pandemic recovery.

Note

1. In the 2019 edition, the tax administrations for Chile and Iceland reported not being responsible for debt collection (OECD, 2019[1]). While this is still the case in Chile, it has changed in Iceland when on 1 May 2019 the debt collection function was transferred from the Directorate of Customs to the Directorate of Internal Revenue.

References

CIAT/IOTA/OECD (2020), *"Tax administration responses to COVID-19: Measures taken to support taxpayers", OECD Policy Responses to Coronavirus (COVID-19)*, OECD Publishing, Paris, http://dx.doi.org/10.1787/adc84188-en. [6]

De Neve, J. et al. (2021), "How to Improve Tax Compliance? Evidence from Population-Wide Experiments in Belgium", *Journal of Political Economy*, Vol. 129/5, pp. 1425-1463, http://dx.doi.org/10.1086/713096. [5]

OECD (2019), *Successful Tax Debt Management: Measuring Maturity and Supporting Change*, OECD, Paris, https://www.oecd.org/tax/forum-on-tax-administration/publications-and-products/successful-tax-debt-management-measuring-maturity-and-supporting-change.htm (accessed on 1 September 2021). [3]

OECD (2019), *Tax Administration 2019: Comparative Information on OECD and other Advanced and Emerging Economies*, OECD Publishing, Paris, https://dx.doi.org/10.1787/74d162b6-en. [1]

OECD (2016), *Advanced Analytics for Better Tax Administration: Putting Data to Work*, OECD Publishing, Paris, https://dx.doi.org/10.1787/9789264256453-en. [4]

OECD (2014), *Working Smarter in Tax Debt Management*, OECD Publishing, Paris, https://dx.doi.org/10.1787/9789264223257-en. [2]

Annex 7.A

Links to supporting material (accessed on 1 September 2021)

- Box 7.1 – Spain:
  - Links to a presentation and a video on the national telephone helpline for assistance and processing in tax collection: presentation: www.oecd.org/tax/forum-on-tax-administration/publications-and-products/spain-helpline-for-assistance-and-processing-in-tax-collection.pdf, and video: https://youtu.be/H9erraJ6s_Y
  - Link to videos on Cl@vepin: www.agenciatributaria.es/AEAT.internet/PIN_24H/videos.shtml
  - Link to AEAT website to register for Cl@vepin: https://www.agenciatributaria.gob.es/AEAT.sede/en_gb/procedimientoini/GC27.shtml
  - Links to a presentation and a video illustrating the new tools in the field of debt collection: presentation: www.oecd.org/tax/forum-on-tax-administration/publications-and-products/spain-new-tools-in-the-field-of-debt-collection.pdf, and video: https://youtu.be/q_xJrGlNeRc
  - Link to the calculators to assist taxpayers in the field of tax collection: www.agenciatributaria.es/AEAT.internet/Inicio/La_Agencia_Tributaria/Campanas/_Campanas_/Herramientas_de_asistencia_virtual/Herramientas_asistencia_Recaudacion/Herramientas_asistencia_Recaudacion.shtml
- Box 7.2 – Belgium: Link to a video describing a series of behavioural experiments run by the Belgian General Administration for Collection and Recovery: https://youtu.be/JedLnJp0NdU
- Box 7.2 – Hungary: Link to a video on a pilot project to test the impact of new types of payment notifications: https://youtu.be/3mnuDHOCi-E

Chapter 8

Disputes

Dispute prevention and resolution are essential features of tax systems. This chapter explores both issues by looking at dispute prevention strategies, the availability of dispute review mechanisms and tax administrations' performance in relation to disputes.

Introduction

Effective access to processes that allow taxpayers to challenge assessments and decisions are an essential feature of a good tax system. They safeguard taxpayer rights and ensure appropriate checks and balances exist on the exercising of tax powers by administrations. At the same time, tax administrations and taxpayers should strive to work to together to prevent disputes from arising in the first place, thus reducing burdens and uncertainty for both parties.

Table 8.1. **Taxpayer's rights and obligations**

Right	Obligation
To be informed, assisted, and heard	To be honest
Of appeal	To be co-operative
To pay no more than the correct amount of tax	To provide accurate information and documents on time
Certainty	To keep records
Privacy	To pay taxes on time
Confidentiality and secrecy	

Source: OECD (2019), *Tax Administration 2019: Comparative Information on OECD and other Advanced and Emerging Economies*, https://doi.org/10.1787/74d162b6-en

This chapter explores both issues. First, it takes a closer look at the dispute prevention strategies put in place by tax administrations, and second it examines the dispute resolution and review mechanisms in the jurisdictions covered by this report, as well as their performance in this area.

Dispute prevention

Prevention is the best form of dispute resolution, and tax administrations have introduced a variety of approaches to provide clarity and certainty to taxpayers with the aim of reducing compliance costs, particularly in relation to litigation. Additionally, as disputes can be resource intensive processes, fewer disputes will free up resources that can be focussed elsewhere.

A key element in the dispute prevention framework is the provision of guidance and advice to taxpayers. Tax administrations often do this as part of their wider service strategy, and it can include putting information and interactive tools on their website, publishing guidelines and taxpayer information briefs, and carrying out educational and business support initiatives.

In addition, many administrations offer specific dispute prevention mechanisms. For example, as noted in the chapter "Innovations in dispute resolution" in the 2019 edition of this series, the Australian Taxation Office explained their independent review of the technical merits of an audit case prior to the finalisation of the audit. The review aims to encourage earlier engagement to resolve disputes (OECD, 2019[1]). Initially this service was only available to large businesses with an annual turnover greater than AUD 250 million. However, following a successful pilot it has now been extended to small business taxpayers, i.e. taxpayers in business with income or turnover of less than AUD 10 million (Australian Taxation Office, 2021[2]).

Rulings

As shown in the 2019 edition of this series (OECD, 2019[1]), as part of tax administrations' commitment to give taxpayers certainty of treatment, it is now common practice for administrations to set out how they will interpret the laws they administer, and how it will interpret the tax law in particular situations, through rulings:

- A ***public ruling*** is a published statement of how an administration will interpret provisions of the tax law in particular situations. They are generally published to clarify application of the law, especially where a large number of taxpayers may be impacted by particular provisions and/or where a provision has caused confusion or uncertainty. Typically, a public ruling is binding on the tax administration if the ruling applies to the taxpayer and the taxpayer relies upon it.
- A ***private ruling*** relates to a specific request from a taxpayer (or their tax representative) seeking greater certainty as to how the law would be applied by the tax administration in relation to a proposed or completed transaction(s). The objective of private rulings is to provide additional support and certainty to taxpayers on the tax consequences of more complex transactions.

Co-operative compliance programmes

Over the last few years, there has been an increasing focus on the use of co-operative arrangements to manage compliance and enhance tax certainty. These programmes often involve a more transparent relationship between tax administration and taxpayer, and can involve more proactive approaches to resolving material tax risks. The concept of co-operative compliance has been the subject of several OECD reports, most recently *Co-operative Tax Compliance: Building Better Tax Control Frameworks* (OECD, 2016[3]).

As the operation of a co-operative compliance programme is resource intensive due to the high level of engagement between tax administration officials and taxpayers, traditionally, those programmes were reserved for large companies. However, technological advancements in risk assessment processes have led to a number of administrations applying this concept to other taxpayer groups (see Figure 8.1).

Figure 8.1. **Existence of co-operative compliance approaches for different taxpayer segments, 2019**

Percent of administrations that have such approaches

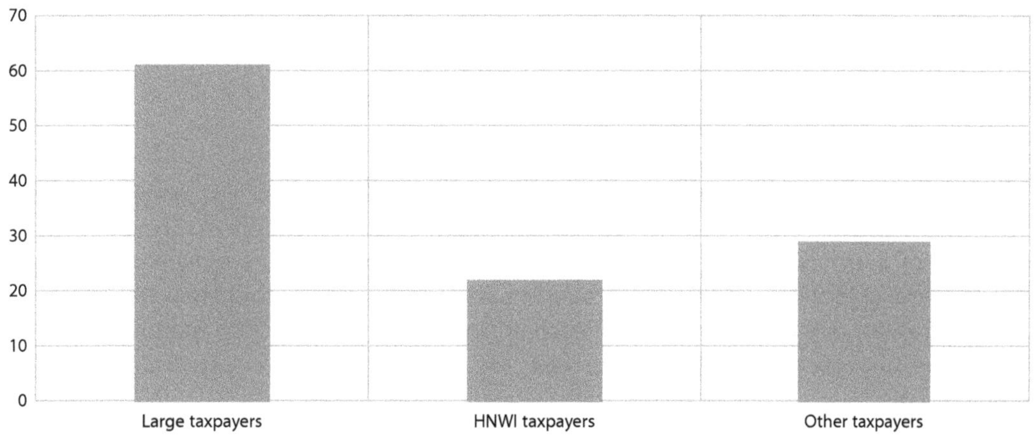

StatLink http://dx.doi.org/10.1787/888934271625

Source: Table A.49 Cooperative compliance approaches.

International Compliance Assurance Programme

The International Compliance Assurance Programme (ICAP) is a voluntary programme for a multilateral co-operative risk assessment and assurance process. It is designed to provide multinational enterprise groups (MNE groups) with increased tax certainty with respect to certain of their activities and transactions as long as they are willing to engage actively, openly and in a fully transparent manner. ICAP does not provide an MNE group with the legal certainty that may be achieved, for example, through an advance pricing arrangement (APA). However, it does give assurance when tax administrations participating in an MNE group's risk assessment consider covered risks to be low risk. (OECD, 2021[4]) As of April 2021, twenty jurisdictions participate in ICAP.[1]

Joint audits

Another tool that can assist in preventing disputes is a joint audit where officials from two or more administrations join to form a single audit team which will examine issues or transactions of taxpayer(s) with cross-border business activities and in which the jurisdictions have a common or complementary interest. By collaborating it may be possible for the participating tax administrations to detect and address differences or potential disputes at an early stage. (OECD, 2019[5])

Box 8.1. **United States: Dispute prevention measures**

On 16 November 2020, the competent authorities of the United States and Mexico announced that they had renewed their prior co-ordination agreement that provides tax certainty for over six hundred multinational groups with "maquiladoras" – Mexican subsidiaries providing contract manufacturing and assembly functions for U.S. principals. Under this renewed Qualified Maquiladora Approach Agreement ("QMA"), double taxation is prevented if the Mexican taxpayer enters into a unilateral advance pricing agreement ("APA") with Mexico's Large Taxpayer Division (Administración General de Grandes Contribuyentes) under terms negotiated in advance between the U.S. and Mexican competent authorities. The competent authorities also announced that they are actively working to extend the QMA framework, with the aid of recently issued OECD guidance (issued 18 December 2020), to provide tax certainty for tax years impacted by current economic, commercial and public health conditions.

Source: United States – Internal Revenue Service (2021).

Dispute resolution review mechanisms

All 59 jurisdictions provide taxpayers with the right to challenge assessments. Almost all administrations report having an internal review mechanism in place, and a large majority of administrations provide taxpayers with the option to seek an independent review by an external body, which can help improve legal certainty for taxpayers. For those administrations that offer both review mechanisms, approximately 70% require taxpayers to seek an internal review before their case can be reviewed by an external body. (See Figure 8.2.)

Figure 8.2. **Dispute resolution: Available review mechanisms, 2019**

Percent of administrations

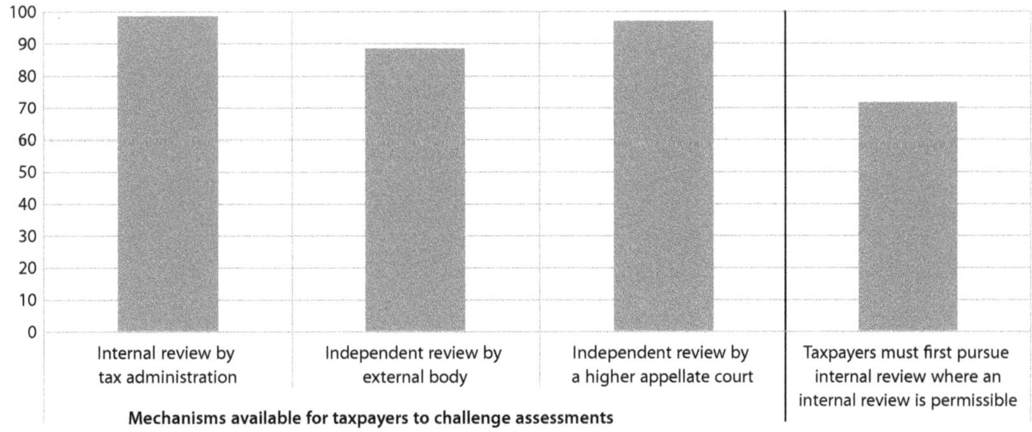

StatLink http://dx.doi.org/10.1787/888934271644

Source: Table A.37 Dispute resolution: Review procedures.

> Box 8.2. **Resolving international tax disputes: Mutual agreement procedures**
>
> Double taxation of the same transaction or income can have significant economic impacts. Tax treaties, also known as double taxation agreements, usually aim to remove double taxation, by setting out mutually agreed rules on the allocation of taxing rights for taxpayers resident in the signatory countries. They can also provide mechanisms to help prevent tax non-compliance.
>
> Given the complexity of these situations, the parties may disagree on the application or interpretation of those rules. To respond to these situations, the vast majority of tax treaties have a formal process for dispute resolution through a mutual agreement procedure (MAP). Such a procedure is set out in Article 25 of the OECD Model Tax Convention, which is used by most countries as the framework for their tax treaties. MAP is critical component in ensuring the effective working of tax treaties, and in helping to reduce double taxation.
>
> *Source:* OECD (2017), "Improving mutual agreement procedures", in *Tax Administration 2017: Comparative Information on OECD and Other Advanced and Emerging Economies*, https://doi.org/10.1787/tax_admin-2017-18-en.

Performance in dispute resolution

While tax administrations cannot generally control the timing of judicial processes, many of them are working on improving dispute resolution processes to make them quicker. The Brazilian example included in Box 8.3. illustrates how technological advancements offer new possibilities for tax administrations to identify similar cases or to understand likely outcomes of disputes; and the examples from Georgia and India show how digitalisation can support the dispute function (see Box 8.3).

Making effective adjustments to dispute resolution processes requires sound reporting and monitoring mechanisms. It is encouraging to see that since the 2015 TAS report, many administrations have been active in improving the level of management information available, and as a result, this report contains performance information from approximately 90% of administrations.

Box 8.3. Country examples: E-dispute resolution

Brazil: Artificial Intelligence in tax dispute resolution

In order to expedite tax dispute resolutions, the Brazilian Tax Administration is working to employ artificial intelligence in this process. With machine-learning algorithms, it is possible to automatically read the taxpayers allegations, compare it with a knowledge base of previous resolutions, cluster similar allegations and also propose, in natural language, the most likely outcome.

Georgia: E-hearing of tax disputes

During the pandemic the Georgia Revenue Service (GRS) introduced remote, electronic tax dispute hearings. Taxpayers were offered the chance to have a remote hearing for their ongoing disputes. This option was further embedded when taxpayers had the possibility to indicate in advance their willingness to participate in a remote hearing for new dispute resolution proceedings.

The solution ensures the business continuity of tax administration processes, the safety of involved parties during the pandemic, as well saving the time and financial resources of the taxpayers. Central to effective implementation was to ensure a smooth, efficient and effective system also taking into account concerns and requirements relating to data protection and confidentiality. GRS decided to build a system using a video-conferencing platform that allowed taxpayers to connect both via computer as well as phone. Taxpayers receive reminders of hearings through their personalised web pages as well as via SMS, which also provides detailed instructions on how to use the platform.

Table 8.2 shows the take up of e-hearings in Georgia, and the GRS expect the take up to grow as taxpayers become more accustomed to the e-hearing service. The e-hearing system has now been incorporated into the tax code of Georgia, meaning it will be maintained after pandemic is over.

Table 8.2. **Georgia: Evolution of the use of e-hearing of tax disputes**

	May 2020	June 2020	August 2020	November 2020	December 2020
Number of cases to be heard	11	14	8	236	235
Number of cases where taxpayers agreed to go through e-hearing	8	13	6	151	130

Source: Georgia Revenue Service (2021).

India: Faceless Appeal Scheme

In 2020, the government of India launched the Faceless Appeal Scheme. This scheme introduces remote filing and hearing of the income tax appeals, and dispenses of the need for the taxpayer to appear in person before the Commissioner of Income Tax (Appeal).

The taxpayer has to supply their supporting material online, through the e-filing portal, and their appeal is heard through the central online Appeal Centre, which is a single point of contact between appellants and the government. Through this scheme, India will deliver greater efficiency, transparency and accountability for both taxpayers and the appeal body.

Sources: Federal Revenue Service of Brazil (2021), Georgia Revenue Service (2021) and India – Income Tax Department (2021).

Figures 8.3 and 8.4. show the change between 2018 and 2019 in the number of review cases on hand at fiscal year-end, for both internal and external reviews. What is interesting to note are the significant increases in the number of review cases reported by a few jurisdictions.

Figure 8.3. **Internal review procedures: Change between 2018 and 2019 in the number of cases at fiscal year-end**

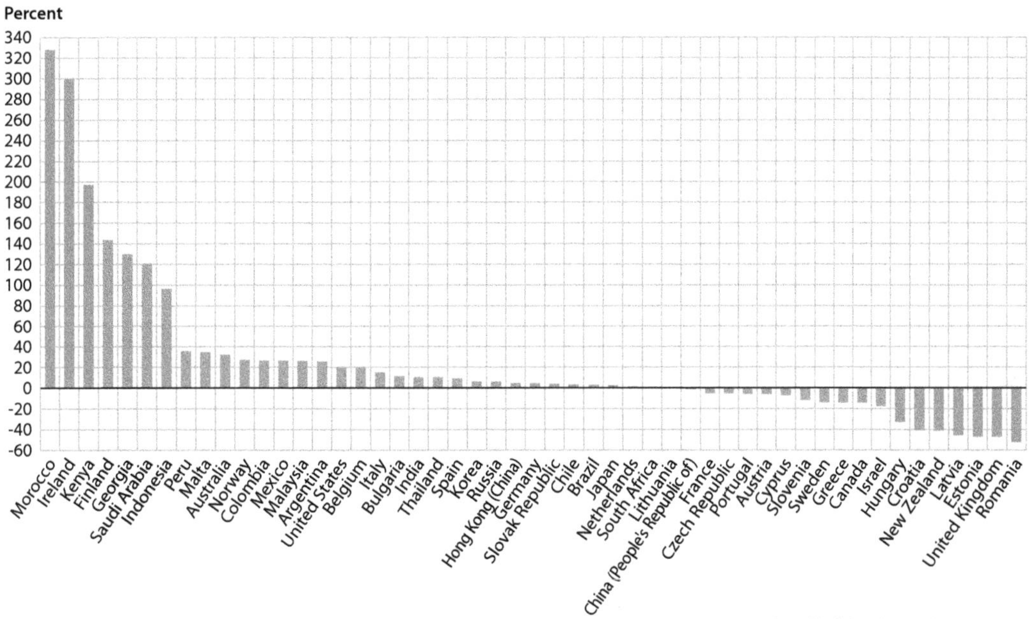

StatLink http://dx.doi.org/10.1787/888934271663

Source: Table A.38 Dispute resolution: Number of cases.

Figure 8.4. **Independent review by external bodies: Change between 2018 and 2019 in the number of cases at fiscal year-end**

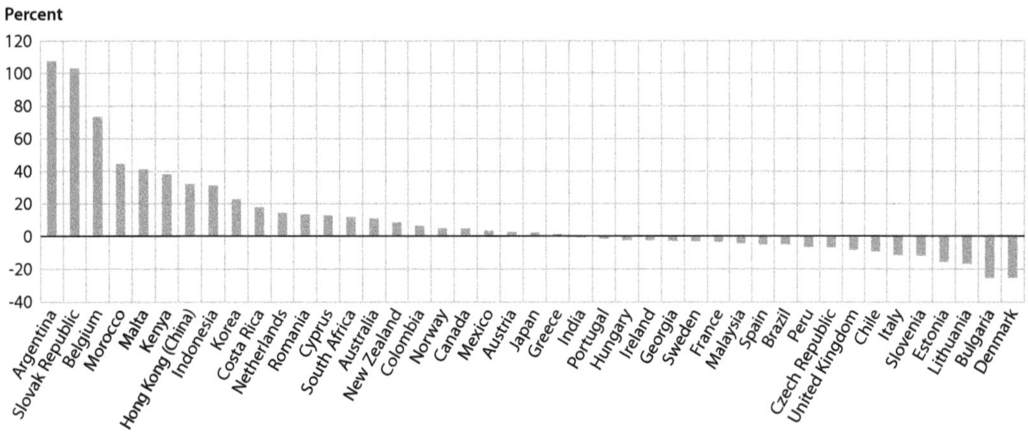

StatLink http://dx.doi.org/10.1787/888934271682

Source: Table A.38 Dispute resolution: Number of cases.

At the same time, it should be pointed out that the volume of cases per jurisdiction varies significantly. For example, Table A.38 shows that Ireland has a very small number of cases under internal review procedure and the 300% increase of cases on hand is actually an increase from one case at the end of 2018 to four cases at the end of 2019. This becomes more evident when looking at Figure 8.5, which highlights the wide differences between jurisdictions in the use of internal review procedures.

Figure 8.5. **Number of internal review cases initiated per 1 000 active PIT and CIT taxpayers, 2019**

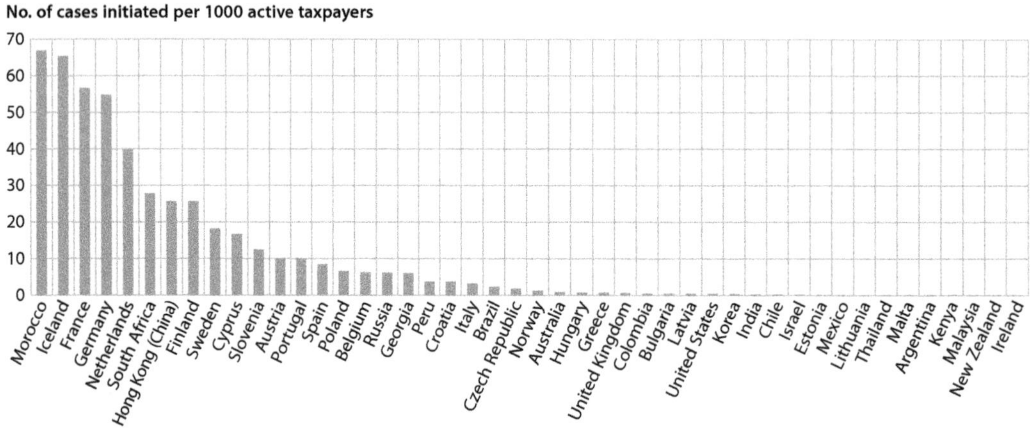

StatLink http://dx.doi.org/10.1787/888934271701

Note: For Iceland and Poland the data relates to the year 2018.

Source: Table D.24 Administrative review cases & litigation.

Figure 8.6. **Percentage of cases resolved in favour of the administration**

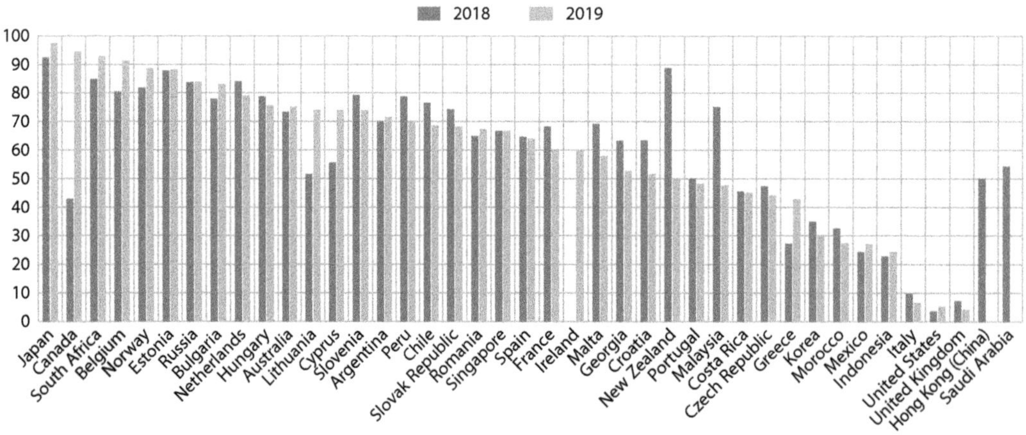

StatLink http://dx.doi.org/10.1787/888934271720

Note: Cases resolved in favour of the administration means those cases where the administration has been successful in more than 50% of the issues contested in each case. For France, the number of cases resolved in favour of the administration includes all decisions totally or partially favourable to the administration. For Korea, the number of cases resolved in favour of the administration refers to decisions where all issues were ruled in favour of the tax administration.

Source: Table D.24 Administrative review cases & litigation.

Different interpretations of tax law by taxpayers and the tax administration are a normal part of tax administration, and it is not uncommon for these differences to become subject to litigation, once the internal and external review procedures have been exhausted. Whilst tax administrations report that most disputes are resolved without the need for litigation, Figure 8.6. reports the performance of administrations for cases decided upon by the courts. This shows that there is little variation between 2018 and 2019, although for some jurisdictions the number of cases decided is very low, meaning results can fluctuate significantly between years.

Note

1. See www.oecd.org/tax/forum-on-tax-administration/international-compliance-assurance-programme.htm (accessed on 29 April 2021).

References

Australian Taxation Office (2021), *Independent review for small businesses with turnover less than $10 million*, www.ato.gov.au/General/Dispute-or-object-to-an-ATO-decision/In-detail/Avoiding-and-resolving-disputes/Independent-review/Independent-review-for-small-businesses-with-turnover-less-than-$10-million/ (accessed on 1 September 2021). [2]

OECD (2021), *International Compliance Assurance Programme – Handbook for tax administrations and MNE*, OECD, Paris, www.oecd.org/tax/forum-on-tax-administration/publications-and-products/international-compliance-assurance-programme-handbook-for-tax-administrations-and-mne-groups.htm (accessed on 1 September 2021). [4]

OECD (2019), *Joint Audit 2019 – Enhancing Tax Co-operation and Improving Tax Certainty: Forum on Tax Administration*, OECD Publishing, Paris, https://dx.doi.org/10.1787/17bfa30d-en. [5]

OECD (2019), *Tax Administration 2019: Comparative Information on OECD and other Advanced and Emerging Economies*, OECD Publishing, Paris, https://dx.doi.org/10.1787/74d162b6-en. [1]

OECD (2016), *Co-operative Tax Compliance: Building Better Tax Control Frameworks*, OECD Publishing, Paris, https://dx.doi.org/10.1787/9789264253384-en. [3]

Chapter 9

Budget and workforce

This chapter looks at the resources devoted to tax administrations and provides information on their workforce. It sets out challenges administrations are managing in increasing their capability while managing a workforce that in general terms is reducing in size and on average is getting older.

Introduction

Central to a tax administration meeting its role in collecting revenue and providing services to citizens and businesses, is sufficient financial resources and a skilled workforce that can deliver quality outputs efficiently and effectively. This chapter looks at those issues. The first part examines the financial resources available to tax administrations, and how those resources are spent. The second part provides information on tax administrations' workforce. This chapter also sets out some of the challenges caused by digitalisation and the COVID-19 crisis.

As already mentioned in other chapters, the International Survey on Revenue Administration (ISORA), which forms the basis of this report, was reduced in size to facilitate a move to an annual survey and to reduce burdens on participating administration (see Reader's Guide for more detailed information). As a result, this report does not look anymore at governance arrangements for tax administrations or human resource management aspects, including staff capability. Readers interested in those topics are invited to look at the 2019 edition of this series (OECD, 2019[1]).

Budget and information and communication technology

Operating expenditures

The overall level of resources devoted to tax administration is an important and topical issue for most governments, external observers, and of course tax administrations themselves. While the budgetary approaches differ, in most jurisdictions the budget allocated is tied to the delivery of performance outputs which are outlined in an annual business plan.

When looking at the budget figures, around three-quarters of tax administrations report an increase of their operational expenditure between the years 2018 and 2019. With the data from the previous ISORA survey it is also possible to look at budgetary developments over the period 2016 to 2019. Here more than 85% of the administrations show an increase in their budget (see Table 9.1).

However, this data should be treated with caution. While on paper a significant number of administrations saw increases in their budget, this does not take into the account the increases in responsibilities that many administrations are reporting, as well as inflation pressures.

This issue is compounded as a significant part of the budgets is needed for salary costs, accounting for on average 73% of operating budgets annually (see Figure 9.1). Any

Table 9.1. **Changes in operating expenditures**

Percent of administrations

Change	Between 2016 and 2019 (based on data for 36 administrations)	Between 2018 and 2019 (based on data for 57 administrations)
Increase in operating expenditure	86%	77%
Decrease in operating expenditure	14%	23%

Note: The comparison of 2016 and 2019 data is only based on information of 36 tax administrations as for some administrations data was not available for all years, or data was not comparable as (i) some administrations received significant new responsibilities or (ii) a number of joint tax and customs administrations utilised a new simplified form for estimating the budget attributed to tax administration alone (something offered through the ISORA 2020 survey tool).

Source: Secretariat calculations based on Tables E.1 and A.7 and OECD (2019), *Tax Administration 2019: Comparative Information on OECD and other Advanced and Emerging Economies*, https://doi.org/10.1787/74d162b6-en, Tables E.1 and A.31.

wider increases in budgets can be rapidly consumed by salary increases, which may be a contractual obligation. This mix of greater responsibility, and pressured budgets, is driving tax administrations to find innovative approaches, often using technology, so they can deliver greater services to taxpayers, and focus on the relevant compliance risks. This approach is allowing tax administrations to meet the budgetary challenges they face.

It will also be interesting to see the impact of the COVID-19 pandemic on tax administrations' budgets as reduced revenue collections (see Chapter 2) coupled with significant government spending on programmes to support citizens and businesses may lead to some governments reducing budgets for some government bodies. The impact of reduced revenue collections may also pose additional challenges for the small number of administrations where the annual budget (or a part of it) is based on a "percentage-of-revenue-collected" formula unless adjustments to that formula are made (OECD, 2019, p. 114[1]).

A potential area for tax administrations for future cost reductions could be real estate management. With an increasing number of staff expected to work remotely even after the COVID-19 crisis is over, tax administrations may consider re-assessing if they need the existing size of office space (whether as owners or tenants). For the immediate future, the required office space may remain unchanged as potential savings due to remote working may be offset by social distancing requirements.

Moving to smart and energy efficient buildings, reducing energy consumption, and sharing infrastructure with other government agencies as described in the country examples included in Box 9.1. are among other possible approaches for reducing costs.

Box 9.1. **Country examples: Reducing operating expenditure**

Chile: Energy Efficiency Project

In August 2019, the Chilean tax administration (Servicio de Impuestos Internos, SII) introduced the Energy Efficiency Project which covers the following aspects: current contracts optimisation, reduction of energy consumption, generation of sustainable lifestyles and reduction of energy costs:

- Twenty-one electricity supply contracts around the country were revised during 2020. Best prices were negotiated, and SII aimed to achieve economies of scale by pooling contracts from different organisations, allowing them to optimise their negotiating position. By the end of 2020, 19 out of 21 contracts were modified.
- SII reduced energy consumption by monitoring 21 facilities distributed around the country, through an online platform of data collection allowing the tracking of peak consumption times and energy costs. SII examined replacing outdated technology with more efficient consumption systems, and adjusting consumption times to take advantage of lower costs.
- Through training workshops, the objective is that 500 public servants of SII may raise awareness about sustainable development, renewable energies and efficient use of resources. Throughout 2020, SII developed a national workshop programme supported by Chilean Ministry of Energy, with all 21 heads of administration at a country level. For 2021, the goal is to implement between 8 to 10 workshop activities of local or national impact.
- The milestone for 2021 is the reduction of energy expenses by 30% (approximately USD 167 000) and 40% (approximately USD 296 000) for 2022. The savings will be used to fund the programmes of reduction in energy consumption.

Box 9.1. **Country examples: Reducing operating expenditure** *(continued)*

United Kingdom: HMRC locations smarter working smarter buildings

In the United Kingdom (UK), Her Majesty's Revenue and Customs' (HMRC) Locations Programme is central to its wider transformation. It is leading the delivery of phase one of the UK's government hubs programme to provide great places to work, with a wide range of flexible workspaces designed to support smarter working and incorporate on-site learning facilities.

High-speed digital infrastructure ensures high levels of resilience and reliability. Gov. uk Wi-Fi networks enable flexible occupation by multiple Government departments. These technologically advanced buildings are an integral component of HMRC's plans to provide better services to the taxpayer at a lower cost, saving GBP 90 million per annum.

The buildings are designed using the standards set out in HMRC's Inclusive Design Guide, which has been commended by the Construction Industry Council, to provide a modern and welcoming working environment that is accessible to the broadest range of people.

All of HMRC's regional centres are designed and constructed in accordance with Building Information Modelling (BIM) processes and procedures. This ensures accuracy and continuity of asset data throughout design, construction and into building operation. This is leading to increased collaboration between HMRC and its suppliers.

For example, all new sites are designed using BIM Level 2, which has meant that every element of design has been co-ordinated before on-site assembly, reducing errors and raising quality. In addition, HMRC is piloting sensor technology at HMRC's Croydon Regional Centre to monitor building performance across four key areas: thermal comfort; CO2 levels in meeting rooms; energy usage and condition-based maintenance of plant and equipment.

Regional Centres have all received Building Research Establishment Environmental Assessment Method (BREEAM) excellent or outstanding ratings. Since 2017, HMRC has reduced overall waste by 64% and achieved a 77% recycle rate from other waste products with only 1% going to landfill. It has also reduced operational carbon emissions by 36% and water usage by 51%. This places HMRC in the top 10 UK Government departments for every Greening Government target area.

Sources: Chile – Servicio de Impuestos Internos (2021) and United Kingdom – Her Majesty's Revenue and Customs (2021).

Components of tax administration operating expenditure

As stated above, the largest reported component of tax administration operating budgets is staff costs, with salary alone accounting for on average 73% of operating budgets annually (see Figure 9.1). Another important component is the operating cost for ICT. On average this accounts for 10% of operating expenditure, with a few countries reporting ICT expenditure between 20 and 25% of their total operating expenditure (see Table D.3). The averages for both items (salary and ICT) have remained stable since 2016 across the administrations covered by this report.

Capital expenditure

Capital expenditure makes-up about 4% of total expenditure on average but varies significantly between administrations. A few administrations report figures below 1% while others report figures above 10% (see Table A.7).

Figure 9.1. **Salary cost as a percent of total operating expenditure, 2019**

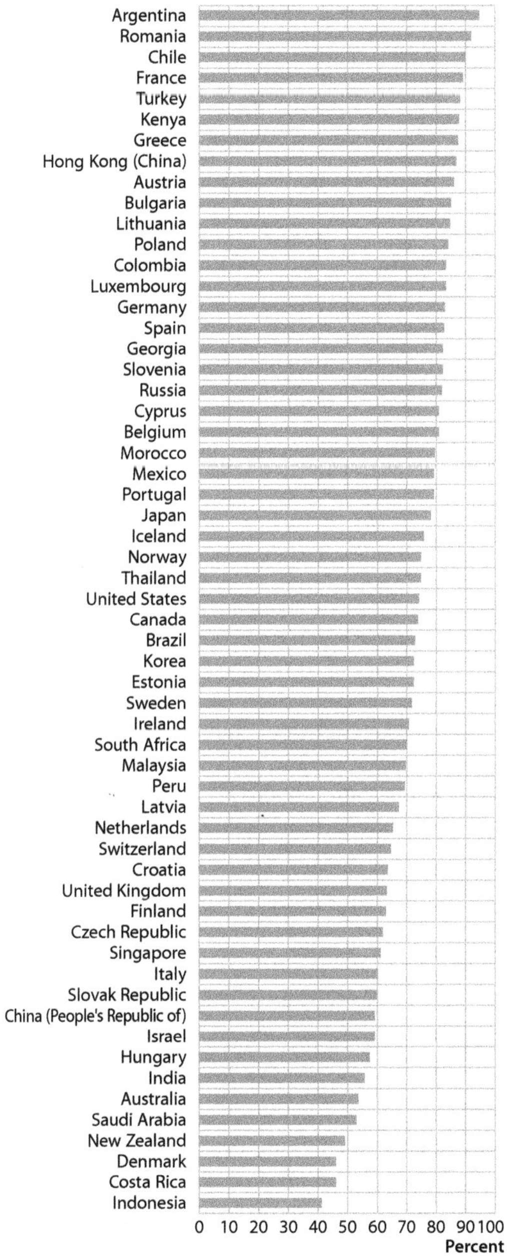

StatLink http://dx.doi.org/10.1787/888934271739

Source: Table D.3 Resource ratios.

Figure 9.2. **Movement in "cost of collection" ratios between 2018 and 2019**

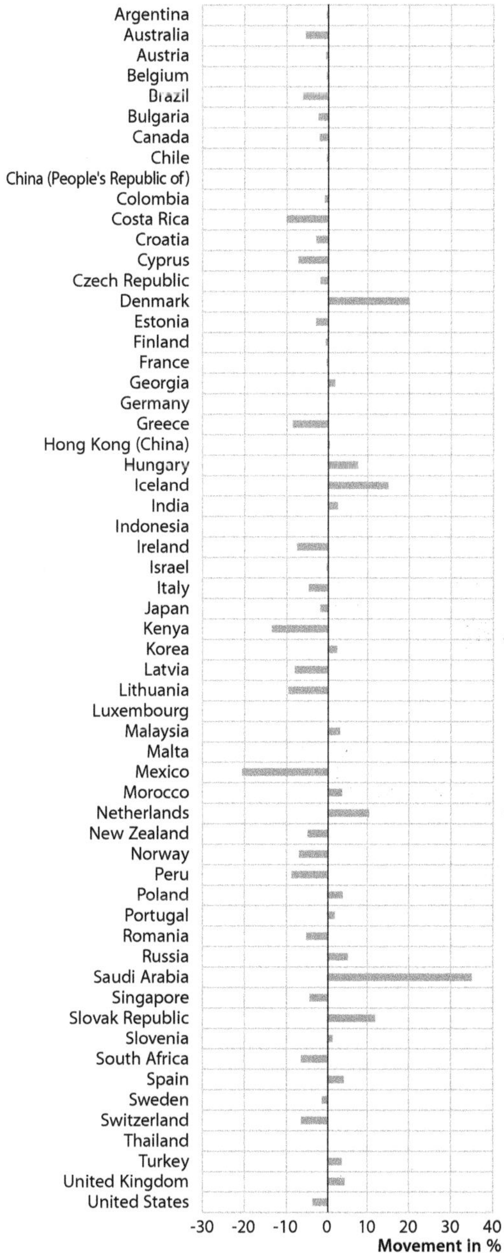

StatLink http://dx.doi.org/10.1787/888934271758

Source: Table D.3 Resource ratios.

Note: When interpreting Figure 9.2 the factors mentioned in Box 9.2. should be taken into account.

Cost of collection

It has become a fairly common practice for tax administrations to compute and publish (e.g. in their annual reports) a "cost of collection" ratio as a surrogate measure of their efficiency/effectiveness. The ratio is computed by comparing the annual expenditure of a tax administration, with the net revenue collected over the course of a fiscal year. Given the many similarities in the taxes administered by tax administrations, there has been a natural tendency by observers to make comparisons of "cost of collection" ratios across jurisdictions. Such comparison have to be treated with a high degree of caution, for reasons explained in Box 9.2.

In practice there are a number of factors that may influence the cost/revenue relationship, but which have nothing to do with relative efficiency or effectiveness. While data for fiscal year 2020 will only be available through the next ISORA survey, it is expected that the COVID-19 crisis may well be one of those factors. Further, international comparisons are difficult to make given a range of variables to be taken into account.

Examples of such factors and variables include macroeconomic changes as well as differences in revenue types administered. These factors are further elaborated in Box 9.2.

Box 9.2. **Difficulties and challenges in using the "cost of collection" ratio as an indicator of efficiency and/or effectiveness**

Observed over time, a downward trend in the "cost of collection" ratio can constitute evidence of a reduction in relative costs (i.e. improved efficiency) and/or improved tax compliance (i.e. improved effectiveness). However, experience has also shown that there are many factors that can influence the ratio which are **not** related to changes in a tax administrations efficiency and/or effectiveness and which render this statistic unreliable in the international context:

- **Changes in tax policy**: Tax policy changes are an important factor in determining the cost/revenue relationship. In theory, a policy decision to increase the overall tax burden should, all other things being equal, improve the ratio by a corresponding amount, but this has nothing to do with improved operational efficiency or effectiveness.
- **Macroeconomic changes**: Abnormal changes in rates of economic growth etc. or inflation over time are likely to impact on the overall revenue collected by the tax administration and the cost/revenue relationship.
- **Abnormal expenditure of the tax administration**: From time to time, a tax administration may be required to undertake an abnormal level of investment (e.g. the building of a new information technology infrastructure, acquisition of more expensive new accommodation). Such investments are likely to increase overall operating costs over the medium term, and short of offsetting efficiencies, will impact on the cost/ revenue relationship.
- **Changes in the scope of revenues collected**: From time to time, governments decide to shift responsibility for the collection of particular revenues from one agency to another which may impact the cost/revenue relationship.

From a fully domestic perspective, an administration may be able to account for those factors by making corresponding adjustments to its cost or collected revenue. This can make tracking the "cost of collection" ratio a helpful measure to see the trend over time of the administration's work to collect revenue. If it were gathered by tax type, it may also help inform policy choices around how particular taxes may be administered and collected.

Box 9.2. Difficulties and challenges in using the "cost of collection" ratio as an indicator of efficiency and/or effectiveness *(continued)*

However, its usefulness with respect to international comparison is very limited. While administrations may be able to account for the above factors from a domestic perspective, it will be difficult to do this at an international level as such analysis would have to consider:

- **Differences in tax rates and structure**: Rates of tax and the actual structure of taxes all will have a bearing on aggregate revenue and, to a lesser extent, cost considerations. For example, comparisons of the ratio involving high-tax jurisdictions and low-tax jurisdictions are hardly realistic given their widely varying tax burdens.
- **Differences in the range and nature of revenues administered**: There are a number of differences that can arise here. In some jurisdictions, more than one major tax authority may operate at the national level, or taxes at the federal level are predominantly of a direct tax nature, while indirect taxes are administered largely by separate regional/state authorities. In other jurisdictions, one national authority will collect taxes for all levels of government, i.e. federal, regional and local governments. Similar issues arise in relation to the collection of social insurance contributions.
- **Differences in the range of functions undertaken**: The range of functions undertaken by tax administrations can vary from jurisdiction to jurisdiction. For example, in some jurisdictions the tax administration is also responsible for carrying out activities not directly related to tax administration (e.g. the administration of certain welfare benefits), while in others some tax-related functions are not carried out by the tax administration (e.g. enforced debt collections). Further, differences in societal views may influence what an administration does, how it can operate and what services is has to offer. The latter may have a particularly significant impact on the cost/revenue relationship.

Finally, it should be pointed out that the "cost of collection" ratio ignores the revenue potential of a tax system, i.e. the difference between the amount of tax actually collected and the maximum potential revenue. This is particularly relevant in the context of international comparisons – administrations with similar cost/revenue ratios can be some distance apart in terms of their relative effectiveness.

Despite those factors, the "cost of collection" ratio is included in this report for two reasons:

1. The "cost of collection" ratio is useful for administrations to track as a domestic measure as it allows them to see the trend over time of their work to collect revenue and, as pointed out in Box 9.2., they may be able to account for the main factors that can influence the ratio.
2. The inclusion of the "cost of collection" ratio and the accompanying comments set out in Box 9.2. can serve as a prominent reminder to stakeholders of the difficulties and challenges in using the easily calculated "cost of collection" ratio for international comparison.

Figure 9.2 illustrates the movement in the "cost of collection" ratios between 2018 and 2019 for the administrations included in this report. It shows that sixty percent of the administrations had decreasing ratios. However, as mentioned in Box 9.2, the chart and the underlying figures have to be interpreted with care.

Information and communication technology

On average ICT expenditure accounts for about 10% of operating expenditure (see above). However, reported levels of ICT expenditure vary enormously between administrations. For those administrations able to provide ICT-related cost, close to 50% reported an annual operating ICT expenditure exceeding 10% of the administration's total operating expenditure in 2019 and another twenty percent reported figures between 5% and 10% (see Table D.3). While some of this variation can be explained by the different sourcing and business approaches, some cannot and point, at least on the surface, to expenditure levels that maybe somewhat low to support the rapidly changing electronic and digital services administrations are increasingly being called upon to provide.

As regards the operational ICT solutions (i.e. solutions that are used to fulfil the tax administration's mandate and include systems for registration, return processing, payment processing and auditing), almost all tax administrations report using custom built ICT solutions, while sixty percent report also using commercial-off-the-shelf (COTS) solutions (see Figure 9.3).

Figure 9.3. **Basis of ICT solutions of tax administrations, 2019**

Percent of administrations that have such solutions

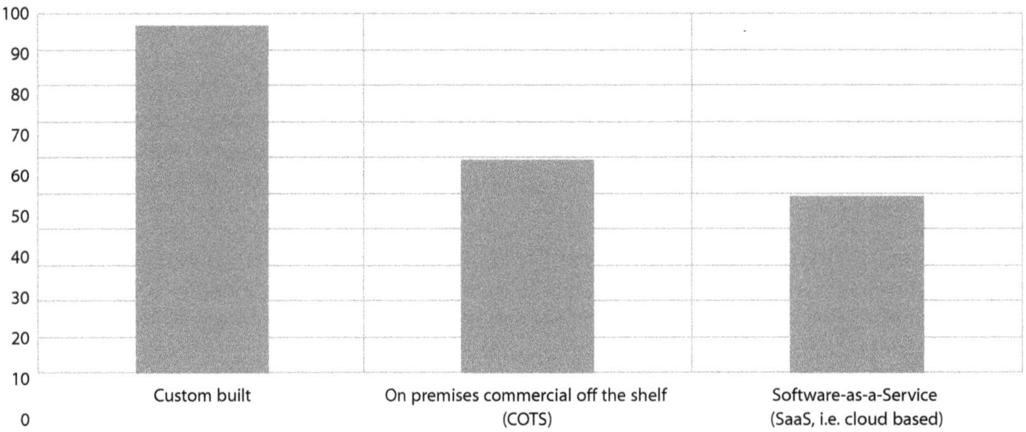

StatLink http://dx.doi.org/10.1787/888934271777

Source: Table A.9 Information and communication technology (ICT) solutions of the tax administration.

In addition, close to half of the administrations report using Software-as-a-service (SaaS) solutions. These are software licensing models where the tax administration pays for a subscription license and the cost depends on the usage. The software is installed on third party computers, not on tax administration computers, and is accessed by users via the internet. One of the main barriers to adopting SaaS more widely, is the storage of sensitive tax data on these third party systems. As more legislative and technological solutions are identified, including regarding the encryption of data, it is likely the use of SaaS will increase.

Box 9.3. Country examples: Developing new ICT approaches

Canada: Leveraging cloud services

The Canada Revenue Agency (CRA) leveraged cloud services to implement a contact centre operation to support the Canadian Emergency Response Benefits (CERB) due to the COVID-19 pandemic. The new contact centre was built to process general enquiries from the public with interactive voice response informational content and the option to transfer to a live agent. Strategically, it also diverted some of the new call demand from the existing programmes during the tax filing season when the IT infrastructure usage is at its peak.

Due to the criticality of the situation, the urgent requirement to respond to public enquiries and the rigidity of the existing infrastructure, the cloud service infrastructure became the clear option of choice very quickly. The CRA was able to develop and implement the contact centre solution within a three-week period. From March 2020 to April 2021 the contact centre has processed over 6.8 million calls from Canadian taxpayers. The ongoing efforts in adopting cloud services through unforeseen events or planned pathfinder projects have proven very valuable in improving the delivery of programmes and generated opportunities that would not have been viable based on traditional IT infrastructure. Cloud services are not without their challenges and constraints, but they certainly stand out as a valuable concept to deliver technology services.

Canada: Adopting Agile processes

In Autumn 2019, IT Architecture at the CRA identified a need to innovate on its current practices to adapt to the Agile approaches to development that were being embraced within the CRA. Its analysis determined that, rather than concentrating on integrating with Agile processes and methods, the focus of IT Architecture's innovations needs to be on the value of the outcome of their services. The service IT Architecture provided to the development teams in the CRA has been redefined to take advantage of the Product-centric mindset consistent with the Agile manifesto. The CRA is beginning to fully embrace the cultural changes associated with the Product-centric mindset, including: changes to its budgeting and funding approaches; adjusting its project gating processes; adopting new roles like Product Owner; and, empowering its development teams to make critical decisions. In conjunction with those changes, IT Architecture will identify initiatives to pilot its new approach. In addition, IT Architecture is practicing a product-centric approach to developing and maintaining some of its key documents and models.

Source: Canada Revenue Agency (2021).

Workforce

In 2019, the administrations included in this report employed approximately 1.8 million staff (see Table A.8) making the effective and efficient management of workforce critical to good tax administration. Having a competent, professional, productive and adaptable workforce is at the heart of most administrations' human resource planning. With salary costs averaging more than 70% of operating expenditures, any budget change invariably impacts staff numbers.

The "double pressure" created from reduced budgets and technology change, mentioned in the 2017 edition (see also Figure 9.4.), continues to be a significant management issue for most administrations. The challenge is compounded for some which, due to contract restrictions or government mandates, may find it difficult to strategically down-size their operations other than through the non-replacement of staff who leave of their own accord.

Figure 9.4. **Double pressure on the workforce**

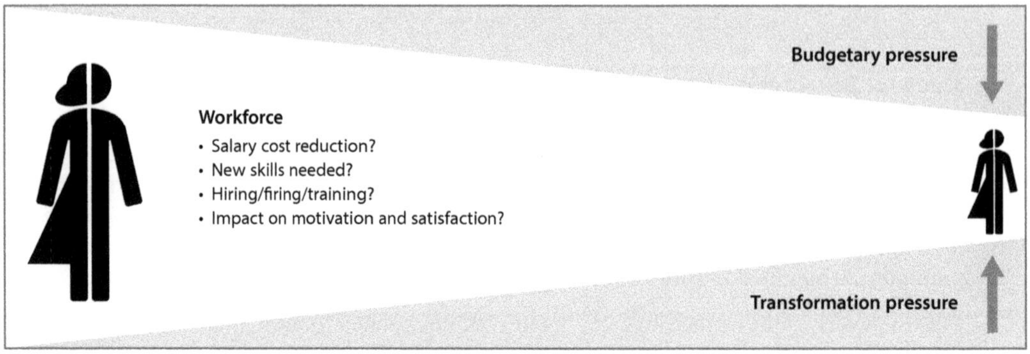

Source: OECD (2017), *Tax Administration 2017: Comparative Information on OECD and Other Advanced and Emerging Economies* https://doi.org/10.1787/tax_admin-2017-en.

Staff usage by function

Figure 9.5 provides average allocation of staff resources (expressed in full-time equivalents) across four functional groupings used to categorise tax administration operations.[1] While the detailed data for each administration in Table D.4 shows a significant spread of values and a number of outliers for each function, generally the "audit, investigation and other verification" function is the most resource intensive, employing on average thirty percent of staff, a ratio that has remained stable over the past years.

Figure 9.5. **Staff usage by function, 2019**

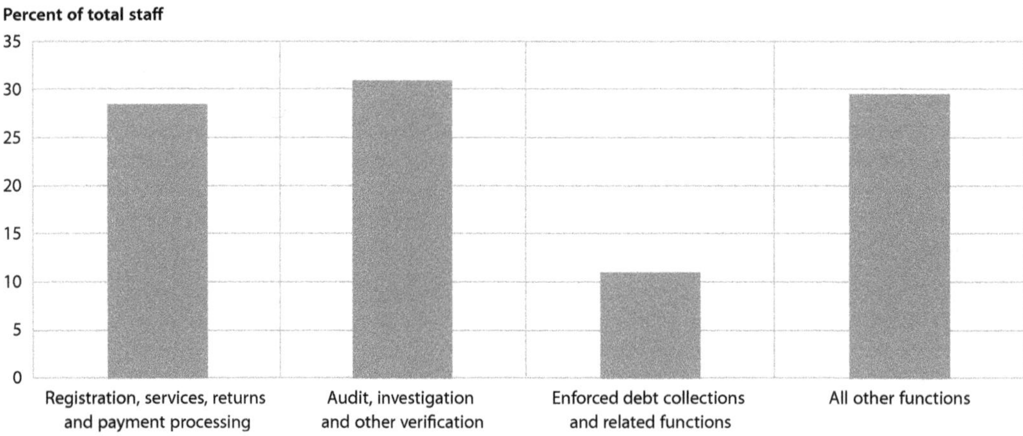

StatLink http://dx.doi.org/10.1787/888934271796

Note: Excluding administrations that were unable to provide the break-down for all functions.

Source: Table D.4 Staff allocation by function.

Staff metrics

ISORA 2020 also gathered key data concerning the age profiles, length of service, gender distribution and educational qualifications of tax administration staff: see Tables D.6 to D.8 and A.11 to A.14. In interpreting this data, there are two main considerations to bear in mind:

- Combined tax and customs administrations were allowed to use their total workforce for answering the underlying survey questions as it may be difficult for them to separate the characteristics of the tax and customs workforce.

- In ISORA 2020, staff metrics information was collected for the total number of staff, whereas in previous ISORA rounds staff metrics information was collected for permanent staff only. Trend analysis comparing staff metrics in the ISORA 2020 data with that of previous ISORA surveys should therefore be conducted with caution. In particular, for administrations that employ a significant number of non-permanent staff, this change in methodology may cause a shift in staff-metric-percentages that is not based on regular staff fluctuations but rather a result of including a different group of staff.

Age profiles

While there are significant variations between the age profiles of tax administration staff (see Table D.6), it is interesting to see that there are also differences when viewed across different regional groupings. This may be the result of a complex mix of cultural, economic, and sociological factors (e.g. economic maturity, recruitment, remuneration, and retirement policies).

Figure 9.6 illustrates that staff are generally younger in administrations in the regional groupings of "Asia-Pacific" and "Middle East and Africa" where, on average, around one third of staff are below 35 years of age, whereas in the "Americas" and "Europe" this percentage drops to below twenty percent. At the same time, administrations in the "Americas" and "Europe" have a large percentage of staff older than 54 years.

Figure 9.6. **Age profiles of tax administration staff, 2019**

Percentage of staff by age bands for selected regional groupings

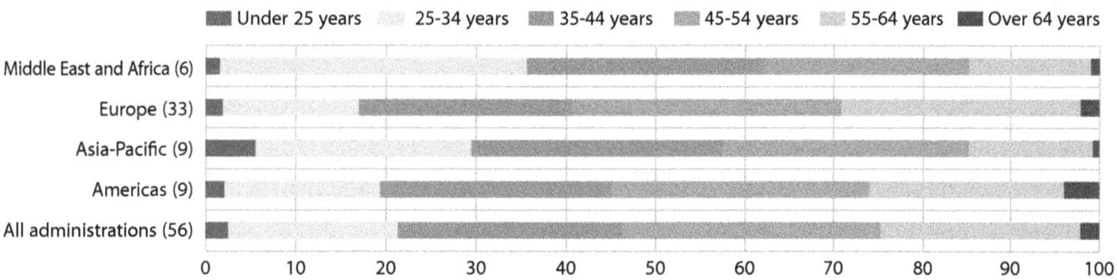

	All administrations (56)	Americas (9)	Asia-Pacific (9)	Europe (33)	Middle East and Africa (6)
Under 25 years	2.5	2.1	5.6	1.9	1.6
25-34 years	18.8	17.3	23.9	15.0	34.0
35-44 years	25.0	25.8	28.1	23.7	26.4
45-54 years	28.9	28.8	27.8	30.2	23.4
55-64 years	22.8	22.2	13.9	27.0	13.7
Over 64 years	2.0	3.9	0.8	2.1	1.0

Percent

StatLink http://dx.doi.org/10.1787/888934271815

Note: The following administrations are included in the regional groupings: Americas (9) – Argentina, Brazil, Canada, Chile, Colombia, Costa Rica, Mexico, Peru and the United States; Asia-Pacific (9) – Australia, China, Hong Kong (China), Indonesia, Korea, Malaysia, New Zealand, Singapore and Thailand; Europe (33) – Austria, Belgium, Bulgaria, Croatia, Cyprus, the Czech Republic, Denmark, Estonia, Finland, France, Georgia, Germany, Greece, Hungary, Iceland, Ireland, Italy, Latvia, Lithuania, Luxembourg, Malta, the Netherlands, Norway, Poland, Portugal, Romania, Russia, the Slovak Republic, Slovenia, Spain, Sweden, Switzerland and the United Kingdom; Middle East and Africa (6): Israel, Kenya, Morocco, Saudi Arabia, South Africa and Turkey.

Source: Table D.6 Staff age distribution.

Looking at the jurisdiction specific data, and keeping in mind the change in methodology mentioned above, it can still be observed that between 2014 and 2019 the percentage of staff older than 54 years grew in a large number of administrations, in some even significantly (see Figure 9.7).

Figure 9.7. **Staff older than 54 years: Movement between 2014 and 2019**

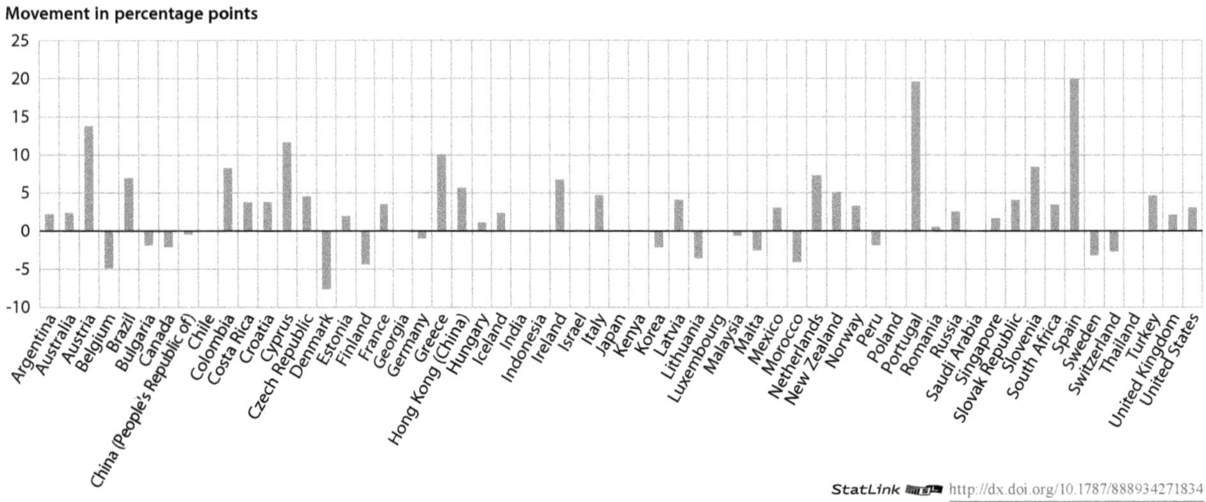

StatLink http://dx.doi.org/10.1787/888934271834

Note: Only includes jurisdictions for which data was available for both years. It is important to note that this comparison should be read with caution as there was a change in methodology in the underlying survey question: In ISORA 2020 (covering fiscal year 2019), staff metrics information was collected for the total number of staff, whereas in ISORA 2016 (covering fiscal year 2014), staff metrics information was collected for permanent staff only.

Source: Table D.6 Staff age distribution and OECD (2017) *Tax Administration 2017: Comparative Information on OECD and Other Advanced and Emerging Economies*, https://doi.org/10.1787/tax_admin-2017-en, Table A.22.

Figure 9.8. **Average length of service vs. average age profile, 2019**

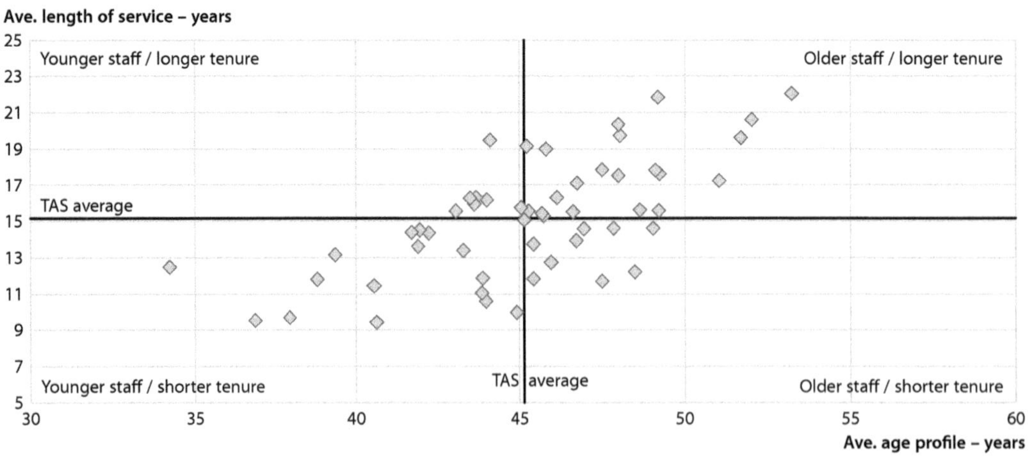

StatLink http://dx.doi.org/10.1787/888934271853

Source: OECD Secretariat calculations based on Tables D.6 Staff age distribution and D.7 Length of service.

Length of service

The difference in age profiles is also largely reflected in the length of service of tax administration staff. Figure 9.8 indicates that a significant number of administrations will not only face a large number of staff retiring over the next years, but that many of these staff will be very experienced, thus raising further issues about retention of key knowledge and experience.

Figure 9.8 also indicates that a small number of administrations have an above-average workforce age, while the length of service is lower than average (see Figure 9.8, Quadrant "Older staff/shorter tenure").

Gender distribution

In light of the strong public interest in gender equality, administrations were invited to report total staff and executive staff respectively by gender. As can be seen in Figure 9.9, while many administrations are close to the proportional line, typically female staff remains proportionally underrepresented in executive positions and significantly underrepresented (black oval) in a number of administrations, something that has remained unchanged since the 2017 edition of this report (OECD, 2017[2]).

Figure 9.9. **Percentage of female staff – total female staff vs. female executives, 2019**

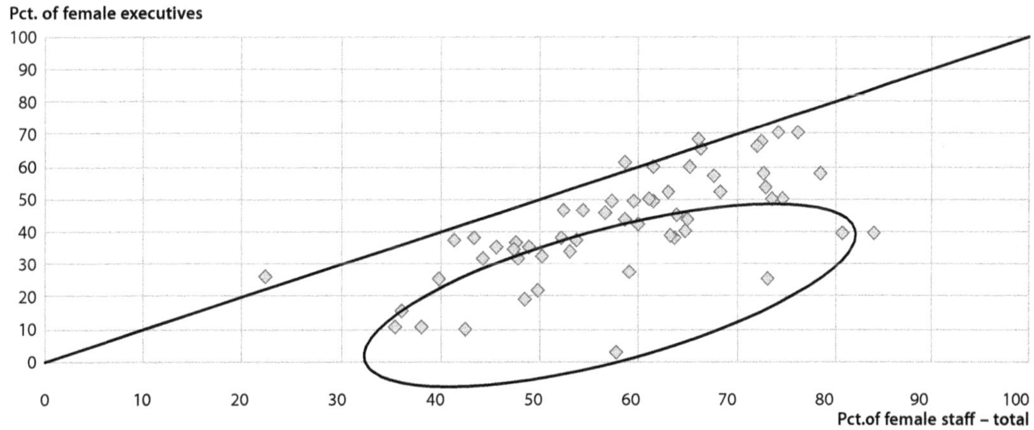

StatLink http://dx.doi.org/10.1787/888934271872

Source: Table D.8 Gender distribution and academic qualifications.

For the first time, the ISORA 2020 survey also asked administrations to indicate whether staff has self-identified as neither female nor male (referred to as "other" gender for the purposes of the survey). Table A.14. shows that two administrations, Australia and New Zealand, had staff who self-identified as "other".

Staff attrition

Staff attrition, also called staff turnover, refers to the rate at which employees leave an organisation during a defined period (normally a year). High attrition rates may result from a variety of factors, such as downsizing policies, demographics or changing staff preferences. The attrition rate should be considered together with other measures, such as the hire rate, which looks at the number of staff recruited during a defined period, when evaluating the human resource trends of an administration.

While a high attrition rate combined with a low hire rate is usually associated with a general downsizing policy – and may therefore be accepted – administrations should be concerned where both rates are high. Recruitment is costly, not only the recruitment process itself but also the cost and time for training and supporting new staff members, and the significant down time before new staff are fully operational or able to perform at the highest level. Having high attritions rates are generally to be avoided.

Having attrition rates that are too low may also not be ideal. While an organisation is growing, a low attrition rate may be accepted. However, in situations where both the attrition rate and the hire rate are low, an organisation may not have the ability to recruit new skills as all positions are filled. This could be an issue particularly for administrations that are undergoing transformation and therefore are in need of staff with skills that are different from what is currently available within the administration.

While what is considered a "healthy" attrition rate differs between industry sectors or jurisdictions, and the general economic conditions also influence this judgement, the average attrition rate for administrations participating in this publication of 7.5% in 2019 and the average hire rate of 7.3%[2] in 2019 (see Table D.5) would seem to present a reasonable range for tax administrations of between 5% and 10%. The average attrition and hire rates are still in-line with average rates seen since 2014 (see the 2017 edition (OECD, 2017[2])).

However, when looking at specific administration data, it becomes apparent that "attrition and hire" rates cover a very broad range. Figure 9.10 shows the relationship between tax administration attrition and hire rates. It illustrates that there are a number of administrations with attrition and hire rates well above 10% (upper-right box), while others show very low attrition and hire rates (lower-left box).

Figure 9.10. **Attrition and hire rates, 2019**

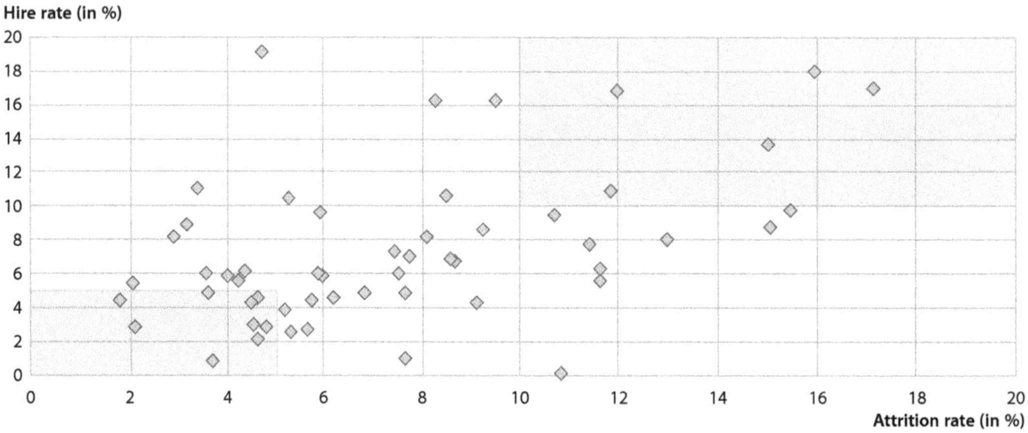

StatLink http://dx.doi.org/10.1787/888934271891

Note: Attrition rate = number of staff departures/average staffing level. Hire rate = number of staff recruitments/ average staffing level. The average staffing level equals opening staff numbers + end-of-year staff numbers/2.

Source: Table D.5 Staff dynamics.

Looking at the data going back to 2014, it is also interesting to see that it is often the same administrations that have very high attrition and hire rates, posing the interesting question of how those administrations address the issues mentioned above concerning recruitment, training and knowledge transfer.

Box 9.4. Canada: Demographic data analytics

In Canada, eligibility to retire at the CRA was previously used as a proxy to estimate future retirements. It was observed, however, that a large proportion of employees who were eligible for retirement continued to work for years, which resulted in an overestimation of the number of employees leaving the agency.

To address this, the CRA developed a new approach to measure future retirement departures using data from retired CRA employees over the past five years. The CRA's new approach of using projected retirement rates has strengthened its capacity to analyse departures due to retirement, and strategic planning ability in terms of future workforce requirements.

The CRA was able to increase its reporting capacity by transitioning from conducting data analysis using spreadsheets to using a statistical analysis software, which was necessary to analyse a database holding millions of observations as well as support timely reporting and decision-making. Not only did the statistical analysis software reduce the amount of time spent on manual labour by approximately 80%, this transformation almost completely eliminated the risk of human error.

Source: Canada Revenue Agency (2021).

Supporting staff

The changes tax administrations are managing, whether technology, policy or budget driven, are significant. These changes are impacting the service expectations of taxpayers, and staff need the right tools and support to adapt. As a result, tax administrations are considering the best way to support staff through these changes, ensuring they have the right tools for the tasks.

Box 9.5. Country examples: Supporting staff through simplifying procedures and providing new tools

Australia: Transformation of frontline procedures and guidance

Transformation of Australian Taxation Office (ATO) frontline procedures and guidance involved reviewing, re-formatting and re-writing over 3 500 pages of content. This has made it quicker, easier and more intuitive for client-facing staff to complete their day-to-day work and provide clients with great service.

Prior to the transformation, an assessment of this content found:

- no consistent writing style – making it hard to digest and understand
- no consistent layout – making it hard to intuitively complete tasks and identify ways to add value (e.g. promote self-help options to clients)
- lack of on-page navigation – making it hard to find information (particularly on content-heavy pages).

To address this, the ATO:

- partnered with experts to understand best practices
- used best practice insights and user-feedback to develop a:
    - consistent writing style that incorporates behavioural insights, readability tools and quantifiable metrics

Box 9.5. **Country examples: Supporting staff through simplifying procedures and providing new tools** *(continued)*

  - page structure to improve usability, promote self-service and support business objectives
  - template with built-in on-page navigation to improve findability of content
- conducted topic reviews to remove duplication and consolidate content (reducing overall page numbers by up to 50% per topic)
- re-wrote and re-formatted pages into new template.

This transformation has improved:

- efficiency – with around a 40% reduction in pages visited per user by per day (through consolidating content)
- readability – with quantifiable metrics (e.g. content now written to Australian grade 7 reading level, previously many pages were written at postgraduate level)
- intuitiveness – consistent structure, format and headings (including promotion of self-help)
- findability – page navigation options were added and search results de-cluttered by removing over 2 000 pages.

Canada: Risk Exposure and Tolerances Assessment (RETA) Tool

In order to support Canadians during the pandemic, the CRA had to quickly adapt and increase its tolerance to risk and adjust controls. This presented an opportunity to evaluate whether these changes resulted in added value to the organisation. When regular business resumes, should the CRA revert to its previous practices or should these crisis practices become the new normal?

To answer this question, the CRA developed the Risk Exposure and Tolerance Assessment (RETA) tool, which provides users with information pertaining to the levels of risk tolerance and exposure. The tool uses a five-point scale to quantify the elements of risk exposure (likelihood, impact, and control effectiveness) and risk tolerance (maturity, sensitivity, and span of control). The tool then calculates an overall score by subtracting the risk tolerance from the risk exposure score. The higher the overall score, the more attention the risk requires. Depending on the overall score, the tool will generate a recommendation on the sufficiency of controls, which is helping guide senior management in their decision making process.

The RETA tool was presented at the Institute of Internal Auditors (IIA) National Conference in 2020, and an article was also accepted for publication in the IIA Magazine.

In the midst of an ever-changing and unpredictable environment, the RETA tool is improving the effectiveness and efficiency of the CRA's risk management practices and is enabling the CRA to quantitatively assess and address new and evolving risks, and ultimately, increase its service and compliance effectiveness.

Sources: Australian Taxation Office (2021) and Canada Revenue Agency (2021).

The COVID-19 crisis added another complication to this as many administrations have moved to a remote working environment, with many officials working from home full-time (see Table 9.2). Many administrations signal that remote working will continue to be part of the normal work environment going forward.

Table 9.2. **Overview of remote working readiness and actual percentages**

Averages across three clusters of administrations that completed the FTA's digital resilience survey

Clusters (based on overall readiness for remote working before the crisis)	Overall readiness for remote working			Actual percentage of remote working			Average number of days per week that staff worked remotely		
	Before the crisis	During the peak of the crisis	Diff.	Before the crisis	During the peak of the crisis	Diff.	Before the crisis	During the peak of the crisis	Diff.
Cluster 1: Overall readiness below 10% (11 administrations)	0.9%	70.0%	+69.1%	0.5%	62.5%	+62.0%	0.5	3.9	+3.4
Cluster 2: Overall readiness between 10% and 50% (7 administrations)	26.3%	75.4%	+49.1%	14.5%	70.5%	+56.0%	1.8	4.2	+2.4
Cluster 3: Overall readiness above 50% (5 administrations)	81.4%	92.4%	+11.0%	30.6%	92.4%	+61.8%	1.0	4.7	+3.7

Source: OECD (2021), "Tax Administration: Digital Resilience in the COVID-19 Environment", *OECD Policy Responses to Coronavirus (COVID-19)*, https://doi.org/10.1787/2f3cf2fb-en.

Anecdotal evidence, gathered through numerous Forum on Tax Administration (FTA) meetings, shows that tax administrations have put considerable efforts into supporting staff during periods of transition, particularly during the COVID-19 crisis, considering issues such as:

- **staff welfare**, which includes looking into staff motivation and satisfaction, health and safety related issues, work-life balance, assistance programmes, and ergonomic office equipment
- **staff training**, which includes how to best support those that have been given new tasks, those that have to perform their tasks from home instead of the office, as well as those that are leading partially or wholly virtual teams for the first time.

A key issue in this respect, is also the availability of sufficient information to managers and team leaders, to allow them to identify where pressure points lie so that informed decisions can be taken swiftly. For example, a recent OECD publication on the digital resilience of tax administrations during the COVID-19 crisis showed that in more than 90% of the administrations covered by that study, tax administration's leadership teams were able to obtain real-time information on the status of employees (OECD, 2021[3]).

Box 9.6. **Country examples: Supporting staff**

Finland: Leading by knowledge – Shared goals and transparent information

The Finnish Tax Administration has renewed its operating model to enable and strengthen two central capacities: 1) agile and continuous improvement and 2) flexible use of resources. Drivers that lead the new operating model are constant learning, and more specifically, self-directed that is goal-driven and based on information.

Box 9.6. **Country examples: Supporting staff** *(continued)*

In the self-directed organisation, teams have a responsibility to participate in planning and developing their own work. Team objectives are derived from the organisation's strategy, and everyone knows what the objectives and measures mean in their everyday work life. Teams decide how they strive to reach the goals within the boundaries of standardised processes.

Shared goals provide the direction for the actions and decision-making is based on information. Digital "status centres" provide transparent metrics for teams on how they are doing on, for example, work progress, employee satisfaction and work culture. Status centres provide real-time and unified operational snapshots from senior management to individual officers, which enables ongoing development in each team. Weekly status centre meetings allow teams to discuss how work is progressing, identify barriers to development, and give and receive feedback.

Status centres contain a vast amount of information on operational progress and results, currently standing at approximately 9 billion data points. With the base these status centres form, senior management can track joint progress towards strategic goals and, therefore, better lead the organisation based on data.

See Annex 9.A. for a link to supporting material.

United Kingdom: COVID-19 HR practices

In the UK, HMRC was at the centre of the UK government's economic response to the COVID-19 pandemic. HMRC played an essential role in supporting businesses, families and the UK economy through the pandemic, including financially supporting the UK's most vulnerable people.

During the pandemic, most of HMRC's workforce were asked to stay home if possible, a move which saw over 90% of people move from office-based activity to home working. Within days, Human Resources (HR) transformed the way they support colleagues to work effectively during these unprecedented personally and professionally challenging times. With health and wellbeing central to HR's response, particular attention was focused on ensuring colleagues had the equipment and support required to complete their work from home and to be able to respond to extraordinary demands at home, including caring responsibilities.

HR exploited a web-based collaborative platform, to move COVID-19 guidance, people policy and support to a cloud-based virtual platform. This enabled all colleagues to access critical support from their tablets, laptops and phones, while allowing HR to continuously improve and evolve the support offered as the pandemic response continued. Another online tool allowed for real-time collaboration and publication of people policies, health and wellbeing guidance and support tools that were responsive to changes in the management of the pandemic at both a national level (i.e. lockdown measures) and at an organisational level. Supplementing this, communities were created on HMRC's social media platform, encouraging connectivity and discussion across the organisation.

This response saw HMRC support colleagues in the moment, communicate in real-time and respond to the ever-changing COVID-19 environment. As of March 2021, the collaborative platform site has had over 1.15 million views, enabling all HMRC colleagues to access a consistent, comprehensive suite of support resources to ensure they can work safely and effectively, while building organisation trust and engagement.

Sources: Finnish Tax Administration (2021) and United Kingdom – Her Majesty's Revenue and Customs (2021).

Developing staff capability

While ISORA 2020 did not survey administrations as regards their strategy and approaches towards increasing staff capability, this remains a key topic for all administrations and, as a result of the new remote working environment, administrations have started reconsidering their approaches to delivering training to staff.

With the increase in remote working, it becomes more difficult to conduct face-to-face training, and tax administrations have started moving their training programmes into a virtual environment, using live online training sessions or pre-recorded videos/webinars. While moving to a virtual training environment may have some up-front costs, it may save costs in the longer term. Once produced, pre-recorded training material or recorded live seminars can be viewed at any time, from anywhere, which may reduce travel expenses (if staff would have otherwise had to be brought to special training centres) and would allow staff to learn at their own pace and convenience. Also, the number of staff members that could follow a course would not be limited, and courses could be expanded over time. Box 9.7. summarises the approaches taken by a few administrations.

Box 9.7. **Country examples: Tax administration's approaches to staff training and development**

Australia: The Spotlight training series

The ATO's Service Delivery Group plays a key role in delivering organisational priorities and delivering value to the community. It does this by leveraging data to shape the work and automate processes. The Spotlight training series (Spotlights) is an excellent example of how the internal Service Delivery Training and Development team have utilised data and customer feedback to shape a series of innovative, best practice, client centred skilling solutions designed to be delivered in a digital environment.

Spotlights are contemporary "bite-sized" skilling packages that focus on Service Delivery pressure points identified through quality assurance, feedback and data from the frontline teams. They have been designed to be delivered in a digital environment and have now been accessed by frontline staff over 35 000 times.

Key differences from traditional "classroom" style training delivered in the ATO:

- Spotlights have been created using a combination of animation and case studies; and includes use of the ATO's in-house designed PowerPit (short for PowerPoint and Sandpit) system emulator.
- They are self-paced learning modules that focus on addressing improvement opportunities as they arise, and are designed to be completed in 3-5 minutes rather than more traditional physical or virtual "classroom style" training packages.
- Spotlights are used as a support tool in the ATO's quality assurance processes and provide a targeted approach to addressing identified skill gaps. This has resulted in some very positive trends in ATO's quality assurance results.

Spotlights created have focused on Proof of Record Ownership, Correspondence and Call Recording Warning.

Canada: Virtual Training

In Canada, for the 2020 fall hiring season, the CRA contact centres leveraged virtual tools to train its new workforce, allowing them all to work remotely. Web conferencing tools in combination with a virtual training environment, coaching, videos, chat functions and support tools, enabled the training programmes to innovate at an extremely fast pace, given that in the past 100% of training was done in a classroom environment.

Box 9.7. **Country examples: Tax administration's approaches to staff training and development** *(continued)*

Singapore: AI-powered skills development and profiling platform

In Singapore, the Inland Revenue Authority of Singapore (IRAS) introduced Jobkred, an AI-powered platform that measures employees' skills proficiency and facilitates career planning by enabling skills-gap analysis, recommending relevant training/courses, and providing career progression options within the organisation. This fosters greater self-awareness in employees and ownership of their career development, employability, and future-readiness. Strategically, Jobkred supports IRAS' workforce transformation by:

- articulating future job roles and skills required to achieve IRAS' objectives as IRAS' work evolves, to build transparency into performance indicators
- aligning job descriptions and skills taxonomy to highlight transferable skills, and facilitate job rotations
- gaining oversight of IRAS' skills profile to assess if the workforce can meet existing and future work demands. This allows for targeted monitoring of growth areas and progress measurements towards key milestones and performance indicators
- facilitating employees' self-assessment on how their current skills level meets future work expectations in their current and alternative job roles in IRAS.

Such transparency on job expectations complements other capability-building efforts (e.g. training, changes to performance grade definitions), making career conversations between staff and supervisors more constructive and effective.

Sources: Australian Taxation Office (2021), Canada Revenue Agency (2021) and Inland Revenue Authority of Singapore (2021).

Notes

1. Previous editions reported the allocation of staff resources across seven functional groupings: (i) Registration and taxpayer services; (ii) Returns and payment processing; (iii) Audit, investigation and other verification; (iv) Debt collection; (v) Dispute and appeals; (vi) Information and communication technology; and (vii) Other functions. Starting with ISORA 2020 those seven groupings were reduced to the four groupings shown in Figure 9.5.
2. The average hire rate for 2019 excludes Iceland given that staff which transferred from the Directorate of Customs to the Directorate of Internal Revenue when the debt collection function was moved in 2019 was recorded as recruitments, thus distorting the 2019 hiring rate for the Iceland Tax Administration.

References

OECD (2021), *"Tax Administration: Digital Resilience in the COVID-19 Environment"*, *OECD Policy Responses to Coronavirus (COVID-19)*, OECD Publishing, Paris, http://dx.doi.org/10.1787/2f3cf2fb-en. [3]

OECD (2019), *Tax Administration 2019: Comparative Information on OECD and other Advanced and Emerging Economies*, OECD Publishing, Paris, https://dx.doi.org/10.1787/74d162b6-en. [1]

OECD (2017), *Tax Administration 2017: Comparative Information on OECD and Other Advanced and Emerging Economies*, OECD Publishing, Paris, https://dx.doi.org/10.1787/tax_admin-2017-en. [2]

Annex 9.A

Links to supporting material (accessed on 1 September 2021)

- Box 9.6 – Finland: Link to a presentation on the new operating model of the Finnish Tax Administration: www.oecd.org/tax/forum-on-tax-administration/publications-and-products/finland-leading-by-knowledge.pdf

Annex A

Data tables

Annex A contains the set of tables which hold the data provided by tax administrations in response to the 2020 International Survey on Revenue Administration (ISORA). It covers the 59 jurisdictions that participate in the 2021 edition of the OECD's Tax Administration Series, including all 53 jurisdictions that are members of the OECD's Forum on Tax Administration (FTA) and the following non-FTA jurisdictions: Bulgaria, Croatia, Cyprus, Malta, Morocco and Thailand.

The first set of tables contains a number of indicators derived from the data submitted via the ISORA survey (tables starting with "D"). The formulae and data points used for calculating the indicators are shown below each of these tables.

The second set of tables contains the raw ISORA 2020 survey data. Those are the tables starting with "A".

The last table holds external data points that were used to calculate some of the D-table indicators. This table starts with "E".

Table D.1 **Revenue related ratios**

	Revenue related ratios									
	Revenue collected by the Tax Administration (in %) [1]									
	Revenue collected to total government revenue		Revenue collected to GDP		Tax collected including SSC to GDP		Tax collected excluding SSC to GDP		Non tax revenue to total revenue collected	
Jurisdiction	2018	2019	2018	2019	2018	2019	2018	2019	2018	2019
Argentina	62.8	60.5	21.3	20.5	19.4	18.7	13.2	13.1	8.8	8.5
Australia	58.1	61.2	20.7	21.1	20.7	21.1	20.7	21.1	0.1	0.0
Austria	46.7	46.4	22.8	22.7	22.8	22.7	22.8	22.7		
Belgium	48.3	47.4	24.8	23.9	23.9	23.0	23.9	23.0	3.7	3.5
Brazil	58.7	56.7	18.3	18.2	18.3	18.2	12.3	12.2		
Bulgaria	55.5	56.8	19.2	20.1	18.8	19.7	10.3	11.0	1.9	1.9
Canada	46.9	47.7	19.4	19.8	19.2	19.6	16.0	16.4	1.0	1.3
Chile	54.4	54.2	13.0	12.6	13.0	12.6	13.0	12.6		
China (People's Republic of)	70.9	73.2	20.0	20.2	19.5	19.6	16.7	15.7	2.7	3.1
Colombia	37.8	39.2	11.4	11.5	11.4	11.5	11.4	11.5		
Costa Rica	67.2	62.7	9.2	9.8	9.2	9.8	9.2	9.8		
Croatia	63.4	63.5	29.5	30.2	29.5	30.2	17.8	18.5	0.0	0.0
Cyprus	39.1	39.8	15.5	16.5	15.5	16.5	15.5	16.5		
Czech Republic	38.3	38.4	15.9	15.9	15.8	15.8	15.8	15.8	0.7	0.5
Denmark	85.6	81.5	44.0	43.6	44.0	43.6	39.9	39.5		
Estonia	86.1	85.1	33.3	32.9	32.7	32.3	19.6	19.1	1.8	1.7
Finland [2]	55.9	55.9	29.4	29.2	29.4	29.2	29.0	29.0		
France	32.4	30.8	17.3	16.2	13.4	13.1	13.4	13.1	22.4	19.3
Georgia	56.5	53.1	14.9	14.2	14.9	14.2	14.9	14.2		
Germany	40.9	40.8	18.9	19.1	18.9	19.1	18.9	19.1		
Greece	52.4	56.7	25.0	26.5	22.6	21.9	22.6	21.9	9.6	17.3
Hong Kong (China)	54.8	60.2	11.6	11.9	11.6	11.9	11.6	11.9		
Hungary	73.6	74.0	32.8	32.5	32.8	32.5	21.9	21.8		
Iceland	44.8	45.4	20.5	19.5	20.5	19.5	17.0	16.2		
India	26.1	28.9	5.3	5.6	5.3	5.6	5.3	5.6		
Indonesia	50.8	52.5	7.6	7.4	7.6	7.4	7.6	7.4		
Ireland	79.4	80.9	20.4	20.3	19.5	19.3	16.1	15.8	4.4	5.0
Israel	52.3	52.5	18.9	18.5	18.9	18.5	18.9	18.5		
Italy	47.7	47.4	22.1	22.3	22.1	22.3	22.1	22.3		
Japan [3]	28.9	29.7	10.1	10.2	10.1	10.2	10.1	10.2		
Kenya	79.2	81.3	14.4	14.4	13.4	13.3	13.4	13.3	7.4	7.5
Korea	55.1	55.1	12.6	12.7	12.6	12.6	12.6	12.6	0.4	0.4
Latvia	85.7	86.2	32.1	32.3	30.6	30.8	19.6	19.3	4.8	4.7
Lithuania	52.8	60.5	17.9	20.8	17.0	19.9	17.0	19.9	5.3	4.3
Luxembourg [4]	56.0	57.5	25.4	25.7	25.1	25.4	25.1	25.4	1.2	1.2
Malaysia	46.3	44.5	9.0	9.0	9.0	9.0	9.0	9.0	0.0	0.0
Malta	74.0	75.2	28.3	28.3	28.3	28.3	20.5	20.5	0.0	0.0
Mexico	57.6	58.0	13.5	13.8	10.0	10.4	10.0	10.4	26.2	24.8

	Revenue related ratios									
	Revenue collected by the Tax Administration (in %)[1]									
	Revenue collected to total government revenue		Revenue collected to GDP		Tax collected including SSC to GDP		Tax collected excluding SSC to GDP		Non tax revenue to total revenue collected	
Jurisdiction	2018	2019	2018	2019	2018	2019	2018	2019	2018	2019
Morocco	52.2	51.9	13.7	13.4	13.7	13.4	13.7	13.4		
Netherlands	77.7	77.0	33.2	33.7	32.5	32.9	20.7	21.6	2.1	2.5
New Zealand	64.6	68.2	24.5	25.5	24.2	25.0	24.2	25.0	1.1	2.0
Norway	53.2	55.3	30.1	32.4	29.8	32.1	25.8	28.0	0.7	0.8
Peru	66.0	66.6	12.8	13.3	12.7	13.1	10.7	11.1	1.1	1.5
Poland	41.5	40.8	17.1	16.8	15.8	15.5	15.8	15.5	8.0	8.2
Portugal	55.0	55.5	23.6	23.8	23.5	23.6	23.5	23.6	0.6	0.6
Romania	84.4	85.1	24.6	24.6	23.1	23.3	12.8	12.8	6.0	5.2
Russia	74.7	75.6	26.3	26.9	26.2	26.6	20.0	20.2	0.7	0.8
Saudi Arabia	9.3	9.9	2.9	3.1	2.9	3.1	2.9	3.1		
Singapore	49.5	50.6	8.9	9.2	8.9	9.2	8.9	9.2		
Slovak Republic	29.1	28.9	11.8	11.9	11.6	11.8	11.6	11.8	2.2	1.1
Slovenia	81.2	82.3	36.0	36.3	35.8	36.1	20.4	20.4	0.6	0.6
South Africa	77.0	77.3	22.4	22.5	22.2	22.3	21.8	21.9	0.7	0.8
Spain	40.7	40.1	16.0	15.7	15.6	15.4	15.6	15.4	2.1	2.1
Sweden[5]	93.3	94.2	46.2	45.7	46.2	45.7	31.7	31.3		
Switzerland	19.1	19.7	6.5	6.7	6.5	6.7	6.5	6.7		
Thailand	39.7	40.3	8.4	8.4	8.4	8.4	8.4	8.4		
Turkey	42.9	43.7	13.3	12.7	13.3	12.7	13.3	12.7		
United Kingdom	73.1	73.4	26.8	26.8	26.6	26.7	20.6	20.6	0.7	0.6
United States	49.2	49.4	14.6	14.5	14.6	14.5	9.1	8.9		

StatLink http://dx.doi.org/10.1787/888934271910

1. Note: To improve comparability with previous ISORA rounds' data and indicators, VAT (gross imports) has been removed from the total net revenue collected.
2. Finland: VAT (gross imports) cannot be separated from VAT (gross domestic). As a result, total net revenue collected includes VAT (gross imports).
3. Japan: VAT (gross imports) cannot be separated from VAT (gross domestic). As a result, total net revenue collected includes VAT (gross imports).
4. Luxembourg: VAT (gross imports) cannot be separated from VAT (gross domestic). As a result, total net revenue collected includes VAT (gross imports).
5. Sweden: VAT (gross imports) cannot be separated from VAT (gross domestic). As a result, total net revenue collected includes VAT (gross imports).

Formula	(Total net revenue collected [A.2] - VAT (gross imports) [A.5]) / Total government revenue [E.1] * 100	(Total net revenue collected [A.2] - VAT (gross imports) [A.5]) / GDP [E.1] * 100	(Total net revenue collected [A.2] - VAT (gross imports) [A.5] - Non-tax revenue [A.6]) / GDP [E.1]* 100	(Total net revenue collected [A.2] - VAT (gross imports) [A.5] - Non-tax revenue [A.6] - Social security contributions [A.6]) / GDP [E.1]* 100	Non-tax revenue [A.6] / (Total net revenue collected [A.2 - VAT (gross imports) [A.5]) * 100

Table D.2 **Tax structure and SSC proportions**

	Tax structure and SSC proportions[1]									
	PIT to total revenue collected		CIT to total revenue collected		VAT to total revenue collected		SSC to total revenue collected		Other taxes to total revenue collected	
Jurisdiction	**2018**	**2019**	**2018**	**2019**	**2018**	**2019**	**2018**	**2019**	**2018**	**2019**
Argentina	7.4	8.3	16.5	16.6	24.0	23.9	29.2	27.6	11.6	12.8
Australia	52.6	53.0	25.5	26.0	15.1	14.5			0.8	0.9
Austria	39.3	40.2	10.4	10.4	33.1	32.9			17.2	16.6
Belgium	40.3	39.6	17.1	17.1	26.8	27.4			12.1	12.4
Brazil	10.9	11.9	16.1	16.2	19.6	17.3	32.7	33.1	19.8	20.7
Bulgaria	15.4	14.8	11.2	10.9	26.2	28.1	44.1	43.3	1.3	1.1
Canada	52.2	52.1	16.3	16.5	10.0	9.5	16.3	16.2	3.3	3.5
Chile	10.9	11.8	47.0	45.2	31.4	30.9			2.3	3.2
China (People's Republic of)	7.6	5.2	19.3	18.6	33.5	31.0	13.9	19.3	17.1	16.5
Colombia	10.9	10.6	46.2	44.8	32.8	32.7			6.6	8.4
Costa Rica	15.1	15.0	28.6	26.9	24.3	26.9			19.1	19.6
Croatia	11.8	12.1	7.5	7.7	37.7	38.6	39.7	38.5	3.2	3.1
Cyprus	17.6	16.6	25.1	24.2	40.6	42.1			16.7	17.2
Czech Republic	25.5	27.0	21.1	20.9	48.0	47.1			4.7	4.5
Denmark	47.7	48.7	6.2	6.6	22.1	23.3	9.2	9.4	3.0	1.3
Estonia	16.3	16.6	6.0	5.5	23.5	23.5	39.2	40.1	1.1	1.0
Finland[2]	44.2	43.8	8.7	8.6	25.9	26.9	1.1	1.0	9.3	9.4
France	17.9	18.3	6.7	8.5	35.1	36.5			18.0	17.3
Georgia	48.9	49.2	11.1	12.2	8.5	12.8			28.9	23.8
Germany	48.7	49.3	15.3	14.4	27.6	27.8			8.3	8.4
Greece	17.5	21.0	6.5	7.3	25.0	20.7			26.1	19.4
Hong Kong (China)	22.9	22.1	40.6	47.1					36.5	30.8
Hungary	15.6	15.9	2.7	2.0	26.1	27.8	33.3	33.0	14.3	13.5
Iceland	32.1	33.7	12.4	11.4	9.8	10.3	16.9	16.8	28.7	27.8
India	40.7	40.6	57.0	58.3					2.3	1.1
Indonesia	13.1	13.8	53.7	51.8	30.9	31.9			2.4	2.5
Ireland	31.9	31.8	15.5	15.1	18.4	18.2	16.7	17.0	5.0	4.8
Israel	34.1	34.0	26.1	26.3	20.7	20.8			11.5	11.2
Italy	43.1	43.2	7.5	7.6	22.8	23.1			26.6	26.1
Japan[3]	34.1	35.2	21.7	21.8	29.0	28.0			15.2	15.0
Kenya	28.4	28.0	12.5	12.0	16.0	16.4			29.2	28.3
Korea	35.3	34.5	29.8	29.9	10.5	11.6			10.3	10.7
Latvia	18.5	19.8	3.3	0.5	25.5	26.2	34.3	35.7	2.6	2.4
Lithuania	22.7	34.2	8.5	7.5	43.2	37.1			2.8	2.3
Luxembourg[4]	36.8	35.9	22.5	24.0	24.4	24.1			15.1	14.8
Malaysia	25.4	27.9	68.8	66.0					5.8	6.0
Malta	25.7	26.9	18.9	19.7	22.5	20.8	27.4	27.6	5.5	5.0
Mexico	26.9	26.4	25.5	24.0	6.5	7.5			4.0	3.6
Morocco	29.0	28.9	34.5	33.7	22.4	22.3			14.2	15.0
Netherlands	23.4	24.1	9.2	9.5	20.0	20.4	35.6	33.4	9.7	10.1

	Tax structure and SSC proportions [1]									
	PIT to total revenue collected		CIT to total revenue collected		VAT to total revenue collected		SSC to total revenue collected		Other taxes to total revenue collected	
Jurisdiction	**2018**	**2019**	**2018**	**2019**	**2018**	**2019**	**2018**	**2019**	**2018**	**2019**
New Zealand	51.4	50.8	21.3	22.3	25.6	24.4			0.6	0.5
Norway	31.7	30.6	7.5	7.3	27.6	26.5	13.3	12.9	10.5	14.1
Peru	14.2	14.4	27.5	27.1	23.7	22.4	15.6	15.2	14.2	14.6
Poland	16.4	17.1	9.5	10.4	44.0	43.1			2.2	2.2
Portugal	27.6	26.9	14.1	13.5	34.1	35.8			12.9	12.3
Romania	9.6	8.9	7.8	7.9	21.9	21.7	41.8	42.9	1.3	1.8
Russia	13.3	13.4	16.7	17.3	13.0	14.4	23.3	23.8	27.7	26.0
Saudi Arabia			19.5	18.7	39.6	36.8			26.0	29.2
Singapore	24.0	25.2	36.9	38.0	12.1	11.1			26.9	25.7
Slovak Republic	30.4	31.4	26.3	24.0	34.4	36.8			6.8	6.7
Slovenia	14.9	15.1	5.1	5.7	22.0	21.5	42.7	43.2	5.2	5.1
South Africa	42.5	43.3	20.2	18.8	13.3	13.1	1.7	1.7	18.2	18.8
Spain	43.1	44.4	12.9	12.1	27.9	27.7			3.2	2.6
Sweden [5]	34.1	32.7	8.6	9.7	20.0	20.0	31.3	31.5	0.0	0.0
Switzerland	24.9	24.3	25.2	25.1	26.3	24.8			23.7	25.8
Thailand	23.2	23.6	52.9	55.8	18.3	15.0			5.6	5.6
Turkey	27.8	29.7	15.8	14.4	11.3	10.1			18.3	19.0
United Kingdom	32.3	32.6	9.3	9.0	17.1	17.3	22.7	22.7	14.4	14.3
United States	52.4	51.0	6.8	7.3			37.6	38.7	0.8	0.5

StatLink http://dx.doi.org/10.1787/888934271929

1. Note: To improve comparability with previous ISORA rounds' data and indicators, VAT (gross imports) has been removed from the total net revenue collected.
2. Finland: VAT (gross imports) cannot be separated from VAT (gross domestic). As a result, total net revenue collected includes VAT (gross imports).
3. Japan: VAT (gross imports) cannot be separated from VAT (gross domestic). As a result, total net revenue collected includes VAT (gross imports).
4. Luxembourg: VAT (gross imports) cannot be separated from VAT (gross domestic). As a result, total net revenue collected includes VAT (gross imports).
5. Sweden: VAT (gross imports) cannot be separated from VAT (gross domestic). As a result, total net revenue collected includes VAT (gross imports).

Formula	Income tax - individuals [A.3] / (Total net revenue collected [A.2] - VAT (gross imports) [A.5]) * 100	Income tax - corporate and other entities [A.3] / (Total net revenue collected [A.2] - VAT (gross imports) [A.5]) * 100	(Value added tax [A.4] - VAT (gross imports) [A.5]) / (Total net revenue collected [A.2] - VAT (gross imports) [A.5]) * 100	Social security contributions [A.6] / (Total net revenue collected [A.2] - VAT (gross imports) [A.5]) * 100	Other taxes [A.4] / (Total net revenue collected [A.2] - VAT (gross imports) [A.5]) * 100

Table D.3 **Resource ratios**

Resource Ratios										
	Population per FTE		Labour force per FTE		Recurrent cost of collection (in %)[1]		Salary cost as percent of operating expenditure		ICT operating cost as percent of operating expenditure	
Jurisdiction	2018	2019	2018	2019	2018	2019	2018	2019	2018	2019
Argentina	3 018.0	2 920.2	1 394.0	1 349.8	1.2	1.2	94.7	94.8	0.3	1.1
Australia	1 370.0	1 456.7	726.8	770.4	0.9	0.9	55.2	53.8	13.0	12.2
Austria	1 121.9	1 123.1	583.9	583.7	0.7	0.7	86.0	86.1	22.2	23.3
Belgium	726.2	738.6	323.5	328.1	0.8	0.8	80.6	81.0	4.5	4.3
Brazil	16 269.5	18 288.5	8 197.5	9 228.8	0.5	0.4	72.5	72.8	2.9	3.1
Bulgaria	890.8	884.6	422.0	417.8	1.0	1.0	85.3	85.3	3.3	17.4
Canada	931.9	915.1	511.6	501.1	1.1	1.1	74.3	74.0	14.4	16.3
Chile	3 762.4	3 779.8	1 886.5	1 906.2	0.9	0.9	89.1	89.9	9.0	10.0
China (People's Republic of)	1 881.6	1 940.6	1 058.4	1 084.4	D	0.5	D	59.1	D	1.6
Colombia	7 287.3	6 839.6	3 849.9	3 639.7	0.9	0.9	83.0	83.6	5.0	7.0
Costa Rica	5 218.6	5 398.5	2 553.1	2 645.8	1.5	1.4	47.2	46.0	22.5	22.9
Croatia	1 035.2	1 043.2	454.5	456.2	0.7	0.7	64.0	63.7	19.0	18.0
Cyprus	1 152.5	1 192.0	575.7	601.6	1.2	1.1	79.5	81.1	1.6	1.5
Czech Republic	684.0	700.5	350.9	357.5	1.4	1.3	61.7	62.0	9.7	10.5
Denmark	723.3	681.3	376.4	354.4	0.7	0.8	51.7	46.3	22.0	25.7
Estonia	1 710.2	1 787.9	913.1	949.3	0.3	0.3	73.6	72.5	0.2	0.3
Finland[2]	1 108.0	1 104.5	551.0	548.0	0.6	0.6	62.3	62.8	23.8	23.9
France	1 462.1	1 498.9	663.6	679.2	0.9	0.9	86.4	89.2	5.7	5.7
Georgia	1 940.9	1 832.7	1 063.0	1 001.4	0.6	0.6	81.1	82.6	2.4	3.2
Germany	753.2	757.3	395.7	397.0	1.5	1.5	83.6	83.2	9.1	9.7
Greece	1 306.3	1 256.0	584.8	559.8	0.7	0.6	87.2	87.5	0.1	0.4
Hong Kong (China)	2 612.6	2 598.6	1 390.2	1 368.6	0.5	0.5	87.1	86.8	10.8	10.7
Hungary	691.7	713.0	334.8	344.5	1.2	1.2	66.4	57.6	D	D
Iceland	1 560.7	1 428.1	942.0	861.0	0.6	0.6	77.7	75.8	13.4	13.7
India	32 030.5	32 415.7	11 547.1	11 725.4	0.6	0.6	59.8	55.8	10.9	12.3
Indonesia	5 903.3	5 817.8	2 927.5	2 897.4	0.6	0.6	38.8	41.3	1.7	0.4
Ireland	987.7	980.4	484.1	479.8	0.5	0.5	71.3	70.9	2.2	2.1
Israel	1 383.2	1 347.2	638.9	622.2	1.1	1.1	59.3	59.0	12.0	12.3
Italy	1 596.2	1 692.6	687.8	728.3	0.8	0.8	57.3	60.2	9.2	9.5
Japan[3]	2 273.0	2 265.9	1 228.0	1 222.8	1.3	1.2	79.9	78.4	7.0	7.1
Kenya	19 241.1	18 376.1	8 632.7	8 346.4	0.8	0.7	88.6	87.8	0.2	0.4
Korea	2 533.7	2 477.2	1 388.1	1 361.1	0.7	0.7	72.6	72.7	5.8	6.2
Latvia	719.4	714.3	373.4	367.1	0.9	0.8	64.7	67.5	14.0	13.3
Lithuania	987.5	1 048.1	519.1	548.1	0.6	0.6	83.5	84.8	14.2	15.9
Luxembourg[4]	539.0	537.6	268.4	268.9	0.8	0.8	85.8	83.4	1.8	2.0
Malaysia	2 446.2	2 418.4	1 193.4	1 186.4	1.7	1.7	71.4	69.6	7.0	6.5
Malta	1 316.9	1 365.9	640.2	661.5	D	D	D	D	D	D
Mexico	3 584.8	3 859.1	1 598.0	1 728.5	0.4	0.3	78.9	79.3	4.7	4.9

Resource Ratios										
	Population per FTE		Labour force per FTE		Recurrent cost of collection (in %)[1]		Salary cost as percent of operating expenditure		ICT operating cost as percent of operating expenditure	
Jurisdiction	2018	2019	2018	2019	2018	2019	2018	2019	2018	2019
Morocco	7 085.4	7 384.4	2 343.8	2 443.3	0.6	0.6	81.9	79.8	10.9	9.6
Netherlands	873.1	850.1	467.6	454.9	0.7	0.8	73.9	65.2	19.9	23.0
New Zealand	942.7	1 005.9	530.1	565.6	0.7	0.7	49.4	49.4	10.6	13.1
Norway	903.4	883.4	476.2	465.5	0.6	0.5	74.4	74.9	19.3	20.6
Peru	4 616.7	4 766.2	2 647.8	2 765.7	1.2	1.1	68.7	69.6	10.9	11.7
Poland	826.0	815.5	400.0	392.2	1.1	1.1	81.8	84.0	1.1	1.1
Portugal	1 064.6	1 040.6	545.3	530.9	1.0	1.1	78.6	79.2	5.2	5.7
Romania	948.6	981.0	441.1	452.7	1.0	0.9	89.7	91.9	D	D
Russia	992.4	993.6	507.1	502.6	0.5	0.5	79.6	82.0	14.0	11.4
Saudi Arabia	11 717.6	12 070.6	4 874.7	5 007.8	1.2	1.7	53.0	53.1	9.8	13.2
Singapore	2 950.6	3 005.0	1 828.3	1 858.3	0.9	0.9	60.7	61.3	26.7	26.4
Slovak Republic	953.1	974.6	481.9	490.2	1.9	2.1	61.3	59.9	7.0	4.2
Slovenia	658.8	667.5	329.6	330.7	0.7	0.7	83.2	82.4	9.3	10.2
South Africa	5 681.9	6 157.5	2 256.6	2 450.1	0.8	0.7	68.9	70.0	0.9	0.8
Spain	2 303.4	2 270.9	1 135.3	1 115.3	0.6	0.6	81.6	82.8	5.5	5.1
Sweden[5]	1 063.7	1 099.3	565.7	584.7	0.4	0.4	73.4	71.9	21.1	19.2
Switzerland	8 062.8	7 859.6	4 691.3	4 562.9	0.6	0.6	62.2	64.8	20.5	15.8
Thailand	3 142.6	3 204.7	1 761.1	1 794.6	0.7	0.7	74.3	74.8	5.3	5.1
Turkey	2 137.8	2 194.4	852.5	877.7	0.6	0.7	83.9	88.3	4.3	4.1
United Kingdom	1 132.8	1 236.0	585.1	638.6	0.6	0.6	62.9	63.4	17.3	16.7
United States	4 443.6	4 462.6	2 250.9	2 255.4	0.4	0.4	73.0	74.3	24.7	25.2

StatLink http://dx.doi.org/10.1787/888934271948

1. Note: To improve comparability with previous ISORA rounds' data and indicators, VAT (gross imports) has been removed from the total net revenue collected.
2. Finland: VAT (gross imports) cannot be separated from VAT (gross domestic). As a result, total net revenue collected includes VAT (gross imports).
3. Japan: VAT (gross imports) cannot be separated from VAT (gross domestic). As a result, total net revenue collected includes VAT (gross imports).
4. Luxembourg: VAT (gross imports) cannot be separated from VAT (gross domestic). As a result, total net revenue collected includes VAT (gross imports).
5. Sweden: VAT (gross imports) cannot be separated from VAT (gross domestic). As a result, total net revenue collected includes VAT (gross imports).

Formula	Population [E.1] / Total FTEs [A.8]	Labour force [E.1] / Total FTEs [A.8]	Total operating expenditure [A.7] / (Total net revenue collected [A.2] - VAT (gross imports) [A.5]) * 100	Salary [A.7] / Total operating expenditure [A.7] * 100	Information and communication technology [A.7] / Total operating expenditure [A.7] * 100

Table D.4 **Staff allocation by function and location**

	Tax administration staff allocation by function									
	Percentage staff allocated to registration, taxpayer services, returns and payment processing		Percentage staff allocated to audit, investigation and other verification		Percentage staff in enforced debt collections and related functions		Percentage staff in all other functions		Percentage staff in headquarters	
Jurisdiction	**2018**	**2019**	**2018**	**2019**	**2018**	**2019**	**2018**	**2019**	**2018**	**2019**
Argentina	6.7	6.3	27.0	26.6	23.2	23.0	43.1	44.1	15.0	17.0
Australia	14.2	12.1	28.9	30.7	7.2	7.2	49.7	50.0	11.0	11.0
Austria	23.6	23.8	50.9	50.4	5.0	5.1	20.6	20.8	2.8	2.8
Belgium	40.1	40.5	39.1	38.7	9.6	9.6	11.2	11.3	12.0	12.0
Brazil	29.2	29.2	25.1	25.1	19.2	19.2	26.5	26.4	7.3	5.5
Bulgaria	4.7	4.6	45.9	45.4	9.8	9.8	39.6	40.2	21.0	22.0
Canada	21.7	22.4	24.5	24.3	25.3	26.0	28.5	27.3	27.6	27.7
Chile	16.5	16.5	45.8	45.7	0.0	0.0	37.6	37.8	23.0	23.0
China (People's Republic of)	D	D	D	D	D	D	D	D	0.2	0.2
Colombia	23.6	23.6	39.7	39.7	14.8	14.8	21.8	21.8	17.5	17.5
Costa Rica	10.4	10.9	47.2	44.9	11.4	12.0	31.0	32.2	26.0	28.0
Croatia	52.5	52.2	20.2	20.2	13.2	13.2	14.1	14.4	8.0	9.0
Cyprus	35.4	35.4	36.2	36.2	16.7	16.6	11.7	11.7	16.0	16.0
Czech Republic	43.0	43.3	21.0	20.9	6.6	6.6	29.4	29.2	1.0	1.0
Denmark	21.1	20.4	20.4	19.8	18.7	18.5	39.9	41.4	8.4	8.0
Estonia	37.5	31.5	43.3	48.5	6.7	7.5	12.4	12.4	17.6	17.6
Finland	18.2	18.0	23.2	23.1	2.3	2.2	56.3	56.7	15.0	17.0
France	28.3	28.7	24.5	24.5	19.3	18.9	27.9	27.9	3.7	3.8
Georgia	23.3	23.9	44.5	43.3	3.3	3.0	29.0	29.9	6.0	9.0
Germany	22.4	22.3	36.2	34.8	7.4	7.4	33.9	35.4	6.4	6.7
Greece	D	D	D	D	D	D	D	D	14.3	11.3
Hong Kong (China)	64.1	63.9	8.4	8.3	7.8	7.7	19.7	20.2	10.9	10.8
Hungary	23.6	23.9	34.9	34.3	23.5	23.5	18.0	18.3	41.2	43.6
Iceland	56.6	48.6	16.4	17.0	0.0	11.5	27.0	22.9	72.0	61.0
India	D	D	D	D	D	D	D	D	D	D
Indonesia	22.9	23.4	15.5	16.9	1.5	1.5	60.1	58.3	14.4	13.3
Ireland	39.1	43.8	36.5	39.7	10.5	11.2	13.9	5.2	32.4	30.4
Israel	27.2	26.7	24.0	25.4	7.2	6.9	41.7	41.0	21.0	20.0
Italy	30.5	30.8	36.1	36.2	2.6	2.6	30.8	30.5	6.2	6.1
Japan	D	D	D	D	D	D	D	D	1.7	1.8
Kenya	20.0	20.0	50.0	50.0	30.0	30.0	0.0	0.0	30.0	40.0
Korea	53.5	54.2	21.7	21.5	6.4	6.0	18.4	18.3	4.3	4.5
Latvia	44.0	41.4	29.4	30.8	8.4	8.3	18.3	19.5	D	D
Lithuania	50.2	36.7	27.0	39.1	6.1	6.2	16.7	18.0	47.0	50.0
Luxembourg	12.6	13.3	60.4	59.8	6.4	6.2	20.7	20.7	19.9	19.7
Malaysia	29.0	31.3	29.7	29.0	9.3	9.2	31.9	30.5	14.8	14.4
Malta	D	D	39.1	39.4	23.6	23.6	D	D	15.5	17.1

Tax administration staff allocation by function										
	Percentage staff allocated to registration, taxpayer services, returns and payment processing		Percentage staff allocated to audit, investigation and other verification		Percentage staff in enforced debt collections and related functions		Percentage staff in all other functions		Percentage staff in headquarters	
Jurisdiction	2018	2019	2018	2019	2018	2019	2018	2019	2018	2019
Mexico	9.7	10.2	29.7	29.8	17.6	16.7	43.0	43.3	12.0	12.0
Morocco	48.9	48.8	12.2	12.1	13.5	13.0	25.4	26.2	11.0	11.0
Netherlands	17.3	16.3	36.3	35.9	8.1	7.5	38.2	40.3	2.4	2.1
New Zealand	30.1	18.0	14.5	2.8	10.7	23.1	44.7	56.2	28.0	29.0
Norway	17.7	16.2	36.3	43.5	5.2	4.8	40.8	35.6	6.4	10.2
Peru	18.0	18.7	36.3	35.5	13.0	13.8	32.7	32.0	15.0	15.1
Poland	29.4	29.2	9.1	9.1	15.5	15.5	46.0	46.2	2.5	2.5
Portugal	53.8	55.0	19.0	18.5	11.8	11.5	15.4	14.9	18.4	18.1
Romania	24.7	24.5	26.9	25.7	13.8	14.7	34.6	35.1	10.9	10.4
Russia	16.6	16.4	54.0	53.9	11.5	11.7	17.9	18.0	10.9	11.1
Saudi Arabia	6.3	14.2	49.4	49.1	0.2	3.2	44.1	33.5	68.0	70.0
Singapore	41.0	40.3	20.3	20.5	10.6	11.0	28.1	28.2	28.0	28.0
Slovak Republic	40.7	41.4	26.4	26.6	5.0	5.1	27.9	26.9	6.6	6.4
Slovenia	40.0	40.8	21.8	21.5	15.6	15.4	22.6	22.3	14.4	14.1
South Africa	36.1	34.7	21.9	22.1	11.5	10.9	30.5	32.4	7.0	8.0
Spain	16.1	16.1	44.2	44.3	20.1	20.3	19.6	19.4	18.2	18.6
Sweden	38.8	38.1	25.1	32.4	2.3	2.3	33.8	27.2	6.3	7.5
Switzerland	7.4	7.8	25.0	25.2	6.0	6.0	61.6	61.0	22.4	22.8
Thailand	27.7	27.4	24.7	25.2	7.7	7.7	39.9	39.7	10.4	10.5
Turkey	D	D	D	D	D	D	D	D	1.2	1.9
United Kingdom	31.0	29.5	27.3	30.3	8.1	8.0	33.6	32.2	9.0	11.0
United States	37.6	38.9	28.3	26.8	11.8	11.5	22.3	22.7	6.3	6.4

StatLink http://dx.doi.org/10.1787/888934271967

Formula	FTEs in registration, taxpayer services, returns and payment processing [A.8] / Total FTEs [A.8] * 100	FTEs in audit, investigation and other verification [A.8] / Total FTEs [A.8] * 100	FTEs in enforced debt collection and related functions [A.8] / Total FTEs [A.8] * 100	FTEs in other functions [A.8] / Total FTEs [A.8] * 100	Percentage of staff in headquarter function [A.8]

Table D.5 **Staff dynamics**

Staff dynamics				
	Hiring rate		Attrition rate	
Jurisdiction	2018	2019	2018	2019
Argentina	0.6	8.1	4.9	2.9
Australia	7.8	5.6	9.4	11.6
Austria	4.5	2.8	4.2	4.8
Belgium	3.6	5.9	7.0	5.9
Brazil	0.0	0.0	4.3	10.8
Bulgaria	9.3	8.1	6.8	8.1
Canada	16.5	16.7	13.3	12.0
Chile	3.6	2.8	3.5	2.1
China (People's Republic of) [1]	68.9	2.6	8.6	5.3
Colombia	3.9	11.1	2.9	3.4
Costa Rica	7.8	4.8	6.3	6.8
Croatia	3.2	3.0	4.8	4.5
Cyprus	2.0	4.8	5.3	3.6
Czech Republic	8.6	6.7	7.9	8.7
Denmark	25.2	16.3	8.8	9.5
Estonia	5.2	7.7	6.8	11.4
Finland	6.5	5.8	6.8	6.0
France	2.3	2.1	4.6	4.6
Georgia	9.3	8.8	4.1	3.2
Germany	D	D	D	D
Greece	2.1	5.4	2.3	2.1
Hong Kong (China)	8.1	7.4	6.7	7.4
Hungary	1.3	2.7	5.0	5.7
Iceland[2]	10.7	25.4	8.0	6.0
India	D	D	D	D
Indonesia	7.1	4.3	1.9	1.8
Ireland	9.9	16.3	8.2	8.3
Israel	4.5	9.6	2.9	6.0
Italy	0.4	1.0	5.3	7.7
Japan	D	D	D	D
Kenya	13.7	19.2	3.6	4.7
Korea	D	D	D	D
Latvia	6.4	7.1	6.5	7.7
Lithuania	5.1	6.3	13.6	11.6
Luxembourg	12.8	6.1	5.5	4.4
Malaysia	4.7	6.0	5.5	3.5
Malta	3.2	4.6	4.1	4.6
Mexico	9.2	8.8	11.1	15.1
Morocco	0.8	0.8	2.8	3.7
Netherlands	6.6	10.5	4.5	5.3

Staff dynamics				
	Hiring rate		Attrition rate	
Jurisdiction	2018	2019	2018	2019
New Zealand	11.3	8.1	16.3	13.0
Norway	6.6	6.9	7.7	8.6
Peru	9.1	13.7	9.6	15.0
Poland	8.4	5.5	4.0	4.2
Portugal	15.2	18.0	15.0	15.9
Romania	4.0	4.9	6.5	7.7
Russia	16.9	16.9	16.9	17.1
Saudi Arabia	16.8	4.5	3.6	5.8
Singapore	7.0	8.6	6.6	9.2
Slovak Republic	6.4	6.0	6.8	7.5
Slovenia	3.7	4.2	4.2	4.5
South Africa	8.0	4.2	9.6	9.1
Spain	3.6	5.8	4.4	4.0
Sweden	15.9	9.7	13.4	15.5
Switzerland	14.5	10.6	10.2	8.5
Thailand	8.5	4.5	5.8	6.2
Turkey	4.1	3.9	5.4	5.2
United Kingdom	6.6	9.4	12.5	10.7
United States	8.7	10.9	11.9	11.9

StatLink http://dx.doi.org/10.1787/888934271986

1. China (People's Republic of): In 2018, the state and local tax administrations were merged. The local tax administrations' staff that was absorbed by the State Tax Administration is recorded as recruitments in 2018 and, therefore, reflected in the 2018 hiring rate.
2. Iceland: On 1 May 2019, debt collection was transferred from the Directorate of Customs to the Directorate of Internal Revenue. The staff that was absorbed by the tax administration is recorded as recruitments in 2019 and, therefore, reflected in the 2019 hiring rate.

Formula	Recruitments in FY [A.10] / ((No. of staff at start of FY [A.10] + No. of staff at end of FY [A.10]) / 2) * 100	Departures in FY [A.10] / ((No. of staff at start of FY [A.10] + No. of staff at end of FY [A.10]) / 2) * 100

Table D.6 **Staff age distribution**

Staff age distribution												
	Percent staff younger than 25		Percent staff 25 to 34		Percent staff 35 to 44		Percent staff 45 to 54		Percent staff 55 to 64		Percent staff over 64	
Jurisdiction	2018	2019	2018	2019	2018	2019	2018	2019	2018	2019	2018	2019
Argentina	0.6	2.2	8.3	11.4	23.3	22.3	37.4	34.5	28.2	27.0	2.2	2.6
Australia	4.6	4.4	20.6	20.0	25.3	25.8	29.6	29.2	18.3	18.7	1.7	1.8
Austria	6.9	6.8	9.9	10.7	11.3	10.5	38.1	36.1	33.8	35.9	0.0	0.1
Belgium	1.2	2.2	16.2	16.6	20.1	20.5	29.8	28.9	32.5	31.4	0.3	0.4
Brazil	0.1	0.1	7.1	6.2	21.9	22.8	33.1	33.5	30.8	30.3	7.0	7.1
Bulgaria	0.8	0.6	15.5	15.8	28.1	26.1	34.4	35.6	20.4	20.9	0.8	1.0
Canada	5.1	5.9	17.8	19.2	25.0	25.2	30.0	28.0	19.8	19.3	2.3	2.4
Chile	0.7	0.6	17.7	16.5	32.3	30.6	28.1	30.4	16.5	16.9	4.7	5.0
China (People's Republic of)	4.7	3.3	18.7	20.3	21.5	19.7	43.0	41.5	12.2	15.2	0.0	0.0
Colombia	1.5	2.2	14.4	17.5	25.5	26.0	28.0	24.4	27.8	27.3	2.9	2.7
Costa Rica	1.0	1.3	17.4	14.9	22.8	29.9	25.8	29.7	20.5	23.1	12.5	1.1
Croatia	0.2	0.1	7.6	7.3	32.8	32.3	27.9	28.4	31.5	31.9	0.0	0.0
Cyprus	0.0	0.0	0.9	2.9	35.0	33.7	28.2	27.7	35.8	35.7	0.0	0.0
Czech Republic	1.1	0.8	11.8	11.2	24.1	22.1	36.2	37.0	25.2	27.0	1.6	2.0
Denmark	3.0	3.1	21.9	24.5	18.8	18.5	26.8	25.1	27.7	26.8	2.0	2.1
Estonia	2.4	3.5	20.7	18.7	25.1	24.9	24.5	26.1	21.9	21.7	5.4	5.1
Finland	2.1	2.6	16.5	17.9	20.3	20.7	25.0	24.0	34.8	33.6	1.2	1.2
France	0.9	0.8	10.7	10.9	20.9	20.5	32.0	32.4	34.9	34.6	0.7	0.9
Georgia	2.0	2.5	54.2	51.9	24.1	25.0	11.8	12.5	6.3	6.3	1.6	1.7
Germany	3.6	3.7	19.4	19.7	20.6	21.2	28.9	27.8	25.4	25.5	2.1	2.1
Greece	0.0	0.0	4.8	3.7	24.0	22.7	31.3	30.3	38.0	38.8	2.0	4.4
Hong Kong (China)	2.5	2.6	23.1	25.2	21.4	21.4	32.5	30.4	20.5	20.4	0.0	0.0
Hungary	1.2	1.5	17.6	15.2	38.4	36.7	30.8	34.3	12.1	12.3	0.0	0.0
Iceland	0.4	0.4	15.0	18.5	21.6	21.4	17.2	17.8	30.8	28.6	15.0	13.4
India	D	D	D	D	D	D	D	D	D	D	D	D
Indonesia	25.8	27.3	32.0	28.4	22.6	24.4	16.0	16.5	3.6	3.4	0.0	0.0
Ireland	0.9	2.0	11.7	13.6	27.3	27.7	25.8	25.8	33.8	30.2	0.5	0.8
Israel	2.2	2.0	18.0	20.4	21.6	21.2	27.0	25.5	26.5	25.9	4.7	5.1
Italy	0.0	0.0	3.4	2.9	21.4	20.9	28.2	29.8	42.8	41.6	4.1	4.7
Japan	D	D	D	D	D	D	D	D	D	D	D	D
Kenya	2.6	3.5	38.7	44.0	29.2	27.5	18.3	15.8	11.2	9.2	0.0	0.0
Korea	1.3	1.1	21.3	21.3	38.4	37.6	32.0	32.6	7.1	7.3	0.0	0.0
Latvia	1.0	1.2	18.2	16.7	29.9	30.4	28.8	29.0	21.1	21.6	0.9	1.1
Lithuania	0.6	2.0	14.0	13.6	19.2	21.1	27.7	30.1	36.6	31.8	1.9	1.3
Luxembourg	4.5	3.4	23.6	24.4	27.8	28.0	31.3	30.9	12.7	13.1	0.1	0.2
Malaysia	1.8	2.4	31.0	34.0	37.1	36.8	17.5	17.0	12.5	9.8	0.0	0.0
Malta	1.9	0.8	16.0	15.5	23.9	23.1	34.0	33.7	18.8	20.1	5.4	6.8
Mexico	3.5	4.1	33.9	33.1	26.4	26.3	23.8	23.8	10.4	10.7	1.9	2.1
Morocco	0.7	0.3	36.0	34.4	21.3	23.1	27.6	27.8	14.3	14.3	0.1	0.1
Netherlands [1]	1.2	1.7	11.4	13.7	15.6	16.3	26.0	23.6	43.9	42.2	1.8	2.4

	Staff age distribution											
	Percent staff younger than 25		Percent staff 25 to 34		Percent staff 35 to 44		Percent staff 45 to 54		Percent staff 55 to 64		Percent staff over 64	
Jurisdiction	**2018**	**2019**	**2018**	**2019**	**2018**	**2019**	**2018**	**2019**	**2018**	**2019**	**2018**	**2019**
New Zealand	8.6	6.1	21.5	21.1	21.6	22.6	26.2	26.1	18.9	20.9	3.1	3.3
Norway	0.2	0.4	9.7	9.8	19.8	19.8	35.8	34.7	29.3	30.8	5.2	4.5
Peru	1.5	1.2	28.5	26.3	26.7	27.5	26.5	26.1	12.7	14.6	4.1	4.2
Poland	1.1	1.3	14.4	14.4	30.1	30.5	33.9	34.2	20.0	19.2	0.5	0.4
Portugal	0.0	0.0	0.9	0.8	17.3	13.7	33.3	34.6	46.2	47.3	2.3	3.5
Romania	0.3	0.2	6.4	5.8	27.8	25.6	43.5	45.6	21.9	22.6	0.2	0.2
Russia	7.2	6.6	34.3	32.5	31.7	33.3	17.7	18.2	9.1	9.4	0.0	0.0
Saudi Arabia	16.3	2.7	65.2	59.0	16.1	26.7	2.3	9.6	0.1	1.9	0.0	0.1
Singapore	0.8	1.4	29.7	27.7	32.2	33.4	19.6	21.2	15.9	14.6	1.8	1.7
Slovak Republic	1.1	1.2	15.5	14.8	29.0	27.8	32.6	33.8	21.2	21.7	0.6	0.8
Slovenia	0.1	0.1	6.6	6.2	19.6	19.2	47.7	45.9	25.7	28.0	0.3	0.6
South Africa	1.2	0.8	19.1	15.7	41.7	41.0	28.9	32.1	9.0	10.2	0.0	0.0
Spain	0.0	0.1	4.3	6.0	13.0	13.4	36.3	31.3	44.1	46.6	2.4	2.7
Sweden	1.4	1.3	20.6	19.5	25.6	25.6	26.6	27.3	24.3	24.8	1.5	1.6
Switzerland	8.3	8.7	20.8	21.7	30.4	28.1	34.1	35.2	6.3	6.2	0.1	0.1
Thailand	1.6	1.6	17.1	16.9	32.8	31.4	34.7	35.6	13.7	14.5	0.0	0.0
Turkey	0.6	0.4	30.8	30.8	19.0	18.7	32.9	29.3	16.7	20.5	0.0	0.4
United Kingdom	5.0	4.8	18.0	18.9	20.4	20.6	31.4	29.5	23.5	24.2	1.6	1.9
United States	1.3	1.7	10.3	10.5	20.5	21.3	29.9	28.3	30.6	30.6	7.4	7.6

StatLink http://dx.doi.org/10.1787/888934272005

1. Netherlands: Figures do not include contractual staff.

Formula	Under 25 years [A.12] / Staff employed at year end [A.10]	25-34 years [A.12] / Staff employed at year end [A.10]	35-44 years [A.12] / Staff employed at year end [A.10]	45-54 years [A.12] / Staff employed at year end [A.10]	55-64 years [A.12] / Staff employed at year end [A.10]	Over 64 years [A.12] /Staff employed at year end [A.10]

Table D.7 **Length of service**

	Length of service							
	Percent staff with less than 5 years of service		Percent staff with 5 to 9 years of service		Percent staff with 10 to 19 years of service		Percent staff with 20 or more years of service	
Jurisdiction	**2018**	**2019**	**2018**	**2019**	**2018**	**2019**	**2018**	**2019**
Argentina	8.9	14.5	13.3	4.1	22.3	30.8	55.6	50.6
Australia	26.2	25.5	17.9	18.4	40.3	40.2	15.6	15.9
Austria	12.5	13.2	7.8	7.7	8.9	9.3	70.7	69.8
Belgium	13.5	16.5	11.8	11.3	22.2	21.0	52.5	51.2
Brazil	D	D	D	D	D	D	D	D
Bulgaria	5.5	5.0	10.3	10.6	29.7	28.7	54.5	55.7
Canada	34.3	37.7	16.9	15.1	27.8	27.9	21.0	19.3
Chile	26.1	25.6	12.8	11.9	32.7	33.0	28.5	29.5
China (People's Republic of)	13.0	12.2	8.4	9.2	11.2	11.5	67.4	67.2
Colombia	47.8	43.8	10.7	12.7	1.6	3.3	40.0	40.2
Costa Rica	18.9	20.0	12.5	11.8	28.7	29.2	39.9	39.1
Croatia	4.4	4.7	4.8	3.3	27.5	28.6	63.4	63.4
Cyprus	5.9	9.1	11.0	6.1	34.6	39.0	48.5	45.8
Czech Republic	24.8	23.0	12.1	13.3	27.8	28.0	35.3	35.8
Denmark	47.5	52.6	1.5	3.0	33.2	27.8	17.8	16.6
Estonia	15.7	17.1	13.2	14.4	31.5	29.4	39.7	39.1
Finland	29.3	30.8	9.2	11.9	20.7	20.3	40.8	37.0
France	15.9	17.1	13.7	13.0	31.9	31.4	38.6	38.6
Georgia	14.2	20.6	50.2	47.5	25.8	22.6	9.9	9.3
Germany	D	D	D	D	D	D	D	D
Greece	12.5	14.6	8.2	10.0	33.8	26.2	45.5	49.2
Hong Kong (China)	23.2	24.4	13.8	14.4	5.9	7.1	57.1	54.1
Hungary	9.4	7.7	20.2	19.6	36.7	36.6	33.7	36.1
Iceland	36.1	37.0	11.9	12.0	23.8	23.9	28.2	27.2
India	D	D	D	D	D	D	D	D
Indonesia	34.9	32.6	11.6	12.6	29.0	29.2	24.5	25.6
Ireland	19.4	27.1	3.7	4.9	30.3	25.2	46.6	42.8
Israel	16.8	19.6	14.1	14.2	17.1	17.5	52.0	48.8
Italy	7.0	5.2	7.0	10.3	25.3	22.8	60.6	61.7
Japan	D	D	D	D	D	D	D	D
Kenya	43.5	52.0	7.8	8.1	27.9	23.0	21.3	16.9
Korea	26.1	24.6	14.6	13.0	31.2	34.4	28.1	28.0
Latvia	17.7	17.1	8.3	11.0	43.0	39.7	31.0	32.1
Lithuania	24.8	25.6	25.5	27.8	21.3	25.3	28.5	21.3
Luxembourg	D	30.5	D	7.9	D	24.1	D	37.5
Malaysia	22.0	25.0	13.8	15.1	35.6	34.5	28.6	25.4
Malta	22.6	20.7	14.4	17.7	26.4	25.5	36.7	36.1
Mexico	34.4	33.3	19.9	22.1	27.8	21.7	17.9	23.0
Morocco	20.0	17.8	26.3	26.3	16.9	18.6	36.9	37.2
Netherlands [1]	14.6	17.8	5.4	8.2	20.4	18.6	59.6	55.3

	Length of service							
	Percent staff with less than 5 years of service		Percent staff with 5 to 9 years of service		Percent staff with 10 to 19 years of service		Percent staff with 20 or more years of service	
Jurisdiction	2018	2019	2018	2019	2018	2019	2018	2019
New Zealand	33.7	29.9	16.7	31.7	30.3	20.3	19.4	18.1
Norway	16.2	17.0	19.8	16.9	22.1	25.1	41.9	41.0
Peru	33.4	29.9	16.5	17.5	17.4	17.8	32.7	34.7
Poland	6.7	7.2	7.9	8.4	26.1	26.3	59.3	58.2
Portugal	0.2	0.4	3.5	3.3	29.1	21.6	67.2	74.7
Romania	15.1	12.8	5.7	8.1	33.8	30.3	45.4	48.7
Russia	30.8	29.7	18.8	18.0	31.5	32.6	18.9	19.6
Saudi Arabia[2]	100.0	100.0	0.0	0.0	0.0	0.0	0.0	0.0
Singapore	18.5	19.3	19.9	19.3	25.6	26.2	36.1	35.2
Slovak Republic	19.7	20.4	15.4	15.5	25.0	23.1	39.9	41.1
Slovenia	3.6	3.8	4.4	4.5	14.1	14.3	77.9	77.4
South Africa	14.8	12.4	16.6	13.3	38.5	41.1	30.1	33.2
Spain	4.3	4.4	5.5	9.7	16.0	15.9	74.2	70.0
Sweden	33.5	31.3	18.5	20.5	25.3	24.8	22.7	23.4
Switzerland	29.2	47.0	20.9	25.2	28.2	6.6	21.7	21.1
Thailand	16.9	17.7	12.1	11.4	26.3	27.4	44.7	43.5
Turkey	19.1	17.8	15.5	20.5	11.3	10.9	54.1	50.9
United Kingdom	21.0	24.6	6.9	5.1	28.6	27.8	43.5	42.4
United States	16.6	20.0	18.2	13.6	31.3	33.7	33.9	32.7

StatLink http://dx.doi.org/10.1787/888934272024

1. Netherlands: Figures do not include contractual staff.
2. Saudi Arabia: Due to the transformation process of GAZT that was finalised in 2019 and based on the new contracts for staff, the length of service for the adminsitration can only be counted after that transformation.

Formula	Under 5 years [A.13] / Staff employed at year end [A.10]*100	5-9 years [A.13] / Staff employed at year end [A.10]*100	10-19 years [A.13] / Staff employed at year end [A.10]*100	Over 19 years [A.13] /Staff employed at year end [A.10] *100

Table D.8 **Gender distribution and academic qualifications**

Gender distribution and academic qualification								
	Percent staff who are female		Percent executives who are female		Percent staff with bachelor's degree or equivalent		Percent staff with master's degree or higher or equivalent	
Jurisdiction	**2018**	**2019**	**2018**	**2019**	**2018**	**2019**	**2018**	**2019**
Argentina	45.1	45.6	25.9	34.7	57.1	58.7	4.4	4.4
Australia	57.3	57.2	48.7	49.1	26.6	27.0	15.7	16.1
Austria	47.0	47.7	30.3	31.8	3.5	3.6	9.9	10.1
Belgium	52.1	52.1	37.1	38.2	34.5	34.5	31.4	33.1
Brazil	37.2	36.1	15.9	15.6	75.9	79.3	0.7	0.9
Bulgaria	74.2	74.6	50.0	50.0	11.0	11.0	77.2	77.2
Canada	59.8	59.4	48.9	49.4	D	D	D	D
Chile	52.2	52.4	46.8	46.3	60.8	60.7	16.4	16.6
China (People's Republic of)	38.2	38.0	11.1	10.6	67.8	69.0	6.3	6.8
Colombia	56.5	56.5	49.3	45.7	76.2	75.4	3.0	3.3
Costa Rica	58.9	58.6	58.6	61.4	79.1	77.6	10.6	8.2
Croatia	75.7	76.2	68.4	70.3	16.3	16.6	55.8	56.3
Cyprus	73.3	73.1	25.0	25.0	36.9	36.6	19.0	21.4
Czech Republic	80.7	80.7	39.7	39.1	9.2	9.6	37.4	37.8
Denmark	63.5	63.6	37.9	38.2	D	D	D	D
Estonia	72.9	72.9	50.8	53.6	11.2	12.3	25.4	24.6
Finland	74.0	73.7	52.5	50.0	20.5	21.5	31.0	31.5
France	59.4	59.0	25.8	27.0	28.6	27.8	22.5	22.4
Georgia	49.6	49.8	21.2	21.9	65.0	65.4	35.0	34.6
Germany	56.9	57.2	D	D	35.5	35.4	21.5	21.8
Greece	62.7	63.1	52.5	52.3	39.3	37.7	24.9	28.9
Hong Kong (China)	68.1	68.2	45.5	52.2	36.1	38.9	3.4	3.3
Hungary [1]	63.6	63.3	31.6	38.7	65.7	67.1	D	D
Iceland	63.4	64.9	50.0	40.0	37.9	34.8	26.4	28.3
India	D	D	D	D	D	D	D	D
Indonesia	34.2	35.3	10.9	10.7	34.7	34.3	13.5	13.8
Ireland	60.9	61.0	41.4	50.2	38.5	39.2	6.5	6.5
Israel	51.2	47.2	31.7	34.3	35.3	38.1	19.9	20.0
Italy	49.7	50.2	30.5	32.1	3.3	3.4	45.9	47.8
Japan	D	D	D	D	D	D	D	D
Kenya	44.1	44.3	29.4	31.8	54.0	91.0	9.8	9.0
Korea	58.9	57.7	0.0	2.9	86.6	87.3	3.2	3.2
Latvia	74.4	74.3	71.2	70.2	26.1	27.5	30.2	30.2
Lithuania	53.9	72.5	65.2	67.7	49.3	38.7	50.7	61.3
Luxembourg	48.4	48.9	33.0	35.0	8.8	8.5	7.4	8.0
Malaysia	58.3	58.6	42.4	43.7	41.1	42.0	5.1	4.9
Malta	46.7	47.6	36.0	36.7	6.0	6.3	10.3	10.3
Mexico	53.9	53.8	30.9	37.2	29.9	63.9	1.2	4.9
Morocco	47.8	48.3	20.1	19.1	11.6	11.7	56.7	56.9

Gender distribution and academic qualification								
	Percent staff who are female		Percent executives who are female		Percent staff with bachelor's degree or equivalent		Percent staff with master's degree or higher or equivalent	
Jurisdiction	2018	2019	2018	2019	2018	2019	2018	2019
Netherlands[2]	40.0	41.3	35.3	37.5	40.2	40.2	19.7	21.5
New Zealand	63.8	63.9	33.9	45.1	D	D	D	D
Norway	61.8	61.4	55.3	59.8	55.0	54.5	30.6	31.8
Peru	42.9	43.4	35.9	38.1	61.3	61.1	9.9	11.6
Poland	71.7	72.1	67.9	66.3	10.6	10.7	70.1	70.6
Portugal	59.1	60.0	41.9	42.3	47.5	46.8	3.8	3.9
Romania	67.2	67.6	56.5	57.1	54.3	53.5	40.6	41.7
Russia	84.0	83.9	39.1	39.2	11.3	13.0	83.2	81.4
Saudi Arabia	8.3	22.3	24.3	25.8	56.1	69.4	4.9	10.9
Singapore	73.2	72.7	60.0	57.9	55.1	57.3	5.3	5.7
Slovak Republic	64.7	65.1	43.1	43.6	9.1	8.9	64.5	65.1
Slovenia	65.9	66.2	68.6	68.2	39.1	38.5	60.9	61.5
South Africa	62.0	61.5	49.1	49.3	26.3	28.8	3.5	3.9
Spain	53.1	53.1	13.9	33.6	63.1	61.5	D	D
Sweden[3]	66.8	66.3	64.8	65.7	57.7	59.3	D	D
Switzerland	42.8	42.4	9.5	9.5	D	D	D	D
Thailand	78.2	78.5	56.1	58.0	76.6	76.8	23.4	23.2
Turkey	39.6	39.7	25.1	25.4	75.8	77.3	6.0	6.7
United Kingdom	55.2	54.3	43.8	46.7	D	D	D	D
United States	65.6	65.1	59.2	59.7	29.1	28.5	13.9	14.4

StatLink http://dx.doi.org/10.1787/888934272043

1. Hungary: Percentage of staff with "Bachelors degree" refers to the total number of staff with academic qualifications (Bachelor and/or Masters degree).
2. Netherlands: Figures do not include contractual staff.
3. Sweden: Percentage of staff with "Bachelors degree" refers to the total number of staff with academic qualifications (Bachelor and/or Masters degree).

Formula	All staff - Female [A.14] / (All staff - Male [A.14] + All staff - Female [A.14] + All staff - Other [A.14) * 100	Executives only - Female [A.14] / (Executives only - Male [A.14] + Executives only - Female [A.14] + Executives only - Other [A.14])*100	Bachelors degree [A.11] / Staff at year end [A.10]*100	Masters degree [A.11] / Staff at year end [A.10]*100

Table D.9 **Segmentation ratios: LTO/Ps**

	Segmentation ratios: LTO/Ps											
	FTEs in LTO/P as percentage of FTEs		FTEs on audit, investigation and other verification function in the LTO/P as percentage of total FTEs in LTO/P		Total value of additional assessments raised through LTO/P as percentage of total value of additional assessments raised from audits		Corporate taxpayers managed through LTO/P as percentage of active corporate income taxpayers		Corporate taxpayers per FTE in LTO/P		Percentage of net revenue administered under LTO/P in relation to total net revenue collected by the tax administration	
Jurisdiction	2018	2019	2018	2019	2018	2019	2018	2019	2018	2019	2018	2019
Argentina	3.1	3.0	53.7	50.4	24.4	13.0	0.2	0.2	1.4	1.6	45.5	49.1
Australia	7.5	7.9	61.0	62.9	17.8	10.0	0.6	0.6	21.3	21.8	D	D
Austria	6.1	6.2	90.0	88.6	48.3	43.5	4.7	4.8	18.8	19.2	56.2	55.8
Belgium	2.3	2.3	63.7	65.4	27.2	21.6	2.8	2.3	44.1	35.8	52.7	49.5
Brazil	1.3	1.4	100.0	100.0	78.3	78.0	0.2	0.1	54.7	40.8	64.0	64.0
Bulgaria	1.8	1.8	61.1	54.9	7.8	1.4	0.4	0.4	9.4	10.0	33.0	34.0
Canada	3.3	3.3	100.0	100.0	45.2	45.3	D	D	14.0	13.6	D	D
Chile	4.4	4.4	85.0	84.5	61.9	58.0	0.1	0.1	4.1	4.4	44.7	43.0
China (People's Republic of)	1.0	2.2	60.0	60.0	D	D	1.3	1.1	37.7	17.7	45.0	45.0
Colombia	4.6	4.7	51.6	50.7	21.7	22.9	0.7	0.7	11.2	10.1	67.3	63.1
Costa Rica	6.4	6.7	91.8	90.5	0.1	0.1	0.3	0.3	7.6	7.1	67.0	62.0
Croatia	2.6	2.5	48.5	53.5	16.0	19.8	0.5	0.5	6.9	7.6	37.3	36.7
Cyprus	3.3	3.4	100.0	100.0	87.4	82.8	0.7	0.7	32.6	35.0	30.2	28.0
Czech Republic	2.3	2.3	51.0	53.4	17.5	15.1	0.3	0.3	5.6	5.9	37.0	37.0
Denmark	3.2	3.0	92.3	92.3	D	D	3.0	2.8	38.5	38.5	40.0	40.0
Estonia												
Finland	3.3	3.5	D	D	D	D	0.7	0.7	18.0	16.9	28.0	28.0
France	D	D	D	D	21.9	19.9	D	D	D	D	D	D
Georgia	0.9	2.7	D	69.1	5.2	6.3	0.3	0.3	15.6	4.9	31.0	33.0
Germany	D	D	D	D	D	D	D	D	D	D	D	D
Greece	2.3	2.1	61.1	61.0	35.4	20.3	0.5	0.9	6.9	13.3	D	D
Hong Kong (China)												
Hungary	3.3	3.2	26.6	27.3	5.9	9.4	0.2	0.2	2.3	2.4	35.3	34.8
Iceland												
India	D	D	D	D	1.3	0.7	0.9	0.9	D	D	0.2	0.2
Indonesia	1.5	1.4	35.1	27.3	44.7	22.6	D	D	4.0	4.2	31.9	30.0
Ireland	5.3	5.4	86.2	86.7	31.3	42.8	6.1	5.9	47.3	46.3	51.0	51.0
Israel	1.1	1.2	56.2	60.0	20.4	25.4	3.7	3.8	113.8	115.4	29.0	28.1
Italy	1.6	1.7	71.8	69.0	7.3	9.2	0.3	0.3	6.2	6.0	28.2	28.0
Japan	4.2	4.2	0.0	0.0	D	D	D	D	13.8	14.2	56.0	55.0
Kenya	7.5	7.5	70.0	69.8	30.0	50.7	0.5	0.4	9.1	8.3	38.5	37.9
Korea												
Latvia	1.8	1.7	D	D	41.8	45.3	1.1	1.1	26.5	27.6	59.1	60.5
Lithuania	1.6	1.6	63.6	61.9	2.2	13.2	0.3	0.3	11.5	11.3	45.0	41.0
Luxembourg												

Segmentation ratios: LTO/Ps												
	FTEs in LTO/P as percentage of FTEs		FTEs on audit, investigation and other verification function in the LTO/P as percentage of total FTEs in LTO/P		Total value of additional assessments raised through LTO/P as percentage of total value of additional assessments raised from audits		Corporate taxpayers managed through LTO/P as percentage of active corporate income taxpayers		Corporate taxpayers per FTE in LTO/P		Percentage of net revenue administered under LTO/P in relation to total net revenue collected by the tax administration	
Jurisdiction	**2018**	**2019**	**2018**	**2019**	**2018**	**2019**	**2018**	**2019**	**2018**	**2019**	**2018**	**2019**
Malaysia	3.8	3.4	59.8	61.5	51.2	57.8	6.1	5.9	100.4	109.5	31.0	33.2
Malta	7.6	9.2	89.3	88.2	16.9	15.7	2.8	3.0	50.4	49.4	20.0	20.0
Mexico	0.2	0.2	100.0	100.0	D	D	0.4	0.4	151.7	132.4	60.5	59.3
Morocco	2.3	2.7	52.1	45.1	66.6	55.3	2.0	1.8	69.5	63.6	70.0	70.0
Netherlands	10.6	10.9	76.1	77.0	50.3	58.2	1.8	1.7	6.9	6.3	68.4	67.3
New Zealand	6.2	6.5	57.2	54.7	D	D	0.1	0.1	3.1	3.1	30.0	30.0
Norway	5.7	5.5	87.0	86.4	43.2	51.1	4.9	4.8	46.1	48.5	D	D
Peru	12.4	13.3	83.7	80.1	92.2	91.2	1.5	1.5	17.6	18.3	76.2	74.8
Poland	4.5	4.5	30.0	30.0	D	D	0.4	0.4	1.2	1.3	70.0	70.0
Portugal	2.2	2.2	45.2	45.7	34.9	40.5	0.5	0.5	12.0	12.4	45.7	44.8
Romania	2.7	2.7	62.4	63.0	28.2	23.5	2.6	2.3	4.9	5.1	42.2	41.8
Russia	2.3	2.4	68.7	66.8	25.9	45.3	0.1	0.1	0.9	0.8	43.5	46.1
Saudi Arabia [1]	0.0	9.6		72.2	9.1	29.8	0.0	113.7		28.3	82.0	81.0
Singapore	4.2	4.3	90.1	88.9	D	D	D	D	23.5	24.7	D	D
Slovak Republic	2.6	2.8	69.5	66.0	6.1	12.4	D	D	5.4	5.4	43.0	41.5
Slovenia	2.2	2.3	88.6	89.0	D	D	0.6	0.6	10.1	9.7	25.0	25.0
South Africa	3.7	3.8	54.9	54.6	82.4	52.1	0.5	0.8	43.1	46.8	35.6	30.5
Spain	3.8	3.7	76.8	76.6	12.5	8.8	0.2	0.2	4.0	4.1	35.3	33.2
Sweden	10.3	11.1	22.4	44.3	68.0	87.6	5.4	5.5	37.9	38.0	49.4	49.5
Switzerland												
Thailand	2.4	2.4	59.2	59.2	51.0	73.1	0.6	0.6	7.4	7.4	45.9	46.3
Turkey	0.6	0.7	5.2	5.3	0.1	0.0	0.1	0.1	3.2	3.0	19.0	20.0
United Kingdom	4.1	4.4	D	D	33.4	39.3	0.1	0.1	0.9	0.8	40.0	40.0
United States	4.7	4.2	100.0	100.0	39.3	38.1	16.6	17.2	103.1	119.9	6.5	7.1

StatLink http://dx.doi.org/10.1787/888934272062

1. Saudi Arabia: As regards the ratio of corporate taxpayers managed through the LTO/P as a percentage of active corporate income taxpayers, the ratio is above 100% as the number of corporate taxpayers managed through LTO/P includes "Zakat payers".

Formula	Number of FTEs in LTO or programme [A.16] / Total FTEs [A.8] * 100	FTEs on audit, investigation and other verification function [A.16] / Number of FTEs in LTO or programme [A.16]*100	Total value of additional assessments raised through LTO programme [A.17] / value of additional assessments raised from audits and verification actions - Total [A.34]*100	Number of corporate taxpayers managed [A.16] / CIT Active taxpayers [A.20] * 100	Number of corporate taxpayers managed [A.16] / Number of FTEs in LTO or programme [A.16]	Percentage revenue collected through LTO/P [A.16]

Table D.10 **Registration of personal income taxpayers**

	Active taxpayers on PIT register as percentage of:			
	Labour Force		Population	
Jurisdiction	2018	2019	2018	2019
Argentina	15.1	16.0	7.0	7.4
Australia	168.4	170.1	89.4	90.0
Austria	179.2	185.7	93.3	96.5
Belgium	139.9	140.2	62.3	62.3
Brazil	27.3	28.2	13.7	14.2
Bulgaria	94.3	94.9	44.6	44.8
Canada	147.9	148.5	81.2	81.3
Chile	108.1	107.9	54.2	54.4
China (People's Republic of)	D	D	D	D
Colombia	12.8	13.8	6.8	7.3
Costa Rica	19.7	19.9	9.6	9.7
Croatia	101.9	106.1	44.7	46.4
Cyprus	98.0	100.5	49.0	50.7
Czech Republic	39.2	40.0	20.1	20.4
Denmark	174.3	174.0	90.7	90.5
Estonia	115.1	129.9	61.4	69.0
Finland	199.3	198.8	99.1	98.7
France	168.9	168.9	76.6	76.6
Georgia	63.3	63.4	34.7	34.6
Germany	91.8	95.2	48.2	49.9
Greece	186.1	182.5	83.3	81.3
Hong Kong (China)	78.3	80.2	41.7	42.2
Hungary	106.2	107.2	51.4	51.8
Iceland	144.5	143.8	87.2	86.7
India	12.0	12.7	4.3	4.6
Indonesia	D	D	D	D
Ireland	155.2	157.5	76.1	77.1
Israel	128.8	129.0	59.5	59.6
Italy	109.3	110.9	47.1	47.7
Japan	D	D	D	D
Kenya	35.7	41.9	16.0	19.0
Korea	24.4	26.7	13.4	14.7
Latvia	91.4	92.7	47.5	47.6
Lithuania	95.4	91.1	50.1	47.7
Luxembourg	D	D	D	D
Malaysia	50.9	52.2	24.9	25.6
Malta	137.5	144.9	66.8	70.2
Mexico	124.0	131.8	55.3	59.0
Morocco	5.8	6.4	1.9	2.1
Netherlands	131.8	134.3	70.6	71.9

	Active taxpayers on PIT register as percentage of:			
	Labour Force		Population	
Jurisdiction	2018	2019	2018	2019
New Zealand	90.1	146.0	50.7	82.1
Norway	171.5	167.4	90.4	88.2
Peru	32.0	31.9	18.4	18.5
Poland	106.6	114.1	51.6	54.9
Portugal	101.6	104.0	52.0	53.0
Romania	D	D	D	D
Russia	10.9	11.7	5.6	5.9
Saudi Arabia				
Singapore	D	D	D	D
Slovak Republic	D	D	D	D
Slovenia	149.1	151.2	74.6	74.9
South Africa	92.0	95.2	36.6	37.9
Spain	105.5	106.8	52.0	52.4
Sweden	144.3	142.9	76.7	76.0
Switzerland	D	D	D	D
Thailand	29.5	28.5	16.5	16.0
Turkey	14.3	14.3	5.7	5.7
United Kingdom	90.9	91.5	46.9	47.3
United States	92.4	92.9	46.8	46.9

StatLink http://dx.doi.org/10.1787/888934272081

Formula	PIT active taxpayers [A.20] / Labour force [E.1] * 100	PIT active taxpayers [A.20] / Population [E.1] * 100

Table D.11 **Percentage inactive taxpayers on registers**

	Percentage inactive taxpayers on registers									
	On PIT register		On CIT register		On VAT register		On PAYE register		On Excise register	
Jurisdiction	**2018**	**2019**	**2018**	**2019**	**2018**	**2019**	**2018**	**2019**	**2018**	**2019**
Argentina	24.0	23.8	12.2	17.0	36.2	38.0	D	D	85.5	84.2
Australia	27.4	27.7	56.8	57.0	24.3	25.1	27.7	28.8	20.5	18.4
Austria	0.0	0.0	0.0	0.0	0.0	0.0	0.0	0.0		
Belgium	24.8	25.8	0.0	0.0	0.0	0.0	D	D		
Brazil	4.3	6.6	33.7	41.5	D	D	D	D	D	D
Bulgaria	D	D	47.7	49.4	0.0	0.0	D	D		
Canada	12.6	12.9	D	D	7.6	7.2	D	D	D	D
Chile	4.5	4.8	29.1	29.7	33.6	34.2	0.0	0.0	0.0	0.0
China (People's Republic of)	D	D	14.1	14.7	11.2	11.2	D	D	18.0	17.7
Colombia	8.8	4.7	57.8	61.4	66.5	67.6	D	D	0.0	8.2
Costa Rica	0.0	0.0	0.0	0.0	0.0	0.0	0.0	0.0	0.0	0.0
Croatia	0.0	0.0	0.0	0.0	0.0	0.0	0.0	0.0		
Cyprus	0.0	0.0	32.6	38.2	0.9	1.0	0.0	0.0		
Czech Republic	39.4	39.3	1.3	1.3	35.1	35.3	20.7	21.0		
Denmark	0.0	0.0	4.9	4.9	0.0	0.0	16.1	10.2	0.0	0.0
Estonia	0.0	0.0	0.0	0.0	0.0	0.0	0.0	0.0	0.0	0.0
Finland	0.0	0.0	0.0	0.0	0.0	0.0	0.0	0.0	D	D
France	0.0	0.0	2.5	1.5	33.7	35.9		D		
Georgia	D	D	60.3	67.3	41.4	46.6	74.1	76.6	0.8	5.3
Germany	0.0	0.0	0.0	0.0	0.0	0.0	0.0	0.0		
Greece	26.4	28.9	41.2	41.6	28.1	28.7	14.2	21.0	74.6	75.1
Hong Kong (China)	18.9	17.9	61.6	57.2						
Hungary	0.0	0.0	4.6	3.4	0.0	0.0	3.3	3.4	0.0	0.0
Iceland	0.0	0.0	27.4	27.2	0.0	0.0	0.0	0.0		
India	26.1	28.1	28.5	34.3			D	D		
Indonesia	D	D	D	D	D	D	D	D		
Ireland	0.1	0.5	3.1	3.3	3.2	6.4	12.4	4.0	0.0	0.0
Israel	D	D	D	D	D	D	D	D	D	D
Italy	0.0	0.0	0.0	0.0	46.4	47.9	0.0	0.0		
Japan	D	D	D	D	D	D	D	D		
Kenya	5.2	0.0	41.5	0.0	5.2	0.0	7.3	0.0	9.1	0.0
Korea	6.1	0.6	9.3	9.9	3.8	3.5	D	D	0.0	0.0
Latvia	0.0	0.0	0.0	0.0	0.0	0.0	D	D	0.0	0.0
Lithuania	26.2	42.6	21.8	23.1	0.0	0.0	2.6	4.1	0.9	0.9
Luxembourg	D	D	D	D	7.3	7.3	D	D		
Malaysia	40.1	39.6	32.9	33.2			29.3	28.7		
Malta	44.4	42.9	43.3	41.1	7.4	7.5	41.1	45.7		
Mexico	10.1	9.8	22.8	22.4	0.0	0.0	0.0	0.0	0.0	0.0
Morocco	D	D	D	D	D	D	D	D		
Netherlands	1.8	1.7	19.5	18.7	24.3	27.4	0.0	0.0		

	Percentage inactive taxpayers on registers									
	On PIT register		On CIT register		On VAT register		On PAYE register		On Excise register	
Jurisdiction	2018	2019	2018	2019	2018	2019	2018	2019	2018	2019
New Zealand	64.8	44.1	28.4	32.2	2.5	2.5	3.3	4.0		
Norway	2.1	5.2	5.9	5.3	0.0	0.0	0.0	0.0	0.0	0.0
Peru	23.7	27.8	11.0	18.3	30.6	32.9	26.1	28.1	18.7	20.4
Poland	37.9	34.5	22.0	24.4	1.2	1.2	34.6	35.2	D	D
Portugal	47.9	47.1	0.0	0.0	0.0	0.0	D	D	D	D
Romania	D	D	61.1	56.4	0.1	0.2	8.4	8.5	19.9	19.9
Russia	D	D	17.1	14.0	14.5	12.4	D	D	D	D
Saudi Arabia			11.8	8.6	9.9	16.7			0.0	0.0
Singapore	D	D	D	D	D	D				
Slovak Republic	D	D	D	D	D	D	D	D		
Slovenia	44.1	44.7	0.0	0.0	0.0	0.0	0.0	0.0	0.0	0.0
South Africa	4.6	4.5	28.3	55.5	20.5	20.3	21.1	21.0	18.0	17.3
Spain	0.0	0.0	0.0	0.0	0.0	0.0	0.0	0.0	0.0	0.0
Sweden	D	D	D	D	D	D	D	D	D	D
Switzerland	D	D	D	D	0.0	0.0	D	D		
Thailand	D	D	D	D	49.0	50.1	D	D		
Turkey	69.5	70.1	63.7	63.8	75.2	75.2	72.2	72.3	88.7	91.2
United Kingdom	D	D	18.8	17.1	5.7	4.7	D	D	D	D
United States	D	D	D	D			D	D	D	D

StatLink http://dx.doi.org/10.1787/888934272100

Formula	(PIT total taxpayers [A.20] - PIT active taxpayers [A.20]) / PIT total taxpayers [A.20] * 100	(CIT total taxpayers [A.20] - CIT active taxpayers [A.20]) / CIT total taxpayers [A.20] * 100	(VAT total taxpayers [A.21] - VAT active taxpayers [A.21]) / VAT total taxpayers [A.21] * 100	(Tax withheld from employees by employers total taxpayers [A.21] - Tax withheld from employees by employers active taxpayers [A.21]) / Tax withheld from employees by employers total taxpayers [A.21] * 100	(Excise total taxpayers [A.21] - Excise active taxpayers [A.21]) / Excise total taxpayers [A.21] * 100

Table D.12 **On-time filing rates**

	On-time filing rates							
	CIT on-time filing rate		PIT on-time filing rate		PAYE on-time filing rate		VAT on-time filing rate	
Jurisdiction	**2018**	**2019**	**2018**	**2019**	**2018**	**2019**	**2018**	**2019**
Argentina	41.2	34.5	60.2	56.6	86.9	87.3	80.3	81.1
Australia	76.3	78.7	83.1	83.8	79.9	79.2	76.6	76.0
Austria	D	D	D	D	D	D	85.8	85.8
Belgium	81.5	83.9	93.4	93.5	D	D	99.2	99.2
Brazil	D	D	97.5	95.8	D	D	D	D
Bulgaria	95.1	95.1	90.7	93.7	D	D	99.5	98.3
Canada	85.4	86.6	91.0	94.9	91.1	92.8	60.7	59.5
Chile	80.7	80.7	D	D	93.0	94.5	76.3	77.2
China (People's Republic of)	97.3	97.0	D	D	D	D	97.1	97.8
Colombia	52.3	51.2	102.1	100.2	D	D	D	D
Costa Rica	75.4	77.8	70.8	66.7	28.9	31.9	78.0	68.6
Croatia	83.8	83.7	88.6	95.1	D	D	88.4	87.8
Cyprus	56.8	55.1	75.4	67.2	D	D	86.1	86.3
Czech Republic	78.3	81.8	96.0	96.5	89.7	90.0	95.3	96.7
Denmark	85.3	83.2	99.2	98.2	97.9	96.7	85.7	86.2
Estonia	D	D	93.8	98.1	94.4	93.3	91.7	90.7
Finland	86.4	90.3	88.4	87.2	93.2	78.0	90.1	90.2
France	94.8	95.0	96.1	95.8		D	91.4	91.1
Georgia	D	67.2	D	64.7	D	58.5	91.7	90.4
Germany	80.4	79.4	82.7	81.7	D	D	80.1	79.2
Greece	97.6	97.9	99.4	99.6	94.4	93.8	66.5	66.3
Hong Kong (China)	65.4	67.2	76.5	74.5				
Hungary	75.8	72.1	D	D	91.3	91.3	86.2	85.4
Iceland	81.8	85.8	93.4	93.7	D	D	95.4	94.2
India	89.3	93.7	95.7	95.1	90.1	80.4		
Indonesia	D	D	D	D	D	D	D	D
Ireland	D	D	82.6	82.6	87.4	94.4	89.2	86.9
Israel	85.8	87.9	91.7	92.0	99.3	98.4	96.9	97.1
Italy	D	D	D	D	D	D	D	D
Japan	D	D	D	D	D	D	D	D
Kenya	56.6	46.5	42.6	32.7	55.1	54.4	80.7	80.3
Korea	D	D	97.8	97.1	D	D	D	D
Latvia	78.3	98.1	94.0	93.7	85.3	87.3	90.2	91.2
Lithuania	49.7	51.2	78.8	75.8	94.6	94.4	97.1	92.9
Luxembourg	D	D	D	D	D	D	89.5	84.9
Malaysia	79.7	78.2	77.0	67.9	92.3	86.8		
Malta	68.2	D	77.3	D	74.1	77.8	71.3	65.1
Mexico	46.2	47.7	29.3	31.9	D	D	D	D
Morocco	90.3	93.2	81.4	97.7	97.8	100.0	90.1	91.8
Netherlands	94.4	96.7	98.6	99.0	99.1	99.1	95.6	95.6

	On-time filing rates							
	CIT on-time filing rate		PIT on-time filing rate		PAYE on-time filing rate		VAT on-time filing rate	
Jurisdiction	**2018**	**2019**	**2018**	**2019**	**2018**	**2019**	**2018**	**2019**
New Zealand	88.7	88.9	88.2	87.3	92.9	92.0	92.7	92.3
Norway	96.1	95.5	99.7	99.6	82.5	81.2	90.0	89.7
Peru	84.1	86.7	69.0	79.0	98.2	97.2	87.2	87.9
Poland	89.9	90.0	98.8	95.8	97.2	96.9	97.3	97.7
Portugal	97.5	98.9	97.0	97.1	97.5	97.6	95.5	95.4
Romania	86.7	90.9	D	D	95.2	95.6	93.4	93.4
Russia	75.7	73.7	115.0	98.3	103.3	103.2	D	D
Saudi Arabia	74.9	72.9					76.8	96.1
Singapore	84.3	84.3	97.0	97.3			95.8	96.0
Slovak Republic	77.8	77.7	99.0	99.2	D	D	103.5	104.7
Slovenia	88.2	93.8	65.3	65.8	96.3	97.7	84.2	85.7
South Africa	13.7	29.5	67.2	61.8	59.0	58.5	52.1	52.0
Spain	D	D	D	D	D	D	D	D
Sweden	D	D	D	D	D	D	D	D
Switzerland	D	D	D	D	D	D	77.6	75.9
Thailand	D	D	D	D	D	D	D	D
Turkey	89.2	89.6	92.8	92.2	94.2	92.6	87.4	86.9
United Kingdom[1]	71.0	71.0	93.7	96.7	D	D	84.8	84.1
United States	103.2	99.7	100.2	99.7	100.4	100.6		

StatLink http://dx.doi.org/10.1787/888934272119

1. United Kingdom: CIT methodology has changed compared to previous years.

Formula	No. of returns filed on time [A.22] / No. of returns expected [A.22] * 100	No. of returns filed on time [A.23] / No. of returns expected [A.23] * 100	No. of returns filed on time [A.24] / No. of returns expected [A.24] * 100	No. of returns filed on time [A.25] / No. of returns expected [A.25] * 100

Table D.13 **Electronic filing**

	Electronic filing					
	Percent CIT returns e-filed		Percent PIT returns e-filed		Percent VAT returns e-filed	
Jurisdiction	**2018**	**2019**	**2018**	**2019**	**2018**	**2019**
Argentina	100.0	100.0	100.0	100.0	100.0	100.0
Australia	D	D	D	D	D	D
Austria	96.4	96.2	79.1	81.3	92.4	92.3
Belgium	99.2	99.4	89.5	91.4	98.6	98.9
Brazil	100.0	100.0	100.0	100.0	100.0	100.0
Bulgaria	100.0	100.0	41.3	46.9	100.0	100.0
Canada	90.0	91.2	87.4	88.3	89.2	91.3
Chile	99.7	99.7	99.9	99.9	99.5	99.8
China (People's Republic of)	D	D	D	D	D	D
Colombia	99.8	100.0	91.5	92.6	100.0	100.0
Costa Rica	100.0	100.0	100.0	100.0	100.0	100.0
Croatia	96.3	97.2	64.0	70.1	99.5	99.7
Cyprus	96.9	96.5	94.1	98.5	94.3	95.9
Czech Republic	92.3	92.6	20.3	21.4	99.9	99.8
Denmark	100.0	100.0	100.0	100.0	100.0	100.0
Estonia	99.8	99.8	96.0	94.6	99.5	99.7
Finland	90.5	93.4	95.7	96.6	95.1	96.2
France	97.7	94.4	60.7	66.5	97.7	97.8
Georgia	100.0	100.0	100.0	100.0	100.0	100.0
Germany	91.8	69.3	68.3	71.3	91.6	92.6
Greece	99.7	99.8	98.7	98.8	99.6	99.6
Hong Kong (China)	0.8	0.6	20.5	21.8		
Hungary	99.4	99.7	79.7	84.6	99.9	100.0
Iceland	99.5	99.5	99.3	99.4	99.3	99.4
India	100.0	100.0	99.2	99.8		
Indonesia	D	D	D	D	D	D
Ireland	99.9	99.9	95.2	94.5	99.7	99.7
Israel	98.4	99.1	71.0	72.6	69.5	77.0
Italy	100.0	100.0	100.0	100.0	100.0	100.0
Japan	73.5	77.4	47.5	51.6	D	D
Kenya	100.0	100.0	100.0	100.0	100.0	100.0
Korea	99.2	99.3	97.3	98.3	D	D
Latvia	99.3	99.6	80.1	84.9	100.0	100.0
Lithuania	100.0	100.0	98.7	99.9	100.0	100.0
Luxembourg	88.2	89.5	90.9	88.4	95.1	98.0
Malaysia	100.0	100.0	96.6	98.2		
Malta	D	D	D	D	D	D
Mexico	100.0	100.0	100.0	100.0	D	D
Morocco	99.9	99.9	67.7	59.3	97.7	100.0
Netherlands	100.0	100.0	97.9	98.1	100.0	100.0

	Electronic filing					
	Percent CIT returns e-filed		Percent PIT returns e-filed		Percent VAT returns e-filed	
Jurisdiction	**2018**	**2019**	**2018**	**2019**	**2018**	**2019**
New Zealand	93.6	95.2	98.3	D	86.5	90.7
Norway	97.4	98.5	98.0	98.4	100.0	100.0
Peru	100.0	100.0	100.0	100.0	100.0	100.0
Poland	72.8	94.3	85.5	91.9	98.3	99.6
Portugal	100.0	100.0	100.0	100.0	100.0	100.0
Romania	93.3	95.1	26.4	71.9	98.3	98.9
Russia	D	D	D	D	D	D
Saudi Arabia	100.0	100.0			100.0	100.0
Singapore	69.5	78.1	98.4	98.4	99.4	99.5
Slovak Republic	93.0	93.7	40.7	43.6	99.9	100.0
Slovenia	100.0	100.0	8.4	13.0	100.0	100.0
South Africa	99.6	99.8	99.7	96.5	88.6	86.0
Spain	100.0	100.0	74.8	75.9	100.0	100.0
Sweden	45.4	50.2	72.8	81.8	71.7	77.8
Switzerland	D	D	D	D	D	D
Thailand	45.3	50.9	80.2	82.1	53.8	58.1
Turkey	99.9	99.9	99.9	99.9	99.7	99.7
United Kingdom	99.1	99.2	88.9	90.4	99.4	99.3
United States	63.4	65.1	87.8	89.1		

StatLink http://dx.doi.org/10.1787/888934272138

Formula	(Fully pre-filled, deemed acceptance [A.44] + Fully pre-filled, confirmation required [A.44] + Partically pre-filled [A.44] + Not prefilled [A.44]) / Total [A.43] * 100	(Fully pre-filled, deemed acceptance [A.45] + Fully pre-filled, confirmation required [A.45] + Partically pre-filled [A.45] + Not prefilled [A.45]) / Total [A.43] * 100	(Fully pre-filled, deemed acceptance [A.46] + Fully pre-filled, confirmation required [A.46] + Partically pre-filled [A.46] + Not prefilled [A.46]) / Total [A.43] * 100

Table D.14 **Proportion of Returns by Channel: CIT**

	Percentage of CIT tax returns received via the channels below									
	Paper returns-CIT		Electronic - fully pre-filled deemed-CIT		Electronic - fully pre-filled confirmation required-CIT		Electronic -not pre-filled or partially pre-filled-CIT		Other-CIT	
Jurisdiction	**2018**	**2019**	**2018**	**2019**	**2018**	**2019**	**2018**	**2019**	**2018**	**2019**
Argentina	0.0	0.0	0.0	0.0	0.0	0.0	100.0	100.0	0.0	0.0
Australia	D	D	D	D	D	D	D	D	D	D
Austria	3.6	3.8	0.0	0.0	0.0	0.0	96.4	96.2	0.0	0.0
Belgium	0.8	0.6	0.0	0.0	0.0	0.0	99.2	99.4	0.0	0.0
Brazil	0.0	0.0	0.0	0.0	0.0	0.0	100.0	100.0	0.0	0.0
Bulgaria	0.0	0.0	0.0	0.0	0.0	0.0	100.0	100.0	0.0	0.0
Canada	10.0	8.8	0.0	0.0	0.0	0.0	90.0	91.2	0.0	0.0
Chile	0.3	0.3	0.0	0.0	0.0	0.0	99.7	99.7	0.0	0.0
China (People's Republic of)	D	D	D	D	D	D	D	D	D	D
Colombia	0.2	0.0	0.0	0.0	0.0	0.0	99.8	100.0	0.0	0.0
Costa Rica	0.0	0.0	0.0	0.0	0.0	0.0	100.0	100.0	0.0	0.0
Croatia	3.7	2.8	0.0	0.0	0.0	0.0	96.3	97.2	0.0	0.0
Cyprus	3.1	3.5	0.0	0.0	0.0	0.0	96.9	96.5	0.0	0.0
Czech Republic	7.7	7.4	0.0	0.0	0.0	0.0	92.3	92.6	0.0	0.0
Denmark	0.0	0.0	0.0	0.0	0.0	0.0	100.0	100.0	0.0	0.0
Estonia	0.2	0.2	0.0	0.0	0.0	0.0	99.8	99.8	0.0	0.0
Finland	9.5	6.6	0.0	0.0	0.0	0.0	90.5	93.4	0.0	0.0
France	2.3	5.6	0.0	0.0	0.0	0.0	97.7	94.4	0.0	0.0
Georgia	0.0	0.0	0.0	0.0	0.0	0.0	100.0	100.0	0.0	0.0
Germany	8.2	30.7	0.0	0.0	0.0	0.0	91.8	69.3	0.0	0.0
Greece	0.3	0.2	0.0	0.0	0.0	0.0	99.7	99.8	0.0	0.0
Hong Kong (China)	99.2	99.4	0.0	0.0	0.0	0.0	0.8	0.6	0.0	0.0
Hungary	0.6	0.3	0.0	0.0	0.0	0.0	99.4	99.7	0.0	0.0
Iceland	0.5	0.5	0.0	0.0	0.0	0.0	99.5	99.5	0.0	0.0
India	0.0	0.0	0.0	0.0	0.0	0.0	100.0	100.0	0.0	0.0
Indonesia	D	D	D	D	D	D	D	D	D	D
Ireland	0.1	0.1	0.0	0.0	0.0	0.0	99.9	99.9	0.0	0.0
Israel	1.6	0.9	0.0	0.0	0.0	0.0	98.4	99.1	0.0	0.0
Italy	0.0	0.0	0.0	0.0	0.0	0.0	100.0	100.0	0.0	0.0
Japan	D	D	D	D	D	D	D	D	D	D
Kenya	0.0	0.0	0.0	0.0	0.0	0.0	100.0	100.0	0.0	0.0
Korea	0.8	0.7	0.0	0.0	0.0	0.0	99.2	99.3	0.0	0.0
Latvia	0.7	0.4	0.0	0.0	0.0	0.0	99.3	99.6	0.0	0.0
Lithuania	0.0	0.0	0.0	0.0	0.0	0.0	100.0	100.0	0.0	0.0
Luxembourg	11.8	10.5	0.0	0.0	0.0	0.0	88.2	89.5	0.0	0.0
Malaysia	0.0	0.0	0.0	0.0	0.0	0.0	100.0	100.0	0.0	0.0
Malta	D	D	D	D	D	D	D	D	D	D
Mexico	0.0	0.0	0.0	0.0	0.0	0.0	100.0	100.0	0.0	0.0

	Percentage of CIT tax returns received via the channels below									
	Paper returns-CIT		Electronic - fully pre-filled deemed-CIT		Electronic - fully pre-filled confirmation required-CIT		Electronic -not pre-filled or partially pre-filled-CIT		Other-CIT	
Jurisdiction	**2018**	**2019**	**2018**	**2019**	**2018**	**2019**	**2018**	**2019**	**2018**	**2019**
Morocco	0.1	0.1	0.0	0.0	0.0	0.0	99.9	99.9	0.0	0.0
Netherlands	0.0	0.0	0.0	0.0	0.0	0.0	100.0	100.0	0.0	0.0
New Zealand	6.4	4.8	0.0	0.0	0.0	0.0	93.6	95.2	0.0	0.0
Norway	2.6	1.5	0.0	0.0	0.0	0.0	97.4	98.5	0.0	0.0
Peru	0.0	0.0	0.0	0.0	0.0	0.0	100.0	100.0	0.0	0.0
Poland [1]	27.2	5.7	0.0	0.0	0.0	0.0	72.8	94.3	0.0	0.0
Portugal	0.0	0.0	0.1	0.0	0.0	0.0	99.9	100.0	0.0	0.0
Romania	6.7	4.9	0.0	0.0	0.0	0.0	93.3	95.1	0.0	0.0
Russia	D	D	D	D	D	D	D	D	D	D
Saudi Arabia	0.0	0.0	0.0	0.0	1.2	34.1	98.8	65.9	0.0	0.0
Singapore	30.5	21.9	0.0	0.0	0.0	0.0	69.5	78.1	0.0	0.0
Slovak Republic	7.0	6.3	0.0	0.0	0.0	0.0	93.0	93.7	0.0	0.0
Slovenia	0.0	0.0	0.0	0.0	0.0	0.0	100.0	100.0	0.0	0.0
South Africa	0.4	0.2	0.0	0.0	0.0	0.0	99.6	99.8	0.0	0.0
Spain	0.0	0.0	0.0	0.0	0.0	0.0	100.0	100.0	0.0	0.0
Sweden [2]	54.6	49.8	0.0	0.0	0.0	0.0	45.4	50.2	0.0	0.0
Switzerland	D	D	D	D	D	D	D	D	D	D
Thailand	54.7	49.1	0.0	0.0	0.0	0.0	45.3	50.9	0.0	0.0
Turkey	0.1	0.1	0.0	0.0	0.0	0.0	99.9	99.9	0.0	0.0
United Kingdom [3]	0.9	0.8	0.0	0.0	0.0	0.0	99.1	99.2	0.0	0.0
United States	36.6	34.9	0.0	0.0	0.0	0.0	63.4	65.1	0.0	0.0

StatLink http://dx.doi.org/10.1787/888934272157

1. Poland: All returns that are filed electronically are included in category "Partially pre-filled" as it is not possible to distinguish between the different e-filing categories.
2. Sweden: All returns that are filed electronically are included in category "Partially pre-filled" as it is not possible to distinguish between the different e-filing categories.
3. United Kingdom: All returns that are filed electronically are included in category "Not pre-filled" as it is not possible to distinguish between partially pre-filled and not pre-filled returns.

Formula	Paper returns [A.44] / Total [A.43] * 100	Fully pre-filled, deemed acceptance [A.44] / Total [A.43] * 100	Fully pre-filled, confirmation required [A.44] / Total [A.43] * 100	(Partially pre-filled [A.44] + Not prefilled [A.44]) / Total [A.43] * 100	Other [A.44] / Total [A.43] * 100

Table D.15 **Proportion of Returns by Channel: PIT**

	Percentage of PIT tax returns received via the channels below											
	Paper returns-PIT		Electronic - fully pre-filled deemed-PIT		Electronic - fully pre-filled confirmation required-PIT		Electronic -not pre-filled or partially pre-filled-PIT		Other-PIT		Percentage of PIT returns prefilled with income information	
Jurisdiction	2018	2019	2018	2019	2018	2019	2018	2019	2018	2019	2018	2019
Argentina	0.0	0.0	0.0	0.0	0.0	0.0	100.0	100.0	0.0	0.0	0.0	0.0
Australia	D	D	D	D	D	D	D	D	D	D	D	D
Austria	20.9	18.7	20.9	23.8	0.0	0.0	58.2	57.5	0.0	0.0	50.0	53.7
Belgium	10.0	8.2	35.1	34.6	0.0	0.0	54.4	56.8	0.5	0.4	89.5	91.4
Brazil	0.0	0.0	0.0	0.0	0.0	0.0	100.0	100.0	0.0	0.0	0.0	0.0
Bulgaria	58.7	53.1	0.0	0.0	0.0	0.0	41.3	46.9	0.0	0.0	0.0	0.0
Canada	12.6	11.7	0.0	0.0	0.0	0.0	87.4	88.3	0.0	0.0	0.0	0.0
Chile	0.1	0.1	0.0	0.0	94.3	94.9	5.5	4.9	0.0	0.0	94.3	94.9
China (People's Republic of)	D	D	D	D	D	D	D	D	D	D	D	D
Colombia	8.5	7.4	0.0	0.0	0.0	0.0	91.5	92.6	0.0	0.0	10.7	43.7
Costa Rica	0.0	0.0	0.0	0.0	0.0	0.0	100.0	100.0	0.0	0.0	0.0	0.0
Croatia	36.0	29.9	0.0	0.0	0.0	0.0	64.0	70.1	0.0	0.0	0.0	0.0
Cyprus	5.9	1.5	0.0	0.0	0.0	0.0	94.1	98.5	0.0	0.0	0.0	0.0
Czech Republic	79.7	78.6	0.0	0.0	0.0	0.0	20.3	21.4	0.0	0.0	0.0	0.0
Denmark	0.0	0.0	100.0	100.0	0.0	0.0	0.0	0.0	0.0	0.0	100.0	100.0
Estonia	4.0	5.4	0.0	0.0	41.6	49.7	54.4	44.9	0.0	0.0	96.0	94.6
Finland	4.3	3.4	74.4	76.0	21.3	20.5	0.0	0.0	0.0	0.0	95.7	96.6
France [1]	39.3	33.5	0.0	0.0	0.0	0.0	60.7	66.5	0.0	0.0	D	D
Georgia	0.0	0.0	0.0	0.0	0.0	0.0	100.0	100.0	0.0	0.0	0.0	0.0
Germany	31.7	28.7	0.0	0.0	0.0	0.0	68.3	71.3	0.0	0.0	68.3	71.3
Greece	1.3	1.2	0.0	0.0	0.0	0.0	98.7	98.8	0.0	0.0	98.7	98.8
Hong Kong (China)	79.5	78.2	0.0	0.0	0.0	0.0	20.5	21.8	0.0	0.0	20.2	21.5
Hungary	20.3	15.4	40.7	41.7	16.4	18.3	22.6	24.6	0.0	0.0	66.3	73.1
Iceland	0.7	0.6	0.0	0.0	99.3	99.4	0.0	0.0	0.0	0.0	99.3	99.4
India	0.8	0.2	0.0	0.0	0.0	0.0	99.2	99.8	0.0	0.0	0.0	0.0
Indonesia	D	D	D	D	D	D	D	D	D	D	D	D
Ireland	4.8	5.5	0.0	0.0	0.0	0.0	95.2	94.5	0.0	0.0	95.2	94.5
Israel	29.0	27.4	0.0	0.0	0.0	0.0	71.0	72.6	0.0	0.0	0.0	0.0
Italy	0.0	0.0	0.0	0.0	9.9	11.0	90.1	89.0	0.0	0.0	9.9	11.0
Japan	D	D	D	D	D	D	D	D	D	D	D	D
Kenya	0.0	0.0	0.0	0.0	0.0	0.0	100.0	100.0	0.0	0.0	0.0	0.0
Korea	2.7	1.7	0.0	0.0	16.0	19.1	81.3	79.3	0.0	0.0	97.3	98.3
Latvia	19.9	15.1	0.0	0.0	0.0	0.0	80.1	84.9	0.0	0.0	80.1	84.9
Lithuania	0.1	0.1	29.2	40.9	29.2	40.9	40.3	18.0	1.3	0.0	94.1	99.9
Luxembourg	9.1	11.6	0.0	0.0	0.0	0.0	90.9	88.4	0.0	0.0	0.0	0.0
Malaysia	3.4	1.8	0.0	0.0	0.0	0.0	96.6	98.2	0.0	0.0	96.6	98.2
Malta	D	D	D	D	D	D	D	D	D	D	D	D
Mexico	0.0	0.0	0.0	0.0	9.8	12.7	90.2	87.3	0.0	0.0	100.0	100.0

Jurisdiction	Percentage of PIT tax returns received via the channels below: Paper returns-PIT 2018	2019	Electronic - fully pre-filled deemed-PIT 2018	2019	Electronic - fully pre-filled confirmation required-PIT 2018	2019	Electronic -not pre-filled or partially pre-filled-PIT 2018	2019	Other-PIT 2018	2019	Percentage of PIT returns prefilled with income information 2018	2019
Morocco	32.3	40.7	0.0	0.0	0.0	0.0	67.7	59.3	0.0	0.0	0.0	0.0
Netherlands	2.1	1.9	0.0	0.0	0.0	0.0	97.9	98.1	0.0	0.0	97.9	98.1
New Zealand	1.7	D	0.0	D	76.2	D	22.1	D	0.0	D	76.2	D
Norway	2.0	1.6	67.8	60.9	21.8	29.7	8.3	7.8	0.0	0.0	98.0	98.4
Peru	0.0	0.0	0.0	0.0	0.0	0.0	100.0	100.0	0.0	0.0	100.0	100.0
Poland [2]	14.5	8.1	0.0	0.0	0.0	0.0	85.5	91.9	0.0	0.0	D	D
Portugal	0.0	0.0	2.2	1.9	30.5	30.1	67.3	68.1	0.0	0.0	100.0	100.0
Romania	73.6	28.1	0.0	0.0	0.0	0.0	26.4	71.9	0.0	0.0	0.0	0.0
Russia	D	D	D	D	D	D	D	D	D	D	D	D
Saudi Arabia												
Singapore	1.6	1.6	62.6	63.2	0.0	0.0	35.9	35.2	0.0	0.0	98.4	98.4
Slovak Republic	59.3	56.4	0.0	0.0	0.0	0.0	40.7	43.6	0.0	0.0	0.0	0.0
Slovenia	91.6	87.0	0.0	0.0	0.0	0.0	8.4	13.0	0.0	0.0	8.4	13.0
South Africa	0.3	0.3	0.0	0.0	99.7	96.5	0.0	0.0	0.0	0.0	99.7	96.5
Spain	1.9	0.4	0.0	0.0	24.6	26.3	50.2	49.6	23.3	23.7	74.8	75.9
Sweden	27.2	18.2	0.0	0.0	58.4	65.7	14.4	16.1	0.0	0.0	72.8	81.8
Switzerland	D	D	D	D	D	D	D	D	D	D	D	D
Thailand	19.8	17.9	0.0	0.0	0.0	0.0	80.2	82.1	0.0	0.0	0.0	0.0
Turkey	0.1	0.1	0.0	0.0	0.0	0.0	99.9	99.9	0.0	0.0	13.1	11.2
United Kingdom [3]	11.1	9.6	0.0	0.0	0.0	0.0	88.9	90.4	0.0	0.0	D	D
United States	12.2	10.9	0.0	0.0	0.0	0.0	87.8	89.1	0.0	0.0	0.0	0.0

StatLink http://dx.doi.org/10.1787/888934272176

1. France: All returns that are filed electronically are included in category "Partially pre-filled" as it is not possible to distinguish between the different e-filing categories.
2. Poland: All returns that are filed electronically are included in category "Partially pre-filled" as it is not possible to distinguish between the different e-filing categories.
3. United Kingdom: All returns that are filed electronically are included in category "Not pre-filled" as it is not possible to distinguish between partially pre-filled and not pre-filled returns.

Formula	Paper returns [A.45] / Total [A.43] * 100	Fully pre-filled, deemed acceptance [A.45] / Total [A.43] * 100	Fully pre-filled, confirmation required [A.45] / Total [A.43] * 100	(Partially pre-filled [A.45] + Not prefilled [A.45]) / Total [A.43] * 100	Other [A.45] / Total [A.43] * 100	(Fully pre-filled, deemed acceptance [A.45] + Fully pre-filled, confirmation required [A.45] + Partically pre-filled [A.45]) / Total [A.43] * 100

Table D.16 **Proportion of Returns by Channel: VAT**

	Percentage of VAT tax returns received via the channels below									
	Paper returns – VAT		Electronic – fully pre-filled deemed-VAT		Electronic - fully pre-filled confirmation required-VAT		Electronic – not pre-filled or partially pre-filled-VAT		Other – VAT	
Jurisdiction	2018	2019	2018	2019	2018	2019	2018	2019	2018	2019
Argentina	0.0	0.0	0.0	0.0	0.0	0.3	100.0	99.7	0.0	0.0
Australia	D	D	D	D	D	D	D	D	D	D
Austria	7.6	7.7	0.0	0.0	0.0	0.0	92.4	92.3	0.0	0.0
Belgium	1.4	1.1	0.0	0.0	0.0	0.0	98.6	98.9	0.0	0.0
Brazil	0.0	0.0	0.0	0.0	0.0	0.0	100.0	100.0	0.0	0.0
Bulgaria	0.0	0.0	0.0	0.0	0.0	0.0	100.0	100.0	0.0	0.0
Canada	10.8	8.7	0.0	0.0	0.0	0.0	89.2	91.3	0.0	0.0
Chile	0.5	0.2	0.0	0.0	60.9	65.4	38.6	34.3	0.0	0.0
China (People's Republic of)	D	D	D	D	D	D	D	D	D	D
Colombia	0.0	0.0	0.0	0.0	0.0	0.0	100.0	100.0	0.0	0.0
Costa Rica	0.0	0.0	0.0	0.0	0.0	0.0	100.0	100.0	0.0	0.0
Croatia	0.5	0.3	0.0	0.0	0.0	0.0	99.5	99.7	0.0	0.0
Cyprus	5.7	4.1	0.0	0.0	0.0	0.0	94.3	95.9	0.0	0.0
Czech Republic	0.1	0.2	0.0	0.0	0.0	0.0	99.9	99.8	0.0	0.0
Denmark	0.0	0.0	0.0	0.0	0.0	0.0	100.0	100.0	0.0	0.0
Estonia	0.5	0.3	0.0	0.0	0.0	0.0	99.5	99.7	0.0	0.0
Finland	4.9	3.8	0.0	0.0	0.0	0.0	95.1	96.2	0.0	0.0
France	2.3	2.2	0.0	0.0	0.0	0.0	97.7	97.8	0.0	0.0
Georgia	0.0	0.0	0.0	0.0	0.0	0.0	100.0	100.0	0.0	0.0
Germany	8.4	7.4	0.0	0.0	0.0	0.0	91.6	92.6	0.0	0.0
Greece	0.4	0.4	0.0	0.0	0.0	0.0	99.6	99.6	0.0	0.0
Hong Kong (China)										
Hungary	0.1	0.0	0.0	0.0	0.0	0.0	99.9	100.0	0.0	0.0
Iceland	0.7	0.6	0.0	0.0	0.0	0.0	99.3	99.4	0.0	0.0
India										
Indonesia	D	D	D	D	D	D	D	D	D	D
Ireland	0.3	0.3	0.0	0.0	0.0	0.0	99.7	99.7	0.0	0.0
Israel	30.5	23.0	0.0	0.0	0.0	0.0	69.5	77.0	0.0	0.0
Italy	0.0	0.0	0.0	0.0	0.0	0.0	100.0	100.0	0.0	0.0
Japan	D	D	D	D	D	D	D	D	D	D
Kenya	0.0	0.0	0.0	0.0	0.0	0.0	100.0	100.0	0.0	0.0
Korea	D	D	D	D	D	D	D	D	D	D
Latvia	0.0	0.0	0.0	0.0	0.0	0.0	100.0	100.0	0.0	0.0
Lithuania	0.0	0.0	0.0	0.0	0.0	0.0	100.0	100.0	0.0	0.0
Luxembourg	4.9	2.0	0.0	0.0	0.0	0.0	95.1	98.0	0.0	0.0
Malaysia										
Malta	D	D	D	D	D	D	D	D	D	D
Mexico	D	D	D	D	D	D	D	D	D	D

	Percentage of VAT tax returns received via the channels below									
	Paper returns – VAT		Electronic – fully pre-filled deemed-VAT		Electronic - fully pre-filled confirmation required-VAT		Electronic – not pre-filled or partially pre-filled-VAT		Other – VAT	
Jurisdiction	**2018**	**2019**	**2018**	**2019**	**2018**	**2019**	**2018**	**2019**	**2018**	**2019**
Morocco	2.3	0.0	0.0	0.0	0.0	0.0	97.7	100.0	0.0	0.0
Netherlands	0.0	0.0	0.0	0.0	0.0	0.0	100.0	100.0	0.0	0.0
New Zealand	13.5	9.3	0.0	0.0	0.0	0.0	86.5	90.7	0.0	0.0
Norway	0.0	0.0	0.0	0.0	0.0	0.0	100.0	100.0	0.0	0.0
Peru	0.0	0.0	0.0	0.0	0.0	0.0	100.0	100.0	0.0	0.0
Poland [1]	1.7	0.4	0.0	0.0	0.0	0.0	98.3	99.6	0.0	0.0
Portugal	0.0	0.0	0.0	0.0	0.0	0.0	100.0	100.0	0.0	0.0
Romania	1.7	1.1	0.0	0.0	0.0	0.0	98.3	98.9	0.0	0.0
Russia	D	D	D	D	D	D	D	D	D	D
Saudi Arabia	0.0	0.0	0.0	0.0	0.0	0.0	100.0	100.0	0.0	0.0
Singapore	0.6	0.5	0.0	0.0	0.0	0.0	99.4	99.5	0.0	0.0
Slovak Republic	0.1	0.0	0.0	0.0	0.0	0.0	99.9	100.0	0.0	0.0
Slovenia	0.0	0.0	0.0	0.0	0.0	0.0	100.0	100.0	0.0	0.0
South Africa	11.4	14.0	0.0	0.0	0.0	0.0	88.6	86.0	0.0	0.0
Spain	0.0	0.0	0.0	0.0	0.0	0.0	100.0	100.0	0.0	0.0
Sweden	28.3	22.2	0.0	0.0	0.0	0.0	71.7	77.8	0.0	0.0
Switzerland	D	D	D	D	D	D	D	D	D	D
Thailand	46.2	41.9	0.0	0.0	0.0	0.0	53.8	58.1	0.0	0.0
Turkey	0.3	0.3	0.0	0.0	0.0	0.0	99.7	99.7	0.0	0.0
United Kingdom [2]	0.6	0.7	0.0	0.0	0.0	0.0	99.4	99.3	0.0	0.0
United States										

StatLink http://dx.doi.org/10.1787/888934272195

1. Poland: All returns that are filed electronically are included in category "Partially pre-filled" as it is not possible to distinguish between the different e-filing categories.
2. United Kingdom: All returns that are filed electronically are included in category "Not pre-filled" as it is not possible to distinguish between partially pre-filled and not pre-filled returns.

Formula	Paper returns [A.46] / Total [A.43] * 100	Fully pre-filled, deemed acceptance [A.46] / Total [A.43] * 100	Fully pre-filled, confirmation required [A.46] / Total [A.43] * 100	(Partially pre-filled [A.46] + Not prefilled [A.46]) / Total [A.43] * 100	Other [A.46] / Total [A.43] * 100

Table D.17 **On-time payment performance**

	On-time payment payment rate (%)							
	PIT		CIT		PAYE		VAT	
Jurisdiction	**2018**	**2019**	**2018**	**2019**	**2018**	**2019**	**2018**	**2019**
Argentina	55.3	57.8	86.9	86.5	82.2	83.2	84.3	83.8
Australia	69.5	71.2	85.8	88.1	95.0	95.0	88.4	88.7
Austria	90.7	90.7	97.1	97.2	99.4	99.5	96.9	97.0
Belgium	71.6	71.4	80.3	64.4	99.3	99.5	98.5	98.5
Brazil	96.4	96.3	96.7	95.9	98.1	98.2	97.3	97.4
Bulgaria	85.2	87.0	85.3	86.5	84.9	86.7	85.2	86.1
Canada	94.0	94.0	85.7	86.6	D	D	D	D
Chile	D	D	D	D	D	D	D	D
China (People's Republic of)	D	D	D	D	D	D	D	D
Colombia	D	D	D	D	D	D	98.5	98.7
Costa Rica	72.8	56.9	25.6	46.3	0.1	0.1	8.1	19.5
Croatia	D	D	D	D	D	D	D	D
Cyprus	D	D	D	D	D	D	D	D
Czech Republic	83.4	82.6	94.6	94.2	D	D	92.2	91.8
Denmark	D	D	93.4	91.2	96.5	96.6	91.0	91.9
Estonia	75.1	79.8	74.4	82.8	79.5	79.9	78.1	77.9
Finland	88.6	76.9	90.7	89.8	95.9	95.7	90.5	90.2
France	93.8	90.1	D	D		99.5	96.5	96.0
Georgia	97.0	96.8	93.8	91.2	98.6	99.3	97.1	96.1
Germany	D	D	D	D	D	D	D	D
Greece	67.9	68.3	88.3	88.8	94.0	94.1	86.8	88.2
Hong Kong (China)	92.2	92.0	94.2	94.2				
Hungary	D	D	D	D	D	D	D	D
Iceland	D	D	D	D	D	D	D	D
India	D	D	D	D	D	D		
Indonesia	83.6	80.2	87.7	89.6	84.8	80.9	80.4	78.8
Ireland	98.4	98.1	99.3	98.1	98.9	98.6	98.1	98.0
Israel	101.5	99.9	103.0	100.3	97.1	99.0	90.1	89.9
Italy	D	D	D	D	D	D	D	D
Japan	D	D	D	D	D	D	D	D
Kenya	100.0	100.0	100.0	100.0	100.0	100.0	100.0	100.0
Korea	D	D	D	D	D	D	D	D
Latvia	D	D	D	D	D	D	D	D
Lithuania	89.9	88.1	96.8	90.3	90.3	88.7	99.1	96.5
Luxembourg	D	D	D	D	D	D	D	D
Malaysia	74.5	78.3	70.2	86.1	D	D		
Malta	70.9	72.6	75.6	80.7	97.1	94.2	72.3	61.9
Mexico	D	D	D	D	D	D	D	D
Morocco	D	D	D	D	D	D	D	D
Netherlands	95.1	95.3	97.9	97.9	99.1	99.0	98.2	98.5

	On-time payment payment rate (%)							
	PIT		CIT		PAYE		VAT	
Jurisdiction	2018	2019	2018	2019	2018	2019	2018	2019
New Zealand	94.4	92.1	97.9	71.2	98.7	98.3	96.4	96.7
Norway	76.9	77.8	90.1	92.1	95.8	95.3	88.4	88.3
Peru	44.0	45.2	87.0	87.9	96.9	97.1	87.5	93.0
Poland	79.1	78.1	92.9	92.1	96.2	95.9	87.9	87.7
Portugal	D	D	D	D	99.2	95.5	97.1	97.8
Romania	86.2	86.9	87.3	89.5	85.7	86.7	86.2	85.4
Russia	99.0	99.2	98.6	98.7	99.0	99.2	96.3	96.4
Saudi Arabia			53.2	38.2			88.6	89.5
Singapore	90.1	91.2	84.9	84.3			89.9	90.4
Slovak Republic	93.4	79.2	88.0	95.9	94.4	95.0	88.6	91.2
Slovenia	90.9	91.4	91.7	92.7	91.9	92.6	91.0	90.4
South Africa	51.5	44.6	28.3	41.0	96.5	96.8	92.2	91.5
Spain	96.5	95.9	91.8	93.3	99.7	99.7	94.5	94.4
Sweden	D	D	D	D	D	D	D	D
Switzerland	D	D	D	D	D	D	D	D
Thailand	D	D	D	D	D	D	D	D
Turkey	D	D	D	D	D	D	D	D
United Kingdom	D	D	D	D	D	D	82.7	82.5
United States	D	D	D	D	D	D		

StatLink http://dx.doi.org/10.1787/888934272214

Formula	Value of payments received on-time [A.26] / Value of payments expected by due date [A.26] * 100	Value of payments received on-time [A.27] / Value of payments expected by due date [A.27] * 100	Value of payments received on-time [A.28] / Value of payments expected by due date [A.28] * 100	Value of payments received on-time [A.29] / Value of payments expected by due date [A.29] * 100

Table D.18 **Electronic payment proportions and third party withholding**

Electronic payment proportions and third party withholding						
	Percentage electronic payments by number		Percentage electronic payments by value		Estimated percentage of total personal income tax withheld by third parties and subsequently paid to the administration	
Jurisdiction	2018	2019	2018	2019	2018	2019
Argentina	77.2	76.8	98.0	98.1	81.7	84.7
Australia	D	D	D	D	D	D
Austria	98.0	98.0	D	D	87.6	86.5
Belgium	100.0	100.0	100.0	100.0	93.2	92.6
Brazil	64.1	67.7	77.6	81.4	77.8	77.8
Bulgaria	100.0	100.0	100.0	100.0	88.0	89.0
Canada	82.1	83.8	89.1	89.5	D	D
Chile	D	D	D	D	86.1	88.7
China (People's Republic of)	84.0	88.0	79.0	81.0	80.0	85.0
Colombia	23.0	29.0	33.0	37.0	84.0	89.0
Costa Rica	99.5	99.6	99.5	99.6	12.2	10.4
Croatia	D	D	D	D	D	D
Cyprus	37.6	52.5	29.9	35.8	50.0	41.0
Czech Republic	87.1	87.9	99.6	99.6	96.0	96.0
Denmark	100.0	100.0	100.0	100.0	95.0	95.0
Estonia	98.1	98.1	100.0	100.0	96.2	95.9
Finland	100.0	100.0	100.0	100.0	89.2	89.0
France	D	D	90.3	92.8	D	79.0
Georgia	100.0	100.0	100.0	100.0	92.8	92.9
Germany	100.0	100.0	100.0	100.0	D	D
Greece	86.6	88.7	87.8	89.3	74.0	75.0
Hong Kong (China)	55.4	55.5	23.2	20.7	D	D
Hungary	86.5	86.6	99.3	99.3	93.3	95.4
Iceland	D	D	D	D	D	D
India	D	D	D	D	48.0	51.0
Indonesia	100.0	100.0	100.0	100.0	54.1	66.1
Ireland	94.6	96.9	93.9	94.4	95.6	95.1
Israel	34.0	41.0	36.0	42.0	70.6	67.0
Italy	66.0	67.0	96.0	96.0	89.0	89.0
Japan	23.2	25.6	D	D	84.0	84.0
Kenya	75.0	80.0	60.0	58.4	72.7	71.1
Korea	68.9	75.7	45.6	50.4	D	D
Latvia	100.0	100.0	100.0	100.0	86.0	83.0
Lithuania	100.0	100.0	100.0	100.0	99.0	97.7
Luxembourg	100.0	100.0	100.0	100.0	41.0	40.0
Malaysia	43.7	56.0	47.4	52.3	22.1	18.1
Malta	16.0	21.0	17.0	19.0	83.4	83.3
Mexico	34.0	35.0	94.0	93.0	42.9	43.7

Electronic payment proportions and third party withholding						
	Percentage electronic payments by number		Percentage electronic payments by value		Estimated percentage of total personal income tax withheld by third parties and subsequently paid to the administration	
Jurisdiction	2018	2019	2018	2019	2018	2019
Morocco	55.5	64.2	80.8	85.2	75.0	80.0
Netherlands	100.0	100.0	100.0	100.0	99.2	98.3
New Zealand [1]	91.0	93.0	97.0	97.0	86.4	86.0
Norway	100.0	100.0	100.0	100.0	93.7	93.5
Peru	51.6	54.5	76.4	77.8	99.3	99.4
Poland	98.9	98.4	99.9	99.9	73.8	72.2
Portugal	84.0	86.0	89.0	91.0	84.1	84.1
Romania	47.2	53.9	84.0	86.3	83.0	81.1
Russia	D	D	D	D	94.8	94.4
Saudi Arabia	98.3	99.0	98.0	99.0	0.0	0.0
Singapore	97.1	97.7	83.5	86.1	D	D
Slovak Republic	100.0	100.0	100.0	100.0	97.8	97.3
Slovenia	100.0	100.0	100.0	100.0	82.8	81.3
South Africa	85.5	98.5	84.1	99.9	95.5	95.8
Spain	100.0	100.0	100.0	100.0	84.1	67.9
Sweden	100.0	100.0	100.0	100.0	D	D
Switzerland	D	D	D	D	D	D
Thailand	D	44.4	D	59.6	90.3	90.4
Turkey	62.5	63.1	81.3	80.5	D	D
United Kingdom	95.0	95.7	98.1	98.6	D	D
United States	D	D	D	D	78.7	79.1

StatLink http://dx.doi.org/10.1787/888934272233

1. New Zealand: Percentages of electronic payments refer to Goods and Services Tax only.

Formula	Percentage electronic payments by number [A.47]	Percentage electronic payments by value [A.47]	Estimated percentage of total personal income tax withheld by third parties and subsequently paid to the administration [A.26]

Table D.19 **Arrears: Closing stock, collectable arrears, and arrears relating to state owned enterprises**

Closing stock of arrears, collectible arrears, and arrears relating to state owned enterprises								
	Closing stock of arrears at year end as percentage of total revenue collected [1]		Closing stock of collectable arrears as percentage of closing stock of arrears		Closing stock of arrears relating to state owned enterprises as percentage of closing stock of arrears		Closing stock of collectable arrears relating to state owned enterprises as percentage of closing stock of arrears relating to state owned enterprises	
Jurisdiction	**2018**	**2019**	**2018**	**2019**	**2018**	**2019**	**2018**	**2019**
Argentina	3.6	3.3	D	D	D	D	D	D
Australia	10.3	10.8	58.7	58.4	0.0	0.1	89.7	97.5
Austria	7.9	7.6	44.8	42.5	D	D	D	D
Belgium	15.2	15.5	84.3	84.7	0.8	0.1	0.2	0.8
Brazil	156.4	149.1	100.0	100.0	0.0	0.0		
Bulgaria	27.1	23.8	55.6	54.1	0.6	0.4	100.0	100.0
Canada	13.4	13.4	66.6	64.9	D	D	D	D
Chile	105.4	102.1	76.9	85.3	0.2	0.2	95.4	100.0
China (People's Republic of)	D	D	D	D	D	D	D	D
Colombia	15.6	15.2	62.6	68.9	0.0	0.0		
Costa Rica	5.4	8.1	70.0	88.0	0.1	0.5	70.0	88.0
Croatia	19.9	16.6	15.7	14.5	D	D	D	D
Cyprus	45.5	45.0	43.2	43.2	0.9	1.1	D	D
Czech Republic	16.8	16.8	28.8	23.0	D	D		
Denmark	8.0	8.4	52.9	60.7	43.7	45.3	42.3	73.8
Estonia	6.1	6.3	85.1	87.8	D	D	D	D
Finland [2]	5.7	5.0	57.3	49.6	D	D	D	D
France	6.6	6.4	D	D	D	D	D	D
Georgia	57.9	62.0	19.0	21.6	5.0	4.5	54.4	58.0
Germany	1.1	1.1	44.4	D	D	D	D	D
Greece 3	225.7	212.3	81.6	78.6	11.2	10.7	99.6	99.6
Hong Kong (China)	12.1	13.3	52.8	56.6	0.0	0.0		
Hungary	13.8	12.5	29.0	30.8	D	D	D	D
Iceland	20.3	17.2	D	D	D	D	D	D
India	102.3	140.0	D	D	D	D	D	D
Indonesia	6.1	D	39.6	D	5.2	D	60.9	D
Ireland	6.5	6.0	23.6	21.3	0.3	0.1	62.4	76.2
Israel	20.5	23.9	74.3	71.9	D	D	D	D
Italy	191.6	200.7	5.0	5.0	D	D	D	D
Japan [4]	1.5	1.4	D	D	D	D	D	D
Kenya	23.8	29.7	22.7	23.2	D	10.2	D	D
Korea	7.0	7.3	54.4	52.4	D	D	D	D
Latvia	11.2	8.8	24.9	24.5	0.0	0.0	100.0	100.0
Lithuania	5.8	4.8	35.4	40.9	1.4	1.4	17.6	19.8
Luxembourg [5]	11.8	12.8	D	D	D	D	D	D
Malaysia	8.3	7.9	90.9	94.5	0.0	0.0		
Malta	102.4	117.6	8.8	10.1	D	D	D	D
Mexico	23.5	21.3	89.1	89.3	0.2	0.2	99.4	99.5

Closing stock of arrears, collectible arrears, and arrears relating to state owned enterprises								
	Closing stock of arrears at year end as percentage of total revenue collected [1]		Closing stock of collectable arrears as percentage of closing stock of arrears		Closing stock of arrears relating to state owned enterprises as percentage of closing stock of arrears		Closing stock of collectable arrears relating to state owned enterprises as percentage of closing stock of arrears relating to state owned enterprises	
Jurisdiction	2018	2019	2018	2019	2018	2019	2018	2019
Morocco	D	D	D	D	D	D	D	D
Netherlands	5.1	6.1	56.5	44.0	D	D	D	D
New Zealand	6.1	6.6	74.5	80.8	D	D	D	D
Norway	2.9	2.8	84.6	85.0	D	D	D	D
Peru	129.9	120.4	29.2	35.3	2.7	2.7	77.3	83.0
Poland	31.3	31.0	D	D	0.0	0.0	100.0	99.8
Portugal	36.8	37.1	31.7	29.7	0.0	0.5	0.0	0.0
Romania	44.4	43.0	15.6	17.5	12.8	13.3	3.7	10.2
Russia	7.0	6.1	99.4	99.7	D	D	D	D
Saudi Arabia	D	49.0	D	100.0	D	0.0	D	0.0
Singapore	1.7	1.6	D	D	D	D	D	D
Slovak Republic	28.2	27.4	7.3	7.4	0.0	0.0	9.1	0.0
Slovenia	7.3	6.8	56.8	53.9	0.1	0.3	4.4	54.4
South Africa	11.8	12.5	76.1	81.6	0.6	0.4	14.6	23.6
Spain	9.6	9.1	D	D	D	D	D	D
Sweden 6	0.2	0.1	D	D	D	D	D	D
Switzerland	D	D	D	D	D	D	D	D
Thailand	24.3	25.2	65.4	56.4	D	D	D	D
Turkey	D	D	D	D	D	D	D	D
United Kingdom	2.4	2.5	83.6	82.5	D	D	D	D
United States	8.2	8.3	41.0	40.4	0.0	0.0		

StatLink http://dx.doi.org/10.1787/888934272252

1. Note: To improve comparability with previous ISORA rounds' data and indicators, VAT (gross imports) has been removed from the total net revenue collected.
2. Finland: VAT (gross imports) cannot be separated from VAT (gross domestic). As a result, total net revenue collected includes VAT (gross imports).
3. Greece: Arrears do not include interest and penalties.
4. Japan: VAT (gross imports) cannot be separated from VAT (gross domestic). As a result, total net revenue collected includes VAT (gross imports).
5. Luxembourg: VAT (gross imports) cannot be separated from VAT (gross domestic). As a result, total net revenue collected includes VAT (gross imports).
6. Sweden: VAT (gross imports) cannot be separated from VAT (gross domestic). As a result, total net revenue collected includes VAT (gross imports).

Formula	Closing stock of arrears at year-end [A.31] / (Total net revenue collected [A.2] - VAT (gross imports) [A.5]) * 100	(Closing stock of arrears at year-end [A.31] - Closing stock of arrears considered non-collectable at year-end [A.31]) / Closing stock of arrears at year-end [A.31]	Total arrears relating to state owned enterprises [A.31] / Closing stock of arrears at year-end [A.31]	(Total arrears relating to state owned enterprises [A.31] - Arrears relating to state owned enterprises considered not collectable [A.31]) / Total arrears relating to state owned enterprises [A.31]

Table D.20 **Arrears in relation to collection by tax type**

	Arrears in relation to collection by tax type							
	CIT arrears as percentage of CIT collected		PIT arrears as percentage of PIT collected		PAYE arrears as percentage of PIT collected		VAT arrears as percentage of VAT collected	
Jurisdiction	**2018**	**2019**	**2018**	**2019**	**2018**	**2019**	**2018**	**2019**
Argentina	1.9	2.0	4.1	3.4	21.8	15.6	3.1	3.2
Australia	9.7	9.9	5.1	5.1	3.0	3.2	8.7	8.7
Austria	9.6	8.9	3.9	3.7	0.8	0.8	8.7	8.0
Belgium	41.8	42.9	4.9	5.0	1.1	1.1	18.7	19.2
Brazil	250.5	218.6	34.0	26.3	91.9	79.0	111.0	123.6
Bulgaria[1]	23.4	22.0	19.1	17.3	D	D	20.1	18.4
Canada	21.7	22.1	11.3	11.2	1.3	1.3	22.6	23.4
Chile	70.3	72.5	171.9	128.4	D	D	80.3	79.3
China (People's Republic of)	D	D	D	D	D	D	D	D
Colombia	7.1	7.6	11.1	12.3	D	D	5.6	5.9
Costa Rica	7.9	9.6	5.8	6.2	0.5	1.0	4.0	8.8
Croatia[2]	7.7	8.9	23.7	19.8	D	D	11.9	10.1
Cyprus	80.9	84.7	29.3	28.6	21.3	21.9	29.6	29.1
Czech Republic	3.4	1.2	1.4	1.2	0.4	0.3	6.7	5.1
Denmark	10.2	10.4	8.1	8.2	4.9	5.2	5.1	5.2
Estonia	5.3	4.8	0.7	0.6	1.2	1.1	6.7	6.3
Finland	13.2	6.9	2.2	2.2	2.0	2.0	9.6	8.6
France	D	D	D	D		D	D	D
Georgia	D	D	D	D	D	D	D	D
Germany	D	D	D	D	D	D	D	D
Greece[3]	365.9	309.3	102.0	80.2	2.6	2.3	159.1	150.2
Hong Kong (China)	24.7	24.0	8.8	9.1				
Hungary	13.3	13.6	7.1	6.1	3.7	3.2	15.9	13.1
Iceland	9.3	5.6	12.9	11.5	D	D	21.4	16.0
India	86.2	120.9	129.9	170.3	0.8	0.9		
Indonesia	2.7	D	1.1	D	0.8	D	4.4	D
Ireland	24.6	26.1	3.0	2.1	1.8	1.0	3.7	3.4
Israel	D	D	D	D	8.1	8.0	12.5	16.8
Italy	D	D	D	D	D	D	D	D
Japan	0.8	0.7	1.3	1.2	0.7	0.6	1.9	1.8
Kenya	D	D	D	D	D	D	D	D
Korea	1.0	1.0	2.8	2.9	0.3	0.3	5.5	5.8
Latvia	23.9	127.3	12.3	10.6	12.9	9.8	18.1	12.4
Lithuania	2.7	3.3	3.7	2.2	0.4	0.2	4.0	3.7
Luxembourg	26.5	31.4	3.4	3.2	D	D	18.8	17.2
Malaysia	7.4	6.0	10.5	12.4	D	D		
Malta	70.3	66.0	31.5	30.2	14.9	16.4	293.8	369.9
Mexico	37.4	39.0	5.6	5.0	4.3	4.4	14.6	13.4
Morocco	D	D	D	D	D	D	D	D

	Arrears in relation to collection by tax type							
	CIT arrears as percentage of CIT collected		PIT arrears as percentage of PIT collected		PAYE arrears as percentage of PIT collected		VAT arrears as percentage of VAT collected	
Jurisdiction	**2018**	**2019**	**2018**	**2019**	**2018**	**2019**	**2018**	**2019**
Netherlands	18.5	28.4	6.1	5.8	2.3	2.5	5.9	5.6
New Zealand[4]	D	D	4.4	4.0	1.0	1.2	2.9	4.0
Norway	7.2	7.3	5.1	4.9	0.1	0.1	2.1	2.1
Peru	104.1	99.1	26.6	22.2	14.8	15.0	63.6	61.3
Poland	14.2	12.5	11.0	9.9	1.6	1.5	51.4	52.3
Portugal	84.2	88.6	16.8	17.0	0.4	0.7	41.1	40.1
Romania	93.6	85.5	22.9	24.8	D	D	71.5	66.6
Russia	5.1	4.2	0.9	0.8	2.3	2.0	18.9	14.5
Saudi Arabia	0.0	0.0					0.0	0.0
Singapore	0.8	0.7	2.1	2.1			2.9	3.1
Slovak Republic	19.1	20.1	2.7	3.3	0.7	0.6	36.8	33.7
Slovenia	7.0	6.5	11.6	11.2	13.8	11.8	11.1	10.5
South Africa	16.3	15.8	7.0	7.2	9.2	10.4	5.0	5.4
Spain	18.7	18.8	3.2	3.1	2.1	1.8	11.2	10.5
Sweden	D	D	D	D	D	D	D	D
Switzerland	D	D	D	D	D	D	D	D
Thailand	8.0	8.0	35.6	36.1	D	D	28.1	32.1
Turkey	D	D	D	D	D	D	D	D
United Kingdom	3.7	4.2	2.4	2.5	1.2	1.4	2.3	2.6
United States	19.1	19.2	13.1	13.3	D	D		

StatLink http://dx.doi.org/10.1787/888934272271

1. Bulgaria: PIT arrears includes PAYE arrears.
2. Croatia: PIT arrears includes PAYE arrears.
3. Greece: Arrears do not include interest and penalties.
4. New Zealand: Corporate income tax arrears are included in personal income tax arrears.

Formula	CIT Total arrears at year-end [A.32] / Income tax - corporate and other entities [A.3] * 100	PIT Total arrears at year-end [A.32] / Income tax - individuals [A.3] * 100	Tax withheld from employees by employers Total arrears at year-end [A.32] / Income tax - individuals [A.3] * 100	VAT Total arrears at year-end [A.32] / Value added tax [A.4] * 100

Table D.21 **Arrears: Movement between 2018 and 2019**

Jurisdiction	Total year-end arrears 2019 / total year-end arrears 2018 (including non-collectible arrears) (in %)	Total year-end arreas 2019 / total year-end arrears 2018 (excluding non-collectible arrears) (in %)
Argentina	127.4	D
Australia	112.4	111.7
Austria	98.6	93.5
Belgium	101.0	101.5
Brazil	100.0	100.0
Bulgaria	99.8	97.3
Canada	106.0	103.3
Chile	97.4	108.0
China (People's Republic of)	D	D
Colombia	105.9	116.7
Costa Rica	165.3	207.8
Croatia	88.9	82.6
Cyprus	110.0	109.9
Czech Republic	106.6	85.1
Denmark	107.7	123.6
Estonia	109.8	113.2
Finland	90.1	78.1
France	92.5	D
Georgia	114.2	129.9
Germany	111.1	D
Greece	101.2	97.5
Hong Kong (China)	114.7	122.8
Hungary	98.8	104.8
Iceland	86.1	D
India	155.3	D
Indonesia	D	D
Ireland	98.5	88.9
Israel	121.1	117.1
Italy	107.0	107.0
Japan	95.2	D
Kenya	136.0	138.9
Korea	105.6	101.6
Latvia	82.8	81.5
Lithuania	103.9	120.1
Luxembourg	116.2	D
Malaysia	99.5	103.4
Malta	123.4	140.9
Mexico	95.4	95.6
Morocco	D	D
Netherlands	127.0	99.1
New Zealand	117.7	127.7

Jurisdiction	Total year-end arrears 2019 / total year-end arrears 2018 (including non-collectible arrears) (in %)	Total year-end arreas 2019 / total year-end arrears 2018 (excluding non-collectible arrears) (in %)
Norway	104.4	104.9
Peru	99.7	120.3
Poland	104.5	D
Portugal	105.7	98.9
Romania	107.6	120.6
Russia	94.0	94.3
Saudi Arabia	D	D
Singapore	102.2	D
Slovak Republic	102.9	103.7
Slovenia	98.0	93.1
South Africa	110.5	118.6
Spain	96.0	D
Sweden	62.2	D
Switzerland	D	D
Thailand	107.5	92.6
Turkey	D	D
United Kingdom	109.6	108.1
United States	104.1	102.4

StatLink http://dx.doi.org/10.1787/888934272290

Formula	Closing stock of arrears at year-end 2019 [A.31] / Closing stock of arrears at year-end 2018 [A.31] * 100	(Closing stock of arrears at year-end 2019 [A.31] - Closing stock of arrears considered non-collectible at year-end 2019 [A.31]) / (Closing stock of arrears at year-end 2018 [A.31] - Closing stock of arrears considered non-collectible at year-end 2018 [A.31]) *100

Table D.22 **Audits: Hit rate and additional assessments raised**

	Audit hit rate and additional assessments raised [1]							
	Audit hit rate		Additional assessments raised through audit as percentage of tax collections		Additional assessment raised through electronic compliance checks as percentage of tax collections		Additional assessments raised through all audits and verification actions as percentage of tax collections	
Jurisdiction	**2018**	**2019**	**2018**	**2019**	**2018**	**2019**	**2018**	**2019**
Argentina	63.7	65.3	2.3	2.4	D	D	D	D
Australia	10.6	12.3	4.3	3.6	D	D	D	D
Austria	27.5	27.5	1.7	1.4	0.4	0.3	2.1	1.8
Belgium	29.3	27.6	7.7	6.5	D	D	D	D
Brazil	99.6	99.7	22.1	22.8	0.0	0.0	22.1	22.8
Bulgaria	88.8	88.1	9.0	7.4	D	D	D	D
Canada	58.0	58.6	4.6	4.5	D	D	D	D
Chile	22.4	21.1	5.2	5.1	3.1	2.9	8.3	8.0
China (People's Republic of)	D	D	D	D	D	D	D	D
Colombia	87.2	78.7	1.5	1.5	D	D	D	D
Costa Rica	71.2	55.4	6.7	4.8	0.0	0.0	6.7	4.8
Croatia	57.0	70.0	1.7	1.7	D	D	D	D
Cyprus	D	D	10.8	11.9	D	D	D	D
Czech Republic [2]	44.6	44.6	1.7	1.2	0.1	0.1	1.8	1.3
Denmark	66.4	69.3	1.0	0.6	D	D	D	D
Estonia	28.1	32.5	1.1	0.6	22.6	23.1	23.7	23.7
Finland	D	D	D	D	D	D	D	D
France	D	D	5.1	4.4	D	D	D	D
Georgia	92.7	67.9	11.4	20.2	0.1	0.0	11.5	20.3
Germany	73.4	72.7	2.6	2.7	0.0	0.0	2.6	2.7
Greece	46.4	47.9	4.5	3.6	1.1	1.2	5.7	4.7
Hong Kong (China)	29.4	35.8	0.9	0.9	D	D	D	D
Hungary	56.5	61.0	2.8	2.3	0.2	0.3	3.0	2.7
Iceland	D	D	D	D	D	D	D	D
India	D	D	18.0	40.7	D	D	D	D
Indonesia	50.8	34.3	9.4	7.2	0.0	0.0	9.4	7.2
Ireland	27.9	21.7	1.0	0.9	0.1	0.1	1.1	1.0
Israel	71.9	74.8	7.0	7.5	0.1	0.1	7.1	7.6
Italy	90.4	90.2	8.4	8.2	0.1	0.1	8.5	8.3
Japan	D	D	D	D	D	D	D	D
Kenya	74.9	81.5	2.2	5.7	0.6	0.4	2.7	6.1
Korea	D	D	2.8	2.8	D	D	D	D
Latvia	83.1	76.2	2.0	1.2	D	D	D	D
Lithuania	22.4	22.8	0.7	0.7	D	D	D	D
Luxembourg [3]	D	D	0.6	0.6	D	D	D	D
Malaysia	26.8	35.5	8.6	14.0	0.0	0.0	8.6	14.0
Malta	58.1	63.0	1.4	1.9	0.4	0.5	1.8	2.4
Mexico	D	D	D	D	D	D	8.2	9.3

Audit hit rate and additional assessments raised [1]								
	Audit hit rate		Additional assessments raised through audit as percentage of tax collections		Additional assessment raised through electronic compliance checks as percentage of tax collections		Additional assessments raised through all audits and verification actions as percentage of tax collections	
Jurisdiction	2018	2019	2018	2019	2018	2019	2018	2019
Morocco	98.4	98.4	5.7	5.2	5.6	4.0	11.3	9.2
Netherlands [4]	25.4	24.9	2.7	2.4	0.3	0.2	3.0	2.6
New Zealand	D	D	D	D	D	D	D	D
Norway	4.6	5.2	3.0	2.8	D	D	D	D
Peru	61.5	62.1	5.4	6.4	0.0	0.0	5.4	6.4
Poland	D	D	5.6	4.7	D	D	D	D
Portugal	64.5	62.6	3.6	3.2	0.0	0.0	3.6	3.2
Romania	88.8	87.7	4.3	3.2	D	D	D	D
Russia	97.7	96.2	1.5	1.3	0.0	0.0	1.5	1.3
Saudi Arabia	48.5	70.3	16.3	9.3	0.0	0.0	16.3	9.3
Singapore	D	D	D	D	D	D	D	D
Slovak Republic	69.1	75.5	6.0	7.0	D	D	D	D
Slovenia	8.8	12.1	D	D	D	D	D	D
South Africa	43.6	71.4	0.8	1.3	2.6	2.1	3.4	3.4
Spain	D	D	7.7	7.9	0.0	0.0	7.7	7.9
Sweden [5]	60.6	65.9	0.5	0.5	D	D	D	D
Switzerland	D	D	D	D	D	D	D	D
Thailand	35.9	40.2	1.7	1.8	D	D	D	D
Turkey	45.2	44.5	5.7	6.2	0.0	0.0	5.7	6.2
United Kingdom	D	D	5.9	6.8	D	D	D	D
United States	96.0	97.0	1.4	0.9	0.0	0.0	1.4	0.9

StatLink http://dx.doi.org/10.1787/888934272309

1. Note: To improve comparability with previous ISORA rounds' data and indicators, VAT (gross imports) has been removed from the total net revenue collected.
2. Czech Republic: The value of assessments raised does not include penalties and interest. Only VAT is reported as regards electronic compliance checks.
3. Luxembourg: VAT (gross imports) cannot be separated from VAT (gross domestic). As a result, total net revenue collected includes VAT (gross imports).
4. Netherlands: The value of assessments raised does not include penalties and interest.
5. Sweden: VAT (gross imports) cannot be separated from VAT (gross domestic). As a result, total net revenue collected includes VAT (gross imports).

Formula	No. of audits where a tax adjustment was made [A.33] / No. of audits completed [A.33] * 100	Value of additional assessments from all audits (excluding electronic compliance checks) in FY [A.34] / (Total net revenue collected [A.2] - VAT (gross imports) [A.5] - Non-tax revenue [A.6] - Social security contributions [A.6]) * 100	Value of additional assessments in FY from electronic compliance checks [A.34] / (Total net revenue collected [A.2] - VAT (gross imports) [A.5] - Non-tax revenue [A.6] - Social security contributions [A.6]) * 100	Total value of additional assessments in FY [A.34] / (Total net revenue collected [A.2] - VAT (gross imports) [A.5] - Non-tax revenue [A.6] - Social security contributions [A.6]) * 100

Table D.23 **Audits: Additional assessments raised by tax type**

	Additional assessments raised through audit by tax type							
	CIT assessements as percentage of CIT collected		PIT assessments as percentage of PIT collected		PAYE assessments as percentage of PIT collected		VAT assessments as percentage of VAT collected	
Jurisdiction	**2018**	**2019**	**2018**	**2019**	**2018**	**2019**	**2018**	**2019**
Argentina	3.25	2.94	1.40	1.30	4.67	5.49	1.20	1.32
Australia	D	D	D	D	D	D	D	D
Austria	3.17	2.81	0.49	0.49	0.23	0.14	1.75	1.22
Belgium	19.31	15.74	8.26	6.66	D	D	2.69	3.31
Brazil	46.90	51.67	2.56	3.87	12.31	6.81	9.52	10.67
Bulgaria	9.89	5.66	1.00	0.67	0.49	0.41	7.09	6.88
Canada	12.05	11.94	1.56	1.47	0.07	0.07	10.15	9.98
Chile	8.81	7.94	0.61	0.73	D	D	1.35	1.68
China (People's Republic of)	D	D	D	D	D	D	D	D
Colombia	2.66	2.48	0.98	0.63	0.83	0.44	0.21	0.61
Costa Rica	20.98	15.65	3.11	0.63	D	D	0.50	1.08
Croatia	0.71	2.79	1.45	1.72	D	D	0.87	0.95
Cyprus	39.40	41.87	D	D	D	D	1.62	3.27
Czech Republic [1]	1.33	1.23	0.06	0.06	0.03	0.04	2.78	1.86
Denmark	6.08	-0.04	0.51	0.49	D	D	1.47	1.15
Estonia	D	D	D	D	D	D	D	D
Finland	D	D	D	D	D	D	D	D
France [2]	13.34	9.03	3.30	2.48		D	2.05	1.98
Georgia	21.13	12.19	2.49	4.48	D	D	3.82	7.48
Germany	2.64	3.77	0.87	0.80	0.26	0.25	1.51	1.35
Greece	17.76	11.98	3.71	2.96	0.03	0.05	3.86	3.14
Hong Kong (China)	1.61	1.41	1.04	1.17				
Hungary	0.91	7.74	0.30	0.32	0.56	0.57	6.05	4.18
Iceland	D	D	D	D	D	D	D	D
India	23.32	50.21	11.61	28.11	D	D		
Indonesia	6.62	D	0.42	D	1.01	D	8.01	D
Ireland	0.78	0.73	0.65	0.55	0.63	0.40	0.89	0.65
Israel	12.10	11.92	5.12	5.78	1.06	1.21	4.57	5.07
Italy	31.43	34.90	3.76	3.20	0.66	0.53	15.76	16.63
Japan	1.62	1.58	0.50	0.48	0.16	0.19	0.64	0.69
Kenya	6.29	31.59	0.35	0.67	0.46	0.16	3.63	4.30
Korea	6.38	6.14	1.80	1.94	D	D	0.43	0.48
Latvia	6.42	16.93	0.14	0.12	1.28	0.44	2.75	1.98
Lithuania	0.85	1.75	0.59	0.72	D	D	0.95	0.73
Luxembourg	D	D	D	D	D	D	2.25	2.24
Malaysia	9.27	15.80	8.31	12.24	0.57	0.45		
Malta	2.25	2.76	1.11	11.65	D	D	1.12	1.97
Mexico	D	D	D	D	D	D	D	D
Morocco	8.87	8.12	1.47	1.79	3.83	2.21	1.92	2.26

	Additional assessments raised through audit by tax type							
	CIT assessments as percentage of CIT collected		PIT assessments as percentage of PIT collected		PAYE assessments as percentage of PIT collected		VAT assessments as percentage of VAT collected	
Jurisdiction	2018	2019	2018	2019	2018	2019	2018	2019
Netherlands[3]	9.28	9.57	2.08	1.24	0.09	0.13	1.56	1.45
New Zealand	D	D	D	D	D	D	D	D
Norway[4]	19.63	24.84	3.25	1.68	0.12	0.10	0.30	0.24
Peru	13.20	10.85	2.29	2.08	0.00	0.00	1.11	4.44
Poland	3.52	3.46	2.46	2.28	D	D	9.24	7.56
Portugal	11.87	12.76	0.98	0.69	0.38	0.33	3.98	3.22
Romania	9.68	6.75	0.56	0.60	2.90	2.05	4.66	3.45
Russia	2.94	1.86	0.09	0.04	0.12	0.05	4.07	2.29
Saudi Arabia	67.56	26.89					4.80	6.72
Singapore	0.54	0.59	0.37	0.44			1.79	1.61
Slovak Republic	5.27	11.50	0.27	1.36	0.00	0.02	7.32	6.00
Slovenia	D	D	D	D	D	D	D	D
South Africa	2.13	4.84	0.39	0.18	0.19	0.18	0.23	0.58
Spain	D	D	D	D	D	D	D	D
Sweden	D	D	D	D	D	D	D	D
Switzerland	D	D	D	D	D	D	D	D
Thailand	0.71	1.33	3.39	2.30	D	D	1.41	1.28
Turkey	2.88	3.58	0.41	0.34	0.51	0.27	9.62	12.75
United Kingdom	6.99	5.34	2.30	2.63	0.62	0.71	6.78	10.27
United States	7.10	3.64	0.57	0.43	0.05	0.07		

StatLink http://dx.doi.org/10.1787/888934272328

1. Czech Republic: The value of assessments raised does not include penalties and interest.
2. France: The value of assessments raised does not include penalties and interest.
3. Netherlands: The value of assessments raised does not include penalties and interest.
4. Norway: The values of CIT and PIT assessments raised do not include penalties and interest.

Formula	CIT Total additional assessments from audits in FY [A.35] / Income tax - corporate and other entities [A.3] * 100	PIT Total additional assessments from audits in FY [A.35] / Income tax - individuals [A.3] * 100	Tax withheld from employees by employers Total additional assessments from audits in FY [A.35] / Income tax - individuals [A.3] * 100	VAT Total additional assessments from audits in FY [A.35] / Value added tax [A.4] * 100

Table D.24 **Administrative review cases & litigation**

Administrative review cases & litigation						
	No. of internal cases initiated during the FY per 1 000 active taxpayers (PIT and CIT)		Ratio of cases under independent review to internal review cases		Number of cases resolved by higher appelate court in favour of the administration as percentage of cases resolved	
Jurisdiction	2018	2019	2018	2019	2018	2019
Argentina	0.03	0.03	9.67	15.98	69.88	71.54
Australia	0.87	0.98	0.12	0.10	73.33	75.00
Austria	10.71	10.22	0.82	0.90	D	D
Belgium	5.74	6.36	0.04	0.06	80.41	91.33
Brazil	2.19	2.34	0.48	0.44	D	D
Bulgaria	0.83	0.57	0.45	0.30	77.71	82.90
Canada	D	D	0.08	0.10	42.93	94.59
Chile	0.40	0.30	1.08	0.95	76.40	68.55
China (People's Republic of)	D	D	D	D	D	D
Colombia	0.70	0.60	2.31	1.93		
Costa Rica	D	D	D	D	45.53	45.12
Croatia	3.98	3.77			63.48	51.64
Cyprus	13.23	16.70	0.02	0.02	55.56	73.91
Czech Republic	2.23	1.82	0.71	0.70	47.32	44.17
Denmark					D	D
Estonia	0.24	0.17	13.18	21.00	87.67	88.24
Finland	19.38	25.64	D	D	D	D
France	53.25	56.66	0.16	0.16	68.26	60.20
Georgia	6.45	6.11	8.61	3.65	63.33	52.83
Germany	54.68	54.72	D	D	D	D
Greece	0.82	0.76	5.47	6.48	27.27	42.86
Hong Kong (China)	22.40	25.69	0.00	0.00	50.00	0.00
Hungary	0.81	0.78	1.55	2.25	78.60	75.68
Iceland	65.32	D	D	D	D	D
India	0.41	0.42	0.30	0.27	D	D
Indonesia	D	D	11.25	7.51	22.81	24.34
Ireland	0.00	0.00	3 459.00	842.50	0.00	60.00
Israel	0.24	0.26			D	D
Italy	3.60	3.23	8.09	6.23	9.78	6.71
Japan	D	D	0.07	0.07	92.45	97.37
Kenya	0.02	0.05	25.44	11.80		
Korea	0.42	0.44	3.01	3.48	34.91	30.09
Latvia	0.66	0.55			D	D
Lithuania	0.15	0.12	0.55	0.45	51.49	73.97
Luxembourg	D	D	D	D	D	D
Malaysia	0.05	0.03	5.81	4.39	75.00	47.62
Malta	0.03	0.06	0.74	0.77	69.23	57.89
Mexico	0.18	0.15	16.04	13.11	24.38	27.13

Administrative review cases & litigation						
	No. of internal cases initiated during the FY per 1 000 active taxpayers (PIT and CIT)		Ratio of cases under independent review to internal review cases		Number of cases resolved by higher appelate court in favour of the administration as percentage of cases resolved	
Jurisdiction	**2018**	**2019**	**2018**	**2019**	**2018**	**2019**
Morocco	97.03	66.91	0.05	0.02	32.57	27.39
Netherlands	45.17	39.86	0.07	0.08	84.06	78.91
New Zealand	0.01	0.01	4.00	7.43	88.89	50.00
Norway	2.34	1.40	1.54	1.27	81.63	88.57
Peru	3.39	3.79	1.08	0.74	78.62	69.76
Poland	6.67	D	D	D	D	D
Portugal	9.47	10.03	3.30	3.46	50.00	48.37
Romania	D	D	4.79	11.48	64.89	67.17
Russia	6.01	6.22	D	D	83.61	83.74
Saudi Arabia [1]	4 781.01	11 158.50			54.34	
Singapore	D	D	D	D	66.67	66.67
Slovak Republic	D	D	0.22	0.43	74.10	68.10
Slovenia	11.58	12.46	0.82	0.82	79.13	73.84
South Africa	22.91	27.69	0.02	0.03	84.62	92.86
Spain	8.94	8.50	7.57	6.59	64.71	64.08
Sweden	18.31	18.22	0.57	0.64	D	D
Switzerland	D	D	D	D	D	D
Thailand	0.07	0.09			D	D
Turkey	D	D	D	D	D	D
United Kingdom	0.84	0.63	7.20	12.54	7.19	4.16
United States	0.60	0.55	D	D	3.62	5.28

StatLink http://dx.doi.org/10.1787/888934272347

1. Saudi Arabia: The number of internal cases initiated during the FY per 1 000 active taxpayers (PIT and CIT) are so high as the number of underlying cases includes Zakat taxpayers which are not part of the PIT and CIT taxpayer base.

Formula	No. of cases initiated during FY [A.38] / (PIT active taxpayers [A.20] + CIT active taxpayers [A.20]) * 1000	No. of tax cases at FY end under independent review by external bodies [A.38] / No. of tax cases at FY end under internal review procedures [A.38]	No. of cases resolved during FY in favor of the administration [A.38] / No. of cases resolved during FY [A.38] * 100

Table A.1. **Revenue types for which the administration has responsibility and employer withholding**

Jurisdiction	Revenue types or categories for which the tax administration has responsibility: Income tax: Individuals		Income tax: Corporate and other entities		Value added tax		Excises (domestic)		Other taxes: Motor vehicle taxes		Other taxes: Real property taxes		Other taxes: Wealth taxes		Other taxes: Estate, inheritance, gift and other taxes		Other taxes: Other taxes on good and services		Other taxes: Other		Social security contributions		Non-tax revenue		Employers withholding taxes on behalf of salaried employees		Joint with Customs?	
	2018	2019	2018	2019	2018	2019	2018	2019	2018	2019	2018	2019	2018	2019	2018	2019	2018	2019	2018	2019	2018	2019	2018	2019	2018	2019	2018	2019
Argentina	■	■	■	■	■	■	■	■					■	■			■	■	■	■	■	■	■	■	■	■	■	■
Australia	■	■	■	■	■	■	■	■	■	■							■	■	■	■			■	■	■	■	□	□
Austria	■	■	■	■	■	■			■	■									■	■					■	■	■	■
Belgium	■	■	■	■	■	■			■	■	■	■			■	■	■	■	■	■			■	■	■	■	■	■
Brazil	■	■	■	■	■	■	■	■			■	■					■	■	■	■	■	■			■	■	■	■
Bulgaria	■	■	■	■	■	■											■	■	■	■	■	■	■	■	■	■	□	□
Canada	■	■	■	■	■	■	■	■											■	■	■	■	■	■	■	■	□	□
Chile	■	■	■	■	■	■	■	■	■	■	■	■			■	■			■	■					■	■	□	□
China (People's Republic of)	■	■	■	■	■	■	■	■	■	■	■	■							■	■	■	■	■	■	■	■	□	□
Colombia	■	■	■	■	■	■	■	■					■	■			■	■	■	■					■	■	■	■
Costa Rica	■	■	■	■	■	■	■	■	■	■	■	■	■	■											■	■	□	□
Croatia	■	■	■	■	■	■			■	■					■	■	■	■	■	■	■	■	■	■	■	■	□	□
Cyprus	■	■	■	■	■	■									■	■			■	■					■	■	□	□
Czech Republic	■	■	■	■	■	■			■	■	■	■			■	■			■	■			■	■	■	■	□	□
Denmark	■	■	■	■	■	■	■	■	■	■	■	■			■	■	■	■	■	■	■	■			■	■	■	■
Estonia	■	■	■	■	■	■	■	■	■	■	■	■								■	■	■	■	■	■	■	■	■
Finland	■	■	■	■	■	■	■	■	■	■	■	■			■	■			■	■	■	■			■	■	□	□
France	■	■	■	■	■	■			■	■	■	■	■	■	■	■	■	■	■	■			■	■	□	■	□	□
Georgia	■	■	■	■	■	■	■	■											■	■					■	■	■	■
Germany	■	■	■	■	■	■					■	■	■	■	■	■	■	■	■	■					■	■	□	□
Greece	■	■	■	■	■	■	■	■	■	■	■	■			■	■	■	■					■	■	■	■	■	■
Hong Kong (China)	■	■	■	■							■	■			■	■			■	■					□	□	□	□

Table A.1. **Revenue types for which the administration has responsibility and employer withholding** *(continued)*

	Revenue types or categories for which the tax administration has responsibility																										Employers withholding taxes on behalf of salaried employees			
	Income tax								Other taxes																					
	Individuals		Corporate and other entities		Value added tax		Excises (domestic)		Motor vehicle taxes		Real property taxes		Wealth taxes		Estate, inheritance, gift and other taxes		Other taxes on good and services		Other		Social security contributions		Non-tax revenue				Joint with Customs?	
Jurisdiction	2018	2019	2018	2019	2018	2019	2018	2019	2018	2019	2018	2019	2018	2019	2018	2019	2018	2019	2018	2019	2018	2019	2018	2019	2018	2019	2018	2019
Hungary	■	■	■	■	■	■	■	■							■	■	■	■	■	■	■	■			■	■	■	■
Iceland	■	■	■	■	■	■			■	■					■	■	■	■	■	■	■	■			■	■	□	□
India	■	■	■	■															■	■					■	■	□	□
Indonesia	■	■	■	■	■	■													■	■					■	■	□	□
Ireland	■	■	■	■	■	■	■	■	■	■	■	■			■	■	■	■			■	■	■	■	■	■	■	■
Israel	■	■	■	■	■	■	■	■	■	■	■	■	■	■			■	■	■	■					■	■	■	■
Italy	■	■	■	■	■	■									■	■			■	■					■	■	□	□
Japan	■	■	■	■	■	■			■	■					■	■	■	■							■	■	□	□
Kenya	■	■	■	■	■	■	■	■	■	■	■	■	■	■	■	■	■	■	■	■			■	■	■	■	■	■
Korea	■	■	■	■	■	■	■	■							■	■			■	■			■	■	■	■	□	□
Latvia	■	■	■	■	■	■	■	■	■	■									■	■	■	■	■	■	■	■	■	■
Lithuania	■	■	■	■	■	■	■	■	■	■	■	■	■	■	■	■	■	■					■	■	■	■	□	□
Luxembourg	■	■	■	■	■	■					■	■	■	■	■	■	■	■	■	■			■	■	■	■	□	□
Malaysia	■	■	■	■							■	■							■	■			■	■	■	■	□	□
Malta	■	■	■	■	■	■			■	■					■	■			■	■	■	■	■	■	■	■	□	□
Mexico	■	■	■	■	■	■	■	■	■	■									■	■			■	■	■	■	■	■
Morocco	■	■	■	■	■	■			■	■									■	■					■	■	□	□
Netherlands	■	■	■	■	■	■			■	■					■	■	■	■	■	■	■	■	■	■	■	■	■	■
New Zealand	■	■	■	■	■	■													■	■			■	■	■	■	□	□
Norway	■	■	■	■	■	■	■	■	■	■			■	■	■	■			■	■	■	■	■	■	■	■	□	□
Peru	■	■	■	■	■	■	■	■					■	■			■	■	■	■	■	■	■	■	■	■	■	■
Poland	■	■	■	■	■	■	■	■							■	■			■	■			■	■	■	■	■	■
Portugal	■	■	■	■	■	■	■	■	■	■	■	■					■	■	■	■			■	■	■	■	■	■
Romania	■	■	■	■	■	■	■	■									■	■	■	■	■	■	■	■	■	■	■	■

Table A.1. **Revenue types for which the administration has responsibility and employer withholding** *(continued)*

	Revenue types or categories for which the tax administration has responsibility																										Employers withholding taxes on behalf of salaried employees		Joint with Customs?	
	Income tax				Value added tax		Excises (domestic)		Other taxes												Social security contributions		Non-tax revenue					
	Individuals		Corporate and other entities						Motor vehicle taxes		Real property taxes		Wealth taxes		Estate, inheritance, gift and other taxes		Other taxes on good and services		Other									
Jurisdiction	2018	2019	2018	2019	2018	2019	2018	2019	2018	2019	2018	2019	2018	2019	2018	2019	2018	2019	2018	2019	2018	2019	2018	2019	2018	2019	2018	2019
Russia	■	■	■	■	■	■	■	■	■	■	■	■					■	■	■	■	■	■	■	■	■	■	□	□
Saudi Arabia			■	■	■	■	■	■											■	■					□	□	□	□
Singapore	■	■	■	■	■	■					■	■			■	■			■	■					□	□	□	□
Slovak Republic	■	■	■	■	■	■			■	■									■	■			■	■	■	■	■	■
Slovenia	■	■	■	■	■	■	■	■	■	■	■	■	■	■	■	■	■	■	■	■	■	■	■	■	■	■	■	■
South Africa	■	■	■	■	■	■	■	■							■	■	■	■	■	■	■	■	■	■	■	■	■	■
Spain	■	■	■	■	■	■	■	■											■	■			■	■	■	■	■	■
Sweden	■	■	■	■	■	■	■	■			■	■							■	■	■	■			■	■	□	□
Switzerland	■	■	■	■	■	■													■	■					■	■	□	□
Thailand	■	■	■	■	■	■									■	■	■	■	■	■					■	■	□	□
Turkey	■	■	■	■	■	■	■	■	■	■					■	■	■	■	■	■					■	■	□	□
United Kingdom	■	■	■	■	■	■	■	■			■	■			■	■			■	■	■	■	■	■	■	■	■	■
United States	■	■	■	■			■	■	■	■					■	■			■	■	■	■			■	■	□	□

StatLink http://dx.doi.org/10.1787/888934272366

■ Yes

□ No

Table A.2. **Net revenue collected by the tax administration: Total**

	Total net revenue collected by the tax administration (in thousands in local currency)	
Jurisdiction	**2018**	**2019**
Argentina	3 462 304 673	4 874 496 097
Australia	397 074 515	425 921 153
Austria	88 203 598	90 893 296
Belgium	114 575 457	113 458 533
Brazil	1 316 295 267	1 382 159 058
Bulgaria	25 489 824	28 136 975
Canada	430 332 316	457 219 829
Chile	33 267 370 025	33 601 031 194
China (People's Republic of)	19 972 493 850	21 655 987 550
Colombia	131 167 827 955	144 051 179 389
Costa Rica	3 912 622 030	4 235 491 540
Croatia	122 231 868	129 130 431
Cyprus	3 790 106	4 171 883
Czech Republic	861 204 471	915 312 947
Denmark	987 502 183	1 008 791 833
Estonia	8 912 494	9 517 829
Finland	68 580 900	70 359 600
France	436 506 197	423 956 009
Georgia	9 996 895	10 809 293
Germany	694 669 721	717 839 394
Greece	48 963 935	55 154 353
Hong Kong (China)	328 619 251	341 441 564
Hungary	14 252 497 700	15 525 090 100
Iceland	746 459 000	762 421 000
India	10 027 384 100	11 377 184 800
Indonesia	1 313 241 933 247	1 353 193 198 130
Ireland	68 709 752	74 141 881
Israel	297 279 590	307 232 273
Italy	390 159 122	398 434 860
Japan	55 302 941 000	56 513 359 000
Kenya	1 435 499 531	1 580 061 751
Korea	284 575 023 000	285 417 077 154
Latvia	9 407 234	9 916 386
Lithuania	8 147 039	10 114 906
Luxembourg	15 265 262	16 348 259
Malaysia	130 033 803	135 710 172
Malta	3 662 891	3 946 598
Mexico	3 895 571 909	4 032 677 446
Morocco	206 072 018	207 571 668
Netherlands	258 132 142	273 762 311
New Zealand	82 398 124	89 736 482

Table A.2. **Net revenue collected by the tax administration: Total** *(continued)*

	Total net revenue collected by the tax administration (in thousands in local currency)	
Jurisdiction	**2018**	**2019**
Norway	1 063 221 536	1 150 722 109
Peru	120 487 417	127 755 318
Poland	378 241 754	398 669 754
Portugal	49 222 338	51 038 048
Romania	242 453 717	269 242 114
Russia	27 745 338 778	29 776 006 488
Saudi Arabia	106 388 180	116 234 218
Singapore	50 226 143	52 426 642
Slovak Republic	13 273 826	13 943 257
Slovenia	16 613 623	17 572 564
South Africa	1 242 532 034	1 315 832 020
Spain	208 684 965	212 807 546
Sweden	2 232 679 151	2 297 116 531
Switzerland	55 773 586	58 020 393
Thailand	1 697 720 659	1 750 490 173
Turkey	621 536 356	673 447 075
United Kingdom	605 819 649	627 895 776
United States	3 001 581 900	3 112 480 051

StatLink http://dx.doi.org/10.1787/888934272385

Table A.3. Net revenue collected by the tax administration by tax type: Income tax

Jurisdiction	Net revenue collected by the tax administration (in thousands in local currency) If USBB			
	Income tax – individuals		Income tax – corporate and other entities	
	2018	2019	2018	2019
Argentina	230 577 489	366 639 687	511 474 897	729 881 547
Australia	206 992 959	223 672 881	100 379 667	109 705 626
Austria	34 530 000	36 396 000	9 162 800	9 384 700
Belgium	45 969 575	44 764 239	19 528 820	19 294 371
Brazil	136 602 438	156 666 573	202 743 290	213 480 928
Bulgaria	3 234 852	3 525 607	2 345 701	2 593 207
Canada	224 820 635	238 216 391	70 113 418	75 238 874
Chile	2 701 415 791	2 937 532 164	11 679 440 540	11 295 293 429
China (People's Republic of)	1 387 196 780	1 038 852 860	3 549 016 220	3 751 557 550
Colombia	12 215 962 644	12 888 179 508	51 827 965 170	54 630 320 332
Costa Rica	483 644 600	535 412 200	915 283 600	955 908 500
Croatia	13 371 647	14 618 499	8 518 878	9 303 537
Cyprus	583 488	609 415	831 821	891 190
Czech Republic	219 894 386	246 640 294	181 278 572	190 874 958
Denmark	471 536 819	491 671 189	61 712 192	67 091 098
Estonia	1 411 185	1 531 587	517 859	509 096
Finland	30 288 800	30 818 000	5 949 400	6 057 100
France	73 009 838	71 743 458	27 386 290	33 465 562
Georgia	3 247 089	3 482 794	736 624	866 289
Germany	309 596 394	324 564 130	97 323 882	94 517 904
Greece	8 077 512	10 440 190	3 007 572	3 631 507
Hong Kong (China)	75 270 013	75 519 924	133 459 326	160 833 150
Hungary	2 177 428 400	2 424 565 200	380 435 300	303 310 900
Iceland	183 396 000	195 301 000	70 981 000	65 883 000
India	4 082 026 800	4 616 517 200	5 712 018 700	6 635 716 200
Indonesia	146 679 023 552	162 699 392 092	602 351 573 533	609 746 704 458
Ireland	21 297 619	22 938 254	10 386 589	10 887 287
Israel	85 728 191	88 756 246	65 633 662	68 645 229
Italy	168 142 000	171 997 000	29 171 000	30 366 000
Japan	18 881 565 000	19 900 578 000	11 995 304 000	12 318 027 000
Kenya	364 103 622	392 692 649	160 059 236	168 783 463
Korea	84 572 734 471	83 700 611 278	71 395 611 764	72 597 278 072
Latvia	1 723 614	1 946 718	304 004	44 777
Lithuania	1 840 347	3 446 158	691 249	759 147
Luxembourg	5 618 025	5 866 391	3 437 040	3 921 156
Malaysia	33 050 179	37 902 221	89 435 944	89 604 538
Malta	907 145	1 020 169	665 998	745 632
Mexico	855 114 357	884 186 968	809 833 508	803 643 118
Morocco	43 804 100	44 335 300	52 119 900	51 741 100
Netherlands	60 184 377	65 772 951	23 655 463	25 949 389

Table A.3. **Net revenue collected by the tax administration by tax type: Income tax** *(continued)*

	Net revenue collected by the tax administration (in thousands in local currency) If USBB			
	Income tax – individuals		Income tax – corporate and other entities	
Jurisdiction	**2018**	**2019**	**2018**	**2019**
New Zealand	37 480 821	40 339 972	15 547 822	17 725 793
Norway	335 965 927	351 798 241	79 244 443	83 677 486
Peru	13 454 072	14 747 162	26 134 664	27 693 389
Poland	59 558 738	65 444 928	34 640 853	39 984 713
Portugal	13 315 923	13 587 605	6 810 424	6 840 275
Romania	22 576 352	23 115 795	18 150 641	20 544 061
Russia	3 652 985 684	3 955 215 621	4 600 274 067	5 116 741 571
Saudi Arabia			16 523 302	17 203 921
Singapore	10 732 223	11 716 204	16 495 817	17 649 927
Slovak Republic	3 217 628	3 534 474	2 787 700	2 700 721
Slovenia	2 455 425	2 626 656	845 734	997 088
South Africa	462 903 133	493 828 780	220 238 556	214 388 377
Spain	82 858 655	86 892 207	24 837 777	23 732 923
Sweden	761 085 553	751 596 905	191 955 598	223 092 626
Switzerland	11 156 566	11 454 534	11 289 311	11 813 348
Thailand	319 200 641	336 508 070	727 222 345	794 351 650
Turkey	138 992 395	162 704 018	78 673 314	78 828 983
United Kingdom	186 000 000	194 000 000	53 300 000	53 500 000
United States	1 574 238 805	1 587 059 261	202 652 958	225 765 409

StatLink http://dx.doi.org/10.1787/888934272404

Table A.4. Net revenue collected by the tax administration by tax type: Value added tax, excises (domestic) and other taxes

Jurisdiction	Net revenue collected by the tax administration (in thousands in local currency)					
	Value added tax (including VAT (gross import) even where collected by customs)		Excises (Domestic)		Other taxes	
	2018	2019	2018	2019	2018	2019
Argentina	1 104 580 290	1 532 596 903	75 323 825	95 832 298	361 106 722	561 616 982
Australia	63 265 148	65 269 562	22 702 968	23 300 321	3 279 220	3 888 221
Austria	29 347 098	30 046 196			15 163 700	15 066 400
Belgium	31 024 414	31 463 399			13 773 602	13 989 095
Brazil	305 318 938	290 821 547	11 938 879	11 992 776	248 448 880	272 766 839
Bulgaria	9 966 988	10 969 736			266 213	265 862
Canada [1]	42 940 492	43 631 505	3 708 749	3 998 776	14 391 599	16 065 543
Chile	16 211 646 000	16 348 943 000	2 106 535 000	2 222 532 000	568 332 694	796 730 601
China (People's Republic of)	7 767 086 820	7 756 789 830	1 080 010 830	1 269 305 890	3 138 892 360	3 315 924 800
Colombia	55 879 110 000	61 938 202 371	3 881 439 487	4 404 758 275	7 363 350 654	10 189 718 903
Costa Rica	1 487 620 010	1 634 985 940	414 622 020	411 399 470	611 451 800	697 785 430
Croatia	51 767 412	54 966 285			3 612 471	3 746 204
Cyprus	1 822 626	2 039 102			552 171	632 176
Czech Republic	413 312 379	431 607 415			40 516 236	41 408 038
Denmark	217 497 897	234 197 010	115 933 595	107 211 508	29 598 742	13 441 432
Estonia	2 312 620	2 454 652	1 040 641	1 066 056	90 720	94 125
Finland	17 760 300	18 950 900	7 414 100	7 197 600	6 407 500	6 637 600
France	171 081 069	174 803 989			73 530 000	68 082 000
Georgia	3 917 490	4 630 474	176 043	143 169	1 919 649	1 686 567
Germany	234 800 469	243 255 526			52 948 976	55 501 834
Greece	14 292 841	15 692 216	7 101 847	7 122 319	12 065 045	9 654 155
Hong Kong (China)	0	0			119 889 912	105 088 490
Hungary	3 928 685 800	4 532 379 000	1 111 884 800	1 176 375 700	2 005 474 500	2 061 159 700
Iceland	231 406 000	242 715 000			164 112 000	161 028 000
India	0	0			233 338 600	124 951 400
Indonesia	537 433 094 789	551 777 415 176			26 778 241 373	28 969 686 404
Ireland	14 207 813	15 167 341	5 433 001	5 865 295	3 307 489	3 453 879
Israel	97 876 300	100 818 000	19 223 000	19 796 000	28 818 437	29 216 798
Italy [2]	89 034 000	91 906 000			103 812 122	104 165 860
Japan	16 043 390 000	15 825 677 000			8 382 682 000	8 469 077 000
Kenya	356 776 808	409 526 230	84 535 089	107 275 130	374 934 332	396 395 461
Korea	70 009 108 134	70 828 267 830	32 738 617 979	31 332 093 839	24 819 395 491	25 954 392 040
Latvia	2 456 969	2 648 347	1 029 214	1 064 055	243 934	238 842
Lithuania	3 540 087	3 775 878	1 420 854	1 465 544	225 255	231 280
Luxembourg	3 723 926	3 948 031			2 299 968	2 420 361
Malaysia	0	0			7 544 968	8 194 950
Malta	927 970	944 741			192 531	189 349
Mexico	922 238 289	933 326 766	347 435 486	460 495 587	127 712 373	120 998 282

Table A.4. **Net revenue collected by the tax administration by tax type: Value added tax, excises (domestic) and other taxes** *(continued)*

	Net revenue collected by the tax administration (in thousands in local currency)					
	Value added tax (including VAT (gross import) even where collected by customs)		Excises (Domestic)		Other taxes	
Jurisdiction	**2018**	**2019**	**2018**	**2019**	**2018**	**2019**
Morocco	88 720 018	88 494 268			21 428 000	23 001 000
Netherlands	52 342 283	56 472 736			24 889 535	27 610 143
New Zealand	28 108 931	29 650 306			425 603	420 784
Norway	295 120 775	305 885 892	92 602 554	90 109 171	111 043 798	162 463 794
Peru	48 031 594	48 444 996	3 508 245	4 964 961	13 460 953	14 911 655
Poland	174 947 071	180 891 751	72 108 486	72 395 920	8 098 695	8 573 408
Portugal	17 414 498	18 628 206	5 170 385	5 443 130	6 212 200	6 224 383
Romania	59 606 124	65 417 176	27 193 167	30 243 891	3 069 747	4 797 468
Russia	3 761 173 371	4 481 741 841	1 493 162 933	1 277 474 684	7 634 597 641	7 672 476 987
Saudi Arabia	55 334 639	58 178 098	12 524 076	14 078 179	22 006 163	26 774 020
Singapore	10 962 571	11 140 464			12 035 532	11 920 047
Slovak Republic	6 316 156	6 830 155			715 918	749 655
Slovenia	3 756 848	3 871 523	1 559 767	1 543 292	856 723	894 898
South Africa	297 997 587	324 765 977	37 355 875	40 829 690	197 968 724	213 877 416
Spain	70 176 790	71 537 923	20 528 164	21 379 728	6 199 684	5 069 108
Sweden	445 643 000	459 887 000	134 295 000	137 940 000	0	0
Switzerland	22 697 291	22 591 343			10 630 418	12 161 168
Thailand	574 750 139	540 273 945			76 547 534	79 356 508
Turkey	178 616 022	180 316 251	133 906 012	147 134 147	91 348 613	104 463 676
United Kingdom	128 619 649	135 595 776	20 300 000	21 300 000	83 000 000	84 900 000
United States	0	0	72 402 321	79 185 812	22 943 348	16 636 554

StatLink http://dx.doi.org/10.1787/888934272423

1. Canada: VAT does not include VAT (gross import)
2. Italy: VAT does not include VAT (gross import)

Table A.5. Composition of value added tax collected by the tax administration

Jurisdiction	Composition of value added tax collected by the tax administration (in thousands in local currency)					
	Value added tax (gross domestic)		Value added tax (gross import) even where collected by customs		Value added tax refunds	
	2018	2019	2018	2019	2018	2019
Argentina	767 719 275	1 097 201 136	360 261 015	481 095 767	23 400 000	45 700 000
Australia	119 142 148	125 075 562	3 900 000	4 200 000	59 777 000	64 006 000
Austria	42 720 890	44 570 270	287 844	276 502	13 661 636	14 800 576
Belgium	46 166 428	47 155 974	455 805	468 730	15 597 819	16 161 305
Brazil	252 235 912	239 132 993	58 957 294	63 250 337	5 874 268	11 561 783
Bulgaria	12 472 423	13 817 983	4 466 758	4 266 867	6 972 193	7 115 114
Canada [1]	42 940 492	43 631 505	D	D	0	0
Chile	14 420 539 000	15 457 314 000	8 413 733 000	8 622 479 000	6 622 626 000	7 730 850 000
China (People's Republic of) [2]	6 143 038 350	6 242 326 130	1 624 048 470	1 514 463 700	0	0
Colombia	40 856 077 708	44 390 408 427	19 061 511 770	22 032 861 844	4 038 479 478	4 485 067 900
Costa Rica [3]	779 416 350	958 750 120	708 203 660	676 235 820	0	0
Croatia	53 851 845	57 879 819	9 208 577	8 439 537	11 293 010	11 353 071
Cyprus	1 831 180	1 943 285	478 336	490 848	486 890	395 031
Czech Republic	732 291 617	765 811 384	299 811	296 338	319 279 049	334 500 307
Denmark	511 118 807	547 524 113	-547 088	-750 609	293 073 822	312 576 494
Estonia	2 038 155	2 180 894	280 934	281 522	6 469	7 764
Finland [4]	30 901 200	32 141 100	0	0	13 140 900	13 190 200
France	198 354 470	203 105 810	27 653 527	31 295 856	54 926 928	59 597 677
Georgia	1 076 847	1 515 661	3 350 062	3 723 360	509 419	608 547
Germany [5]	175 437 173	183 112 738	59 363 296	60 142 788	0	0
Greece	13 489 141	12 381 294	2 730 893	5 411 144	1 927 193	2 100 222
Hong Kong (China)						
Hungary	6 654 796 300	7 385 481 100	276 725 600	298 930 100	3 002 836 100	3 152 032 200
Iceland	76 879 000	83 201 000	175 577 000	183 120 000	21 050 000	23 606 000
India						
Indonesia	428 576 029 238	457 342 570 305	190 522 489 882	176 100 269 202	81 665 424 331	81 665 424 331
Ireland	17 434 671	18 926 454	1 905 539	2 008 117	5 132 397	5 767 230
Israel	85 889 000	91 349 000	45 889 300	46 455 000	33 902 000	36 986 000
Italy	119 367 000	122 990 000	D	D	30 333 000	31 084 000
Japan [6]	22 233 872 000	22 446 204 000	0	0	6 190 482 000	6 620 527 000
Kenya	219 499 363	244 748 287	151 677 445	179 177 943	14 400 000	14 400 000
Korea [7]	25 283 853 896	28 278 557 991	44 725 254 238	42 549 709 839	0	0
Latvia	3 268 105	3 472 386	76 067	72 976	887 203	897 015
Lithuania	4 728 954	4 972 425	36 812	36 254	1 225 679	1 232 801
Luxembourg [8]	5 347 663	5 614 888	0	0	1 623 737	1 666 857
Malaysia						
Malta	986 273	1 060 621	131 689	154 546	189 992	270 426
Mexico	934 305 675	953 802 962	714 696 806	680 779 401	726 764 192	701 255 597
Morocco	38 877 000	41 339 000	54 792 800	54 229 200	4 949 782	7 073 932
Netherlands	83 659 332	89 947 796	846 663	843 523	32 163 712	34 318 583

Table A.5. **Composition of value added tax collected by the tax administration** *(continued)*

	Composition of value added tax collected by the tax administration (in thousands in local currency)					
	Value added tax (gross domestic)		Value added tax (gross import) even where collected by customs		Value added tax refunds	
Jurisdiction	2018	2019	2018	2019	2018	2019
New Zealand	31 774 795	33 397 969	9 420 487	10 257 202	13 086 351	14 004 865
Norway	393 509 089	414 407 679	1 820 214	1 712 327	100 208 528	110 234 114
Peru	35 124 963	37 891 702	25 541 126	25 612 562	12 634 495	15 059 268
Poland	256 692 275	278 182 217	14 959 551	15 825 185	96 704 755	113 115 651
Portugal	22 444 119	23 883 993	947 982	523 492	5 977 603	5 779 279
Romania	67 727 188	75 223 143	8 285 721	8 984 038	16 406 785	18 790 005
Russia 9	3 574 613 815	4 257 770 868	186 559 556	223 970 973	0	0
Saudi Arabia	38 311 184	47 341 498	21 853 081	24 400 669	4 829 626	13 564 069
Singapore	14 670 703	15 086 779	5 563 684	5 961 804	9 271 816	9 908 119
Slovak Republic	10 301 542	10 954 630	2 673 078	2 694 428	6 658 464	6 818 903
Slovenia	5 645 985	5 836 718	129 152	124 324	2 018 289	2 089 519
South Africa	336 206 554	378 732 651	152 861 677	175 184 585	191 070 644	229 151 259
Spain	79 671 246	82 359 627	16 484 357	17 281 728	25 978 813	28 103 432
Sweden [10]	674 535 000	704 180 000	0	0	228 892 000	244 293 000
Switzerland	21 483 112	21 614 500	10 898 311	10 918 883	9 684 132	9 942 040
Thailand	469 972 530	473 551 483	323 026 080	326 116 763	218 248 471	259 394 301
Turkey	128 359 938	144 851 653	122 301 655	124 888 514	72 045 571	89 423 916
United Kingdom	184 799 962	194 534 329	30 263 271	32 811 765	86 443 584	91 750 318
United States						

StatLink http://dx.doi.org/10.1787/888934272442

D Data not available

1. Canada: VAT (gross domestic) includes VAT refunds
2. China (People's Republic of): VAT (gross domestic) includes VAT refunds
3. Costa Rica: VAT (gross domestic) includes VAT refunds
4. Finland: VAT (gross domestic) includes VAT (on imports)
5. Germany: VAT (gross domestic) includes VAT refunds
6. Japan: VAT (gross domestic) includes VAT (on imports)
7. Korea: VAT (gross domestic) includes VAT refunds
8. Luxembourg: VAT (gross domestic) includes VAT (on imports)
9. Russia: VAT (gross domestic) includes VAT refunds
10. Sweden: VAT (gross domestic) includes VAT (on imports)

Table A.6. **Net revenue collected by the tax administration by tax type: SSC and non-tax revenue**

Jurisdiction	Net revenue collected by the tax administration (in thousands in local currency)			
	Social security contributions		Non-tax revenue	
	2018	2019	2018	2019
Argentina	905 447 455	1 212 552 621	273 793 995	375 376 059
Australia			454 553	84 542
Austria				
Belgium			4 279 046	3 947 429
Brazil	411 242 842	436 430 395		
Bulgaria	9 277 149	10 332 067	398 921	450 496
Canada	70 047 286	73 986 222	4 310 137	6 082 518
Chile				
China (People's Republic of)	2 554 761 830	3 889 792 470	495 529 010	633 764 150
Colombia				
Costa Rica				
Croatia	44 923 758	46 452 490	37 702	43 416
Cyprus				
Czech Republic			6 202 898	4 782 242
Denmark	91 222 938	95 179 596		
Estonia	3 383 640	3 705 927	155 829	156 386
Finland	760 800	698 400		
France			91 499 000	75 861 000
Georgia				
Germany				
Greece			4 419 118	8 613 966
Hong Kong (China)				
Hungary	4 648 588 900	5 027 299 600		
Iceland	96 564 000	97 494 000		
India				
Indonesia				
Ireland	11 155 104	12 252 225	2 922 137	3 577 600
Israel				
Italy				
Japan				
Kenya			95 090 444	105 388 818
Korea			1 039 555 161	1 004 434 095
Latvia	3 204 464	3 509 877	445 035	463 770
Lithuania			429 247	436 899
Luxembourg			186 303	192 320
Malaysia			2 712	8 463
Malta	967 830	1 046 139	1 417	568
Mexico			833 237 896	830 026 725
Morocco				
Netherlands	91 532 696	91 230 072	5 527 788	6 727 020

Table A.6. **Net revenue collected by the tax administration by tax type: SSC and non-tax revenue** *(continued)*

	Net revenue collected by the tax administration (in thousands in local currency)			
	Social security contributions		Non-tax revenue	
Jurisdiction	2018	2019	2018	2019
New Zealand			834 947	1 599 627
Norway	141 693 806	147 759 046	7 550 233	9 028 479
Peru	14 816 264	15 478 438	1 081 625	1 514 717
Poland			28 887 911	31 379 034
Portugal			298 908	314 449
Romania	97 782 107	111 556 689	14 075 579	13 567 034
Russia	6 416 843 367	7 038 733 168	186 301 715	233 622 616
Saudi Arabia				
Singapore				
Slovak Republic			236 424	128 252
Slovenia	7 034 924	7 530 764	104 202	108 343
South Africa	18 271 131	19 116 523	7 797 028	9 025 257
Spain			4 083 895	4 195 657
Sweden	699 700 000	724 600 000		
Switzerland				
Thailand				
Turkey				
United Kingdom	130 500 000	135 000 000	4 100 000	3 600 000
United States	1 129 344 468	1 203 833 015		

StatLink http://dx.doi.org/10.1787/888934272461

Table A.7. **Tax administration expenditures**

Jurisdiction	Tax administration expenditures (in thousands in local currency)[1]							
	Operating expenditure		Salary expenditure		Information and communications technology (ICT) expenditure		Capital expenditure	
	2018	2019	2018	2019	2018	2019	2018	2019
Argentina	38 742 701	54 665 678	36 676 060	51 833 002	131 337	585 716	63 629	624 413
Australia	3 581 480	3 630 168	1 977 679	1 953 172	465 956	443 669	201 685	144 866
Austria	586 078	601 182	503 745	517 671	130 000	140 000	632	517
Belgium	922 789	909 649	743 517	736 560	41 513	39 233	D	D
Brazil	5 900 217	5 810 120	4 274 939	4 231 599	170 373	179 543	2 669	2 222
Bulgaria	207 787	230 552	177 190	196 754	6 868	40 213	9 606	35 005
Canada	4 915 828	5 115 836	3 651 742	3 784 269	706 104	831 423	89 687	71 606
Chile	222 346 081	222 886 291	198 201 025	200 334 499	19 971 852	22 181 328	5 631 037	5 441 472
China (People's Republic of)	D	110 564 273	D	65 293 499	D	1 759 569	D	3 686 407
Colombia	1 048 964 985	1 131 507 943	870 920 283	945 635 574	52 358 259	78 890 651	104 928 785	121 888 289
Costa Rica	48 162 090	48 182 732	22 750 263	22 174 921	10 812 977	11 045 717	1 132 057	1 210 983
Croatia	791 721	821 315	506 903	523 355	150 816	147 514	41 994	63 066
Cyprus	38 648	39 898	30 712	32 375	607	585	24	76
Czech Republic	11 695 399	12 197 041	7 217 945	7 559 634	1 138 606	1 285 034	401 244	455 590
Denmark	6 885 052	8 449 573	3 556 589	3 913 153	1 515 696	2 168 439	1 497 846	1 808 020
Estonia[2]	27 169	28 199	19 997	20 447	58	77	304	100
Finland	414 448	422 753	258 124	265 664	98 479	100 993	86	28
France	3 580 419	3 422 846	3 093 061	3 054 018	203 098	196 546	D	D
Georgia	37 651	40 853	30 522	33 742	902	1 327	998	2 272
Germany	9 669 547	10 029 757	8 081 300	8 340 986	879 254	975 035	287 700	277 336
Greece[3]	320 346	315 645	279 197	276 288	223	1 317	412	1 498
Hong Kong (China)	1 539 230	1 605 078	1 340 026	1 393 159	166 876	171 366	77 070	61 289
Hungary	161 126 093	188 858 773	106 940 802	108 716 387	D	D	D	D
Iceland	3 162 188	3 686 179	2 456 194	2 793 807	422 417	504 272	191 080	372 114
India	60 876 480	70 758 899	36 392 489	39 464 346	6 661 290	8 680 778	1 816 771	2 440 458
Indonesia	6 192 874 803	6 504 839 684	2 400 520 431	2 683 779 258	103 062 389	29 001 042	541 494 885	433 184 402
Ireland	342 545	342 474	244 311	242 957	7 615	7 354	1 645	1 729

Table A.7. **Tax administration expenditures** *(continued)*

Jurisdiction	Tax administration expenditures (in thousands in local currency)[1]							
	Operating expenditure		Salary expenditure		Information and communications technology (ICT) expenditure		Capital expenditure	
	2018	2019	2018	2019	2018	2019	2018	2019
Israel	2 800 192	2 896 099	1 659 226	1 710 062	336 448	357 385	97 732	100 144
Italy	3 111 672	3 027 825	1 782 871	1 824 105	286 300	286 531	95 530	11 775
Japan	700 416 000	702 647 000	559 804 000	550 548 000	48 820 000	49 561 000	D	D
Kenya	10 060 326	9 504 340	8 916 003	8 342 550	21 067	36 546	124 244	1 326
Korea	1 613 431 330	1 669 286 179	1 171 131 137	1 213 281 278	93 617 638	104 081 637	25 401 141	42 871 005
Latvia	82 467	79 964	53 393	53 965	11 574	10 654	8 734	4 992
Lithuania	52 653	59 128	43 941	50 116	7 453	9 393	3 959	6 235
Luxembourg	123 580	136 306	106 000	113 731	2 231	2 756	563	394
Malaysia	2 261 698	2 361 110	1 614 301	1 644 104	158 170	153 919	116 151	59 678
Malta	D	D	7 791 021	9 102 754	2 400	2 050	D	D
Mexico	12 754 449	10 673 737	10 060 723	8 468 185	602 950	525 149	0	4 961
Morocco	843 071	885 120	690 462	706 191	91 493	84 961	64 314	89 514
Netherlands	1 899 427	2 224 396	1 403 654	1 450 171	377 450	510 747	49 497	50 578
New Zealand	543 676	563 235	268 386	278 173	57 725	73 851	70 286	73 112
Norway	6 055 634	6 102 977	4 505 882	4 571 936	1 169 212	1 256 595	529 263	523 352
Peru	1 132 110	1 110 398	777 272	772 443	123 883	130 290	70 644	90 710
Poland	4 014 933	4 389 223	3 283 641	3 687 739	42 515	47 129	4 694	4 054
Portugal	502 548	535 315	394 849	423 923	26 029	30 355	24 225	18 558
Romania	2 290 384	2 410 453	2 054 316	2 215 332	D	D	D	D
Russia	141 400 000	159 100 000	112 500 000	130 500 000	19 792 369	18 161 976	3 700 000	4 100 000
Saudi Arabia	1 042 386	1 526 861	552 265	810 483	102 195	202 187	82 135	91 394
Singapore	424 259	421 950	257 418	258 719	113 345	111 234	16 576	16 191
Slovak Republic	203 359	241 725	124 578	144 904	14 301	10 032	5 452	12 210
Slovenia	118 873	127 168	98 911	104 783	11 055	12 939	9 829	11 884
South Africa	8 205 145	8 032 382	5 649 829	5 623 829	72 324	62 329	26 959	49 018
Spain	1 076 214	1 138 158	878 625	942 578	59 080	57 550	30 709	24 629
Sweden	8 488 562	8 612 181	6 228 075	6 188 971	1 793 000	1 656 000	291 264	311 079

Table A.7. **Tax administration expenditures** *(continued)*

Jurisdiction	Tax administration expenditures (in thousands in local currency)[1]							
	Operating expenditure		Salary expenditure		Information and communications technology (ICT) expenditure		Capital expenditure	
	2018	2019	2018	2019	2018	2019	2018	2019
Switzerland	265 824	261 273	165 407	169 308	54 451	41 316	1 806	494
Thailand	9 280 645	9 634 815	6 892 408	7 209 961	495 000	495 000	332 914	53 105
Turkey	3 226 727	3 672 736	2 708 687	3 243 681	137 490	149 477	152 213	159 848
United Kingdom	3 361 694	3 624 556	2 116 159	2 299 303	580 816	605 108	273 270	353 478
United States	11 202 194	11 204 900	8 172 955	8 328 385	2 772 321	2 821 332	544 254	620 342

StatLink http://dx.doi.org/10.1787/888934272480

D Data not available

1. Note: Expenditure figures were estimated by some administrations.
2. Estonia: ICT is provided by the "Information Technology Centre for the Ministry of Finance". All the expenditure and investments are handled by the ITC centre.
3. Greece: ICT expenditure does not include the payroll costs for ITC staff

Table A.8. Staff of the tax administration: Total and by function

Jurisdiction	Total tax administration FTEs 1		FTEs by function of the tax administration [1]: Registration, taxpayer services, returns and payment processing		Audit, investigation and other verification		Enforced debt collection and related functions		Other functions		Percentage of staff working on headquarter functions [1]	
	2018	2019	2018	2019	2018	2019	2018	2019	2018	2019	2018	2019
Argentina	14 743	15 389	982	969	3 986	4 094	3 425	3 535	6 350	6 791	15.0	17.0
Australia	18 236	17 412	2 581	2 107	5 277	5 337	1 321	1 259	9 057	8 709	11.0	11.0
Austria	7 880	7 904	1 857	1 880	4 009	3 981	394	401	1 620	1 642	2.8	2.8
Belgium	15 735	15 548	6 303	6 290	6 156	6 012	1 517	1 489	1 759	1 757	12.0	12.0
Brazil	12 875	11 540	3 765	3 375	3 228	2 894	2 476	2 220	3 406	3 051	7.3	5.5
Bulgaria	7 886	7 886	373	365	3 621	3 577	769	771	3 123	3 173	21.0	22.0
Canada	39 765	41 075	8 611	9 201	9 757	9 962	10 074	10 699	11 323	11 213	27.6	27.7
Chile	4 978	5 014	823	828	2 281	2 291	0	0	1 874	1 895	23.0	23.0
China (People's Republic of)	740 196	720 258	D	D	D	D	D	D	D	D	0.2	0.2
Colombia	6 813	7 360	1 610	1 739	2 707	2 924	1 010	1 091	1 486	1 606	17.5	17.5
Costa Rica	958	935	100	102	452	420	109	112	297	301	26.0	28.0
Croatia	3 949	3 899	2 075	2 037	799	787	520	514	555	561	8.0	9.0
Cyprus	760	745	269	264	275	270	127	124	89	87	16.0	16.0
Czech Republic	15 540	15 232	6 686	6 598	3 256	3 185	1 028	1 008	4 570	4 441	1.0	1.0
Denmark	8 010	8 540	1 688	1 741	1 632	1 687	1 494	1 577	3 196	3 535	8.4	8.0
Estonia	773	742	290	234	335	360	52	56	96	92	17.6	17.6
Finland	4 978	4 998	905	898	1 157	1 156	114	109	2 802	2 835	15.0	17.0
France	45 800	44 739	12 966	12 834	11 227	10 944	8 842	8 478	12 765	12 483	3.7	3.8
Georgia	1 920	2 030	447	485	854	878	63	60	556	607	6.0	9.0
Germany	110 071	109 769	24 639	24 533	39 897	38 183	8 199	8 143	37 336	38 910	6.4	6.7
Greece	8 216	8 532	D	D	D	D	D	D	D	D	14.3	11.3
Hong Kong (China)	2 852	2 889	1 828	1 845	239	239	222	222	563	583	10.9	10.8
Hungary	14 132	13 702	3 335	3 278	4 927	4 700	3 320	3 223	2 550	2 501	41.2	43.6
Iceland[2]	226	253	128	123	37	43	0	29	61	58	72.0	61.0
India	42 229	42 153	D	D	D	D	D	D	D	D	D	D
Indonesia	45 341	46 517	10 383	10 887	7 028	7 853	700	677	27 230	27 100	14.4	13.3
Ireland	4 928	5 040	1 926	2 210	1 799	2 003	516	565	687	262	32.4	30.4

Table A.8. Staff of the tax administration: Total and by function *(continued)*

Jurisdiction	Total tax administration FTEs 1		FTEs by function of the tax administration [1]: Registration, taxpayer services, returns and payment processing		Audit, investigation and other verification		Enforced debt collection and related functions		Other functions		Percentage of staff working on headquarter functions [1]	
	2018	2019	2018	2019	2018	2019	2018	2019	2018	2019	2018	2019
Israel	6 422	6 720	1 744	1 794	1 539	1 706	461	467	2 678	2 753	21.0	20.0
Italy	37 853	35 625	11 554	10 957	13 650	12 893	987	913	11 662	10 862	6.2	6.1
Japan	55 667	55 724	D	D	D	D	D	D	D	D	1.7	1.8
Kenya	2 671	2 861	534	572	1 336	1 431	801	858	0	0	30.0	40.0
Korea	20 368	20 874	10 897	11 314	4 430	4 496	1 298	1 253	3 743	3 811	4.3	4.5
Latvia	2 679	2 678	1 178	1 108	787	826	225	223	489	521	D	D
Lithuania [3]	2 837	2 659	1 425	976	766	1 039	172	166	474	478	47.0	50.0
Luxembourg	1 128	1 153	142	153	681	690	72	71	233	239	19.9	19.7
Malaysia	12 889	13 211	3 736	4 136	3 831	3 834	1 205	1 217	4 117	4 024	14.8	14.4
Malta	368	368	D	D	144	145	87	87	D	D	15.5	17.1
Mexico	35 202	33 058	3 424	3 373	10 462	9 855	6 186	5 523	15 130	14 307	12.0	12.0
Morocco	5 085	4 939	2 486	2 408	621	598	685	640	1 293	1 293	11.0	11.0
Netherlands	19 736	20 390	3 419	3 318	7 172	7 318	1 606	1 531	7 539	8 223	2.4	2.1
New Zealand	5 135	4 888	1 545	878	747	136	547	1 128	2 296	2 746	28.0	29.0
Norway	5 880	6 054	1 038	978	2 135	2 633	308	288	2 399	2 155	6.4	10.2
Peru	6 929	6 821	1 245	1 274	2 517	2 422	898	940	2 269	2 185	15.0	15.1
Poland	45 976	46 561	13 509	13 612	4 183	4 249	7 132	7 199	21 152	21 501	2.5	2.5
Portugal	9 660	9 869	5 195	5 431	1 835	1 830	1 141	1 137	1 489	1 471	18.4	18.1
Romania	20 527	19 732	5 063	4 832	5 522	5 073	2 837	2 904	7 105	6 923	10.9	10.4
Russia	145 584	145 299	24 187	23 798	78 594	78 348	16 728	17 012	26 075	26 141	10.9	11.1
Saudi Arabia	2 876	2 839	181	404	1 421	1 394	7	91	1 267	950	68.0	70.0
Singapore	1 911	1 898	784	764	387	390	203	208	537	536	28.0	28.0
Slovak Republic	5 715	5 596	2 326	2 317	1 510	1 491	285	285	1 594	1 503	6.6	6.4
Slovenia	3 148	3 128	1 260	1 276	686	672	492	483	710	697	14.4	14.1
South Africa	10 169	9 510	3 670	3 299	2 225	2 097	1 173	1 034	3 101	3 080	7.0	8.0
Spain	20 317	20 730	3 276	3 331	8 984	9 178	4 076	4 207	3 981	4 014	18.2	18.6

Table A.8. **Staff of the tax administration: Total and by function** *(continued)*

	Total tax administration FTEs 1		FTEs by function of the tax administration [1]								Percentage of staff working on headquarter functions [1]	
			Registration, taxpayer services, returns and payment processing		Audit, investigation and other verification		Enforced debt collection and related functions		Other functions			
Jurisdiction	**2018**	**2019**	**2018**	**2019**	**2018**	**2019**	**2018**	**2019**	**2018**	**2019**	**2018**	**2019**
Sweden	9 566	9 356	3 714	3 569	2 401	3 031	221	214	3 230	2 542	6.3	7.5
Switzerland	1 056	1 091	78	85	264	275	63	65	651	666	22.4	22.8
Thailand	22 093	21 726	6 115	5 957	5 461	5 472	1 701	1 666	8 816	8 631	10.4	10.5
Turkey	38 507	38 019	D	D	D	D	D	D	D	D	1.2	1.9
United Kingdom	58 670	54 072	18 165	15 940	16 025	16 366	4 753	4 331	19 727	17 435	9.0	11.0
United States	73 519	73 554	27 671	28 644	20 782	19 742	8 662	8 454	16 404	16 714	6.3	6.4

StatLink http://dx.doi.org/10.1787/888934272499

D Data not available

1. Note: FTE and staff related figures were estimated by some administrations.
2. Iceland: On 1 May 2019, debt collection was transferred from the Directorate of Customs to the Directorate of Internal Revenue.
3. Lithuania: In 2019, the tax administration has undergone a major structural change as a result of which a number of employees performing taxpayer service functions have been moved to perform primary verification functions.

Table A.9. **Information and communication technology (ICT) solutions of the tax administration**

	Operational ICT solutions of the administration are...					
	Custom built		On premises commercial off the shelf (COTS)		Software-as-a-Service (SaaS, i.e. cloud based)	
Jurisdiction	**2018**	**2019**	**2018**	**2019**	**2018**	**2019**
Argentina	■	■	□	□	□	□
Australia	■	■	■	■	■	■
Austria	■	■	□	□	□	□
Belgium	■	■	■	■	■	■
Brazil	■	■	■	■	■	■
Bulgaria	■	■	■	■	□	□
Canada	■	■	■	■	■	■
Chile	■	■	■	■	■	■
China (People's Republic of)	■	■	■	■	■	■
Colombia	■	■	□	□	■	■
Costa Rica	□	□	□	□	□	■
Croatia	■	■	□	□	□	□
Cyprus	■	■	□	□	□	□
Czech Republic	■	■	□	□	□	□
Denmark	■	■	■	■	■	■
Estonia	■	■	■	■	■	■
Finland	■	■	■	■	■	■
France	■	■	□	□	■	■
Georgia	■	■	□	□	□	□
Germany	■	■	■	■	■	■
Greece	■	■	■	■	□	□
Hong Kong (China)	■	■	■	■	□	□
Hungary	■	■	□	□	□	□
Iceland	■	■	■	■	□	□
India	■	■	□	□	■	■
Indonesia	■	■	■	■	■	■
Ireland	■	■	■	■	□	□
Israel	■	■	■	■	□	□
Italy	■	■	■	■	□	□
Japan	■	■	□	□	□	□
Kenya	■	■	■	■	□	□
Korea	■	■	□	□	□	□
Latvia	■	■	■	■	□	□
Lithuania	■	■	■	■	□	□
Luxembourg	■	■	□	□	□	□
Malaysia	■	■	■	■	■	■
Malta	□	□	□	□	□	□
Mexico	■	■	■	■	■	■
Morocco	■	■	□	□	□	□

Table A.9. **Information and communication technology (ICT) solutions of the tax administration** *(continued)*

	Operational ICT solutions of the administration are...					
	Custom built		On premises commercial off the shelf (COTS)		Software-as-a-Service (SaaS, i.e. cloud based)	
Jurisdiction	**2018**	**2019**	**2018**	**2019**	**2018**	**2019**
Netherlands	■	■	■	■	□	□
New Zealand	■	■	■	■	■	■
Norway	■	■	■	■	■	■
Peru	■	■	□	□	■	■
Poland	■	■	□	□	□	□
Portugal	■	■	□	□	□	□
Romania	■	■	□	□	□	□
Russia	■	■	□	□	□	□
Saudi Arabia	■	■	■	■	■	■
Singapore	■	■	■	■	■	■
Slovak Republic	■	■	■	■	■	■
Slovenia	■	■	■	■	■	■
South Africa	■	■	■	■	■	■
Spain	■	■	□	□	□	□
Sweden	■	■	□	□	■	■
Switzerland	■	■	■	■	■	■
Thailand	■	■	■	■	□	□
Turkey	■	■	□	□	□	□
United Kingdom	■	■	■	■	■	■
United States	■	■	■	■	■	■

StatLink http://dx.doi.org/10.1787/888934272518

■ Yes

□ No

Table A.10. **Staff metrics: Staff strength levels**

	Staff strength levels [1]							
	No. at start of FY		Departures in FY		Recruitments in FY		No. at end of FY	
Jurisdiction	2018	2019	2018	2019	2018	2019	2018	2019
Argentina	21 756	20 838	1 045	619	127	1 742	20 838	21 961
Australia	20 682	20 350	1 928	2 297	1 596	1 104	20 350	19 157
Austria	9 374	9 408	392	447	426	258	9 408	9 219
Belgium	21 421	20 712	1 466	1 217	757	1 230	20 712	20 725
Brazil	21 797	20 878	919	2 146	0	5	20 878	18 737
Bulgaria	7 686	7 886	527	640	727	640	7 886	7 886
Canada	43 216	44 632	5 851	5 471	7 267	7 659	44 632	46 820
Chile	4 971	4 978	172	104	179	140	4 978	5 014
China (People's Republic of) [2]	397 491	740 196	49 186	38 736	391 891	18 798	740 196	720 258
Colombia	9 704	9 797	286	344	379	1 131	9 797	10 584
Costa Rica	947	961	60	65	74	46	961	942
Croatia	3 998	3 934	190	176	126	119	3 934	3 877
Cyprus	773	748	40	27	15	36	748	757
Czech Republic	15 465	15 571	1 233	1 340	1 339	1 036	15 571	15 267
Denmark	7 144	8 417	688	829	1 961	1 419	8 417	9 007
Estonia	1 459	1 436	98	161	75	109	1 436	1 384
Finland	5 150	5 133	349	306	332	300	5 133	5 127
France	106 492	104 112	4 832	4 734	2 452	2 177	104 112	101 555
Georgia	3 318	3 513	138	114	316	320	3 496	3 719
Germany	105 241	110 071	D	D	D	D	110 071	109 769
Greece	11 971	11 942	276	249	247	653	11 942	12 346
Hong Kong (China)	2 772	2 813	186	209	227	207	2 813	2 811
Hungary	20 043	19 313	987	1 081	257	506	19 313	18 738
Iceland [3]	221	227	18	15	24	64	227	276
India	D	D	D	D	D	D	D	D
Indonesia	43 052	45 341	858	821	3 147	1 997	45 341	46 517
Ireland	6 007	6 110	499	528	602	1 037	6 110	6 619
Israel	5 760	5 871	168	356	261	577	5 853	6 092
Italy	38 661	36 771	1 990	2 726	163	340	36 834	34 385
Japan	55 253	55 695	D	D	2 106	2 234	D	D
Kenya	5 196	6 911	219	350	829	1 427	6 911	7 988
Korea	20 175	20 602	D	D	D	D	20 602	20 804
Latvia	3 639	3 636	235	280	232	256	3 636	3 612
Lithuania	3 062	2 813	400	319	151	173	2 813	2 667
Luxembourg	1 164	1 251	67	55	154	77	1 251	1 273
Malaysia	12 985	12 889	710	461	614	783	12 889	13 211
Malta	371	368	15	17	12	17	368	368
Mexico	35 898	35 202	3 953	5 139	3 257	2 995	35 202	33 058
Morocco	5 190	5 085	145	185	40	39	5 085	4 939
Netherlands	32 271	32 967	1 457	1 789	2 153	3 553	32 967	34 731

Table A.10. **Staff metrics: Staff strength levels** *(continued)*

	Staff strength levels [1]							
	No. at start of FY		Departures in FY		Recruitments in FY		No. at end of FY	
Jurisdiction	2018	2019	2018	2019	2018	2019	2018	2019
New Zealand	5 401	5 135	861	651	595	404	5 135	4 888
Norway [4]	6 581	6 509	507	555	435	445	6 509	6 399
Peru	10 742	10 689	1 027	1 598	974	1 456	10 689	10 547
Poland	52 467	54 778	2 167	2 335	4 478	3 047	54 778	55 490
Portugal	10 995	11 015	1 654	1 774	1 674	2 002	11 015	11 243
Romania	24 342	23 736	1 562	1 794	956	1 136	23 736	23 078
Russia	145 580	145 584	24 613	24 915	24 617	24 630	145 584	145 299
Saudi Arabia	2 518	2 876	96	165	454	128	2 876	2 839
Singapore	1 903	1 911	126	176	134	163	1 911	1 898
Slovak Republic	9 097	9 058	621	676	582	543	9 058	8 925
Slovenia	3 647	3 630	152	162	135	153	3 630	3 621
South Africa	13 583	13 379	1 279	1 190	1 075	555	13 379	12 744
Spain	25 152	24 939	1 114	1 007	901	1 468	24 939	25 400
Sweden	10 486	10 746	1 423	1 615	1 683	1 012	10 746	10 143
Switzerland	1 104	1 153	115	99	164	124	1 153	1 178
Thailand	21 503	22 093	1 273	1 358	1 863	991	22 093	21 726
Turkey	38 983	38 507	2 080	1 983	1 604	1 495	38 507	38 019
United Kingdom	68 722	64 785	8 341	6 886	4 404	6 052	64 785	63 951
United States	81 310	78 748	9 522	9 292	6 960	8 548	78 748	78 004

StatLink http://dx.doi.org/10.1787/888934272537

D Data not available

1. Note: The ISORA survey allowed combined tax and customs administration to use their total workforce when responding to the questions underlying this table.
2. China (People's Republic of): In 2018, the state and local tax administrations were merged. The local tax administrations' staff that was absorbed by the State Tax Administration is recorded as recruitments in 2018.
3. Iceland: On 1 May 2019, debt collection was transferred from the Directorate of Customs to the Directorate of Internal Revenue. The staff that was absorbed by the tax administration is recorded as recruitments in 2019.
4. Norway: In 2018, the Norwegian Tax Adminstration took over new tasks from the Collection Agency and Welfare Administration including 170 new employees which are recorded as recruitments in 2018.

Table A.11. **Staff metrics: Academic qualifications**

Jurisdiction	Academic qualifications (No. of staff at the end of FY)[1]			
	Masters degree (or above) or equivalent		Bachelors degree or equivalent	
	2018	2019	2018	2019
Argentina	916	971	11 901	12 896
Australia	3 201	3 076	5 404	5 174
Austria	929	932	328	334
Belgium	6 510	6 860	7 147	7 140
Brazil	145	160	15 840	14 852
Bulgaria	6 089	6 087	869	866
Canada	D	D	D	D
Chile	816	833	3 026	3 046
China (People's Republic of)	46 834	48 675	501 517	497 207
Colombia	293	345	7 469	7 980
Costa Rica	102	77	760	731
Croatia	2 194	2 183	640	645
Cyprus	142	162	276	277
Czech Republic	5 830	5 775	1 432	1 468
Denmark	D	D	D	D
Estonia	365	341	161	170
Finland	1 591	1 617	1 053	1 100
France	23 389	22 793	29 780	28 243
Georgia	1 224	1 286	2 272	2 433
Germany	23 676	23 964	39 025	38 867
Greece	2 977	3 564	4 694	4 658
Hong Kong (China)	96	93	1 016	1 093
Hungary[2]	D	D	12 694	12 571
Iceland	60	78	86	96
India	D	D	D	D
Indonesia	6 120	6 411	15 745	15 942
Ireland	398	431	2 355	2 595
Israel	1 162	1 217	2 064	2 322
Italy	16 907	16 432	1 216	1 176
Japan	D	D	D	D
Kenya	680	719	3 731	7 269
Korea	665	659	17 841	18 170
Latvia	1 099	1 092	949	992
Lithuania	1 426	1 636	1 387	1 031
Luxembourg	93	102	110	108
Malaysia	653	643	5 293	5 553
Malta	38	38	22	23
Mexico	432	1 604	10 511	21 122
Morocco	2 881	2 812	590	580
Netherlands[3]	5 847	6 673	11 961	12 464

Table A.11. **Staff metrics: Academic qualifications** *(continued)*

	Academic qualifications (No. of staff at the end of FY) [1]			
	Masters degree (or above) or equivalent		Bachelors degree or equivalent	
Jurisdiction	**2018**	**2019**	**2018**	**2019**
New Zealand	D	D	D	D
Norway	1 995	2 038	3 582	3 489
Peru	1 054	1 224	6 553	6 446
Poland	38 397	39 187	5 812	5 953
Portugal	423	444	5 237	5 264
Romania	9 637	9 622	12 896	12 356
Russia	121 182	118 262	16 413	18 859
Saudi Arabia	140	309	1 613	1 971
Singapore	101	108	1 053	1 088
Slovak Republic	5 843	5 808	822	790
Slovenia	2 209	2 226	1 421	1 395
South Africa	474	498	3 524	3 666
Spain	D	D	15 743	15 609
Sweden [4]	D	D	6 204	6 012
Switzerland	D	D	D	D
Thailand	5 163	5 049	16 930	16 677
Turkey	2 316	2 550	29 193	29 383
United Kingdom	D	D	D	D
United States	10 953	11 212	22 882	22 234

StatLink http://dx.doi.org/10.1787/888934272556

D Data not available

1. Note: The ISORA survey allowed combined tax and customs administration to use their total workforce when responding to the questions underlying this table.
2. Hungary: Number of staff under "Bachelors degree" refers to the total number of staff with academic qualifications (Bachelor and/or Masters degree).
3. Netherlands: Figures do not include contractual staff.
4. Sweden: Number of staff under "Bachelors degree" refers to the total number of staff with academic qualifications (Bachelor and/or Masters degree).

Table A.12. Staff metrics: Age distribution

Jurisdiction	Age distribution (No. of staff at the end of FY)[1]											
	Under 25 years		25-34 years		35-44 years		45-54 years		55-64 years		Over 64 years	
	2018	2019	2018	2019	2018	2019	2018	2019	2018	2019	2018	2019
Argentina	121	475	1 725	2 510	4 859	4 905	7 786	7 576	5 882	5 933	465	562
Australia	944	850	4 182	3 837	5 141	4 944	6 017	5 603	3 715	3 574	351	349
Austria	649	629	931	983	1 060	965	3 580	3 325	3 184	3 311	4	6
Belgium	248	450	3 345	3 447	4 157	4 247	6 182	5 995	6 724	6 502	56	84
Brazil	28	14	1 481	1 161	4 572	4 274	6 908	6 280	6 420	5 672	1 469	1 336
Bulgaria	61	48	1 225	1 249	2 215	2 057	2 709	2 811	1 609	1 645	67	76
Canada	2 298	2 764	7 960	8 995	11 146	11 777	13 386	13 125	8 824	9 045	1 018	1 114
Chile	33	32	879	829	1 609	1 533	1 399	1 522	823	847	235	251
China (People's Republic of)	34 439	23 447	138 499	146 500	158 895	141 987	318 325	298 760	90 038	109 564	0	0
Colombia	143	236	1 408	1 847	2 498	2 751	2 740	2 581	2 725	2 885	283	284
Costa Rica	10	12	167	140	219	282	248	280	197	218	120	10
Croatia	6	2	298	282	1 289	1 253	1 099	1 102	1 241	1 237	1	1
Cyprus	0	0	7	22	262	255	211	210	268	270	0	0
Czech Republic	172	117	1 837	1 711	3 759	3 368	5 637	5 647	3 917	4 116	249	308
Denmark	249	275	1 840	2 204	1 581	1 668	2 252	2 259	2 328	2 414	167	187
Estonia	35	48	297	259	361	345	352	361	314	300	77	71
Finland	110	131	846	918	1 042	1 061	1 285	1 231	1 786	1 725	64	61
France	891	843	11 163	11 038	21 723	20 798	33 311	32 882	36 287	35 126	737	868
Georgia	71	94	1 894	1 930	844	930	411	465	220	236	56	64
Germany	3 915	4 048	21 357	21 651	22 722	23 222	31 795	30 493	28 011	28 000	2 271	2 355
Greece	0	0	569	462	2 868	2 804	3 732	3 747	4 534	4 795	239	538
Hong Kong (China)	70	73	649	708	602	601	914	855	578	574	0	0
Hungary	229	287	3 392	2 842	7 414	6 877	5 940	6 423	2 331	2 303	7	6
Iceland	1	1	34	51	49	59	39	49	70	79	34	37
India	D	D	D	D	D	D	D	D	D	D	D	D
Indonesia	11 684	12 694	14 505	13 228	10 235	11 342	7 268	7 655	1 649	1 598	0	0
Ireland	58	132	713	899	1 666	1 833	1 578	1 706	2 066	1 996	29	53
Israel	128	120	1 053	1 243	1 263	1 294	1 583	1 551	1 552	1 576	274	308

Table A.12. **Staff metrics: Age distribution** *(continued)*

	Age distribution (No. of staff at the end of FY)[1]											
	Under 25 years		25-34 years		35-44 years		45-54 years		55-64 years		Over 64 years	
Jurisdiction	2018	2019	2018	2019	2018	2019	2018	2019	2018	2019	2018	2019
Italy	14	13	1 238	1 011	7 891	7 176	10 385	10 251	15 783	14 302	1 523	1 632
Japan	D	D	D	D	D	D	D	D	D	D	D	D
Kenya	178	278	2 675	3 512	2 020	2 196	1 267	1 265	771	734	0	3
Korea	270	239	4 384	4 432	7 909	7 829	6 586	6 776	1 453	1 528	0	0
Latvia	38	42	661	604	1 087	1 097	1 047	1 049	769	781	34	39
Lithuania	17	54	394	363	539	564	779	804	1 030	848	54	34
Luxembourg	56	43	295	311	348	357	392	393	159	167	1	2
Malaysia	238	311	3 994	4 490	4 780	4 866	2 261	2 251	1 616	1 293	0	0
Malta	7	3	59	57	88	85	125	124	69	74	20	25
Mexico	1 244	1 350	11 935	10 927	9 276	8 708	8 385	7 865	3 677	3 530	685	678
Morocco	34	13	1 831	1 698	1 084	1 141	1 402	1 374	729	708	5	5
Netherlands[2]	365	516	3 394	4 257	4 651	5 057	7 728	7 327	13 046	13 070	535	756
New Zealand	442	297	1 105	1 030	1 109	1 104	1 345	1 276	973	1 022	161	159
Norway	15	26	629	629	1 292	1 267	2 328	2 218	1 909	1 969	336	290
Peru	155	125	3 047	2 779	2 856	2 904	2 837	2 754	1 361	1 539	433	446
Poland	612	699	7 871	7 996	16 502	16 922	18 589	18 950	10 935	10 680	269	243
Portugal	0	1	99	94	1 910	1 538	3 673	3 894	5 085	5 322	248	394
Romania	76	57	1 508	1 341	6 602	5 898	10 321	10 519	5 191	5 222	38	41
Russia	10 425	9 611	49 879	47 182	46 190	48 391	25 770	26 380	13 296	13 706	24	29
Saudi Arabia	470	78	1 874	1 675	464	758	65	272	3	53	0	3
Singapore	15	27	568	526	616	634	374	402	303	277	35	32
Slovak Republic	97	105	1 406	1 321	2 631	2 482	2 949	3 014	1 919	1 935	56	68
Slovenia	3	2	241	225	710	697	1 732	1 662	933	1 014	11	21
South Africa	167	104	2 552	2 004	5 580	5 231	3 870	4 094	1 204	1 305	6	6
Spain	0	17	1 064	1 518	3 236	3 402	9 044	7 948	10 999	11 828	596	687
Sweden	151	127	2 214	1 977	2 754	2 597	2 857	2 772	2 613	2 512	157	158
Switzerland	96	102	240	256	350	331	393	415	73	73	1	1

Table A.12. **Staff metrics: Age distribution** *(continued)*

Jurisdiction	Age distribution (No. of staff at the end of FY)[1]											
	Under 25 years		25-34 years		35-44 years		45-54 years		55-64 years		Over 64 years	
	2018	2019	2018	2019	2018	2019	2018	2019	2018	2019	2018	2019
Thailand	362	344	3 769	3 680	7 250	6 828	7 675	7 726	3 037	3 148	0	0
Turkey	246	151	11 847	11 710	7 300	7 107	12 666	11 137	6 435	7 779	13	135
United Kingdom	3 232	3 071	11 685	12 116	13 236	13 174	20 346	18 874	15 218	15 495	1 068	1 221
United States	996	1 333	8 104	8 166	16 168	16 582	23 539	22 104	24 108	23 887	5 833	5 932

StatLink http://dx.doi.org/10.1787/888934272575

D Data not available

1. Note: The ISORA survey allowed combined tax and customs administration to use their total workforce when responding to the questions underlying this table.
2. Netherlands: Figures do not include contractual staff.

Table A.13. **Staff metrics: Length of service**

	Length of service (No. of staff at the end of FY)[1]							
	Under 5 years		5-9 years		10-19 years		Over 19 years	
Jurisdiction	2018	2019	2018	2019	2018	2019	2018	2019
Argentina	1 845	3 187	2 762	894	4 637	6 762	11 594	11 118
Australia	5 338	4 892	3 633	3 523	8 207	7 694	3 172	3 048
Austria	1 179	1 213	738	713	838	855	6 653	6 438
Belgium	2 801	3 429	2 440	2 345	4 588	4 343	10 883	10 608
Brazil	D	D	D	D	D	D	D	D
Bulgaria	434	395	815	836	2 340	2 262	4 297	4 393
Canada	15 299	17 646	7 557	7 063	12 416	13 056	9 360	9 055
Chile	1 298	1 286	635	596	1 626	1 655	1 419	1 477
China (People's Republic of)	96 399	87 747	62 055	66 069	82 811	82 546	498 931	483 896
Colombia	4 686	4 636	1 044	1 347	152	348	3 915	4 253
Costa Rica	182	188	120	111	276	275	383	368
Croatia	172	182	187	128	1 082	1 110	2 493	2 457
Cyprus	44	69	82	46	259	295	363	347
Czech Republic	3 866	3 504	1 887	2 024	4 328	4 269	5 490	5 470
Denmark	3 996	4 734	127	269	2 794	2 508	1 500	1 496
Estonia	225	237	189	199	452	407	570	541
Finland	1 503	1 580	471	608	1 063	1 043	2 096	1 896
France	16 512	17 346	14 223	13 178	33 209	31 858	40 168	39 173
Georgia	495	766	1 755	1 767	901	840	345	346
Germany	D	D	D	D	D	D	D	D
Greece	1 490	1 801	982	1 231	4 041	3 237	5 429	6 077
Hong Kong (China)	654	686	387	404	167	199	1 605	1 522
Hungary	1 806	1 441	3 905	3 672	7 095	6 855	6 507	6 770
Iceland	82	102	27	33	54	66	64	75
India	D	D	D	D	D	D	D	D
Indonesia	15 833	15 181	5 266	5 848	13 156	13 597	11 086	11 891
Ireland	1 187	1 791	226	325	1 852	1 668	2 845	2 835
Israel	983	1 194	826	863	1 001	1 064	3 043	2 971
Italy	2 594	1 799	2 592	3 533	9 326	7 827	22 322	21 226
Japan	D	D	D	D	D	D	D	D
Kenya	3 003	4 151	541	650	1 931	1 841	1 475	1 346
Korea	5 383	5 123	3 010	2 713	6 418	7 152	5 791	5 816
Latvia	644	618	302	399	1 562	1 434	1 128	1 161
Lithuania	697	682	716	741	598	676	802	568
Luxembourg	D	388	D	100	D	307	D	478
Malaysia	2 835	3 300	1 782	1 989	4 583	4 560	3 689	3 362
Malta	83	76	53	65	97	94	135	133
Mexico	12 114	10 999	6 995	7 293	9 790	7 165	6 303	7 601
Morocco	1 016	881	1 335	1 299	857	921	1 877	1 838
Netherlands[2]	4 352	5 527	1 610	2 556	6 054	5 775	17 703	17 125

Table A.13. **Staff metrics: Length of service** *(continued)*

	Length of service (No. of staff at the end of FY) [1]							
	Under 5 years		5-9 years		10-19 years		Over 19 years	
Jurisdiction	**2018**	**2019**	**2018**	**2019**	**2018**	**2019**	**2018**	**2019**
New Zealand	1 728	1 461	858	1 550	1 554	991	995	886
Norway	1 053	1 087	1 287	1 079	1 440	1 609	2 729	2 624
Peru	3 571	3 158	1 762	1 849	1 856	1 879	3 500	3 661
Poland	3 677	3 978	4 326	4 644	14 309	14 591	32 466	32 277
Portugal	26	44	384	373	3 201	2 430	7 404	8 396
Romania	3 596	2 954	1 344	1 876	8 026	7 004	10 770	11 244
Russia	44 857	43 224	27 396	26 182	45 797	47 424	27 534	28 469
Saudi Arabia [3]	2 876	2 839	0	0	0	0	0	0
Singapore	353	367	380	366	489	497	689	668
Slovak Republic	1 781	1 819	1 397	1 381	2 264	2 058	3 616	3 667
Slovenia	130	138	160	164	511	517	2 829	2 802
South Africa	1 986	1 581	2 218	1 694	5 149	5 236	4 026	4 233
Spain	1 074	1 106	1 369	2 466	3 994	4 036	18 502	17 792
Sweden	3 605	3 176	1 987	2 079	2 716	2 514	2 438	2 374
Switzerland	337	554	241	297	325	78	250	249
Thailand	3 730	3 849	2 674	2 481	5 803	5 953	9 886	9 443
Turkey	7 354	6 757	5 964	7 790	4 341	4 132	20 848	19 340
United Kingdom	13 623	15 760	4 440	3 270	18 527	17 800	28 195	27 121
United States	13 093	15 620	14 366	10 621	24 629	26 282	26 660	25 481

StatLink http://dx.doi.org/10.1787/888934272594

D Data not available

1. Note: The ISORA survey allowed combined tax and customs administration to use their total workforce when responding to the questions underlying this table.
2. Netherlands: Figures do not include contractual staff.
3. Saudi Arabia: Due to the transformation process of GAZT that was finalised in 2019 and based on the new contracts for staff, the length of service for the adminsitration is counted from the moment of transformation.

Table A.14. Staff metrics: Gender distribution

Jurisdiction	Gender distribution (No. of staff at the end of FY) [1]											
	All staff						Executives only					
	Male		Female		Other		Male		Female		Other	
	2018	2019	2018	2019	2018	2019	2018	2019	2018	2019	2018	2019
Argentina	11 449	11 949	9 389	10 012	0	0	83	77	29	41	0	0
Australia	8 686	8 199	11 658	10 951	6	7	2 404	2 256	2 285	2 175	0	0
Austria	4 989	4 817	4 419	4 402	0	0	605	580	263	270	0	0
Belgium	9 911	9 925	10 801	10 800	0	0	1 350	1 254	796	774	0	0
Brazil	13 111	11 971	7 767	6 766	0	0	138	130	26	24	0	0
Bulgaria	2 036	2 002	5 850	5 884	0	0	2	2	2	2	0	0
Canada	17 934	19 029	26 698	27 791	0	0	217	215	208	210	0	0
Chile	2 379	2 386	2 599	2 628	0	0	269	270	237	233	0	0
China (People's Republic of)	457 603	446 647	282 593	273 611	0	0	31 336	30 370	3 900	3 616	0	0
Colombia	4 264	4 601	5 533	5 983	0	0	34	38	33	32	0	0
Costa Rica	395	390	566	552	0	0	53	51	75	81	0	0
Croatia	957	921	2 977	2 956	0	0	122	118	264	279	0	0
Cyprus	200	204	548	553	0	0	3	3	1	1	0	0
Czech Republic	3 008	2 949	12 563	12 318	0	0	82	84	54	54	0	0
Denmark	3 068	3 279	5 349	5 728	0	0	41	42	25	26	0	0
Estonia	389	375	1 047	1 009	0	0	30	32	31	37	0	0
Finland	1 334	1 348	3 799	3 779	0	0	19	21	21	21	0	0
France	42 232	41 599	61 880	59 956	0	0	138	135	48	50	0	0
Georgia	1 761	1 868	1 735	1 851	0	0	242	253	65	71	0	0
Germany	47 459	46 985	62 612	62 784	0	0	D	D	D	D	D	D
Greece	4 450	4 557	7 492	7 789	0	0	589	607	651	665	0	0
Hong Kong (China)	896	894	1 917	1 917	0	0	12	11	10	12	0	0
Hungary	7 022	6 885	12 291	11 853	0	0	52	46	24	29	0	0
Iceland	83	97	144	179	0	0	5	6	5	4	0	0
India	D	D	D	D	D	D	D	D	D	D	D	D
Indonesia	29 841	30 112	15 500	16 405	0	0	49	50	6	6	0	0
Ireland	2 391	2 583	3 719	4 036	0	0	401	323	283	325	0	0

Table A.14. **Staff metrics: Gender distribution** *(continued)*

Jurisdiction	Gender distribution (No. of staff at the end of FY)[1]											
	All staff						Executives only					
	Male		Female		Other		Male		Female		Other	
	2018	2019	2018	2019	2018	2019	2018	2019	2018	2019	2018	2019
Israel	2 857	3 215	2 996	2 877	0	0	71	69	33	36	0	0
Italy	18 536	17 136	18 298	17 249	0	0	685	1 119	301	530	0	0
Japan	D	D	D	D	D	D	D	D	D	D	D	D
Kenya	3 862	4 450	3 049	3 538	0	0	89	90	37	42	0	0
Korea	8 459	8 792	12 143	12 012	0	0	37	34	0	1	0	0
Latvia	931	929	2 705	2 683	0	0	147	154	363	362	0	0
Lithuania	1 298	734	1 515	1 933	0	0	150	41	281	86	0	0
Luxembourg	646	651	605	622	0	0	77	76	38	41	0	0
Malaysia	5 369	5 464	7 520	7 747	0	0	167	166	123	129	0	0
Malta	196	193	172	175	0	0	16	19	9	11	0	0
Mexico	16 214	15 274	18 988	17 784	0	0	65	81	29	48	0	0
Morocco	2 654	2 551	2 431	2 388	0	0	449	457	113	108	0	0
Netherlands[2]	17 824	18 188	11 895	12 795	0	0	910	1 017	497	609	0	0
New Zealand	1 859	1 758	3 274	3 122	2	8	39	39	20	32	0	0
Norway	2 486	2 471	4 023	3 928	0	0	250	174	309	259	0	0
Peru	6 108	5 970	4 581	4 577	0	0	660	649	369	399	0	0
Poland	15 489	15 471	39 289	40 019	0	0	1 133	1 343	2 399	2 643	0	0
Portugal	4 505	4 497	6 510	6 746	0	0	157	154	113	113	0	0
Romania	7 796	7 469	15 940	15 609	0	0	877	836	1 138	1 113	0	0
Russia	23 288	23 368	122 296	121 931	0	0	3 995	4 011	2 563	2 585	0	0
Saudi Arabia	2 636	2 205	240	634	0	0	56	89	18	31	0	0
Singapore	513	519	1 398	1 379	0	0	8	8	12	11	0	0
Slovak Republic	3 194	3 119	5 864	5 806	0	0	491	469	372	362	0	0
Slovenia	1 238	1 224	2 392	2 397	0	0	107	107	234	230	0	0
South Africa	5 080	4 911	8 299	7 833	0	0	2 023	2 049	1 954	1 993	0	0
Spain	11 697	11 924	13 242	13 476	0	0	99	97	16	49	0	0

Table A.14. **Staff metrics: Gender distribution** *(continued)*

Jurisdiction	Gender distribution (No. of staff at the end of FY)[1]											
	All staff						Executives only					
	Male		Female		Other		Male		Female		Other	
	2018	2019	2018	2019	2018	2019	2018	2019	2018	2019	2018	2019
Sweden	3 565	3 423	7 181	6 720	0	0	248	228	457	436	0	0
Switzerland	659	678	494	500	0	0	19	19	2	2	0	0
Thailand	4 826	4 679	17 267	17 047	0	0	76	79	97	109	0	0
Turkey	23 259	22 912	15 248	15 107	0	0	1 236	1 215	415	414	0	0
United Kingdom	29 015	29 209	35 770	34 742	0	0	205	200	160	175	0	0
United States	27 077	27 217	51 671	50 787	0	0	2 986	2 927	4 341	4 333	0	0

StatLink http://dx.doi.org/10.1787/888934272613

D Data not available

1. Note: The ISORA survey allowed combined tax and customs administration to use their total workforce when responding to the questions underlying this table.
2. Netherlands: Figures do not include contractual staff.

Table A.15. **Large taxpayer office/programme: Existence and functions**

Jurisdiction	Large taxpayer office/ programme exists		Tax administration functions carried out by LTO or programme: Registration		Return and payment processing		Taxpayer services		Audit, Investigation and other verifications		Enforced debt collection and related functions		Dispute resolution	
	2018	2019	2018	2019	2018	2019	2018	2019	2018	2019	2018	2019	2018	2019
Argentina	■	■			■	■	■	■	■	■	■	■	■	■
Australia	■	■					■	■	■	■			■	■
Austria	■	■							■	■				
Belgium	■	■			■	■	■	■	■	■			■	■
Brazil	■	■					■	■	■	■	■	■		
Bulgaria	■	■	■	■	■	■	■	■	■	■	■	■	■	■
Canada	■	■							■	■				
Chile	■	■					■	■	■	■	■	■	■	■
China (People's Republic of)	■	■					■	■	■	■			■	■
Colombia	■	■					■	■	■	■	■	■	■	■
Costa Rica	■	■	■	■	■	■	■	■	■	■	■	■	■	■
Croatia	■	■			■	■	■	■	■	■	■	■		
Cyprus	■	■					■	■	■	■			■	■
Czech Republic	■	■	■	■	■	■	■	■	■	■	■	■	■	■
Denmark	■	■					■	■	■	■			■	■
Estonia	□	□												
Finland	■	■					■	■	■	■			■	■
France	■	■							■	■				
Georgia	■	■			■	■	■	■	■	■				
Germany	■	■							■	■			■	
Greece	■	■			■	■			■	■	■	■		
Hong Kong (China)[1]	□	□												
Hungary	■	■	■	■	■	■	■	■	■	■	■	■	■	■
Iceland	□	□												
India	■	■					■	■	■	■	■	■		
Indonesia	■	■			■	■	■	■	■	■	■	■	■	■

Table A.15. **Large taxpayer office/programme: Existence and functions** *(continued)*

	Large taxpayer office/ programme exists		Tax administration functions carried out by LTO or programme: Registration		Return and payment processing		Taxpayer services		Audit, Investigation and other verifications		Enforced debt collection and related functions		Dispute resolution	
Jurisdiction	**2018**	**2019**	**2018**	**2019**	**2018**	**2019**	**2018**	**2019**	**2018**	**2019**	**2018**	**2019**	**2018**	**2019**
Ireland	■	■	■	■	■	■	■	■	■	■	■	■	■	■
Israel	■	■	■	■	■	■	■	■	■	■	■	■	■	■
Italy	■	■	■	■	■	■	■	■	■	■	■	■	■	■
Japan	■	■					■	■	■	■			■	■
Kenya	■	■	■	■	■	■	■	■	■	■	■	■		
Korea	□	□												
Latvia	■	■	■	■	■	■	■	■						
Lithuania	■	■					■	■	■	■				
Luxembourg	□	□												
Malaysia	■	■	■	■	■	■	■	■	■	■	■	■	■	■
Malta	■	■	■	■	■	■	■	■	■	■	■	■	■	■
Mexico	■	■					■	■	■	■	■	■	■	■
Morocco	■	■	■	■	■	■	■	■	■	■	■	■	■	■
Netherlands	■	■					■	■	■	■	■	■	■	■
New Zealand	■	■	■	■	■	■	■	■	■	■	■	■	■	■
Norway	■	■					■	■	■	■			■	■
Peru	■	■	■	■	■	■	■	■	■	■	■	■	■	■
Poland	■	■	■	■	■	■	■	■	■	■	■	■	■	■
Portugal	■	■	■	■	■	■	■	■	■	■	■	■	■	■
Romania	■	■	■	■	■	■	■	■	■	■	■	■	■	■
Russia	■	■	■	■	■	■	■	■	■	■	■	■	■	■
Saudi Arabia	■	■					■	■	■	■	■			
Singapore	■	■					■	■	■	■			■	■
Slovak Republic	■	■	■	■	■	■	■	■	■	■	■	■	■	■
Slovenia	■	■	■	■	■	■	■	■	■	■	■	■	■	■

Table A.15. **Large taxpayer office/programme: Existence and functions** *(continued)*

Jurisdiction	Large taxpayer office/ programme exists		Tax administration functions carried out by LTO or programme: Registration		Return and payment processing		Taxpayer services		Audit, Investigation and other verifications		Enforced debt collection and related functions		Dispute resolution	
	2018	2019	2018	2019	2018	2019	2018	2019	2018	2019	2018	2019	2018	2019
South Africa	■	■	■	■	■	■	■	■	■	■	■	■	■	■
Spain	■	■	■	■	■	■	■	■	■	■	■	■	■	■
Sweden	■	■	■	■	■	■	■	■	■	■			■	■
Switzerland	□	□												
Thailand	■	■					■	■	■	■	■	■	■	■
Turkey	■	■	■	■	■	■	■	■	■	■	■	■	■	■
United Kingdom	■	■					■	■	■	■			■	■
United States	■	■					■	■	■	■				

StatLink http://dx.doi.org/10.1787/888934272632

■ Yes

□ No

1. Hong Kong (China): A Large Business office was established during Fiscal Year 2020.

Table A.16. **Large taxpayer office/programme: Staff, taxpayers and revenue collected**

Jurisdiction	No. of FTEs in LTO/programme				No. of taxpayers included under the LTO/programme				Percentage (actual or estimated) of net revenue administered under LTO/ programme in relation to total net revenue collected by the tax administration	
	Total		In the audit, investigation and other verification activities		Corporate taxpayers		Individual taxpayers			
	2018	2019	2018	2019	2018	2019	2018	2019	2018	2019
Argentina	454	464	244	234	622	764	815	835	45.5	49.1
Australia	1 359	1 378	829	867	29 000	30 000	0	0	D	D
Austria	478	490	430	434	8 977	9 421	894	934	56.2	55.8
Belgium	355	361	226	236	15 647	12 916	0	0	52.7	49.5
Brazil	164	166	164	166	8 969	6 777	30 700	27 446	64.0	64.0
Bulgaria	144	144	88	79	1 360	1 433	0	0	33.0	34.0
Canada	1 308	1 343	1 308	1 343	18 300	18 200	D	D	D	D
Chile	220	220	187	186	891	970	0	0	44.7	43.0
China (People's Republic of)	7 300	15 570	4 380	9 340	275 000	275 000	0	0	45.0	45.0
Colombia	316	349	163	177	3 535	3 542	57	49	67.3	63.1
Costa Rica	61	63	56	57	461	448	0	0	67.0	62.0
Croatia	101	99	49	53	701	750	0	0	37.3	36.7
Cyprus	25	25	25	25	816	874	0	0	30.2	28.0
Czech Republic	365	352	186	188	2 044	2 086	0	0	37.0	37.0
Denmark	260	260	240	240	10 000	10 000	0	0	40.0	40.0
Estonia										
Finland	166	174	D	D	2 982	2 948	0	0	28.0	28.0
France	D	D	502	502	D	D	D	D	D	D
Georgia	17	55	D	38	265	267	0	0	31.0	33.0
Germany	D	D	D	D	D	D	D	D	D	D
Greece	185	182	113	111	1 285	2 415	0	0	D	D
Hong Kong (China)										
Hungary	463	444	123	121	1 059	1 066	0	0	35.3	34.8
Iceland										
India	D	D	D	D	7 246	7 246	9 466	9 466	0.2	0.2

Table A.16. **Large taxpayer office/programme: Staff, taxpayers and revenue collected** *(continued)*

	No. of FTEs in LTO/programme				No. of taxpayers included under the LTO/programme				Percentage (actual or estimated) of net revenue administered under LTO/ programme in relation to total net revenue collected by the tax administration	
	Total		In the audit, investigation and other verification activities		Corporate taxpayers		Individual taxpayers			
Jurisdiction	2018	2019	2018	2019	2018	2019	2018	2019	2018	2019
Indonesia	684	664	240	181	2 714	2 792	1 315	1 309	31.9	30.0
Ireland	260	270	224	234	12 300	12 500	D	D	51.0	51.0
Israel	73	80	41	48	8 305	9 228	1 323	1 311	29.0	28.1
Italy	588	622	422	429	3 648	3 732	0	0	28.2	28.0
Japan	2 325	2 326	0	0	32 000	33 000	0	0	56.0	55.0
Kenya	200	215	140	150	1 820	1 783	0	0	38.5	37.9
Korea										
Latvia	47	46	D	D	1 247	1 270	0	0	59.1	60.5
Lithuania	44	42	28	26	508	473	0	0	45.0	41.0
Luxembourg										
Malaysia	490	454	293	279	49 178	49 721	3 743	4 801	31.0	33.2
Malta	28	34	25	30	1 410	1 679	9 880	10 583	20.0	20.0
Mexico	59	69	59	69	8 952	9 135	D	D	60.5	59.3
Morocco	119	133	62	60	8 268	8 459	0	0	70.0	70.0
Netherlands 1	2 096	2 224	1 596	1 713	14 500	14 100	44 800	44 300	68.4	67.3
New Zealand	320	316	183	173	985	995	0	0	30.0	30.0
Norway	338	330	294	285	15 571	15 996	0	0	D	D
Peru	859	908	719	727	15 082	16 608	13	10	76.2	74.8
Poland	2 050	2 108	615	632	2 561	2 746	0	0	70.0	70.0
Portugal	217	221	98	101	2 609	2 735	758	758	45.7	44.8
Romania 2	548	527	342	332	2 700	2 700	0	0	42.2	41.8
Russia	3 339	3 523	2 295	2 352	2 895	2 881	0	0	43.5	46.1
Saudi Arabia 3	0	273	0	197	0	7 723			82.0	81.0
Singapore	81	81	73	72	1 900	2 000	0	0	D	D
Slovak Republic	151	159	105	105	809	865	4	5	43.0	41.5

Table A.16. **Large taxpayer office/programme: Staff, taxpayers and revenue collected** *(continued)*

Jurisdiction	No. of FTEs in LTO/programme				No. of taxpayers included under the LTO/programme				Percentage (actual or estimated) of net revenue administered under LTO/ programme in relation to total net revenue collected by the tax administration	
	Total		In the audit, investigation and other verification activities		Corporate taxpayers		Individual taxpayers			
	2018	2019	2018	2019	2018	2019	2018	2019	2018	2019
Slovenia	70	73	62	65	704	705	0	0	25.0	25.0
South Africa[4]	379	359	208	196	16 323	16 812	1 513	1 513	35.6	30.5
Spain	776	768	596	588	3 099	3 114	248	240	35.3	33.2
Sweden	981	1 038	220	460	37 135	39 491	0	0	49.4	49.5
Switzerland										
Thailand	530	530	314	314	3 920	3 920	0	0	45.9	46.3
Turkey	250	263	13	14	800	793	0	0	19.0	20.0
United Kingdom	2 395	2 367	D	D	2 043	1 945	D	D	40.0	40.0
United States	3 423	3 071	3 423	3 071	352 768	368 350	49 949	56 342	6.5	7.1

StatLink http://dx.doi.org/10.1787/888934272651

D Data not available

1. Netherlands: Netherlands: With respect ot the number of corporate taxpayers managed, the LTO manages 14 500 (2018) / 14 100 (2019) group entities that each may consist of several entities.
2. Romania: As regards the percentage of net revenue administered under the LTO / programme, the percentage reported refers to the LTO performance in relation to the net revenue reported in ISORA (excluding customs), therefore the reported indicator may slightly differ from the same indicator presented in the institution performance reports.
3. Saudi Arabia: The number of corporate taxpayers includes "Zakat payers".
4. South Africa: The LTO headcount reported for the 2018 fiscal year is at December 2018 (the commencement of the re-establishment of the Large Business unit via seconded resources from other divisions within the organisation). For both fiscal years, the number of corporate taxpayers for Large Tax Office excludes inactive cases.

Table A.17. **Large taxpayer office/ programme: Audits**

	Audits undertaken by the LTO/programme (excluding electronic compliance checks)			
	Total number completed		Total value of additional assessments raised (including penalties and interest) (in thousands in local currency)	
Jurisdiction	2018	2019	2018	2019
Argentina	2 206	1 536	10 674 972	8 654 356
Australia	44	56	3 003 875	1 529 418
Austria	3 670	3 556	726 900	565 800
Belgium	6 566	5 364	2 285 765	1 524 348
Brazil	1 466	1 511	146 436 503	156 924 162
Bulgaria	64	53	79 388	13 352
Canada	3 605	3 252	7 442 200	7 707 228
Chile	464	361	803 370 000	735 372 000
China (People's Republic of)	2 051	34 836	D	D
Colombia	1 064	1 031	371 702 762	427 977 243
Costa Rica	50	61	159 453	118 647
Croatia	78	117	183 317	244 399
Cyprus	896	839	312 232	364 009
Czech Republic	174	172	2 512 059	1 644 880
Denmark	4 100	3 900	D	D
Estonia				
Finland	D	D	D	D
France	1 244	1 096	3 540 640	2 762 994
Georgia	79	96	39 180	90 500
Germany	D	D	D	D
Greece	417	455	672 225	297 480
Hong Kong (China)				
Hungary	1 516	1 265	15 516 138	22 228 590
Iceland				
India	299	416	23 504 112	32 407 614
Indonesia	1 842	1 616	47 030 924 714	19 222 561 979
Ireland	2 949	3 080	166 702	209 012
Israel	840	767	3 614 356	4 953 599
Italy	304	292	2 367 000	2 982 000
Japan	2 538	2 422	82 207 345	80 355 344
Kenya	1 190	1 040	7 792 239	37 588 646
Korea				
Latvia	84	64	46 862	32 231
Lithuania	45	41	1 287	8 930
Luxembourg				
Malaysia	19 139	25 515	5 751 478	10 970 766
Malta	10	12	6 000	8 000
Mexico	1 182	1 093	D	D
Morocco	573	426	5 762 428	4 406 785

Table A.17. **Large taxpayer office/ programme: Audits** *(continued)*

	Audits undertaken by the LTO/programme (excluding electronic compliance checks)			
	Total number completed		Total value of additional assessments raised (including penalties and interest) (in thousands in local currency)	
Jurisdiction	**2018**	**2019**	**2018**	**2019**
Netherlands [1]	99 767	82 804	2 172 285	2 449 277
New Zealand	541	625	167 000	312 000
Norway	502	287	12 002 943	14 183 041
Peru	2 529	2 105	3 956 631	4 981 735
Poland	D	D	D	D
Portugal	215	225	594 711	660 289
Romania	262	303	1 496 436	1 000 869
Russia	669	436	81 559 028	135 222 587
Saudi Arabia	5 662	6 407	1 257 311	2 545 904
Singapore	D	D	D	D
Slovak Republic	52	41	37 919	96 305
Slovenia [2]	37 710	11 979	8 973	77 024
South Africa	605	533	6 685 907	7 309 689
Spain	541	512	1 817 730	1 327 650
Sweden	258	211	4 707 262	6 944 290
Switzerland				
Thailand	2 954	3 208	12 253 000	18 439 000
Turkey	76	27	22 456	11 686
United Kingdom	2 637	1 906	8 726 608	12 258 257
United States	7 189	5 697	10 420 924	6 581 555

StatLink http://dx.doi.org/10.1787/888934272670

D Data not available

1. Netherlands: The value of additional assessments raised excludes interest and penalties.
2. Slovenia: The value of additional assessments raised excludes penalties.

Table A.18. **High net wealth individuals (HNWIs) programme**

Jurisdiction	HNWI programme exists		HNWI programme is part of the large taxpayer programme		Percentage of net revenue administered under HNWI program in relation to total tax revenue collected by the tax administration	
	2018	2019	2018	2019	2018	2019
Argentina	■	■	■	■	D	D
Australia	■	■	■	■	4.70	4.50
Austria	□	□				
Belgium	□	□				
Brazil	■	■	■	■	5.00	6.00
Bulgaria	□	□				
Canada	■	■	□	□	D	D
Chile	■	■	□	□	4.10	4.87
China (People's Republic of)	□	□				
Colombia	□	□				
Costa Rica	■	■	■	■	D	D
Croatia	□	□				
Cyprus	□	□				
Czech Republic	□	□				
Denmark	□	□				
Estonia	□	□				
Finland	■	■	□	□	D	D
France	□	□				
Georgia	□	□				
Germany	■	■	■	■	D	D
Greece	■	■	□	□	D	D
Hong Kong (China)	□	□				
Hungary	□	□				
Iceland	□	□				
India	□	□				
Indonesia	■	■	■	■	0.90	0.90
Ireland	■	■	□	□	0.50	0.50
Israel	□	□				
Italy	■	■	□	□	D	D
Japan	■	■	□	□	D	D
Kenya	■	■	□	□	0.06	0.05
Korea	□	□				
Latvia	□	□				
Lithuania	■	■	□	□	2.28	D
Luxembourg	□	□				
Malaysia	■	■	■	■	1.08	1.11
Malta	■	■	□	□	20.00	20.00
Mexico	□	□				

Table A.18. **High net wealth individuals (HNWIs) programme** *(continued)*

Jurisdiction	HNWI programme exists		HNWI programme is part of the large taxpayer programme		Percentage of net revenue administered under HNWI program in relation to total tax revenue collected by the tax administration	
	2018	2019	2018	2019	2018	2019
Morocco	□	□				
Netherlands	■	■	■	■	D	D
New Zealand	■	■	■	■	1.31	1.21
Norway	□	□				
Peru	□	□				
Poland	□	□				
Portugal	■	■	■	■	D	D
Romania	■	■	□	□	D	D
Russia	□	□				
Saudi Arabia	□	□				
Singapore	□	□				
Slovak Republic	□	□				
Slovenia	□	□				
South Africa	■	■	■	■	1.21	0.97
Spain	■	■	■	■	D	D
Sweden	□	□				
Switzerland	□	□				
Thailand	□	□				
Turkey	□	□				
United Kingdom	■	■	□	□	9.00	13.00
United States	■	■	■	■	4.44	4.50

StatLink http://dx.doi.org/10.1787/888934272689

■ Yes

□ No

D Data not available

Table A.19. **Small and medium enterprises (SMEs) and small taxpayers**

Jurisdiction	Specific service initiatives aimed at SMEs exist		Simplified income tax regime for small taxpayers exists	
	2018	2019	2018	2019
Argentina	■	■	■	■
Australia	■	■	■	■
Austria	□	□	■	■
Belgium	□	□	■	■
Brazil	■	■	■	■
Bulgaria	□	□	■	■
Canada	■	■	□	□
Chile	■	■	■	■
China (People's Republic of)	■	■	■	■
Colombia	□	□	□	■
Costa Rica	■	■	■	■
Croatia	■	■	■	■
Cyprus	□	□	□	□
Czech Republic	□	□	□	□
Denmark	■	■	□	□
Estonia	□	□	□	■
Finland	□	□	□	□
France	■	■	■	■
Georgia	■	■	■	■
Germany	□	□	□	□
Greece	■	■	□	□
Hong Kong (China)	□	□	□	□
Hungary	■	■	■	■
Iceland	■	■	□	□
India	□	□	■	■
Indonesia	■	■	■	■
Ireland	□	□	□	□
Israel	■	■	■	■
Italy	■	■	■	■
Japan	□	□	□	□
Kenya	■	■	■	■
Korea	■	■	■	■
Latvia	□	□	■	■
Lithuania	■	■	■	■
Luxembourg	□	□	□	□
Malaysia	■	■	□	□
Malta	□	□	□	□
Mexico	■	■	■	■
Morocco	□	□	■	■
Netherlands	■	■	□	□

Table A.19. **Small and medium enterprises (SMEs) and small taxpayers** *(continued)*

Jurisdiction	Specific service initiatives aimed at SMEs exist		Simplified income tax regime for small taxpayers exists	
	2018	2019	2018	2019
New Zealand	■	■	□	□
Norway	□	□	□	□
Peru	■	■	■	■
Poland	■	■	■	■
Portugal	■	■	■	■
Romania	□	□	□	□
Russia	■	■	■	■
Saudi Arabia	■	■	□	□
Singapore	■	■	■	■
Slovak Republic	□	□	■	■
Slovenia	□	□	■	■
South Africa	■	■	■	■
Spain	■	■	■	■
Sweden	■	■	■	■
Switzerland	□	□	□	□
Thailand	■	■	□	□
Turkey	□	□	□	□
United Kingdom	□	□	■	■
United States	■	■	□	□

StatLink http://dx.doi.org/10.1787/888934272708

■ Yes

□ No

Table A.20. **Number of taxpayers by tax type: Personal income tax and corporate income tax**

	Number of taxpayers by tax type							
	Personal Income tax				Corporate Income tax			
	Registered taxpayers		Active taxpayers		Registered taxpayers		Active taxpayers	
Jurisdiction	**2018**	**2019**	**2018**	**2019**	**2018**	**2019**	**2018**	**2019**
Argentina[1]	4 085 714	4 368 350	3 106 873	3 330 771	410 082	441 530	360 030	366 272
Australia	30 763 272	31 566 781	22 325 930	22 823 877	10 512 549	10 847 850	4 538 779	4 669 944
Austria	8 247 467	8 565 293	8 247 467	8 565 293	189 619	197 396	189 619	197 396
Belgium	9 470 257	9 637 209	7 119 341	7 151 559	555 959	572 143	555 959	572 143
Brazil	30 109 336	32 120 750	28 800 842	30 011 981	8 206 785	8 408 032	5 442 886	4 918 187
Bulgaria	D	D	3 136 523	3 125 755	698 035	742 786	364 744	375 829
Canada	34 431 166	35 088 821	30 087 051	30 567 800	3 590 417	3 721 194	D	D
Chile	10 626 784	10 841 072	10 150 899	10 317 528	2 061 517	2 164 526	1 460 920	1 521 022
China (People's Republic of)	D	D	D	D	24 964 324	29 603 184	21 440 319	25 244 714
Colombia	3 692 756	3 873 230	3 366 185	3 692 756	1 227 389	1 293 689	518 398	499 986
Costa Rica	482 153	491 225	482 153	491 225	178 706	168 364	178 706	168 364
Croatia	1 829 297	1 887 665	1 829 297	1 887 665	154 119	158 834	154 119	158 834
Cyprus	428 952	450 481	428 952	450 481	183 536	195 458	123 763	120 701
Czech Republic	3 525 175	3 582 707	2 136 634	2 176 238	646 186	667 978	637 968	659 327
Denmark	5 253 856	5 267 310	5 253 856	5 267 310	350 000	369 000	333 000	351 000
Estonia	812 166	914 783	812 166	914 783	322 933	349 041	322 933	349 041
Finland	5 467 555	5 446 294	5 467 555	5 446 294	450 754	450 998	450 754	450 998
France[2]	51 325 573	51 334 785	51 325 573	51 334 785	2 390 000	2 519 000	2 330 000	2 480 000
Georgia	D	D	1 291 310	1 288 122	266 799	290 021	105 890	94 954
Germany	39 988 839	41 495 682	39 988 839	41 495 682	1 561 705	1 588 524	1 561 705	1 588 524
Greece	12 147 933	12 257 519	8 941 081	8 715 110	442 593	461 034	260 255	269 323
Hong Kong (China)	3 830 000	3 860 000	3 105 761	3 170 111	1 272 000	1 261 000	488 468	540 034
Hungary	5 027 227	5 061 292	5 027 227	5 061 292	483 521	480 919	461 367	464 365
Iceland	307 699	313 338	307 699	313 338	62 633	64 110	45 492	46 652
India	79 477 324	87 235 122	58 723 101	62 701 418	1 179 525	1 273 633	843 552	836 349
Indonesia	D	D	D	D	D	D	D	D
Ireland	3 706 581	3 828 203	3 701 950	3 809 154	209 603	218 827	203 094	211 628

Table A.20. **Number of taxpayers by tax type: Personal income tax and corporate income tax** *(continued)*

Jurisdiction	Number of taxpayers by tax type							
	Personal Income tax				Corporate Income tax			
	Registered taxpayers		Active taxpayers		Registered taxpayers		Active taxpayers	
	2018	2019	2018	2019	2018	2019	2018	2019
Israel[3]	D	D	5 283 445	5 394 358	D	D	227 279	242 471
Italy	28 460 000	28 767 000	28 460 000	28 767 000	1 359 000	1 361 000	1 359 000	1 361 000
Japan	D	D	D	D	3 106 000	3 132 000	D	D
Kenya	8 684 796	10 013 954	8 231 851	10 013 954	665 741	505 216	389 703	505 216
Korea	7 362 000	7 640 000	6 911 000	7 595 000	816 370	874 245	740 215	787 438
Latvia	914 463	911 291	914 463	911 291	117 599	115 348	117 599	115 348
Lithuania	1 903 993	2 312 467	1 404 288	1 328 259	193 974	202 830	151 600	156 006
Luxembourg	295 491	296 799	D	D	98 292	100 273	D	D
Malaysia	13 085 395	13 553 460	7 836 371	8 186 427	1 198 516	1 254 333	804 049	838 245
Malta	582 552	617 366	323 967	352 780	88 503	95 026	50 163	55 972
Mexico	77 595 276	83 484 527	69 743 073	75 298 562	2 659 546	2 763 497	2 052 832	2 143 999
Morocco	D	D	687 797	775 897	D	D	419 903	475 342
Netherlands	12 387 606	12 669 575	12 165 559	12 457 331	976 652	1 002 183	785 926	814 757
New Zealand	6 971 947	7 216 889	2 453 828	4 036 414	1 140 458	1 179 010	816 993	799 388
Norway	4 906 890	4 974 894	4 802 810	4 717 769	337 828	350 829	317 742	332 060
Peru	7 704 084	8 335 852	5 875 212	6 015 294	1 159 195	1 341 080	1 032 167	1 095 947
Poland	31 585 596	31 832 783	19 611 875	20 843 290	789 178	831 127	615 631	628 321
Portugal	10 276 617	10 295 909	5 351 618	5 446 716	501 428	507 940	501 428	507 940
Romania	D	D	D	D	267 056	266 302	103 993	115 987
Russia	D	D	8 064 548	8 508 037	4 085 035	3 744 617	3 386 702	3 219 939
Saudi Arabia					7 103	7 436	6 265	6 795
Singapore	2 532 034	2 591 238	D	D	325 256	344 658	D	D
Slovak Republic	665 801	686 048	D	D	322 235	340 389	D	D
Slovenia	2 768 150	2 830 393	1 547 325	1 564 197	112 408	112 393	112 408	112 393
South Africa	22 121 177	23 217 721	21 104 375	22 170 513	4 464 488	4 545 046	3 202 007	2 020 759
Spain	24 341 503	24 685 574	24 341 503	24 685 574	1 806 805	1 926 633	1 806 805	1 926 633

Table A.20. **Number of taxpayers by tax type: Personal income tax and corporate income tax** *(continued)*

	Number of taxpayers by tax type							
	Personal Income tax				Corporate Income tax			
	Registered taxpayers		Active taxpayers		Registered taxpayers		Active taxpayers	
Jurisdiction	**2018**	**2019**	**2018**	**2019**	**2018**	**2019**	**2018**	**2019**
Sweden	D	D	7 806 350	7 814 069	D	D	686 563	713 607
Switzerland	D	D	D	D	D	D	D	D
Thailand	D	D	11 460 408	11 124 159	D	D	664 058	704 018
Turkey	15 356 631	16 006 467	4 677 791	4 778 268	2 220 462	2 347 386	806 622	848 904
United Kingdom	D	D	31 200 000	31 600 000	4 161 866	4 336 819	3 378 871	3 595 291
United States	D	D	152 937 949	154 094 555	D	D	2 127 673	2 146 904

StatLink http://dx.doi.org/10.1787/888934272727

D Data not available

1. Argentina: The number of registered and active taxpayers includes 2 013 319 (for 2018) / 2 264 478 (for 2019) employees who had their PIT retained directly from the salary by their employers. These PIT taxpayers are not obliged to be registered for tax.
2. France: PIT taxpayer numbers are estimated.
3. Israel: The number of active PIT taxpayers is estimated.

Table A.21. **Number of taxpayers by tax type: Employers that withhold tax from employees, value added tax and excise**

	Number of taxpayers by tax type											
	Employers that withhold tax from employees				Value added tax				Excise (domestic manufacturers / producers)			
	Registered employers		Active employers		Registered taxpayers		Active taxpayers		Registered taxpayers		Active taxpayers	
Jurisdiction	2018	2019	2018	2019	2018	2019	2018	2019	2018	2019	2018	2019
Argentina	D	D	41 394	40 212	1 685 471	1 744 652	1 075 583	1 081 931	16 291	17 033	2 366	2 697
Australia	1 608 812	1 646 059	1 163 164	1 172 049	2 606 991	2 680 991	1 973 983	2 009 357	2 913	3 184	2 316	2 599
Austria	402 898	407 688	402 898	407 688	922 887	949 532	922 887	949 532				
Belgium	D	D	D	D	983 287	974 910	983 287	974 910				
Brazil	D	D	D	D	D	D	D	D	D	D	D	D
Bulgaria	D	D	D	D	297 464	310 709	297 464	310 709				
Canada	D	D	D	D	3 542 783	3 930 551	3 272 236	3 646 941	D	D	D	D
Chile	358 206	369 381	358 206	369 381	1 615 685	1 697 568	1 073 225	1 117 247	115	104	115	104
China (People's Republic of)	D	D	D	D	53 018 817	62 177 487	47 060 866	55 194 001	220 222	257 526	180 660	211 824
Colombia	D	D	D	D	1 323 244	1 406 341	443 837	455 671	34 192	37 194	34 192	34 126
Costa Rica	23 590	21 643	23 590	21 643	103 120	548 798	103 120	548 798	277	576	277	576
Croatia	102 831	117 248	102 831	117 248	147 794	154 717	147 794	154 717				
Cyprus	127 926	136 879	127 926	136 879	95 280	99 023	94 438	98 031				
Czech Republic	716 380	727 114	568 338	574 351	907 815	934 068	588 813	604 740				
Denmark	226 803	215 200	190 198	193 337	521 160	522 915	521 160	522 915	19 473	19 300	19 473	19 300
Estonia	63 997	73 387	63 997	73 387	96 670	100 157	96 670	100 157	590	584	590	584
Finland	242 182	238 622	242 182	238 622	529 130	611 470	529 130	611 470	D	D	D	D
France		D		1 050 000	6 020 000	6 400 000	3 990 000	4 100 000				
Georgia	619 383	743 853	160 116	173 898	120 502	134 138	70 609	71 669	842	2 125	835	2 012
Germany	2 559 853	2 564 642	2 559 853	2 564 642	6 083 972	6 087 993	6 083 972	6 087 993				
Greece	329 285	346 366	282 526	273 730	1 393 626	1 415 624	1 002 257	1 009 293	3 709	3 782	943	943
Hong Kong (China)												
Hungary	512 192	523 922	495 189	506 028	530 833	512 520	530 833	512 520	4 151	4 180	4 151	4 180
Iceland	38 040	39 286	38 040	39 286	33 267	33 690	33 267	33 690				
India	754 837	681 261	D	D								
Indonesia	D	D	D	D	D	D	D	D				
Ireland	226 958	210 766	198 781	202 298	268 874	273 365	260 359	255 949	33 910	35 015	33 910	35 015

Table A.21. **Number of taxpayers by tax type: Employers that withhold tax from employees, value added tax and excise** *(continued)*

	Number of taxpayers by tax type											
	Employers that withhold tax from employees				Value added tax				Excise (domestic manufacturers / producers)			
	Registered employers		Active employers		Registered taxpayers		Active taxpayers		Registered taxpayers		Active taxpayers	
Jurisdiction	**2018**	**2019**	**2018**	**2019**	**2018**	**2019**	**2018**	**2019**	**2018**	**2019**	**2018**	**2019**
Israel	D	D	356 075	337 547	D	D	847 247	886 573	D	D	51 801	53 798
Italy	4 122 000	4 080 000	4 122 000	4 080 000	8 920 000	9 018 000	4 785 000	4 700 000				
Japan	3 536 000	3 532 000	D	D	D	D	3 345 000	3 377 000				
Kenya	118 791	134 097	110 099	134 097	205 719	215 051	195 060	215 051	960	1 083	873	1 083
Korea	D	D	D	D	6 731 117	7 001 193	6 478 314	6 753 201	2 416	2 571	2 416	2 571
Latvia	D	D	D	D	83 554	78 897	83 554	78 897	7 111	7 050	7 111	7 050
Lithuania	106 543	108 763	103 774	104 313	86 848	90 015	86 848	90 015	1 592	1 709	1 577	1 693
Luxembourg	37 258	38 939	D	D	82 868	85 492	76 854	79 238				
Malaysia	1 069 623	1 134 315	755 742	809 086								
Malta	48 412	51 803	28 514	28 133	76 885	89 846	71 168	83 071				
Mexico	195 103	206 534	195 103	206 534	9 314 967	9 728 920	9 314 967	9 728 920	118 261	128 294	118 261	128 294
Morocco	D	D	366 320	376 812	D	D	619 615	680 482				
Netherlands	695 659	715 929	695 659	715 929	2 519 892	2 751 620	1 906 705	1 997 205				
New Zealand	222 606	223 590	215 184	214 753	658 770	665 981	642 242	649 080				
Norway	248 452	250 384	248 452	250 384	365 263	368 416	365 263	368 416	2 068	2 084	2 068	2 084
Peru	557 588	591 919	412 259	425 771	1 282 602	1 431 370	890 600	960 968	1 358	1 387	1 104	1 104
Poland	1 998 951	2 053 067	1 307 676	1 329 463	2 140 286	2 166 399	2 114 367	2 141 182	D	D	D	D
Portugal	D	D	432 896	448 643	1 435 236	1 644 535	1 435 236	1 644 535	D	D	1 547	1 800
Romania	583 998	603 306	535 089	551 926	404 921	423 892	404 713	423 134	2 668	2 702	2 137	2 163
Russia	D	D	3 745 630	3 881 721	1 644 214	1 514 258	1 406 517	1 326 821	D	D	D	D
Saudi Arabia					158 194	229 645	142 513	191 311	19	43	19	43
Singapore					100 243	101 293	D	D				
Slovak Republic	270 568	272 854	D	D	221 190	232 703	D	D				
Slovenia	96 453	97 579	96 453	97 579	112 661	116 380	112 661	116 380	1 103	1 595	1 103	1 595
South Africa	660 446	699 942	520 918	552 611	973 243	1 007 943	773 783	802 957	3 524	3 690	2 388	3 051
Spain	2 514 918	2 546 286	2 514 918	2 546 286	7 301 485	7 107 361	7 301 485	7 107 361	78 608	80 504	78 608	80 504

Table A.21. **Number of taxpayers by tax type: Employers that withhold tax from employees, value added tax and excise** *(continued)*

	Number of taxpayers by tax type											
	Employers that withhold tax from employees				Value added tax				Excise (domestic manufacturers / producers)			
	Registered employers		Active employers		Registered taxpayers		Active taxpayers		Registered taxpayers		Active taxpayers	
Jurisdiction	2018	2019	2018	2019	2018	2019	2018	2019	2018	2019	2018	2019
Sweden	D	D	460 211	456 948	D	D	1 131 219	1 152 580	D	D	72 300	71 840
Switzerland	D	D	D	D	386 662	395 036	386 662	395 036				
Thailand	D	D	192 854	207 439	1 175 400	1 244 776	599 662	620 720				
Turkey	10 655 887	11 116 258	2 964 862	3 082 199	11 525 277	11 981 727	2 856 889	2 965 674	70 990	77 890	7 991	6 850
United Kingdom	D	D	D	D	2 331 730	2 352 250	2 199 382	2 240 672	D	D	D	D
United States	D	D	6 884 725	6 905 030					D	D	1 049 493	1 073 183

StatLink http://dx.doi.org/10.1787/888934272746

D Data not available

Table A.22. **On-time return filing: Corporate income tax**

Jurisdiction	On-time return filing			
	Corporate income tax			
	No. of returns expected		No. of returns filed on time	
	2018	2019	2018	2019
Argentina	370 202	380 856	152 620	131 393
Australia [1]	D	D	D	D
Austria	189 619	197 396	D	D
Belgium	555 959	572 143	452 933	479 959
Brazil	D	D	1 333 482	1 282 372
Bulgaria	375 000	390 000	356 544	370 976
Canada	1 018 980	1 084 546	870 060	939 424
Chile	1 142 323	1 118 271	922 297	902 813
China (People's Republic of)	20 183 179	23 633 394	19 637 409	22 924 492
Colombia	868 053	889 314	454 175	455 721
Costa Rica	178 706	168 364	134 698	130 935
Croatia	154 123	158 835	129 107	132 949
Cyprus	123 763	120 701	70 259	66 554
Czech Republic	557 634	554 082	436 431	453 088
Denmark	333 000	351 000	284 000	292 000
Estonia	D	D	D	D
Finland	294 900	300 500	254 800	271 400
France	2 330 000	2 480 000	2 210 000	2 356 000
Georgia	D	1 031 188	D	693 256
Germany	1 351 895	1 391 483	1 087 199	1 105 498
Greece	247 404	259 193	241 503	253 770
Hong Kong (China)	488 468	540 034	319 464	362 867
Hungary	483 521	480 919	366 587	346 510
Iceland	45 492	46 652	37 197	40 019
India	843 552	836 349	753 226	783 284
Indonesia	D	D	D	D
Ireland	202 795	212 630	D	D
Israel	198 870	275 646	170 593	242 250
Italy	D	D	1 488 000	1 599 000
Japan	D	D	D	D
Kenya	389 703	505 216	220 698	235 067
Korea	D	D	D	D
Latvia	102 449	107 338	80 230	105 299
Lithuania	193 974	202 830	96 309	103 901
Luxembourg	D	D	D	D
Malaysia	484 690	511 059	386 447	399 866
Malta	50 163	55 972	34 196	D
Mexico	1 653 993	1 713 156	763 925	817 999
Morocco	271 008	265 294	244 655	247 163

Table A.22. **On-time return filing: Corporate income tax** *(continued)*

	On-time return filing			
	Corporate income tax			
	No. of returns expected		No. of returns filed on time	
Jurisdiction	2018	2019	2018	2019
Netherlands	785 926	814 757	742 219	788 231
New Zealand	817 069	799 419	725 030	710 953
Norway	321 955	338 503	309 329	323 306
Peru	741 194	753 153	623 404	652 963
Poland	591 653	587 407	532 138	528 574
Portugal	500 026	509 121	487 590	503 517
Romania	408 014	357 478	353 686	324 811
Russia	9 104 993	8 434 059	6 893 546	6 216 986
Saudi Arabia	6 101	6 238	4 567	4 545
Singapore	219 966	230 744	185 375	194 606
Slovak Republic	322 235	340 389	250 762	264 432
Slovenia	112 408	112 393	99 133	105 390
South Africa	2 733 331	1 555 435	375 819	458 271
Spain	D	D	1 605 088	1 597 585
Sweden	D	D	D	D
Switzerland	D	D	D	D
Thailand	D	D	D	D
Turkey	4 033 110	4 244 520	3 596 031	3 804 085
United Kingdom[2]	3 550 648	3 780 543	2 520 013	2 685 303
United States	2 062 100	2 154 300	2 127 673	2 146 904

StatLink http://dx.doi.org/10.1787/888934272765

D Data not available

1. Australia: The on-time filing percentage for CIT was 76.29% (FY 2018) and 78.74% (FY 2019).
2. United Kingdom: CIT methodology has changed compared to previous years.

Table A.23. **On-time return filing: Personal income tax**

Jurisdiction	On-time return filing: Personal income tax: No. of returns expected 2018	No. of returns expected 2019	No. of returns filed on time 2018	No. of returns filed on time 2019
Argentina	1 309 209	1 285 831	788 764	727 841
Australia [1]	D	D	D	D
Austria	8 247 467	8 565 293	D	D
Belgium	7 119 341	7 151 559	6 647 691	6 685 912
Brazil	28 800 000	30 500 000	28 086 790	29 232 838
Bulgaria	650 000	670 000	589 364	627 639
Canada	27 847 908	27 153 000	25 340 128	25 780 047
Chile	D	D	1 764 619	1 827 604
China (People's Republic of)	D	D	D	D
Colombia	3 062 456	3 140 302	3 127 050	3 147 901
Costa Rica	482 153	491 225	341 168	327 589
Croatia	117 487	125 055	104 128	118 883
Cyprus	360 180	394 634	271 500	265 292
Czech Republic	2 264 842	2 286 260	2 173 442	2 206 925
Denmark	5 252 671	5 267 310	5 208 947	5 171 850
Estonia	752 944	755 272	706 028	741 026
Finland	1 712 900	1 489 200	1 513 500	1 298 000
France	39 037 176	39 394 542	37 533 908	37 734 067
Georgia	D	2 517 599	D	1 629 075
Germany	21 121 312	21 664 714	17 468 727	17 697 816
Greece	6 368 152	6 447 321	6 327 119	6 422 078
Hong Kong (China)	3 105 761	3 170 111	2 374 882	2 361 122
Hungary	D	D	D	D
Iceland	307 699	313 338	287 534	293 528
India	58 723 101	62 701 418	56 201 805	59 624 154
Indonesia	D	D	D	D
Ireland	674 359	673 860	557 021	556 460
Israel	1 136 152	1 223 998	1 041 994	1 125 573
Italy	D	D	29 258 000	30 123 000
Japan	D	D	D	D
Kenya	8 231 851	10 013 954	3 503 551	3 277 406
Korea	6 911 000	7 595 000	6 759 000	7 373 000
Latvia	768 863	961 274	722 633	900 271
Lithuania	770 487	538 417	606 775	408 083
Luxembourg	D	D	D	D
Malaysia	5 401 460	6 294 120	4 157 740	4 275 492
Malta	161 066	78 194	124 546	D
Mexico	10 320 092	12 107 985	3 020 996	3 862 555
Morocco	307 527	197 867	250 383	193 367

Table A.23. **On-time return filing: Personal income tax** *(continued)*

	On-time return filing			
	Personal income tax			
	No. of returns expected		No. of returns filed on time	
Jurisdiction	**2018**	**2019**	**2018**	**2019**
Netherlands	8 072 697	8 324 512	7 961 000	8 243 247
New Zealand	1 243 624	1 206 998	1 096 806	1 053 295
Norway	4 903 431	4 971 693	4 886 621	4 951 602
Peru	568 766	591 818	392 455	467 589
Poland	24 074 191	24 277 771	23 790 859	23 258 359
Portugal	5 346 422	5 430 582	5 185 648	5 275 003
Romania	757 366	697 850	D	D
Russia	8 064 548	8 508 037	9 272 229	8 367 481
Saudi Arabia				
Singapore	2 404 539	2 466 392	2 332 197	2 400 038
Slovak Republic	939 740	948 224	930 221	940 661
Slovenia	18 553	20 588	12 109	13 537
South Africa	3 364 765	3 929 213	2 261 105	2 427 511
Spain	D	D	19 920 599	20 635 885
Sweden	D	D	D	D
Switzerland	D	D	D	D
Thailand	D	D	D	D
Turkey	12 230 243	12 504 636	11 345 827	11 531 850
United Kingdom	11 564 363	11 122 967	10 833 177	10 760 043
United States	152 558 000	154 601 100	152 937 949	154 094 555

StatLink http://dx.doi.org/10.1787/888934272784

D Data not available

1. Australia: The on-time filing percentage for PIT was 83.14% (FY 2018) and 83.77% (FY 2019).

Table A.24. **On-time return filing: Employers that withhold tax from employees**

	On-time return filing			
	Employers that withhold tax from employees			
	No. of returns expected		No. of returns filed on time	
Jurisdiction	**2018**	**2019**	**2018**	**2019**
Argentina	7 619 631	7 414 025	6 621 829	6 475 253
Australia [1]	D	D	D	D
Austria	D	D	D	D
Belgium	D	D	D	D
Brazil	D	D	D	D
Bulgaria	D	D	D	D
Canada	1 378 190	1 371 035	1 255 144	1 271 947
Chile	825 630	850 319	767 666	803 614
China (People's Republic of)	D	D	D	D
Colombia	D	D	470 663	545 395
Costa Rica	23 590	21 643	6 812	6 902
Croatia	D	D	D	D
Cyprus	D	D	D	D
Czech Republic	367 167	367 760	329 309	331 106
Denmark	2 562 077	2 378 271	2 507 420	2 298 600
Estonia	1 351 255	1 264 131	1 275 320	1 179 824
Finland	1 459 700	1 438 700	1 360 900	1 122 200
France		D		24 820 808
Georgia	D	1 897 671	D	1 109 856
Germany	D	D	D	D
Greece	3 292 663	3 414 489	3 108 112	3 201 444
Hong Kong (China)				
Hungary	6 146 304	6 287 064	5 612 460	5 740 044
Iceland	D	D	D	D
India	2 319 911	2 167 068	2 091 117	1 742 167
Indonesia	D	D	D	D
Ireland	1 809 888	1 650 104	1 581 901	1 558 340
Israel	293 791	298 148	291 688	293 429
Italy	D	D	4 909 000	5 137 000
Japan	D	D	D	D
Kenya	1 321 188	1 609 164	728 405	876 014
Korea	D	D	D	D
Latvia	1 012 057	1 020 531	863 330	891 153
Lithuania	1 137 066	1 140 706	1 075 479	1 077 236
Luxembourg	D	D	D	D
Malaysia	569 832	591 097	526 221	512 993
Malta	28 514	28 133	21 121	21 881
Mexico	D	D	D	D
Morocco	366 320	376 812	358 287	376 812

Table A.24. **On-time return filing: Employers that withhold tax from employees** *(continued)*

	On-time return filing			
	Employers that withhold tax from employees			
	No. of returns expected		No. of returns filed on time	
Jurisdiction	**2018**	**2019**	**2018**	**2019**
Netherlands	8 149 126	8 271 363	8 071 784	8 197 340
New Zealand	4 635 245	5 975 107	4 308 232	5 496 107
Norway	2 360 790	2 382 092	1 947 856	1 933 387
Peru	918 003	963 610	901 410	936 984
Poland	1 249 301	1 255 865	1 213 815	1 217 457
Portugal	4 732 224	4 884 537	4 614 631	4 769 191
Romania	6 190 158	6 303 442	5 891 920	6 028 533
Russia	3 745 630	3 881 721	3 867 448	4 007 368
Saudi Arabia				
Singapore				
Slovak Republic	D	D	2 020 618	2 101 893
Slovenia	1 752 866	1 805 913	1 687 586	1 765 086
South Africa	5 946 753	6 333 025	3 511 508	3 702 887
Spain	D	D	9 016 484	9 169 869
Sweden	D	D	D	D
Switzerland	D	D	D	D
Thailand	D	D	D	D
Turkey	13 842 749	14 256 106	13 039 870	13 201 154
United Kingdom	D	D	D	D
United States	30 833 000	31 380 600	30 942 654	31 566 173

StatLink http://dx.doi.org/10.1787/888934272803

D Data not available

1. Australia: The on-time filing percentage for Employer Withholding Tax was 79.88% (FY 2018) and 79.16% (FY 2019).

Table A.25. **On-time return filing: Value added tax**

	On-time return filing			
	Value added tax			
	No. of returns expected		No. of returns filed on time	
Jurisdiction	**2018**	**2019**	**2018**	**2019**
Argentina	12 725 465	12 830 502	10 224 633	10 409 639
Australia [1]	D	D	D	D
Austria	4 807 657	4 920 066	4 126 857	4 222 066
Belgium	3 672 990	3 752 907	3 644 618	3 721 634
Brazil	D	D	12 523 352	12 408 838
Bulgaria	3 570 000	3 750 000	3 553 894	3 686 355
Canada	8 582 129	8 830 463	5 207 495	5 258 387
Chile	11 466 276	12 004 380	8 749 067	9 262 134
China (People's Republic of)	307 487 616	337 523 421	298 707 077	330 182 109
Colombia	D	D	1 252 111	1 232 272
Costa Rica	1 237 800	2 634 230	964 902	1 806 694
Croatia	1 532 595	1 588 940	1 355 557	1 394 881
Cyprus	357 063	374 095	307 438	323 005
Czech Republic	4 423 626	4 590 598	4 215 950	4 441 265
Denmark	1 415 525	1 440 487	1 212 678	1 241 610
Estonia	1 073 164	1 111 159	983 684	1 007 687
Finland	3 361 200	3 252 100	3 029 500	2 933 000
France	19 000 000	19 416 000	17 370 000	17 690 000
Georgia	710 141	782 552	651 041	707 645
Germany	6 248 248	6 273 200	5 002 316	4 969 003
Greece	6 866 650	7 034 406	4 566 849	4 663 270
Hong Kong (China)				
Hungary	3 538 744	3 555 392	3 049 428	3 037 724
Iceland	151 074	151 037	144 125	142 277
India				
Indonesia	D	D	D	D
Ireland	804 819	866 523	718 217	752 961
Israel	4 018 578	4 137 540	3 893 836	4 017 981
Italy	D	D	5 172 000	5 334 000
Japan	D	D	D	D
Kenya	2 340 720	2 580 612	1 888 078	2 071 280
Korea	D	D	D	D
Latvia	734 511	730 373	662 256	666 409
Lithuania	882 105	909 519	856 440	845 196
Luxembourg	361 595	376 403	323 695	319 528
Malaysia				
Malta	200 645	214 898	143 066	139 978
Mexico	D	D	D	D
Morocco	1 909 391	1 901 918	1 721 166	1 745 725

Table A.25. **On-time return filing: Value added tax** *(continued)*

Jurisdiction	On-time return filing – Value added tax – No. of returns expected – 2018	No. of returns expected – 2019	No. of returns filed on time – 2018	No. of returns filed on time – 2019
Netherlands	8 725 822	9 123 881	8 343 926	8 726 006
New Zealand	3 029 671	3 068 416	2 807 854	2 832 962
Norway	1 484 145	1 532 797	1 335 022	1 374 949
Peru	11 323 819	11 839 980	9 875 600	10 404 054
Poland	17 284 643	17 939 022	16 817 286	17 530 948
Portugal	3 682 012	3 827 648	3 514 789	3 653 118
Romania	3 030 907	3 157 346	2 830 736	2 950 465
Russia	D	D	7 990 646	7 341 333
Saudi Arabia	515 841	722 461	395 955	694 161
Singapore	386 816	385 541	370 411	369 997
Slovak Republic	1 757 762	1 836 299	1 818 568	1 922 312
Slovenia	848 592	889 313	714 461	761 725
South Africa	4 822 639	5 038 532	2 513 243	2 618 867
Spain	D	D	14 161 892	14 258 233
Sweden	D	D	D	D
Switzerland	1 261 442	1 287 632	979 475	977 549
Thailand	599 662	620 720	D	D
Turkey	34 282 668	35 588 088	29 975 283	30 939 217
United Kingdom	8 828 318	8 945 228	7 490 372	7 523 893
United States				

StatLink http://dx.doi.org/10.1787/888934272822

D Data not available

1. Australia: The on-time filing percentage for VAT was 76.63% (FY 2018) and 75.97% (FY 2019).

Table A.26. **Personal income tax withheld by third parties, and on-time payments: Personal income tax**

	Estimated percentage of total personal income tax withheld by third parties and subsequently paid to the administration		On-time payment: Personal income tax: Value of payments expected by due date (in thousands in local currency)		On-time payment: Personal income tax: Value of payments made on time (in thousands in local currency)	
Jurisdiction	**2018**	**2019**	**2018**	**2019**	**2018**	**2019**
Argentina	81.7	84.7	45 794 768	64 369 299	25 324 994	37 216 348
Australia	D	D	45 133 387	49 309 629	31 362 796	35 098 867
Austria	87.6	86.5	8 280 237	9 016 937	7 512 477	8 176 558
Belgium	93.2	92.6	4 607 023	5 041 543	3 299 444	3 599 171
Brazil	77.8	77.8	151 944 124	163 467 772	146 535 778	157 377 081
Bulgaria	88.0	89.0	3 453 032	3 740 072	2 941 827	3 254 757
Canada	D	D	182 156 456	189 592 933	171 191 477	178 286 878
Chile	86.1	88.7	D	D	319 296 456	445 140 291
China (People's Republic of)	80.0	85.0	D	D	D	D
Colombia	84.0	89.0	D	D	12 215 962 644	12 888 179 508
Costa Rica	12.2	10.4	63 225 084	69 626 560	46 002 501	39 603 241
Croatia	D	D	D	D	D	D
Cyprus	50.0	41.0	D	D	48 698	59 443
Czech Republic	96.0	96.0	20 695 216	23 129 364	17 250 201	19 111 363
Denmark	95.0	95.0	D	D	D	D
Estonia	96.2	95.9	53 538	62 230	40 214	49 641
Finland	89.2	89.0	3 607 400	3 459 600	3 195 200	2 659 500
France	D	79.0	81 203 259	10 466 643	76 149 292	9 429 048
Georgia	92.8	92.9	63 967	58 271	62 064	56 404
Germany	D	D	D	D	D	D
Greece	74.0	75.0	3 629 250	3 702 422	2 465 912	2 530 241
Hong Kong (China)	D	D	76 877 828	78 609 555	70 905 278	72 342 966
Hungary	93.3	95.4	D	D	D	D
Iceland	D	D	189 297 000	199 295 000	D	D
India	48.0	51.0	4 981 308 211	5 206 791 615	D	D
Indonesia	54.1	66.1	135 302 740 515	149 246 057 762	113 141 456 576	119 686 696 088
Ireland	95.6	95.1	3 470 541	3 657 398	3 415 715	3 589 135
Israel	70.6	67.0	19 227 000	21 395 375	19 524 890	21 380 816
Italy	89.0	89.0	D	D	D	D
Japan	84.0	84.0	D	D	D	D
Kenya	72.7	71.1	345 597 569	367 954 259	345 597 569	367 954 259
Korea	D	D	D	D	D	D
Latvia	86.0	83.0	1 705 908	1 930 489	D	D
Lithuania	99.0	97.7	1 854 310	3 510 383	1 666 124	3 093 481
Luxembourg	41.0	40.0	D	D	D	D
Malaysia	22.1	18.1	3 350 328	3 828 553	2 495 169	2 997 127
Malta	83.4	83.3	570 644	697 086	404 842	506 057
Mexico	42.9	43.7	D	D	D	D

Table A.26. **Personal income tax withheld by third parties, and on-time payments: Personal income tax** *(continued)*

	Estimated percentage of total personal income tax withheld by third parties and subsequently paid to the administration		On-time payment: Personal income tax			
			Value of payments expected by due date (in thousands in local currency)		Value of payments made on time (in thousands in local currency)	
Jurisdiction	**2018**	**2019**	**2018**	**2019**	**2018**	**2019**
Morocco	75.0	80.0	D	D	7 563 560	9 731 760
Netherlands	99.2	98.3	17 249 589	18 675 959	16 401 685	17 791 409
New Zealand	86.4	86.0	5 000 655	5 128 911	4 722 650	4 724 180
Norway	93.7	93.5	57 247 863	59 467 468	44 045 240	46 288 514
Peru	99.3	99.4	2 223 211	2 260 937	978 238	1 022 431
Poland	73.8	72.2	42 325 496	48 931 820	33 468 543	38 223 315
Portugal	84.1	84.1	D	D	1 751 101	1 796 742
Romania	83.0	81.1	20 480 424	21 804 471	17 663 271	18 949 681
Russia	94.8	94.4	191 842 229	224 347 868	189 978 347	222 459 709
Saudi Arabia	0.0	0.0				
Singapore [1]	D	D	D	D	D	D
Slovak Republic	97.8	97.3	240 655	296 409	224 866	234 622
Slovenia	82.8	81.3	2 480 506	2 636 252	2 255 709	2 408 272
South Africa	95.5	95.8	24 041 023	26 487 713	12 379 582	11 813 658
Spain	84.1	67.9	40 808 853	41 623 363	39 392 024	39 908 400
Sweden	D	D	D	D	D	D
Switzerland	D	D	D	D	D	D
Thailand	90.3	90.4	D	D	D	D
Turkey	D	D	D	D	D	D
United Kingdom	D	D	D	D	D	D
United States	78.7	79.1	D	D	3 051 554 159	3 137 078 983

StatLink http://dx.doi.org/10.1787/888934272841

D Data not available

1. Singapore: The on-time payment rate for PIT was 90.1% (for FY 2018) and 91.2% (for FY 2019).

Table A.27. **On-time payment: Corporate income tax**

	On-time payment			
	Corporate income tax			
	Value of payments expected by due date (in thousands in local currency)		Value of payments made on time (in thousands in local currency)	
Jurisdiction	2018	2019	2018	2019
Argentina	214 131 200	288 592 233	186 068 241	249 679 466
Australia	90 818 000	102 645 098	77 894 408	90 460 258
Austria	11 939 943	12 548 199	11 587 715	12 199 359
Belgium	7 324 317	5 821 383	5 883 051	3 749 077
Brazil	125 258 607	146 252 157	121 120 559	140 195 214
Bulgaria	2 580 822	2 594 642	2 201 828	2 244 157
Canada	84 769 898	88 913 605	72 683 445	76 974 391
Chile	D	D	1 991 254 174	2 579 276 884
China (People's Republic of)	D	D	D	D
Colombia	D	D	55 844 952 795	58 773 414 489
Costa Rica	1 181 986 602	1 255 188 533	302 272 025	581 167 917
Croatia	D	D	D	D
Cyprus	D	D	628 568	676 271
Czech Republic	164 630 385	172 441 027	155 662 541	162 508 930
Denmark	113 200 000	107 500 000	105 700 000	98 000 000
Estonia	519 352	510 176	386 373	422 336
Finland	5 947 300	5 965 900	5 395 900	5 357 800
France	D	D	60 852 000	64 654 000
Georgia	802 181	972 701	752 524	887 255
Germany	D	D	D	D
Greece	4 241 172	4 493 881	3 744 509	3 991 410
Hong Kong (China)	147 891 243	175 508 094	139 345 001	165 272 607
Hungary	D	D	D	D
Iceland	75 702 000	67 802 000	D	D
India	7 688 196 344	6 776 629 941	D	D
Indonesia	266 257 585 543	260 580 703 229	233 465 633 411	233 391 743 824
Ireland	17 177 393	19 925 557	17 051 868	19 542 219
Israel	48 001 000	50 425 295	49 446 229	50 579 914
Italy	D	D	D	D
Japan	D	D	D	D
Kenya	145 427 380	152 051 119	145 427 380	152 051 119
Korea	D	D	D	D
Latvia	146 532	198 616	D	D
Lithuania	686 592	753 465	664 821	680 070
Luxembourg	D	D	D	D
Malaysia	63 410 659	62 733 412	44 517 176	54 007 692
Malta	463 310	605 520	350 426	488 483
Mexico	D	D	D	D
Morocco	D	D	46 892 971	46 912 714

Table A.27. **On-time payment: Corporate income tax** *(continued)*

Jurisdiction	On-time payment – Corporate income tax – Value of payments expected by due date (in thousands in local currency) 2018	2019	Value of payments made on time (in thousands in local currency) 2018	2019
Netherlands	24 954 535	27 449 967	24 438 715	26 876 958
New Zealand	12 658 170	9 903 232	12 396 428	7 051 688
Norway	83 897 037	90 661 376	75 557 431	83 514 088
Peru	19 127 365	19 451 966	16 635 761	17 091 455
Poland	47 322 975	54 950 843	43 943 133	50 629 613
Portugal	D	D	5 123 909	6 576 806
Romania	14 613 522	16 108 170	12 761 274	14 417 123
Russia	4 664 268 342	5 181 538 288	4 600 274 067	5 116 741 571
Saudi Arabia	16 120 000	17 000 000	8 580 000	6 500 000
Singapore [1]	D	D	D	D
Slovak Republic	4 447 193	4 299 359	3 911 711	4 124 978
Slovenia	848 619	996 207	777 991	923 104
South Africa	50 123 194	54 746 579	14 177 432	22 445 126
Spain	25 973 853	24 782 175	23 846 753	23 112 091
Sweden	D	D	D	D
Switzerland	D	D	D	D
Thailand	D	D	D	D
Turkey	D	D	D	D
United Kingdom	D	D	D	D
United States	D	D	262 742 024	277 057 735

StatLink http://dx.doi.org/10.1787/888934272860

D Data not available

1. Singapore: The on-time payment rate for CIT was 84.9% (for FY 2018) and 84.3% (for FY 2019).

Table A.28. **On-time payment: Employers that withhold tax from employees**

	On-time payment			
	Employers that withhold tax from employees			
	Value of payments expected by due date (in thousands in local currency)		Value of payments made on time (in thousands in local currency)	
Jurisdiction	2018	2019	2018	2019
Argentina	854 106 894	1 137 409 865	702 413 829	945 795 040
Australia	197 898 177	210 583 569	187 928 695	199 989 642
Austria	27 022 222	28 313 954	26 867 211	28 178 047
Belgium	45 401 762	45 033 009	45 072 746	44 801 931
Brazil	213 713 134	227 406 407	209 551 857	223 302 283
Bulgaria	9 251 296	10 302 734	7 852 132	8 933 568
Canada	D	D	D	D
Chile	D	D	3 081 379 357	3 384 757 357
China (People's Republic of)	D	D	D	D
Colombia	D	D	D	D
Costa Rica	324 750 536	306 981 152	209 433	198 468
Croatia	D	D	D	D
Cyprus	D	D	450 527	503 397
Czech Republic	D	D	D	D
Denmark	520 100 000	499 400 000	502 000 000	482 400 000
Estonia	4 837 812	5 358 843	3 845 104	4 280 614
Finland	29 014 800	29 274 500	27 827 600	28 006 700
France		59 636 000		59 332 000
Georgia	3 252 185	3 506 971	3 205 819	3 481 411
Germany	D	D	D	D
Greece	6 436 980	6 143 249	6 050 112	5 782 241
Hong Kong (China)				
Hungary	D	D	D	D
Iceland	D	D	D	D
India	2 438 764 109	2 670 304 905	D	D
Indonesia	120 516 131 378	133 865 351 353	102 234 098 044	108 300 898 219
Ireland	25 576 878	28 091 280	25 299 484	27 708 577
Israel	100 723 884	103 872 650	97 775 171	102 852 857
Italy	D	D	D	D
Japan	D	D	D	D
Kenya	362 627 562	395 206 680	362 627 562	395 206 680
Korea	D	D	D	D
Latvia	1 728 756	2 034 459	D	D
Lithuania	1 834 586	3 422 255	1 656 453	3 034 608
Luxembourg	D	D	D	D
Malaysia	D	D	26 262 002	30 309 428
Malta	671 976	765 238	652 343	720 791
Mexico	D	D	D	D
Morocco	D	D	30 406 485	30 439 015

Table A.28. **On-time payment: Employers that withhold tax from employees** *(continued)*

	On-time payment			
	Employers that withhold tax from employees			
	Value of payments expected by due date (in thousands in local currency)		Value of payments made on time (in thousands in local currency)	
Jurisdiction	2018	2019	2018	2019
Netherlands	153 029 885	156 998 869	151 669 493	155 430 268
New Zealand	31 188 619	33 258 826	30 773 099	32 705 221
Norway	461 500 490	481 364 225	442 153 417	458 915 101
Peru	10 280 325	10 893 369	9 958 399	10 577 791
Poland	80 723 408	87 822 771	77 654 768	84 207 187
Portugal	16 207 452	16 980 692	16 072 718	16 210 520
Romania	17 109 189	17 733 281	14 665 151	15 372 795
Russia	3 496 982 975	3 764 438 217	3 463 007 337	3 732 755 912
Saudi Arabia				
Singapore				
Slovak Republic	2 985 502	3 156 856	2 819 545	2 999 604
Slovenia	7 040 694	7 526 982	6 471 426	6 971 982
South Africa	438 544 773	473 107 982	423 077 222	457 740 313
Spain	73 384 314	77 406 906	73 158 596	77 160 624
Sweden	D	D	D	D
Switzerland	D	D	D	D
Thailand	D	D	D	D
Turkey	D	D	D	D
United Kingdom	D	D	D	D
United States	D	D	2 402 897 198	2 480 089 706

StatLink http://dx.doi.org/10.1787/888934272879

D Data not available

Table A.29. On-time payment: Value added tax

	On-time payment If USBB			
	Value added tax			
	Value of payments expected by due date (in thousands in local currency)		Value of payments made on time (in thousands in local currency)	
Jurisdiction	2018	2019	2018	2019
Argentina	418 094 665	582 014 138	352 427 643	487 624 049
Australia	128 435 514	132 144 486	113 520 240	117 173 823
Austria	47 526 507	49 738 801	46 029 600	48 271 506
Belgium	41 559 169	42 555 693	40 932 355	41 931 852
Brazil	264 160 417	270 794 568	256 933 481	263 736 256
Bulgaria	13 897 447	15 305 150	11 836 397	13 181 541
Canada	D	D	D	D
Chile	D	D	10 152 127 139	11 154 889 150
China (People's Republic of)	D	D	D	D
Colombia	41 462 842 233	44 946 735 365	40 856 075 768	44 349 481 098
Costa Rica	2 113 986 069	2 395 626 317	170 386 369	467 682 865
Croatia	D	D	D	D
Cyprus	D	D	1 306 604	1 378 375
Czech Republic	721 390 269	752 058 375	665 275 969	690 245 632
Denmark	403 300 000	416 000 000	366 900 000	382 400 000
Estonia	3 630 775	3 836 208	2 836 575	2 990 070
Finland	30 803 400	32 057 900	27 861 700	28 916 700
France	210 883 000	220 370 000	203 572 000	211 492 000
Georgia	2 643 645	2 985 113	2 568 111	2 868 694
Germany	D	D	D	D
Greece	18 507 711	18 165 537	16 064 369	16 022 168
Hong Kong (China)				
Hungary	D	D	D	D
Iceland	237 368 000	242 216 000	D	D
India				
Indonesia	561 152 348 365	574 547 310 683	451 030 881 526	452 698 709 419
Ireland	16 766 054	18 372 413	16 439 407	18 011 161
Israel	87 476 607	82 115 840	78 816 718	73 848 017
Italy	D	D	D	D
Japan	D	D	D	D
Kenya	137 957 201	198 608 615	137 957 201	198 608 615
Korea	D	D	D	D
Latvia	2 423 762	2 571 306	D	D
Lithuania	3 182 471	3 453 702	3 154 529	3 332 595
Luxembourg	D	D	D	D
Malaysia				
Malta	1 007 821	1 164 711	728 918	720 791
Mexico	D	D	D	D

Table A.29. **On-time payment: Value added tax** *(continued)*

	On-time payment If USBB			
	Value added tax			
	Value of payments expected by due date (in thousands in local currency)		Value of payments made on time (in thousands in local currency)	
Jurisdiction	**2018**	**2019**	**2018**	**2019**
Morocco	D	D	91 102 221	92 775 157
Netherlands	82 322 587	88 651 554	80 866 383	87 279 098
New Zealand	31 254 859	32 980 692	30 142 354	31 880 993
Norway	373 681 551	399 256 872	330 275 201	352 435 843
Peru	26 206 245	26 013 269	22 926 529	24 192 738
Poland	258 565 039	285 382 587	227 285 777	250 406 974
Portugal	22 765 635	24 043 766	22 116 379	23 525 167
Romania	72 359 442	80 832 391	62 369 281	69 055 584
Russia	3 904 068 142	4 647 804 170	3 761 173 371	4 481 741 841
Saudi Arabia	45 668 834	47 465 837	40 455 601	42 489 194
Singapore [1]	D	D	D	D
Slovak Republic	11 322 337	11 603 641	10 034 021	10 579 057
Slovenia	3 797 957	3 963 632	3 455 924	3 584 254
South Africa	333 806 396	375 196 740	307 614 240	343 462 125
Spain	34 696 975	37 218 555	32 799 364	35 146 552
Sweden	D	D	D	D
Switzerland	D	D	D	D
Thailand	D	D	D	D
Turkey	D	D	D	D
United Kingdom	99 014 313	104 813 926	81 855 477	86 471 933
United States				

StatLink http://dx.doi.org/10.1787/888934272898

D Data not available

1. Singapore: The on-time payment rate for VAT was 89.9% (for FY 2018) and 90.4% (for FY 2019).

Table A.30. **VAT refunds**

Jurisdiction	Treatment of approved VAT refunds 2018	Treatment of approved VAT refunds 2019	Value of all VAT "credits" at year end (in thousands in local currency) 2018	Value of all VAT "credits" at year end (in thousands in local currency) 2019
Argentina	Established as "credit", refunded on request	Established as "credit", refunded on request	D	D
Australia	Automatically paid out	Automatically paid out		
Austria	Established as "credit", refunded on request	Established as "credit", refunded on request	D	D
Belgium	Established as "credit", refunded on request	Established as "credit", refunded on request	14 780	15 339
Brazil	Automatically paid out	Automatically paid out		
Bulgaria	Automatically paid out	Automatically paid out		
Canada	Automatically paid out	Automatically paid out		
Chile	Automatically paid out	Automatically paid out		
China (People's Republic of)	Established as "credit", refunded subject to funds	Established as "credit", refunded on request	0	0
Colombia	Established as "credit", refunded on request	Established as "credit", refunded on request	0	0
Costa Rica	Automatically paid out	Automatically paid out		
Croatia	Automatically paid out	Automatically paid out		
Cyprus	Established as "credit", refunded on request	Established as "credit", refunded on request	157 379	184 950
Czech Republic	Automatically paid out	Automatically paid out		
Denmark	Automatically paid out	Automatically paid out		
Estonia	Established as "credit", refunded on request	Established as "credit", refunded on request	D	D
Finland	Established as "credit", refunded on request	Established as "credit", refunded on request	721 209	767 668
France	Automatically paid out	Automatically paid out		
Georgia	Established as "credit", refunded on request	Established as "credit", refunded on request	538 877	426 877
Germany	Automatically paid out	Automatically paid out		
Greece	Automatically paid out	Automatically paid out		
Hong Kong (China)				
Hungary	Automatically paid out	Automatically paid out		
Iceland	Automatically paid out	Automatically paid out		
India				
Indonesia	Automatically paid out	Automatically paid out		
Ireland	Automatically paid out	Automatically paid out		
Israel	Automatically paid out	Automatically paid out		
Italy	Automatically paid out	Automatically paid out		
Japan				
Kenya	Established as "credit", refunded subject to funds	Established as "credit", refunded subject to funds	2 284	3 649
Korea	Automatically paid out	Automatically paid out		
Latvia	Automatically paid out	Automatically paid out		
Lithuania	Established as "credit", refunded on request	Established as "credit", refunded on request	10	216
Luxembourg	Automatically paid out	Automatically paid out		
Malaysia				

Table A.30. **VAT refunds** *(continued)*

Jurisdiction	Treatment of approved VAT refunds		Value of all VAT "credits" at year end (in thousands in local currency)	
	2018	2019	2018	2019
Malta	Paid out, subject to funds	Paid out, subject to funds	D	D
Mexico [1]	Established as "credit", refunded on request	Established as "credit", refunded on request	281 561	1 120 437
Morocco	Established as "credit", refunded on request	Established as "credit", refunded on request	37 955 600	14 033 400
Netherlands	Automatically paid out	Automatically paid out		
New Zealand	Automatically paid out	Automatically paid out		
Norway	Automatically paid out	Automatically paid out		
Peru	Established as "credit", refunded on request	Established as "credit", refunded on request	57 370	169 187
Poland	Established as "credit", refunded on request	Established as "credit", refunded on request	D	D
Portugal	Established as "credit", refunded on request	Established as "credit", refunded on request	92 704	113 701
Romania	Established as "credit", refunded subject to funds	Established as "credit", refunded subject to funds	5 603	6 187
Russia	Automatically paid out	Automatically paid out		
Saudi Arabia	Established as "credit", refunded on request	Established as "credit", refunded on request	1 059 931	3 700 000
Singapore	Automatically paid out	Automatically paid out		
Slovak Republic	Automatically paid out	Automatically paid out		
Slovenia	Established as "credit", refunded on request	Established as "credit", refunded on request	223 759	296 312
South Africa	Automatically paid out	Automatically paid out		
Spain	Established as "credit", refunded on request	Established as "credit", refunded on request	D	D
Sweden	Automatically paid out	Automatically paid out		
Switzerland	Automatically paid out	Automatically paid out		
Thailand	Established as "credit", refunded on request	Established as "credit", refunded on request	186 029 090	2 055 397 490
Turkey	Established as "credit", refunded on request	Established as "credit", refunded on request	72 005 175	89 402 791
United Kingdom	Automatically paid out	Automatically paid out		
United States				

StatLink http://dx.doi.org/10.1787/888934272917

Automatically paid out VAT refunds are automatically paid out immediately

Paid out, subject to funds VAT refunds are paid out immediately subject to the availability of funds

Established as "credit", refunded on request VAT refund are established as a "credit" in the taxpayer's account, until such time as the taxpayer may legally request the refund

Established as "credit", refunded subject to funds VAT refund are established as a "credit" in the taxpayer's account, until such time as the taxpayer may legally request the refund, subject to the availability of funds

D Data not available

1. Mexico: VAT refunds are automatically paid out for all taxpayers, with the exception of large taxpayers. For large taxpayers, VAT refund are established as a "credit" in the taxpayer's account, until such time as the taxpayer may legally request the refund. The value of VAT "credits" at year-end refers to large taxpayers.

Table A.31. **Closing stock of arrears: Total and non-collectable**

Jurisdiction	Closing stock of arrears at year-end (in thousands in local currency)							
	Total arrears		Arrears considered non-collectable		Total arrears relating to state owned enterprises		Arrears relating to state owned enterprises considered not collectable	
	2018	2019	2018	2019	2018	2019	2018	2019
Argentina	112 172 014	142 954 574	D	D	D	D	D	D
Australia	40 400 259	45 397 768	16 679 501	18 899 549	8 138	35 815	841	894
Austria	6 955 329	6 855 855	3 841 172	3 944 503	D	D	D	D
Belgium	17 358 788	17 539 139	2 732 689	2 687 153	136 072	10 313	135 777	10 234
Brazil	1 966 420 000	1 966 420 000	0	0	0	0	0	0
Bulgaria [1]	5 690 208	5 679 764	2 528 937	2 604 514	36 866	23 654	0	0
Canada	57 801 415	61 267 625	19 332 516	21 529 589	D	D	D	D
Chile	26 187 706 000	25 506 902 000	6 044 782 000	3 759 126 354	42 644 105	44 806 608	1 974 271	3 810
China (People's Republic of)	D	D	D	D	D	D	D	D
Colombia	17 476 121 760	18 513 822 555	6 538 509 076	5 749 085 359	0	0	0	0
Costa Rica	173 795 054	287 332 155	52 138 516	34 479 859	257 344	1 535 472	77 203	184 257
Croatia	22 540 146	20 042 390	19 010 418	17 127 643	D	D	D	D
Cyprus [2]	1 506 994	1 657 089	856 036	941 934	13 449	18 851	D	D
Czech Republic	144 558 063	154 038 458	102 938 164	118 638 321	D	D	D	D
Denmark	78 899 000	84 981 000	37 189 000	33 426 000	34 500 000	38 500 000	19 900 000	10 100 000
Estonia	529 793	581 555	78 868	71 092	D	D	D	D
Finland	3 906 000	3 521 000	1 669 000	1 774 000	D	D	D	D
France	27 120 512	25 080 187	D	D	D	D	D	D
Georgia	3 846 966	4 392 885	3 116 323	3 443 867	192 040	197 192	87 587	82 769
Germany	6 678 907	7 417 583	3 715 971	D	D	D	D	D
Greece [3]	104 365 020	105 617 906	19 254 238	22 635 089	11 678 987	11 286 684	48 882	48 067
Hong Kong (China)	39 690 439	45 512 352	18 716 963	19 752 459	0	0	0	0
Hungary	1 928 488 140	1 905 160 537	1 368 567 786	1 318 547 967	D	D	D	D
Iceland	115 871 000	99 773 000	D	D	D	D	D	D
India	10 257 608 000	15 926 346 000	D	D	D	D	D	D
Indonesia	68 090 740 726	D	41 098 667 933	D	3 513 544 753	D	1 372 244 761	D
Ireland	4 368 088	4 301 132	3 335 912	3 383 708	11 954	6 385	4 496	1 520

Table A.31. **Closing stock of arrears: Total and non-collectable** *(continued)*

Jurisdiction	Closing stock of arrears at year-end (in thousands in local currency)							
	Total arrears		Arrears considered non-collectable		Total arrears relating to state owned enterprises		Arrears relating to state owned enterprises considered not collectable	
	2018	2019	2018	2019	2018	2019	2018	2019
Israel	51 472 604	62 321 516	13 234 591	17 529 009	D	D	D	D
Italy	747 393 639	799 526 756	710 023 957	759 550 418	D	D	D	D
Japan	853 060 000	811 788 000	D	D	D	D	D	D
Kenya	305 909 000	415 948 513	236 399 000	319 406 000	D	42 529 000	D	D
Korea	16 787 184 138	17 721 573 899	7 647 754 618	8 437 145 513	D	D	D	D
Latvia	1 044 219	865 037	784 047	653 123	141	237	0	0
Lithuania	470 491	488 799	304 033	288 850	6 358	6 917	5 241	5 550
Luxembourg	1 803 187	2 096 012	D	D	D	D	D	D
Malaysia	10 778 838	10 721 290	983 762	590 985	0	0	0	0
Malta	3 615 593	4 460 900	3 295 695	4 010 133	D	D	D	D
Mexico	747 177 371	712 490 139	81 762 541	76 246 205	1 684 696	1 625 864	9 947	7 885
Morocco	D	D	D	D	D	D	D	D
Netherlands	13 007 259	16 525 305	5 662 158	9 248 730	D	D	D	D
New Zealand	4 425 976	5 210 539	1 130 285	1 001 322	D	D	D	D
Norway	30 684 641	32 022 871	4 738 302	4 805 075	D	D	D	D
Peru	123 344 656	122 969 986	87 304 168	79 611 890	3 379 213	3 327 534	765 633	565 348
Poland	113 649 847	118 728 471	D	D	17 777	18 037	3	28
Portugal	17 745 713	18 753 835	12 112 902	13 182 493	6 339	93 307	6 339	93 270
Romania	103 954 956	111 885 072	87 755 900	92 351 319	13 304 081	14 845 772	12 814 883	13 330 642
Russia	1 916 637 504	1 800 859 424	11 838 987	5 500 721	D	D	D	D
Saudi Arabia	D	45 000 000	D	0	D	0	D	0
Singapore	737 077	753 641	D	D	D	D	D	D
Slovak Republic	2 993 239	3 081 078	2 774 048	2 853 733	22	20	20	20
Slovenia	1 204 717	1 180 361	520 694	543 774	1 492	3 059	1 426	1 394
South Africa	128 716 919	142 272 706	30 823 941	26 138 130	809 720	592 566	691 515	452 621
Spain	18 476 910	17 732 940	D	D	D	D	D	D

Table A.31. **Closing stock of arrears: Total and non-collectable** *(continued)*

	Closing stock of arrears at year-end (in thousands in local currency)							
	Total arrears		Arrears considered non-collectable		Total arrears relating to state owned enterprises		Arrears relating to state owned enterprises considered not collectable	
Jurisdiction	2018	2019	2018	2019	2018	2019	2018	2019
Sweden	5 522 923	3 437 289	D	D	D	D	D	D
Switzerland	D	D	D	D	D	D	D	D
Thailand	334 452 730	359 600 453	115 588 970	156 899 810	D	D	D	D
Turkey	D	D	D	D	D	D	D	D
United Kingdom	13 742 155	15 061 367	2 247 726	2 638 774	D	D	D	D
United States	246 771 138	256 973 778	145 498 000	153 226 000	0	0	0	0

StatLink http://dx.doi.org/10.1787/888934272936

D Data not available

1. Bulgaria: Total stock of arrears refers to arrears from tax returns only.
2. Cyprus: The total amount of arrears is the sum of arrears for PIT, CIT, VAT and Employer Withholding Tax.
3. Greece: Arrears do not include interest and penalties.

Table A.32. Closing stock of arrears: By tax type

Jurisdiction	Closing stock of arrears at year-end by tax type (in thousands in local currency)							
	Corporate income tax		Personal income tax		Value added tax		Tax withheld from employees by employers	
	2018	2019	2018	2019	2018	2019	2018	2019
Argentina	9 822 322	14 740 155	9 437 333	12 367 046	33 811 091	49 465 594	50 297 152	57 258 725
Australia	9 691 947	10 905 847	10 553 940	11 312 477	5 529 227	5 667 982	6 237 551	7 230 710
Austria	875 734	838 610	1 357 108	1 343 330	2 553 672	2 417 015	283 533	274 755
Belgium	8 160 181	8 283 592	2 240 240	2 236 836	5 809 190	6 027 157	493 750	484 631
Brazil	507 790 000	466 690 000	46 460 000	41 190 000	338 910 000	359 340 000	125 480 000	123 790 000
Bulgaria [1]	548 465	569 702	616 681	609 002	2 005 414	2 014 332	D	D
Canada	15 220 263	16 658 862	25 442 071	26 667 140	9 687 947	10 200 938	2 968 065	3 123 056
Chile	8 211 660 734	8 186 561 410	4 644 923 280	3 771 441 997	13 014 692 369	12 962 144 040	D	D
China (People's Republic of)	D	D	D	D	D	D	D	D
Colombia	3 696 815 106	4 164 968 917	1 354 065 180	1 590 138 599	3 118 408 989	3 655 373 514	D	D
Costa Rica	72 301 520	91 628 892	27 888 382	33 200 912	58 995 773	143 440 076	2 253 632	5 451 769
Croatia [2]	655 556	831 527	3 175 267	2 896 329	6 141 992	5 536 779	D	D
Cyprus	672 644	755 014	170 795	174 063	538 997	594 292	124 558	133 720
Czech Republic	6 186 080	2 262 709	3 111 173	2 898 163	27 497 486	22 087 076	896 173	819 620
Denmark	6 317 000	6 984 000	38 353 000	40 238 000	11 020 000	12 066 000	23 208 000	25 693 000
Estonia	27 551	24 250	10 368	9 591	154 177	154 390	16 491	17 601
Finland	786 300	418 000	671 400	693 400	1 698 800	1 636 500	607 800	615 500
France	D	D	D	D	D	D		D
Georgia	D	D	D	D	D	D	D	D
Germany	D	D	D	D	D	D	D	D
Greece [3]	11 005 725	11 230 929	8 237 070	8 376 154	22 746 714	23 572 817	210 977	244 711
Hong Kong (China)	33 029 515	38 637 697	6 660 924	6 874 655				
Hungary	50 722 319	41 255 540	155 526 189	147 345 878	623 357 499	595 971 942	80 050 362	78 633 352
Iceland	6 590 000	3 680 000	23 715 000	22 384 000	49 465 000	38 853 000	D	D
India	4 922 468 000	8 021 103 000	5 301 890 000	7 861 532 000			33 250 000	43 710 000
Indonesia	16 109 153 823	D	1 583 276 185	D	23 743 183 930	D	1 179 013 937	D
Ireland	2 558 808	2 842 735	634 077	487 156	527 599	517 378	375 203	233 199

Table A.32. **Closing stock of arrears: By tax type** *(continued)*

Jurisdiction	Closing stock of arrears at year-end by tax type (in thousands in local currency)							
	Corporate income tax		Personal income tax		Value added tax		Tax withheld from employees by employers	
	2018	2019	2018	2019	2018	2019	2018	2019
Israel	D	D	D	D	12 274 442	16 982 699	6 918 968	7 060 172
Italy	D	D	D	D	D	D	D	D
Japan [4]	91 273 000	91 843 000	254 304 000	245 545 000	302 781 000	290 411 000	130 476 000	117 583 000
Kenya	D	D	D	D	D	D	D	D
Korea	696 090 559	739 891 298	2 374 816 950	2 445 131 840	3 874 844 053	4 113 977 482	244 446 202	226 367 022
Latvia	72 592	56 980	212 792	206 921	445 009	329 495	222 127	190 995
Lithuania	18 614	25 258	67 776	75 259	142 175	138 632	6 976	6 564
Luxembourg	912 019	1 230 066	191 116	188 090	700 052	677 856	D	D
Malaysia	6 658 418	5 352 274	3 467 796	4 715 656			D	D
Malta	468 509	491 882	285 457	307 776	2 726 688	3 494 233	134 937	167 008
Mexico	303 179 606	313 414 527	48 065 267	44 406 658	135 105 714	124 948 032	36 635 799	38 481 652
Morocco	D	D	D	D	D	D	D	D
Netherlands	4 364 927	7 370 765	3 665 518	3 788 839	3 102 059	3 145 207	1 398 889	1 675 755
New Zealand [5]	D	D	1 651 300	1 609 800	814 909	1 180 600	374 896	465 900
Norway	5 678 595	6 092 972	17 030 820	17 241 192	6 076 770	6 483 730	194 194	196 441
Peru	27 210 053	27 454 937	3 573 242	3 275 030	30 528 375	29 685 541	1 985 154	2 215 475
Poland	4 920 271	4 981 494	6 548 448	6 479 229	89 975 907	94 521 978	967 503	1 011 427
Portugal	5 736 694	6 062 657	2 236 861	2 304 069	7 162 698	7 469 982	54 229	93 256
Romania	16 987 270	17 570 732	5 176 871	5 737 808	42 590 492	43 568 602	D	D
Russia	233 894 966	214 541 475	31 403 043	31 775 230	709 304 555	649 935 620	83 789 531	79 740 168
Saudi Arabia	0	0			0	0		
Singapore	139 681	115 209	225 958	244 250	314 496	342 250		
Slovak Republic	532 602	542 396	87 907	117 414	2 324 177	2 298 722	23 786	22 902
Slovenia	58 894	64 600	285 767	295 068	417 339	406 630	338 613	309 038
South Africa	35 969 654	33 925 795	32 544 456	35 533 913	15 012 587	17 498 251	42 372 005	51 159 950
Spain	4 642 210	4 451 750	2 636 600	2 691 000	7 863 640	7 500 540	1 738 490	1 599 360
Sweden	D	D	D	D	D	D	D	D

Table A.32. **Closing stock of arrears: By tax type** *(continued)*

Jurisdiction	Closing stock of arrears at year-end by tax type (in thousands in local currency)							
	Corporate income tax		Personal income tax		Value added tax		Tax withheld from employees by employers	
	2018	2019	2018	2019	2018	2019	2018	2019
Switzerland	D	D	D	D	D	D	D	D
Thailand	57 850 740	63 646 230	113 724 690	121 330 090	161 709 530	173 591 290	D	D
Turkey	D	D	D	D	D	D	D	D
United Kingdom	1 982 289	2 228 121	4 413 294	4 774 069	3 022 304	3 569 287	2 185 828	2 657 336
United States	38 719 087	43 343 385	206 013 190	211 372 233			D	D

StatLink http://dx.doi.org/10.1787/888934272955

D Data not available

1. Bulgaria: Closing stock of arrears refers to arrears from tax returns only. Personal income tax includes tax withheld from employees by employers
2. Croatia: Personal income tax includes tax withheld from employees by employers
3. Greece: Arrears do not include interest and penalties.
4. Japan: Tax withheld by employers from employees also includes the amounts of withholding tax from sources other than salary income.
5. New Zealand: Corporate income tax arrears are included in personal income tax arrears.

Table A.33. **Verification/audit activity: All audits (excluding electronic compliance checks)**

	Details on all audits and verifiction actions undertaken (excluding electronic compliance checks)			
	No. of audits completed		No. of audits where a tax adjustment was made	
Jurisdiction	2018	2019	2018	2019
Argentina	98 173	94 055	62 515	61 387
Australia	3 400 000	4 300 000	361 107	530 508
Austria	72 517	69 905	19 966	19 214
Belgium	1 774 290	2 128 531	519 523	587 103
Brazil	345 926	482 893	344 662	481 572
Bulgaria	7 985	7 544	7 094	6 645
Canada	4 011 848	3 817 540	2 327 792	2 237 933
Chile	46 601	60 320	10 439	12 733
China (People's Republic of)	D	D	D	D
Colombia	21 972	21 439	19 168	16 872
Costa Rica	6 439	2 830	4 586	1 569
Croatia	2 690	2 393	1 533	1 675
Cyprus	78 047	73 610	D	D
Czech Republic	33 674	30 364	15 013	13 540
Denmark	63 012	61 261	41 831	42 454
Estonia	75 614	35 954	21 282	11 698
Finland	D	D	D	D
France	1 364 423	1 222 615	D	D
Georgia	4 061	4 847	3 765	3 293
Germany	372 266	355 802	273 200	258 739
Greece	26 364	27 058	12 236	12 968
Hong Kong (China)	48 079	51 666	14 128	18 510
Hungary	17 063	11 917	9 638	7 268
Iceland	D	D	D	D
India	272 178	408 793	D	D
Indonesia	160 247	158 042	81 406	54 209
Ireland	86 008	68 388	23 998	14 865
Israel	26 548	23 757	19 083	17 767
Italy	558 868	510 486	505 373	460 708
Japan	D	D	D	D
Kenya	35 018	26 159	26 230	21 324
Korea	16 306	16 008	D	D
Latvia	899	709	747	540
Lithuania	8 058	7 023	1 801	1 598
Luxembourg	33 920	45 964	D	D
Malaysia	2 019 431	2 152 451	540 649	764 496
Malta	3 100	4 050	1 800	2 550
Mexico	D	D	D	D
Morocco	7 622	7 481	7 498	7 363
Netherlands	867 343	775 243	219 939	192 850

Table A.33. **Verification/audit activity: All audits (excluding electronic compliance checks)** *(continued)*

	Details on all audits and verifiction actions undertaken (excluding electronic compliance checks)			
	No. of audits completed		No. of audits where a tax adjustment was made	
Jurisdiction	2018	2019	2018	2019
New Zealand	D	D	D	D
Norway	1 269 931	1 001 850	58 817	51 959
Peru	9 138	7 611	5 619	4 724
Poland	1 888 814	1 804 636	D	D
Portugal	32 975	30 932	21 284	19 378
Romania [1]	17 675	18 391	15 700	16 124
Russia	14 167	9 332	13 847	8 975
Saudi Arabia	17 498	53 990	8 485	37 969
Singapore	D	D	D	D
Slovak Republic	7 916	10 261	5 469	7 745
Slovenia	610 104	226 381	53 469	27 382
South Africa	26 302	9 436	11 461	6 737
Spain	1 516 764	1 511 359	D	D
Sweden	2 502	2 151	1 515	1 417
Switzerland	D	D	D	D
Thailand	77 318	76 897	27 794	30 894
Turkey [2]	135 103	128 420	61 061	57 159
United Kingdom	474 490	390 917	D	D
United States	991 168	771 095	951 521	747 962

StatLink http://dx.doi.org/10.1787/888934272974

D Data not available

1. Romania: The reported data refer to the activity carried out by the fiscal inspection and do not include information about the anti-fraud component.
2. Turkey: The Tax Inspection Board is a separate body which is not attached to the Revenue Administration. It is responsible for conducting tax audits with 8262 personnel. Information from the Tax Inspection Board is not included in the ISORA survey except for the audit related figures in Tables A.33 to A.35 which were provided by the board.

Table A.34. **Verification/audit activity: Value of additional assessments raised by audit/verification type**

	Value of additional assessments raised from audits and verification actions (including penalties and interest) (in thousands in local currency)					
	All audits (excluding electronic compliance checks)		Electronic compliance checks		Total	
Jurisdiction	**2018**	**2019**	**2018**	**2019**	**2018**	**2019**
Argentina	43 830 901	66 594 706	D	D	D	D
Australia	16 894 195	15 369 447	D	D	D	D
Austria	1 504 096	1 299 387	318 230	312 922	1 822 326	1 612 309
Belgium	8 404 243	7 057 243	D	D	D	D
Brazil	186 935 941	201 105 677	0	0	186 935 941	201 105 677
Bulgaria	1 019 141	965 016	D	D	D	D
Canada	16 477 212	17 021 044	D	D	D	D
Chile	1 298 391 748	1 268 004 709	767 709 000	723 587 000	2 066 100 748	1 991 591 709
China (People's Republic of)	D	D	D	D	D	D
Colombia	1 716 457 662	1 864 993 799	D	D	D	D
Costa Rica	214 522 709	170 746 806	0	0	214 522 709	170 746 806
Croatia	1 146 552	1 235 125	D	D	D	D
Cyprus	357 209	439 751	D	D	D	D
Czech Republic [1]	14 370 659	10 916 679	746 888	689 010	15 117 547	11 605 689
Denmark	9 342 672	5 069 527	D	D	D	D
Estonia	56 424	31 131	1 148 455	1 243 602	1 204 879	1 274 733
Finland	D	D	D	D	D	D
France	16 151 326	13 868 799	D	D	D	D
Georgia	757 760	1 432 490	3 416	2 976	761 176	1 435 466
Germany	16 245 291	17 579 664	0	0	16 245 291	17 579 664
Greece	1 898 377	1 466 349	465 673	476 601	2 364 050	1 942 950
Hong Kong (China)	2 930 617	3 154 728	D	D	D	D
Hungary	264 314 438	237 231 999	17 401 879	34 673 731	281 716 317	271 905 730
Iceland	D	D	D	D	D	D
India	1 805 980 000	4 629 920 000	D	D	D	D
Indonesia	105 227 767 539	84 986 514 986	0	0	105 227 767 539	84 986 514 986
Ireland	533 031	488 776	31 901	51 757	564 932	540 533
Israel	17 707 041	19 498 769	160 323	218 797	17 867 364	19 717 566
Italy	32 606 117	32 586 479	490 257	489 714	33 096 374	33 076 193
Japan	D	D	D	D	D	D
Kenya	25 973 692	74 191 691	6 633 369	5 366 362	32 607 061	79 558 053
Korea	6 718 444 711	6 772 528 399	D	D	D	D
Latvia	112 169	71 147	D	D	D	D
Lithuania	57 318	67 598	D	D	D	D
Luxembourg	92 427	97 239	D	D	D	D
Malaysia	11 229 591	18 965 703	0	0	11 229 591	18 965 703
Malta	35 400	51 100	10 100	13 500	45 500	64 600
Mexico [2]	D	D	D	D	191 563 500	233 481 700
Morocco	8 647 427	7 969 701	8 415 909	6 065 872	17 063 336	14 035 573

Table A.34. **Verification/audit activity: Value of additional assessments raised by audit/verification type** *(continued)*

Jurisdiction	Value of additional assessments raised from audits and verification actions (including penalties and interest) (in thousands in local currency)					
	All audits (excluding electronic compliance checks)		Electronic compliance checks		Total	
	2018	2019	2018	2019	2018	2019
Netherlands [3]	4 318 819	4 207 156	444 142	299 498	4 762 961	4 506 654
New Zealand	D	D	D	D	D	D
Norway	27 794 233	27 768 720	D	D	D	D
Peru	4 289 705	5 460 557	0	0	4 289 705	5 460 557
Poland	18 857 958	16 551 048	D	D	D	D
Portugal	1 706 044	1 630 727	0	0	1 706 044	1 630 727
Romania [4]	5 314 834	4 257 215	D	D	D	D
Russia	314 772 113	298 523 811	0	0	314 772 113	298 523 811
Saudi Arabia	13 819 890	8 533 284	0	0	13 819 890	8 533 284
Singapore	D	D	D	D	D	D
Slovak Republic	618 611	776 149	D	D	D	D
Slovenia	D	D	D	D	D	D
South Africa	8 114 887	14 017 497	27 992 928	23 823 889	36 107 815	37 841 386
Spain	14 489 000	15 101 000	0	0	14 489 000	15 101 000
Sweden	6 927 074	7 923 197	D	D	D	D
Switzerland	D	D	D	D	D	D
Thailand	24 038 379	25 211 453	D	D	D	D
Turkey [5]	28 585 413	33 929 863	10 986	18 521	28 596 399	33 948 384
United Kingdom	26 129 964	31 176 539	D	D	D	D
United States	26 514 334	17 282 170	0	0	26 514 334	17 282 170

StatLink http://dx.doi.org/10.1787/888934272993

D Data not available

1. Czech Republic: The value of assessments raised does not include penalties and interest. Only VAT is reported in electronic compliance checks.
2. Mexico: Total audits include traditional audits (such as comprehensive audits and desk audits) and electronic compliance checks for the following areas: large taxpayers, foreign trade, hydrocarbons and small and medium-sized taxpayers. The total sum includes payments received by the administration as well as those payments that were offset against tax credits.
3. Netherlands: The value of assessments raised does not include penalties and interest.
4. Romania: The reported data refer to the activity carried out by the fiscal inspection and do not include information about the anti-fraud component.
5. Turkey: The Tax Inspection Board is a separate body which is not attached to the Revenue Administration. It is responsible for conducting tax audits with 8262 personnel. Information from the Tax Inspection Board is not included in the ISORA survey except for the audit related figures in Tables A.33 to A.35 which were provided by the board.

Table A.35. **Verification/audit activity: Value of additional assessment raised by tax type**

Jurisdiction	Value of additional assessments raised from audits and verification actions by tax type (including penalties and interest) (in thousands in local currency)							
	Corporate income tax		Personal income tax		Value added tax		Tax withheld by employers from employees	
	2018	2019	2018	2019	2018	2019	2018	2019
Argentina	16 620 859	21 468 165	3 221 014	4 749 290	13 220 965	20 251 514	10 768 063	20 125 737
Australia	D	D	D	D	D	D	D	D
Austria	290 689	263 381	168 682	177 834	513 374	367 054	79 798	49 714
Belgium	3 770 687	3 036 076	3 798 397	2 979 308	835 159	1 041 859	D	D
Brazil	95 087 080	110 312 640	3 498 918	6 055 983	29 061 194	31 032 126	16 817 019	10 671 970
Bulgaria	231 972	146 728	32 284	23 577	706 837	754 473	15 820	14 628
Canada	8 448 341	8 987 079	3 518 366	3 505 785	4 356 627	4 352 539	153 878	175 641
Chile	1 028 812 451	896 326 597	16 350 472	21 575 706	219 582 618	274 312 100	D	D
China (People's Republic of)	D	D	D	D	D	D	D	D
Colombia	1 378 802 057	1 352 258 789	119 895 831	81 125 268	116 531 301	374 946 318	101 228 473	56 663 423
Costa Rica	192 067 576	149 643 163	15 039 905	3 368 897	7 415 228	17 734 746	D	D
Croatia	60 496	259 827	193 554	250 840	448 257	519 583	D	D
Cyprus	327 720	373 127	D	D	29 489	66 624	D	D
Czech Republic [1]	2 405 483	2 353 852	128 035	150 840	11 484 195	8 024 262	67 638	88 450
Denmark	3 753 509	-28 847	2 390 518	2 404 581	3 198 645	2 693 793	D	D
Estonia	D	D	D	D	D	D	D	D
Finland	D	D	D	D	D	D	D	D
France [2]	3 652 331	3 020 292	2 411 546	1 781 223	3 507 531	3 456 954		D
Georgia	155 678	105 642	80 977	156 166	149 692	346 174	D	D
Germany	2 565 691	3 559 405	2 697 630	2 581 691	3 534 851	3 288 610	793 400	810 200
Greece	534 287	434 964	299 804	309 002	551 293	493 052	2 370	4 798
Hong Kong (China)	2 145 442	2 271 762	785 175	882 966				
Hungary	3 458 712	23 468 355	6 513 379	7 640 009	237 613 354	189 520 305	12 245 685	13 835 666
Iceland	D	D	D	D	D	D	D	D
India	1 332 030 000	3 332 070 000	473 950 000	1 297 850 000			D	D
Indonesia	39 891 797 227	D	622 472 674	D	43 044 013 309	D	1 485 550 689	D
Ireland	81 493	79 271	138 676	126 558	125 763	99 046	134 343	92 856

Table A.35. **Verification/audit activity: Value of additional assessment raised by tax type** *(continued)*

Jurisdiction	Value of additional assessments raised from audits and verification actions by tax type (including penalties and interest) (in thousands in local currency)							
	Corporate income tax		Personal income tax		Value added tax		Tax withheld by employers from employees	
	2018	2019	2018	2019	2018	2019	2018	2019
Israel	7 940 350	8 181 282	4 388 809	5 132 851	4 473 378	5 111 952	904 504	1 072 684
Italy	9 167 241	10 597 423	6 326 224	5 509 998	14 029 428	15 284 947	1 114 751	919 576
Japan [3]	194 800 000	194 300 000	94 700 000	96 100 000	102 100 000	109 900 000	30 400 000	37 000 000
Kenya	10 071 755	53 313 212	1 291 868	2 628 313	12 943 701	17 602 723	1 666 367	647 441
Korea	4 556 630 993	4 459 007 544	1 521 596 542	1 623 158 853	299 587 176	339 460 002	D	D
Latvia	19 506	7 582	2 470	2 386	67 449	52 451	22 012	8 484
Lithuania	5 865	13 310	10 870	24 816	33 720	27 752	D	D
Luxembourg	D	D	D	D	83 838	88 343	D	D
Malaysia	8 294 312	14 156 455	2 745 644	4 638 882			189 635	170 365
Malta	15 000	20 600	10 050	118 850	10 350	18 650	D	D
Mexico	D	D	D	D	D	D	D	D
Morocco	4 624 079	4 198 861	642 235	793 177	1 705 461	1 997 700	1 675 652	979 963
Netherlands [4]	2 194 749	2 484 295	1 251 660	815 867	817 102	818 640	55 308	88 354
New Zealand	D	D	D	D	D	D	D	D
Norway [5]	15 553 869	20 785 714	10 922 677	5 901 497	898 285	730 131	419 402	351 348
Peru	3 448 833	3 005 151	308 463	306 650	532 409	2 148 756	0	0
Poland	1 220 467	1 381 560	1 466 841	1 494 497	16 170 649	13 674 990	D	D
Portugal	808 187	872 846	130 026	93 875	692 800	600 752	50 607	45 321
Romania [6]	1 757 488	1 385 769	126 880	138 743	2 775 698	2 257 736	654 766	474 966
Russia	135 382 080	95 337 497	3 146 661	1 745 584	153 197 359	102 847 718	4 496 218	1 997 549
Saudi Arabia	11 162 566	4 626 547			2 657 324	3 906 737		
Singapore	89 334	103 814	40 111	51 483	195 839	179 822		
Slovak Republic	146 858	310 596	8 842	48 108	462 227	409 921	100	607
Slovenia	D	D	D	D	D	D	D	D
South Africa	4 699 491	10 366 303	1 823 697	888 751	694 239	1 874 527	897 460	887 916
Spain	D	D	D	D	D	D	D	D
Sweden	D	D	D	D	D	D	D	D

Table A.35. **Verification/audit activity: Value of additional assessment raised by tax type** *(continued)*

	Value of additional assessments raised from audits and verification actions by tax type (including penalties and interest) (in thousands in local currency)							
	Corporate income tax		Personal income tax		Value added tax		Tax withheld by employers from employees	
Jurisdiction	2018	2019	2018	2019	2018	2019	2018	2019
Switzerland	D	D	D	D	D	D	D	D
Thailand	5 138 649	10 574 933	10 820 294	7 740 744	8 079 439	6 895 776	D	D
Turkey[7]	2 262 246	2 820 431	573 266	559 720	17 184 848	22 986 183	706 874	442 870
United Kingdom	3 725 304	2 856 491	4 286 072	5 101 656	8 726 473	13 927 774	1 146 643	1 373 581
United States	14 380 571	8 225 478	9 050 651	6 897 890			795 419	1 077 302

StatLink http://dx.doi.org/10.1787/888934273012

D Data not available

1. Czech Republic: The value of assessments raised does not include penalties and interest.
2. France: The value of assessments raised does not include penalties and interest.
3. Japan: Tax withheld by employers from employees also includes the amounts of withholding tax from sources other than salary income.
4. Netherlands: The value of assessments raised does not include penalties and interest.
5. Norway: The values of CIT and PIT assessments raised do not include penalties and interest.
6. Romania: The reported data refer to the activity carried out by the fiscal inspection and do not include information about the anti-fraud component.
7. Turkey: The Tax Inspection Board is a separate body which is not attached to the Revenue Administration. It is responsible for conducting tax audits with 8262 personnel. Information from the Tax Inspection Board is not included in the ISORA survey except for the audit related figures in Tables A.33 to A.35 which were provided by the board.

Table A.36. **Tax crime investigations: Role of the administration and number of cases**

	Role of the administration in tax crime investigations		No. of tax crime investigation cases referred for prosecution during the fiscal year (where the tax administration has responsibility)	
Jurisdiction	**2018**	**2019**	**2018**	**2019**
Argentina	Other agency conducts investigations	Other agency conducts investigations		
Australia	Directing and conducting investigations	Directing and conducting investigations	57	77
Austria	Conducting investigations, under direction of other agency	Conducting investigations, under direction of other agency	935	775
Belgium	Other agency conducts investigations	Other agency conducts investigations		
Brazil	Other agency conducts investigations	Other agency conducts investigations		
Bulgaria	Other agency conducts investigations	Other agency conducts investigations		
Canada	Directing and conducting investigations	Directing and conducting investigations	36	49
Chile	Other agency conducts investigations	Other agency conducts investigations		
China (People's Republic of)	Other agency conducts investigations	Other agency conducts investigations		
Colombia	Other agency conducts investigations	Other agency conducts investigations		
Costa Rica	Other agency conducts investigations	Other agency conducts investigations		
Croatia	Conducting investigations, under direction of other agency	Conducting investigations, under direction of other agency	6	7
Cyprus	Directing and conducting investigations	Directing and conducting investigations	35	50
Czech Republic	Other agency conducts investigations	Other agency conducts investigations		
Denmark	Other agency conducts investigations	Other agency conducts investigations		
Estonia	Conducting investigations, under direction of other agency	Conducting investigations, under direction of other agency	15	13
Finland	Other agency conducts investigations	Other agency conducts investigations		
France	Other agency conducts investigations	Other agency conducts investigations		
Georgia	Other agency conducts investigations	Other agency conducts investigations		
Germany	Directing and conducting investigations	Directing and conducting investigations	6 333	6 180
Greece	Directing and conducting investigations	Directing and conducting investigations	76	110
Hong Kong (China)	Directing and conducting investigations	Directing and conducting investigations	4	4
Hungary	Conducting investigations, under direction of other agency	Conducting investigations, under direction of other agency	1 590	1 436

Table A.36. **Tax crime investigations: Role of the administration and number of cases** *(continued)*

Jurisdiction	Role of the administration in tax crime investigations		No. of tax crime investigation cases referred for prosecution during the fiscal year (where the tax administration has responsibility)	
	2018	2019	2018	2019
Iceland	Other agency conducts investigations	Other agency conducts investigations		
India	Directing and conducting investigations	Directing and conducting investigations	4 527	3 512
Indonesia	Directing and conducting investigations	Directing and conducting investigations	124	138
Ireland	Directing and conducting investigations	Directing and conducting investigations	13	14
Israel	Directing and conducting investigations	Directing and conducting investigations	2 242	2 539
Italy	Other agency conducts investigations	Other agency conducts investigations		
Japan	Directing and conducting investigations	Directing and conducting investigations	113	121
Kenya	Directing and conducting investigations	Directing and conducting investigations	130	123
Korea	Directing and conducting investigations	Directing and conducting investigations	336	188
Latvia	Directing and conducting investigations	Directing and conducting investigations	221	182
Lithuania	Other agency conducts investigations	Other agency conducts investigations		
Luxembourg	Other agency conducts investigations	Other agency conducts investigations		
Malaysia	Directing and conducting investigations	Directing and conducting investigations	24	53
Malta	Conducting investigations, under direction of other agency	Conducting investigations, under direction of other agency	3	6
Mexico	Other agency conducts investigations	Other agency conducts investigations		
Morocco	Other agency conducts investigations	Other agency conducts investigations		
Netherlands	Conducting investigations, under direction of other agency	Conducting investigations, under direction of other agency	155	141
New Zealand	Directing and conducting investigations	Directing and conducting investigations	186	89
Norway	Other agency conducts investigations	Other agency conducts investigations		
Peru	Other agency conducts investigations	Other agency conducts investigations		
Poland	Conducting investigations, under direction of other agency	Conducting investigations, under direction of other agency	15 048	15 897
Portugal	Conducting investigations, under direction of other agency	Conducting investigations, under direction of other agency	4 352	3 431
Romania	Other agency conducts investigations	Other agency conducts investigations		

Table A.36. **Tax crime investigations: Role of the administration and number of cases** *(continued)*

Jurisdiction	Role of the administration in tax crime investigations		No. of tax crime investigation cases referred for prosecution during the fiscal year (where the tax administration has responsibility)	
	2018	2019	2018	2019
Russia	Other agency conducts investigations	Other agency conducts investigations		
Saudi Arabia	Other agency conducts investigations	Other agency conducts investigations		
Singapore	Directing and conducting investigations	Directing and conducting investigations	25	69
Slovak Republic	Conducting investigations, under direction of other agency	Conducting investigations, under direction of other agency	600	623
Slovenia	Other agency conducts investigations	Other agency conducts investigations		
South Africa	Directing and conducting investigations	Directing and conducting investigations	411	459
Spain	Directing and conducting investigations	Directing and conducting investigations	177	173
Sweden	Other agency conducts investigations	Other agency conducts investigations		
Switzerland	Directing and conducting investigations	Directing and conducting investigations	7505	9 898
Thailand	Directing and conducting investigations	Directing and conducting investigations	139	199
Turkey	Other agency conducts investigations	Other agency conducts investigations		
United Kingdom	Directing and conducting investigations	Directing and conducting investigations	1 007	836
United States	Directing and conducting investigations	Directing and conducting investigations	2 130	1 893

StatLink http://dx.doi.org/10.1787/888934273031

Directing and conducting investigations Tax administration has responsibility for directing and conducting tax crime investigations

Conducting investigations, under direction of other agency Tax administration has responsibility for conducting investigations, under the direction or authority of another agency, such as the police or public prosecutor

Other agency conducts investigations Another agency outside of tax administration, such as the police or public prosecutor, has responsibility for conducting tax crime investigations

D Data not available

Table A.37. Dispute resolution: Review procedures

Jurisdiction	Mechanisms available for taxpayers to challenge assessments: Internal review by tax administration 2018	Internal review by tax administration 2019	Independent review by external body 2018	Independent review by external body 2019	Independent review by a higher appellate court 2018	Independent review by a higher appellate court 2019	Taxpayers must first pursue internal review where an internal review is permissible 2018	Taxpayers must first pursue internal review where an internal review is permissible 2019
Argentina	■	■	■	■	■	■	□	□
Australia	■	■	■	■	■	■	■	■
Austria	■	■	■	■	■	■	■	■
Belgium	■	■	■	■	■	■	■	■
Brazil	■	■	■	■	■	■	□	□
Bulgaria	■	■	■	■	■	■	■	■
Canada	■	■	■	■	■	■	■	■
Chile	■	■	■	■	■	■	□	□
China (People's Republic of)	■	■	■	■	■	■	■	■
Colombia	■	■	■	■	□	□	□	□
Costa Rica	■	■	■	■	■	■	□	□
Croatia	■	■	□	□	■	■	■	■
Cyprus	■	■	■	■	■	■	■	■
Czech Republic	■	■	■	■	■	■	■	■
Denmark [1]	□	□	■	■	■	■		
Estonia	■	■	■	■	■	■	□	□
Finland	■	■	■	■	■	■	■	■
France	■	■	■	■	■	■	■	■
Georgia	■	■	■	■	■	■	■	■
Germany	■	■	■	■	■	■	■	■
Greece	■	■	■	■	■	■	■	■
Hong Kong (China)	■	■	■	■	■	■	■	■
Hungary	■	■	■	■	■	■	■	■
Iceland	■	■	■	■	■	■	■	■
India	■	■	■	■	■	■	■	■
Indonesia	■	■	■	■	■	■	■	■
Ireland	■	■	■	■	■	■	■	■
Israel	■	■	□	□	■	■	■	■
Italy	■	■	■	■	■	■	■	■
Japan	■	■	■	■	■	■	■	■
Kenya	■	■	■	■	□	□	■	■
Korea	■	■	■	■	■	■	□	□
Latvia	■	■	□	□	■	■	■	■
Lithuania	■	■	■	■	■	■	■	■
Luxembourg	■	■	■	■	■	■	■	■
Malaysia	■	■	■	■	■	■	■	■
Malta	■	■	■	■	■	■	■	■
Mexico	■	■	■	■	■	■	□	□

Table A.37. **Dispute resolution: Review procedures** *(continued)*

	Mechanisms available for taxpayers to challenge assessments						Taxpayers must first pursue internal review where an internal review is permissible	
	Internal review by tax administration		Independent review by external body		Independent review by a higher appellate court			
Jurisdiction	2018	2019	2018	2019	2018	2019	2018	2019
Morocco	■	■	■	■	■	■	■	■
Netherlands	■	■	■	■	■	■	■	■
New Zealand	■	■	■	■	■	■	■	■
Norway	■	■	■	■	■	■	□	□
Peru	■	■	■	■	■	■	■	■
Poland	■	■	■	■	■	■	■	■
Portugal	■	■	■	■	■	■	□	□
Romania	■	■	■	■	■	■	■	■
Russia	■	■	■	■	■	■	■	■
Saudi Arabia	■	■	□	□	■	■	□	□
Singapore	■	■	■	■	■	■	■	■
Slovak Republic	■	■	■	■	■	■	■	■
Slovenia	■	■	■	■	■	■	■	■
South Africa	■	■	■	■	■	■	■	■
Spain	■	■	■	■	■	■	□	□
Sweden	■	■	■	■	■	■	□	□
Switzerland	■	■	□	□	■	■	■	■
Thailand	■	■	□	□	■	■	■	■
Turkey	■	■	□	□	■	■	□	□
United Kingdom	■	■	■	■	■	■	□	□
United States	■	■	■	■	■	■	□	□

StatLink http://dx.doi.org/10.1787/888934273050

■ Yes

□ No

1. Denmark: In Denmark, all disputes are handled by the Tax Appeals Agency, a body independent to the Danish Tax Administration but part of the Ministry of Taxation.

Table A.38. **Dispute resolution: Number of cases**

Jurisdiction	Tax cases under internal procedures				Tax cases under independent review by external bodies				Tax cases under independent review by a higher appellate court			
	No. of cases initiated in FY		No. of cases on hand at FY end		No. of cases initiated in FY		No. of cases on hand at FY end		No. of cases resolved		No. of cases resolved in favour of the administration in FY	
	2018	2019	2018	2019	2018	2019	2018	2019	2018	2019	2018	2019
Argentina	110	127	51	64	493	1 023	493	1 023	1 484	882	1 037	631
Australia	23 483	27 016	4 681	6 174	385	370	575	337	15	12	11	9
Austria	90 388	89 516	36 863	34 587	1 524	1 489	30 321	31 071	D	D	D	D
Belgium	44 048	49 120	20 133	24 011	1 543	2 780	863	1 497	2 889	2 619	2 323	2 392
Brazil	74 831	81 659	257 960	265 350	25 244	20 570	123 254	117 034	D	D	D	D
Bulgaria	2 902	1 996	883	985	1 214	999	400	298	884	503	687	417
Canada	79 088	68 338	149 155	127 398	4 374	4 417	11 849	12 377	198	111	85	105
Chile	4 656	3 586	1 721	1 778	419	482	1 857	1 686	267	283	204	194
China (People's Republic of)	1 078	1 063	224	221	822	817	D	D	D	D	D	D
Colombia	2 708	2 498	1 795	2 274	791	816	4 140	4 394				
Costa Rica	D	D	D	D	718	840	330	388	738	707	336	319
Croatia	7 900	7 725	25 075	14 817					1 424	1 801	904	930
Cyprus	7 315	9 538	13 349	12 393	108	67	258	291	36	23	20	17
Czech Republic	6 192	5 173	3 351	3 161	1 014	834	2 368	2 205	429	557	203	246
Denmark					6 886	6 359	17 350	12 925	D	D	293	160
Estonia	272	214	17	9	172	161	224	189	146	136	128	120
Finland	114 700	151 200	68 800	167 400	D	D	D	D	D	D	979	1 080
France [1]	2 857 411	3 049 066	230 305	218 029	21 089	19 549	36 669	35 354	293	294	200	177
Georgia	9 012	8 444	356	817	637	791	3 066	2 979	120	159	76	84
Germany	2 272 125	2 357 392	2 357 392	2 465 231	D	D	D	D	D	D	D	D
Greece	7 552	6 789	2 399	2 050	2 533	4 536	13 116	13 280	11	21	3	9
Hong Kong (China)	80 497	95 314	41 303	43 233	54	49	31	41	2	3	1	0
Hungary	4 472	4 330	630	421	1 015	1 032	974	949	285	185	224	140
Iceland	23 069	D	2 907	D	D	D	D	D	D	D	D	D
India	24 125	26 884	304 436	336 088	49 693	50 735	92 766	92 205	D	D	D	D
Indonesia	22 573	23 815	1 586	3 116	11 541	17 840	17 840	23 400	469	2 523	107	614

Table A.38. **Dispute resolution: Number of cases** *(continued)*

	Tax cases under internal procedures				Tax cases under independent review by external bodies				Tax cases under independent review by a higher appellate court			
	No. of cases initiated in FY		No. of cases on hand at FY end		No. of cases initiated in FY		No. of cases on hand at FY end		No. of cases resolved		No. of cases resolved in favour of the administration in FY	
Jurisdiction	2018	2019	2018	2019	2018	2019	2018	2019	2018	2019	2018	2019
Ireland	7	12	1	4	1 689	1 495	3 459	3 370	1	5	0	3
Israel[2]	1 329	1 474	1 161	953					D	D	1 040	1 150
Italy	107 231	97 221	27 625	31 712	104 322	85 468	223 482	197 611	53 861	55 180	5 267	3 705
Japan	4 767	5 147	3 012	3 086	199	181	199	203	106	76	98	74
Kenya	155	512	39	116	769	1 190	992	1 369				
Korea[3]	3 245	3 727	535	568	5 090	4 598	1 613	1 975	2 243	2 456	783	739
Latvia	679	563	114	62					D	D	395	357
Lithuania	237	174	22	22	133	92	12	10	134	146	69	108
Luxembourg	1 730	1 944	D	D	253	302	D	D	57	76	D	D
Malaysia	427	290	144	182	283	169	836	799	12	21	9	10
Malta	11	23	23	31	28	17	17	24	13	19	9	11
Mexico	13 163	11 896	3 295	4 167	26 446	23 856	52 860	54 644	68 103	58 499	16 606	15 873
Morocco	107 481	83 723	10 052	43 074	1 268	1 219	527	762	175	314	57	86
Netherlands	585 000	529 000	212 000	215 000	11 500	12 900	14 250	16 270	552	531	464	419
New Zealand	35	44	12	7	26	20	48	52	18	2	16	1
Norway	12 001	7 073	1 652	2 100	3 077	1 079	2 550	2 673	49	35	40	31
Peru	23 388	26 937	5 686	7 728	5 115	5 211	6 146	5 743	304	291	239	203
Poland	134 900	D	D	D	D	D	D	D	D	D	D	D
Portugal	55 448	59 715	6 516	6 127	3 552	3 815	21 531	21 175	362	399	181	193
Romania	8 438	5 965	2 246	1 062	5 818	5 736	10 765	12 197	3 967	4 070	2 574	2 734
Russia	68 803	72 953	4 757	5 043	138 000	147 000	D	D	1 635	1 728	1 367	1 447
Saudi Arabia	29 953	75 822	8 523	18 811					357	0	194	65
Singapore	D	D	D	D	D	D	D	D	3	3	2	2
Slovak Republic	6 514	6 702	2 632	2 738	978	1 588	573	1 164	444	464	329	316
Slovenia	19 224	20 886	4 130	3 636	4 964	5 217	3 378	2 982	484	558	383	412

Table A.38. **Dispute resolution: Number of cases** *(continued)*

Jurisdiction	Tax cases under internal procedures				Tax cases under independent review by external bodies				Tax cases under independent review by a higher appellate court			
	No. of cases initiated in FY		No. of cases on hand at FY end		No. of cases initiated in FY		No. of cases on hand at FY end		No. of cases resolved		No. of cases resolved in favour of the administration in FY	
	2018	2019	2018	2019	2018	2019	2018	2019	2018	2019	2018	2019
South Africa	556 750	669 810	55 464	55 570	3 948	4 822	1 338	1 496	13	14	11	13
Spain	233 797	226 100	37 297	40 688	154 996	145 172	282 253	268 174	14 865	16 616	9 519	10 647
Sweden	155 481	155 378	14 589	12 525	15 006	13 132	8 313	8 052	2 023	1 955	D	D
Switzerland	D	D	D	D					D	D	D	D
Thailand	814	1 121	1 121	1 235					D	D	D	D
Turkey	D	D	D	D					D	D	D	D
United Kingdom	29 014	22 226	3 142	1 650	6 698	6 808	22 625	20 598	1 127	1 202	81	50
United States	92 430	85 286	58 643	70 010	D	D	D	D	359	360	13	19

StatLink http://dx.doi.org/10.1787/888934273069

D Data not available

1. France: The number of cases resolved in favour of the administration includes all decisions totally or partially favourable to the administration. The number of decisions partially favorable to the administration was 31 in 2018 and 11 in 2019.
2. Israel: The number of cases resolved in favour of the administration includes all decisions where at least one of the issues was ruled in favour of the tax administration
3. Korea: Figures related to "Tax cases under independent review by external bodies" only refer to cases dealt with by the tax tribunal. The number of cases resolved in favour of the administration refers to decisions where all issues were ruled in favour of the tax administration.

Table A.39. **Registration channels**

Jurisdiction	Availability of registration channels for taxpayers [1]											
	Online		Telephone		Email		Mail/post		In-person		Other	
	2018	2019	2018	2019	2018	2019	2018	2019	2018	2019	2018	2019
Argentina	■	■	□	□	□	□	□	□	■	■	□	□
Australia	■	■	■	■	□	□	■	■	■	■	□	□
Austria	■	■	■	■	□	□	■	■	■	■	□	□
Belgium	■	■	■	■	■	■	■	■	■	■	□	□
Brazil	■	■	■	■	■	■	■	■	■	■	■	■
Bulgaria	■	■	□	□	■	■	■	■	■	■	□	□
Canada	■	■	■	■	□	□	■	■	■	■	■	■
Chile	■	■	□	□	□	□	□	□	■	■	□	□
China (People's Republic of)	■	■	□	□	□	□	□	□	■	■	□	□
Colombia	■	■	□	□	■	■	□	□	■	■	■	■
Costa Rica	■	■	□	□	□	□	□	□	■	■	□	□
Croatia	■	■	■	■	■	■	■	■	■	■	□	□
Cyprus	□	□	□	□	□	□	■	■	■	■	□	□
Czech Republic	■	■	□	□	□	□	□	□	■	■	□	□
Denmark	■	■	■	■	■	■	■	■	■	■	□	□
Estonia	■	■	■	■	■	■	■	■	■	■	■	■
Finland	■	■	□	□	□	□	□	□	■	■	□	□
France	■	■	■	■	■	■	■	■	■	■	□	□
Georgia	□	□	□	□	□	□	■	■	■	■	■	■
Germany	■	■	■	■	■	■	■	■	■	■	□	□
Greece	■	■	■	■	■	■	■	■	■	■	■	■
Hong Kong (China)	■	■	■	■	■	■	■	■	■	■	■	■
Hungary	■	■	□	□	□	□	□	□	■	■	□	□
Iceland	■	■	■	■	■	■	■	■	■	■	□	□
India	■	■	■	■	■	■	■	■	■	■	□	□
Indonesia	■	■	□	□	□	□	■	■	■	■	□	□
Ireland	■	■	■	■	■	■	■	■	■	■	□	□
Israel	■	■	□	□	□	□	■	■	■	■	□	□
Italy	■	■	□	□	□	□	□	□	■	■	■	■
Japan	■	■	□	□	□	□	■	■	■	■	□	□
Kenya	■	■	■	■	■	■	■	■	■	■	□	□
Korea	■	■	■	■	□	□	□	□	■	■	□	□
Latvia	■	■	■	■	■	■	■	■	■	■	■	■
Lithuania	■	■	■	■	■	■	■	■	□	□	□	□
Luxembourg	■	■	□	□	■	■	■	■	■	■	■	■
Malaysia	■	■	■	■	■	■	■	■	■	■	■	■
Malta	■	■	■	■	■	■	■	■	■	■	□	□
Mexico	■	■	■	■	□	□	□	□	□	□	■	■
Morocco	■	■	■	■	■	■	■	■	■	■	□	□

Table A.39. **Registration channels** *(continued)*

	Availability of registration channels for taxpayers [1]											
	Online		Telephone		Email		Mail/post		In-person		Other	
Jurisdiction	2018	2019	2018	2019	2018	2019	2018	2019	2018	2019	2018	2019
Netherlands	■	■	□	□	□	□	■	■	■	■	□	□
New Zealand	■	■	■	■	■	■	■	■	■	■	□	□
Norway	■	■	□	□	□	□	□	□	■	□	□	■
Peru	■	■	■	■	□	□	□	□	■	■	□	□
Poland	■	■	■	■	■	■	■	■	■	■	■	■
Portugal	■	■	■	■	■	■	■	■	■	■	■	■
Romania	■	■	□	□	□	□	■	■	■	■	□	□
Russia	■	■	■	■	■	■	■	■	■	■	■	■
Saudi Arabia	■	■	□	□	□	□	□	□	□	□	□	□
Singapore	■	■	■	■	■	■	■	■	■	■	■	■
Slovak Republic	■	■	□	□	□	□	■	■	■	■	■	■
Slovenia	■	■	□	□	■	■	■	■	■	■	■	■
South Africa	■	■	■	■	■	■	■	■	■	■	□	□
Spain	■	■	■	■	■	■	■	■	■	■	■	■
Sweden	■	■	■	■	■	■	■	■	■	■	□	□
Switzerland	■	■	■	■	■	■	■	■	■	■	■	■
Thailand	■	■	■	■	■	■	■	■	■	■	□	□
Turkey	■	■	□	□	□	□	■	■	■	■	□	□
United Kingdom	■	■	■	■	□	□	■	■	□	□	□	□
United States	■	■	■	■	□	□	■	■	■	■	□	□

StatLink http://dx.doi.org/10.1787/888934273088

■ Yes

□ No

1. Note: The registration channels may not be available for all tax types or taxpayer segments.

Table A.40. **Incoming service contacts: Monitoring and number of contacts by channel (online, digital assistance, telephone)**

Jurisdiction	Administration monitors incoming service contacts		No. of incoming service contacts by channel					
			Online via taxpayer account		Digital assistance (e.g. chat, digital assistant)		Telephone call	
	2018	2019	2018	2019	2018	2019	2018	2019
Argentina	■	■	D	D	16 460	24 410	356 549	357 950
Australia	■	■	D	D	1 544 615	1 460 361	7 820 527	7 810 586
Austria	■	■	22 400	18 800	0	6 000	5 400 000	4 800 000
Belgium	■	■	8 437 163	12 054 383	0	0	1 947 061	2 193 188
Brazil	■	■	180 309 571	230 356 664	0	49 492	5 208 364	5 315 212
Bulgaria	■	■	24 901 400	25 372 787	D	D	435 941	485 318
Canada	■	■	72 685 049	87 887 084	16 198	17 441	42 229 821	32 009 786
Chile	■	■	1667170	1592702	19 650	62 714	1 296 097	1 262 856
China (People's Republic of)	■	■	D	D	167 300	10 094 000	52 803 793	62 668 617
Colombia	■	■	83 827	112 230	443 823	528 727	833 169	1 358 794
Costa Rica	■	■	0	0	0	0	76 046	94 826
Croatia	■	■	5 961	8 255	18 018	20 205	28 442	23 101
Cyprus	□	□						
Czech Republic	■	■	D	D	D	D	13 227	12 173
Denmark	■	■	53 420 000	65 420 000	63 665	106 095	3 003 115	3 489 083
Estonia	■	■	D	26 361	D	D	258 121	221 594
Finland	■	■	D	19 750 000	289 300	315 300	3 339 300	3 526 600
France	■	■	7 220 376	8 203 596	20 218	89 647	10 483 916	12 657 632
Georgia	■	■	193 962	232 832	D	D	315 400	351 447
Germany	□	□						
Greece	■	■	92 719	78 720	0	0	428 654	459 942
Hong Kong (China)	■	■	3 521 335	4 350 789	0	0	1 441 615	1 505 263
Hungary	■	■	13 214 068	13 699 999	D	D	1 040 657	1 022 101
Iceland[1]	■	■	D	D	D	D	197 771	257 077
India	■	■	24 278	14 387	68 881	19 580	1 295 867	1 198 602
Indonesia	■	■	0	0	49 675	95 187	721 910	702 999
Ireland	■	■	18 907 541	19 432 158	7 280	9 997	2 244 965	2 480 858

Table A.40. **Incoming service contacts: Monitoring and number of contacts by channel (online, digital assistance, telephone)** *(continued)*

Jurisdiction	Administration monitors incoming service contacts		No. of incoming service contacts by channel: Online via taxpayer account		Digital assistance (e.g. chat, digital assistant)		Telephone call	
	2018	2019	2018	2019	2018	2019	2018	2019
Israel	■	■	165 593	359 647	D	D	2 131 491	2 009 532
Italy	■	■	1 286 000	1 400 000	D	D	2 409 000	2 372 000
Japan	■	■	D	D	D	D	5 570 000	5 440 000
Kenya	■	■	D	41 290	47 057	631 863	337 625	294 084
Korea	■	■	287 027	360 210	D	D	4 406 554	4 447 252
Latvia	■	■	D	D	0	0	399 776	327 675
Lithuania[2]	■	■	23 744	24 252	831	6 878	978 832	827 223
Luxembourg	□	□						
Malaysia	■	■	134 136	211 600	0	33 051	425 580	499 507
Malta	■	■	D	D	D	D	175 113	220 768
Mexico	■	■	D	0	5 092 719	4 261 576	6 012 808	4 345 061
Morocco	■	■	D	D	11 860	15 245	73 351	70 404
Netherlands[3]	■	■	0	0	0	0	12 963 000	11 704 000
New Zealand	■	■	28 530 512	27 034 249	0	0	4 228 286	4 349 209
Norway	■	■	27 779 627	31 979 449	193 575	320 186	2 246 000	2 362 000
Peru	■	■	29 544 990	33 946 553	339 238	233 057	3 227 537	3 303 019
Poland	■	■	0	0	4 925	33 506	1 612 755	1 691 237
Portugal	■	■	471 278	532 813	D	D	1 768 673	1 870 569
Romania	■	■	D	D	0	0	410 710	402 052
Russia[4]	■	■	4 654 145	17 213 187	0	0	9 284 076	12 058 795
Saudi Arabia	■	■	0	89 869	100 684	22 164	851 577	967 882
Singapore	■	■	16 249 146	19 862 453	389 860	511 746	904 287	770 676
Slovak Republic	■	■	0	0	203 893	758 906	223 292	286 250
Slovenia	□	□						
South Africa	■	■	0	0	255 278	199 436	4 638 114	4 347 345
Spain	■	■	3 909 413	2 970 458	D	D	11 823 078	8 509 019

Table A.40. **Incoming service contacts: Monitoring and number of contacts by channel (online, digital assistance, telephone)** *(continued)*

Jurisdiction	Administration monitors incoming service contacts		No. of incoming service contacts by channel					
			Online via taxpayer account		Digital assistance (e.g. chat, digital assistant)		Telephone call	
	2018	2019	2018	2019	2018	2019	2018	2019
Sweden	■	■	0	0	97 682	436 725	4 997 086	4 940 329
Switzerland	■	■	D	D	D	D	D	D
Thailand	■	■	D	D	D	D	441 759	377 173
Turkey	■	■	D	D	D	D	932 658	966 902
United Kingdom	■	■	5 567 939	4 058 969	1 479 386	1 419 856	46 745 705	42 691 993
United States	■	■	440 658 352	531 483 065	0	0	65 606 011	58 613 382

StatLink http://dx.doi.org/10.1787/888934273107

■ Yes

□ No

D Data not available

1. Iceland: The increase in telephone calls in 2019 is a result of the transfer of the tax collection function from the customs authority to the tax authority.
2. Lithuania: Online via taxpayer account also includes incoming contact via email and mail/post.
3. Netherlands: Incoming contacts refer to the whole revenue administration (incl. customs and benefits).
4. Russia: For 2018, online contacts via taxpayer account only refers to the period 10 August to 31 December 2018.

Table A.41. **Incoming service contacts: Number of contacts by channel (e-mail, mail/post, in-person)**

	No. of incoming service contacts by channel					
	E-mail		Mail/post		In-person	
Jurisdiction	**2018**	**2019**	**2018**	**2019**	**2018**	**2019**
Argentina	335 529	292 583	D	D	4 546 497	3 933 620
Australia	D	D	D	D	151 849	114 455
Austria	D	D	D	D	2 300 000	2 500 000
Belgium [1]	120 808	139 640	D	D	99 539	619 445
Brazil	1 636 315	1 600 570	D	D	14 673 382	13 625 710
Bulgaria	28 695	44 141	D	D	2 444 858	2 346 646
Canada	0	0	142 374	131 828	D	D
Chile	D	D	1 261	1 386	2 060 209	1 660 452
China (People's Republic of)	D	D	D	D	D	D
Colombia	0	0	D	D	2 507 238	2 441 090
Costa Rica	34 500	54 486	5 539	8 605	204 360	152 336
Croatia	D	D	D	D	D	D
Cyprus						
Czech Republic	D	D	D	D	D	D
Denmark	574 387	642 269	11 798	8 121	96 960	98 441
Estonia	56 863	55 792	15 653	18 383	103 594	108 901
Finland	D	D	D	D	658 700	588 600
France	4 704 668	5 810 360	D	D	13 834 812	12 915 008
Georgia	17 576	12 429	16 777	21 246	298 808	313 582
Germany						
Greece	1 517	4 458	D	D	D	D
Hong Kong (China)	230 670	207 991	644 928	688 300	243 756	268 299
Hungary	33 036	30 102	9 961	8 165	2 363 887	2 279 624
Iceland	D	D	D	D	D	D
India	119 263	99 431	916 460	930 493	D	D
Indonesia	56 470	81 408	0	0	0	0
Ireland	1 743 439	1 914 646	1 163 922	1 088 844	410 276	393 168
Israel	D	D	D	D	D	D
Italy	57 000	69 000	D	D	10 335 000	11 905 000
Japan	410	485	D	D	D	D
Kenya	222 333	239 853	D	D	1 472 785	1 426 575
Korea	0	0	0	0	D	D
Latvia	D	D	D	D	213 536	267 274
Lithuania	D	D	D	D	D	D
Luxembourg						
Malaysia	20 972	40 498	6 863	791	3 413 906	3 504 972
Malta	33 048	58 169	D	D	47 244	56 651
Mexico	D	D	D	D	D	D
Morocco	117 519	78 696	D	D	D	D
Netherlands [2]	0	0	6 222 000	6 091 000	57 000	50 000

Table A.41. **Incoming service contacts: Number of contacts by channel (e-mail, mail/post, in-person)** *(continued)*

	No. of incoming service contacts by channel					
	E-mail		Mail/post		In-person	
Jurisdiction	2018	2019	2018	2019	2018	2019
New Zealand	D	D	474 538	306 454	133 427	111 118
Norway	487 636	555 620	811 274	730 247	485 407	362 934
Peru	0	0	0	0	8 510 666	8 773 990
Poland	28 684	45 127	30 590	30 482	D	D
Portugal	D	D	D	D	9 839 849	9 690 223
Romania	54 106	45 931	7 895	7 221	4 056 928	3 683 811
Russia	D	D	14 262 756	12 948 702	D	D
Saudi Arabia	7 241	39 793	0	0	100 025	27 356
Singapore	473 640	442 246	164 810	92 004	62 491	51 183
Slovak Republic	95 146	117 597	368	289	20	20
Slovenia						
South Africa	758 825	723 749	0	0	4 914 350	6 536 253
Spain	D	D	D	D	13 386 481	12 733 067
Sweden	475 369	463 393	D	D	3 356 718	3 142 528
Switzerland	D	D	D	D	D	D
Thailand	D	D	D	D	D	D
Turkey	42 626	49 417	D	D	D	D
United Kingdom	D	D	18 180 451	19 029 213	D	D
United States	0	0	7 282 176	6 995 510	2 194 650	2 359 217

StatLink http://dx.doi.org/10.1787/888934273126

D Data not available

1. Belgium: For 2018, in-person contacts only refers to the period September to December 2018.
2. Netherlands: Incoming contacts refer to the whole revenue administration (incl. customs and benefits).

Table A.42. **Pre-fill of tax returns**

Jurisdiction	Administration pre-fills returns or assessments		Categories of third party information used to pre-fill PIT returns or assessments: Taxpayer personal information		Wage and salary		Pension		Interest		Dividends		Capital gains/ losses		Other income		Tax deductible expenses (e.g. school fees, donations)	
	2018	2019	2018	2019	2018	2019	2018	2019	2018	2019	2018	2019	2018	2019	2018	2019	2018	2019
Argentina[1]	□	■																
Australia	■	■	■	■	■	■			■	■	■	■						
Austria	■	■	■	■	■	■	■	■							■	■	■	■
Belgium	■	■	■	■	■	■	■	■									■	■
Brazil	■	■	■	■	■	■	■	■	■	■	■	■			■	■	■	■
Bulgaria	□	□																
Canada	■	■	■	■	■	■	■	■	■	■	■	■	■	■	■	■		
Chile	■	■	■	■	■	■	■	■	■	■	■	■	■	■	■	■	■	■
China (People's Republic of)	□	■		■		■										■		
Colombia	■	■	■	■	■	■	■	■		■				■		■		
Costa Rica	□	□																
Croatia	■	■	■	■	■	■	■	■							■	■		
Cyprus	■	■	■	■			■	■										
Czech Republic	■	■	■	■														
Denmark	■	■	■	■	■	■	■	■	■	■	■	■	■	■	■	■	■	■
Estonia	■	■	■	■	■	■	■	■	■	■	■	■	■	■	■	■	■	■
Finland	■	■	■	■	■	■	■	■	■	■	■	■	■	■	■	■		
France	■	■	■	■	■	■	■	■	■	■	■	■				■	■	■
Georgia	□	□																
Germany	■	■	■	■	■	■	■	■									■	■
Greece	■	■	■	■	■	■	■	■							■	■		
Hong Kong (China)	■	■	■	■	■	■	■	■										
Hungary	■	■	■	■	■	■									■	■		
Iceland	■	■	■	■	■	■	■	■	■	■	■	■			■	■	■	■
India	■	■	■	■	■	■	■	■	■	■								

Table A.42. **Pre-fill of tax returns** *(continued)*

	Administration pre-fills returns or assessments		Categories of third party information used to pre-fill PIT returns or assessments																
			Taxpayer personal information		Wage and salary		Pension		Interest		Dividends		Capital gains/ losses		Other income		Tax deductible expenses (e.g. school fees, donations)	
Jurisdiction	2018	2019	2018	2019	2018	2019	2018	2019	2018	2019	2018	2019	2018	2019	2018	2019	2018	2019
Indonesia	■	■	■	■														
Ireland	■	■	■	■	■	■	■	■							■	■	■	■
Israel	■	■	■	■														
Italy	■	■	■	■	■	■	■	■	■	■					■	■	■	■
Japan	□	□																
Kenya	■	■	■	■													■	■
Korea	■	■	■	■	■	■	■	■	■	■	■	■			■	■	■	■
Latvia	■	■	■	■	■	■	■	■	■	■	■	■	■	■	■	■	■	■
Lithuania	■	■	■	■	■	■	■	■	■	■	■	■	■	■	■	■	■	■
Luxembourg	□	□																
Malaysia	■	■	■	■	■	■											■	■
Malta	■	■	■	■	■	■	■	■	■	■	■	■					■	■
Mexico	■	■	■	■	■	■	■	■	■	■	■	■			■	■	■	■
Morocco	□	□																
Netherlands	■	■	■	■	■	■	■	■							■	■	■	■
New Zealand	■	■	■	■	■	■	■	■		■								■
Norway	■	■	■	■	■	■	■	■	■	■	■	■	■	■			■	■
Peru	■	■	■	■	■	■									■	■	■	■
Poland	■	■	■	■	■	■	■	■										
Portugal	■	■	■	■	■	■	■	■									■	■
Romania	□	□																
Russia	□	□																
Saudi Arabia	□	■		■														
Singapore	■	■	■	■	■	■	■	■			■	■			■	■	■	■
Slovak Republic	□	□																

Table A.42. **Pre-fill of tax returns** *(continued)*

Jurisdiction	Administration pre-fills returns or assessments		Categories of third party information used to pre-fill PIT returns or assessments: Taxpayer personal information		Wage and salary		Pension		Interest		Dividends		Capital gains/ losses		Other income		Tax deductible expenses (e.g. school fees, donations)	
	2018	2019	2018	2019	2018	2019	2018	2019	2018	2019	2018	2019	2018	2019	2018	2019	2018	2019
Slovenia	■	■	■	■	■	■	■	■									■	■
South Africa	■	■	■	■	■	■	■	■	■	■							■	■
Spain	■	■	■	■	■	■	■	■	■	■	■	■	■	■	■	■	■	■
Sweden	■	■	■	■	■	■	■	■	■	■	■	■	■	■				
Switzerland	■	■	■	■														
Thailand	□	□																
Turkey	■	■			■	■			■	■	■	■	■	■	■	■		
United Kingdom	■	■	■	■	■	■	■	■										
United States	□	□																

StatLink http://dx.doi.org/10.1787/888934273145

■ Yes

□ No

1. Argentina: In 2019, the administration started pre-filling monthly VAT tax return for small taxpayers ("IVA Listo").

Table A.42 ADD. Categories of tax deductible expenses used to pre-fill PIT returns or assessments

Jurisdiction	Administration pre-fills returns with tax deductible expenses		Categories of tax deductible expenses used to pre-fill PIT returns or assessments Categories of third party information used to pre-fill PIT returns or assessments															
			Donations		School and university fees		Childcare expenses		Selected insurance premiums		Health and medical expenes (other than insurance premiums)		Pension/ retirement contributions and savings		Interest on loans and mortgages		Other	
	2018	2019	2018	2019	2018	2019	2018	2019	2018	2019	2018	2019	2018	2019	2018	2019	2018	2019
Argentina																		
Australia																		
Austria	■	■	■	■					■	■							■	■
Belgium	■	■	■	■			■	■	■	■					■	■		
Brazil	■	■									■	■						
Bulgaria																		
Canada																		
Chile	■	■	■	■	■	■							■	■	■	■	■	■
China (People's Republic of)																		
Colombia																		
Costa Rica																		
Croatia																		
Cyprus																		
Czech Republic																		
Denmark	■	■	■	■					■	■			■	■	■	■	■	■
Estonia	■	■	■	■									■	■	■	■		
Finland																		
France	■	■															■	■
Georgia																		
Germany	■	■							■	■								
Greece																		
Hong Kong (China)																		
Hungary																		
Iceland	■	■											■	■			■	■

Table A.42 ADD. **Categories of tax deductible expenses used to pre-fill PIT returns or assessments** *(continued)*

			Categories of tax deductible expenses used to pre-fill PIT returns or assessments Categories of third party information used to pre-fill PIT returns or assessments															
	Administration pre-fills returns with tax deductible expenses		Donations		School and university fees		Childcare expenses		Selected insurance premiums		Health and medical expenes (other than insurance premiums)		Pension/ retirement contributions and savings		Interest on loans and mortgages		Other	
Jurisdiction	2018	2019	2018	2019	2018	2019	2018	2019	2018	2019	2018	2019	2018	2019	2018	2019	2018	2019
India																		
Indonesia																		
Ireland	■	■									■	■						
Israel																		
Italy	■	■	■	■	■	■	■	■	■	■	■	■			■	■	■	■
Japan																		
Kenya	■	■															■	■
Korea	■	■			■	■			■	■	■	■	■	■			■	■
Latvia	■	■			■	■						■	■	■				
Lithuania	■	■			■	■									■	■		
Luxembourg																		
Malaysia	■	■					■	■	■	■							■	■
Malta	■	■			■	■	■	■									■	■
Mexico	■	■	■	■	■	■			■	■	■	■	■	■	■	■	■	■
Morocco																		
Netherlands	■	■							■	■					■	■		
New Zealand		■																■
Norway	■	■	■	■			■	■										
Peru	■	■							■	■	■	■			■	■	■	■
Poland																		
Portugal	■	■	■	■	■	■	■	■			■	■	■	■	■	■		
Romania																		
Russia																		

Table A.42 ADD. **Categories of tax deductible expenses used to pre-fill PIT returns or assessments** *(continued)*

Jurisdiction	Administration pre-fills returns with tax deductible expenses		Categories of tax deductible expenses used to pre-fill PIT returns or assessments Categories of third party information used to pre-fill PIT returns or assessments															
			Donations		School and university fees		Childcare expenses		Selected insurance premiums		Health and medical expenes (other than insurance premiums)		Pension/ retirement contributions and savings		Interest on loans and mortgages		Other	
	2018	2019	2018	2019	2018	2019	2018	2019	2018	2019	2018	2019	2018	2019	2018	2019	2018	2019
Saudi Arabia																		
Singapore	■	■	■	■														
Slovak Republic																		
Slovenia	■	■					■	■	■	■			■	■				
South Africa	■	■									■	■						
Spain	■	■	■	■					■	■			■	■	■	■	■	■
Sweden																		
Switzerland																		
Thailand																		
Turkey																		
United Kingdom																		
United States																		

StatLink http://dx.doi.org/10.1787/888934273164

■ Yes

Table A.43. **Number of returns received by tax type**

Jurisdiction	Total number of returns received by tax type					
	Corporate income tax		Personal income tax		Value added tax	
	2018	2019	2018	2019	2018	2019
Argentina	326 584	261 089	1 172 916	940 260	13 432 257	13 214 411
Australia	1 042 419	1 085 293	14 957 367	15 349 796	10 564 891	10 866 392
Austria	148 649	154 926	6 015 147	6 295 095	702 109	719 778
Belgium	493 613	507 780	6 900 898	6 964 838	3 635 608	3 710 883
Brazil	1 333 482	1 282 372	28 800 842	30 011 981	12 523 352	12 408 838
Bulgaria	364 745	375 828	649 174	641 382	3 553 894	3 686 355
Canada	2 389 695	2 425 961	31 243 958	29 711 995	7 599 862	7 923 761
Chile	1 399 991	1 406 406	2 685 049	2 718 922	15 673 643	16 186 920
China (People's Republic of)	19 833 366	23 081 707	D	D	304 220 122	333 828 765
Colombia	571 205	500 511	3 366 185	3 692 756	1 408 385	1 451 214
Costa Rica	134 698	130 935	341 168	327 589	964 902	1 806 694
Croatia	139 779	141 356	113 312	119 987	1 523 538	1 588 715
Cyprus	118 318	107 277	310 121	305 804	328 618	336 359
Czech Republic	548 490	559 948	2 371 721	2 404 445	4 508 409	4 735 527
Denmark	311 000	317 000	4 629 575	4 649 747	1 582 150	1 605 347
Estonia	1 368 509	1 281 689	667 695	741 621	1 319 959	1 348 578
Finland	298 200	311 700	5 409 100	5 429 000	3 940 400	3 968 500
France	2 334 384	2 563 455	38 074 285	38 281 207	24 573 753	25 302 268
Georgia	673 085	750 320	1 365 603	1 724 593	684 491	736 326
Germany	1 108 000	166 000	27 197 000	28 457 000	5 905 000	5 893 000
Greece	250 199	262 277	6 397 748	6 488 325	4 623 961	4 706 999
Hong Kong (China)	428 798	497 771	2 960 791	3 021 466		
Hungary	461 367	445 869	5 123 901	5 152 726	4 101 097	4 240 752
Iceland	37 111	40 019	293 528	293 528	151 074	151 037
India	843 552	836 469	62 346 872	63 973 630		
Indonesia	D	D	D	D	D	D
Ireland	177 270	148 610	599 644	214 818	1 144 666	1 223 368
Israel	189 646	204 129	1 124 534	1 200 635	4 214 865	4 332 541
Italy	1 488 000	1 599 000	29 258 000	30 123 000	5 172 000	5 334 000
Japan	2 896 000	2 929 000	21 977 000	22 218 000	D	D
Kenya	220 698	235 067	3 503 551	3 277 406	1 888 780	2 071 280
Korea	740 828	787 788	7 445 000	8 094 000	6 478 314	6 753 201
Latvia	95 055	177 225	906 581	1 056 024	750 772	741 293
Lithuania	201 133	180 899	1 876 841	2 243 408	872 040	899 679
Luxembourg	80 369	100 593	232 389	253 503	353 634	336 211
Malaysia	365 205	377 772	3 491 984	3 710 425		
Malta	D	D	D	D	D	D
Mexico	1 105 421	1 195 093	7 951 260	8 460 275	D	D
Morocco	271 008	265 294	307 527	197 867	1 909 391	1 901 918
Netherlands	785 900	814 800	12 078 000	12 676 000	8 839 000	9 276 000

Table A.43. **Number of returns received by tax type** *(continued)*

	Total number of returns received by tax type					
	Corporate income tax		Personal income tax		Value added tax	
Jurisdiction	2018	2019	2018	2019	2018	2019
New Zealand	365 623	374 058	4 857 489	D	3 073 003	2 985 024
Norway	332 884	342 699	4 720 382	4 943 249	1 764 146	1 815 836
Peru	741 194	753 153	568 766	591 818	11 323 819	11 839 980
Poland	911 148	967 080	57 070 840	59 353 666	25 595 161	26 610 582
Portugal	500 042	509 040	5 356 971	5 412 731	3 682 012	3 827 648
Romania	3 844 320	4 063 643	1 012 139	1 308 142	3 003 869	3 136 797
Russia	D	D	D	D	D	D
Saudi Arabia	856 789	1 733 007			515 841	673 173
Singapore	176 822	189 607	2 150 000	2 213 000	407 858	414 892
Slovak Republic	257 886	264 432	948 224	940 661	1 836 299	1 941 083
Slovenia	107 524	107 134	54 966	50 899	843 540	883 484
South Africa	1 003 823	1 340 952	6 474 665	7 017 599	3 440 647	3 760 303
Spain	1 653 380	1 682 945	20 636 339	21 137 393	14 215 612	14 473 327
Sweden	744 126	763 533	7 911 356	8 006 184	4 783 441	4 837 355
Switzerland	D	D	D	D	D	D
Thailand	5 575 193	5 920 140	11 460 408	11 838 170	7 365 532	7 670 424
Turkey	3 685 603	3 890 881	10 918 595	10 935 043	30 584 690	31 481 869
United Kingdom	2 752 759	2 950 429	11 846 309	11 879 890	8 605 052	8 703 733
United States	2 127 673	2 146 904	152 937 949	154 094 555		

StatLink http://dx.doi.org/10.1787/888934273183

D Data not available

Table A.44. **Tax return receipt channels: Corporate income tax**

	Number of returns received by tax type and channel											
	Corporate income tax											
			Electronic returns									
	Paper returns		Fully pre-filled, deemed acceptance		Fully pre-filled, confirmation required		Partially pre-filled with income and/or expense information		Not prefilled		Other	
Jurisdiction	2018	2019	2018	2019	2018	2019	2018	2019	2018	2019	2018	2019
Argentina	0	0	0	0	0	0	0	0	326 584	261 089	0	0
Australia	D	D	D	D	D	D	D	D	D	D	D	D
Austria	5 392	5 871	0	0	0	0	0	0	143 257	149 055	0	0
Belgium	3 997	3 162	0	0	0	0	0	0	489 616	504 618	0	0
Brazil	0	0	0	0	0	0	0	0	1 333 482	1 282 372	0	0
Bulgaria	0	0	0	0	0	0	0	0	364 745	375 828	0	0
Canada	239 570	214 163	0	0	0	0	0	0	2 150 125	2 211 798	0	0
Chile	4 293	3 660	0	0	0	0	863 206	962 594	532 492	440 152	0	0
China (People's Republic of)	D	D	D	D	D	D	D	D	D	D	D	D
Colombia	956	240	0	0	0	0	0	0	570 249	500 271	0	0
Costa Rica	0	0	0	0	0	0	0	0	134 698	130 935	0	0
Croatia	5 233	3 948	0	0	0	0	0	0	134 546	137 408	0	0
Cyprus	3 672	3 716	0	0	0	0	0	0	114 646	103 561	0	0
Czech Republic	42 307	41 321	0	0	0	0	0	0	506 183	518 627	0	0
Denmark	0	0	0	0	0	0	0	0	311 000	317 000	0	0
Estonia	2 961	2 210	0	0	0	0	1 365 548	1 279 479	0	0	0	0
Finland	28 300	20 700	0	0	0	0	269 900	291 000	0	0	0	0
France	52 562	144 610	0	0	0	0	0	0	2 281 822	2 418 845	0	0
Georgia	0	0	0	0	0	0	0	0	673 085	750 320	0	0
Germany	91 000	51 000	0	0	0	0	1 017 000	115 000	0	0	0	0
Greece	676	509	0	0	0	0	0	0	249 523	261 768	0	0
Hong Kong (China)	425 274	494 871	0	0	0	0	0	0	3 524	2 900	0	0
Hungary	2 912	1 317	0	0	0	0	0	0	458 455	444 552	0	0
Iceland	167	200	0	0	0	0	36 944	39 819	0	0	0	0
India	0	0	0	0	0	0	0	0	843 552	836 469	0	0

Table A.44. **Tax return receipt channels: Corporate income tax** *(continued)*

Jurisdiction	Number of returns received by tax type and channel											
	Corporate income tax											
			Electronic returns									
	Paper returns		Fully pre-filled, deemed acceptance		Fully pre-filled, confirmation required		Partially pre-filled with income and/or expense information		Not prefilled		Other	
	2018	2019	2018	2019	2018	2019	2018	2019	2018	2019	2018	2019
Indonesia	D	D	D	D	D	D	D	D	D	D	D	D
Ireland	177	95	0	0	0	0	177 093	148 515	0	0	0	0
Israel	3 091	1 804	0	0	0	0	0	0	186 555	202 325	0	0
Italy	0	0	0	0	0	0	0	0	1 488 000	1 599 000	0	0
Japan	D	D	0	0	0	0	0	0	2 128 054	2 268 473	0	0
Kenya	0	0	0	0	0	0	0	0	220 698	235 067	0	0
Korea	5 745	5 428	0	0	0	0	0	0	735 083	782 360	0	0
Latvia	647	719	0	0	0	0	94 408	176 506	0	0	0	0
Lithuania	0	0	0	0	0	0	0	0	201 133	180 899	0	0
Luxembourg	9 465	10 540	0	0	0	0	0	0	70 904	90 053	0	0
Malaysia	0	0	0	0	0	0	0	0	365 205	377 772	0	0
Malta	281	0	D	D	D	D	D	D	31 657	11 555	D	D
Mexico	0	0	0	0	0	0	0	0	1 105 421	1 195 093	0	0
Morocco	261	239	0	0	0	0	0	0	270 747	265 055	0	0
Netherlands	0	0	0	0	0	0	0	0	785 900	814 800	0	0
New Zealand	23 263	18 138	0	0	0	0	0	0	342 360	355 920	0	0
Norway	8 606	5 159	0	0	0	0	0	0	324 278	337 540	0	0
Peru	0	0	0	0	0	0	0	0	741 194	753 153	0	0
Poland [1]	248 207	55 502	0	0	0	0	662 941	911 578	0	0	0	0
Portugal	0	0	258	206	0	0	499 784	508 834	0	0	0	0
Romania	256 798	200 028	0	0	0	0	0	0	3 587 522	3 863 615	0	0
Russia	D	D	D	D	D	D	D	D	5 705 649	5 316 197	D	D
Saudi Arabia	0	0	0	0	9 937	590 460	0	0	846 852	1 142 547	0	0
Singapore	53 914	41 588	0	0	0	0	0	148 019	122 908	0	0	0

Table A.44. **Tax return receipt channels: Corporate income tax** *(continued)*

	Number of returns received by tax type and channel											
	Corporate income tax											
			Electronic returns									
	Paper returns		Fully pre-filled, deemed acceptance		Fully pre-filled, confirmation required		Partially pre-filled with income and/or expense information		Not prefilled		Other	
Jurisdiction	2018	2019	2018	2019	2018	2019	2018	2019	2018	2019	2018	2019
Slovak Republic	18 075	16 532	0	0	0	0	0	0	239 811	247 900	0	0
Slovenia	2	2	0	0	0	0	0	0	107 522	107 132	0	0
South Africa	4 231	3 312	0	0	0	0	999 592	1 337 640	0	0	0	0
Spain	0	0	0	0	0	0	0	0	1 653 380	1 682 945	0	0
Sweden[2]	406 160	380 457	0	0	0	0	337 966	383 076	0	0	0	0
Switzerland	D	D	D	D	D	D	D	D	D	D	D	D
Thailand	3 048 087	2 908 497	0	0	0	0	0	0	2 527 106	3 011 643	0	0
Turkey	4 557	4 903	0	0	0	0	0	0	3 681 046	3 885 978	0	0
United Kingdom[3]	24 495	23 913	0	0	0	0	0	0	2 728 264	2 926 516	0	0
United States	778 224	750 031	0	0	0	0	0	0	1 349 449	1 396 873	0	0

StatLink http://dx.doi.org/10.1787/888934273202

D Data not available

1. Poland: All returns that are filed electronically are included in category "Partially pre-filled" as it is not possible to distinguish between the different e-filing categories.
2. Sweden: All returns that are filed electronically are included in category "Partially pre-filled" as it is not possible to distinguish between the different e-filing categories.
3. United Kingdom: All returns that are filed electronically are included in category "Not pre-filled" as it is not possible to distinguish between partially pre-filled and not pre-filled returns.

Table A.45. Tax return receipt channels: Personal income tax

Jurisdiction	Number of returns received by tax type and channel											
	Personal income tax											
	Paper returns		Electronic returns								Other	
			Fully pre-filled, deemed acceptance		Fully pre-filled, confirmation required		Partially pre-filled with income and/or expense information		Not prefilled			
	2018	2019	2018	2019	2018	2019	2018	2019	2018	2019	2018	2019
Argentina	0	0	0	0	0	0	0	0	1 172 916	940 260	0	0
Australia	D	D	D	D	D	D	D	D	D	D	D	D
Austria	1 256 652	1 176 482	1 255 936	1 495 799	0	0	1 749 386	1 883 596	1 753 173	1 739 218	0	0
Belgium	691 209	572 646	2 424 000	2 410 506	0	0	3 752 889	3 954 401	0	0	32 800	27 285
Brazil	0	0	0	0	0	0	0	0	28 800 842	30 011 981	0	0
Bulgaria	381 387	340 514	0	0	0	0	0	0	267 787	300 868	0	0
Canada	3 943 400	3 485 808	0	0	0	0	0	0	27 300 558	26 226 187	0	0
Chile	3 931	3 394	0	0	2 532 739	2 581 616	0	0	148 379	133 912	0	0
China (People's Republic of)	D	D	D	D	D	D	D	D	D	D	D	D
Colombia	286 709	272 300	0	0	0	0	361 222	1 612 739	2 718 254	1 807 717	0	0
Costa Rica	0	0	0	0	0	0	0	0	341 168	327 589	0	0
Croatia	40 819	35 858	0	0	0	0	0	0	72 493	84 129	0	0
Cyprus	18 307	4 640	0	0	0	0	0	0	291 814	301 164	0	0
Czech Republic	1 890 422	1 888 732	0	0	0	0	0	0	481 299	515 713	0	0
Denmark	0	0	4 629 575	4 649 747	0	0	0	0	0	0	0	0
Estonia	26 622	39 917	0	0	277 905	368 879	363 168	332 825	0	0	0	0
Finland	230 200	185 900	4 025 100	4 128 500	1 153 800	1 114 600	0	0	0	0	0	0
France 1	14 959 433	12 812 962	0	0	0	0	23 114 852	25 468 245	0	0	0	0
Georgia	0	0	0	0	0	0	0	0	1 365 603	1 724 593	0	0
Germany	8 624 000	8 171 000	0	0	0	0	18 573 000	20 286 000	0	0	0	0
Greece	82 136	77 305	0	0	0	0	6 315 612	6 411 020	0	0	0	0
Hong Kong (China)	2 353 937	2 362 779	0	0	0	0	598 283	649 867	8 571	8 820	0	0
Hungary	1 042 661	794 570	2 083 518	2 149 825	838 186	940 841	475 037	676 400	684 499	591 090	0	0
Iceland	2 011	1 807	0	0	291 517	291 721	0	0	0	0	0	0
India	512 443	103 825	0	0	0	0	0	0	61 834 429	63 869 805	0	0

Table A.45. **Tax return receipt channels: Personal income tax** *(continued)*

Jurisdiction	Number of returns received by tax type and channel											
	Personal income tax											
	Paper returns		Electronic returns								Other	
			Fully pre-filled, deemed acceptance		Fully pre-filled, confirmation required		Partially pre-filled with income and/or expense information		Not prefilled			
	2018	2019	2018	2019	2018	2019	2018	2019	2018	2019	2018	2019
Indonesia	D	D	D	D	D	D	D	D	D	D	D	D
Ireland	28 530	11 839	0	0	0	0	571 114	202 979	0	0	0	0
Israel	325 562	329 117	0	0	0	0	0	0	798 972	871 518	0	0
Italy	0	0	0	0	2 900 000	3 300 000	0	0	26 358 000	26 823 000	0	0
Japan	D	D	0	0	0	0	0	0	10 430 168	11 472 798	0	0
Kenya	0	0	0	0	0	0	0	0	3 503 551	3 277 406	0	0
Korea	203 000	135 000	0	0	1 192 000	1 543 000	6 050 000	6 416 000	0	0	0	0
Latvia	180 760	159 659	0	0	0	0	725 821	896 365	0	0	0	0
Lithuania	1 403	1 733	547 860	918 438	547 860	918 438	670 335	404 799	85 702	0	23 681	0
Luxembourg	21 137	29 429	0	0	0	0	0	0	211 252	224 074	0	0
Malaysia	117 166	66 955	0	0	0	0	3 374 818	3 643 470	0	0	0	0
Malta	94 691	52 093	207 984	125 435	D	D	3 702	6 768	D	D	D	D
Mexico	0	0	0	0	777 085	1 073 891	7 174 175	7 386 384	0	0	0	0
Morocco	99 445	80 510	0	0	0	0	0	0	208 082	117 357	0	0
Netherlands	253 000	247 000	0	0	0	0	11 825 000	12 429 000	0	0	0	0
New Zealand	84 044	62 476	0	2 500 000	3 700 000	0	0	D	1 073 445	1 071 787	0	0
Norway	96 212	80 498	3 200 867	3 008 432	1 030 293	1 470 284	393 010	384 035	0	0	0	0
Peru	0	0	0	0	0	0	568 766	591 818	0	0	0	0
Poland 2	8 252 593	4 808 919	0	0	0	0	48 818 247	54 544 747	0	0	0	0
Portugal	0	0	118 933	100 275	1 635 186	1 626 648	3 602 852	3 685 808	0	0	0	0
Romania	745 136	367 191	0	0	0	0	0	0	267 003	940 951	0	0
Russia	D	D	D	D	D	D	D	D	3 032 730	3 474 840	D	D
Saudi Arabia												
Singapore	34 000	35 000	1 345 000	1 398 000	0	0	771 000	780 000	0	0	0	0

Table A.45. **Tax return receipt channels: Personal income tax** *(continued)*

Jurisdiction	Number of returns received by tax type and channel											
	Personal income tax											
			Electronic returns									
	Paper returns		Fully pre-filled, deemed acceptance		Fully pre-filled, confirmation required		Partially pre-filled with income and/or expense information		Not prefilled		Other	
	2018	2019	2018	2019	2018	2019	2018	2019	2018	2019	2018	2019
Slovak Republic	561 837	530 597	0	0	0	0	0	0	386 387	410 064	0	0
Slovenia	50 325	44 257	0	0	0	0	4 641	6 642	0	0	0	0
South Africa	20 710	19 846	0	0	6 453 955	6 769 464	0	0	0	0	0	0
Spain	397 340	80 529	0	0	5 067 248	5 552 317	10 366 736	10 493 712	0	0	4 805 015	5 010 835
Sweden	2 153 278	1 456 102	0	0	4 622 585	5 263 952	1 135 493	1 286 130	0	0	0	0
Switzerland	D	D	D	D	D	D	D	D	D	D	D	D
Thailand	2 270 482	2 115 251	0	0	0	0	0	0	9 189 926	9 722 919	0	0
Turkey	10 274	5 596	0	0	0	0	1 433 002	1 222 779	9 475 319	9 706 668	0	0
United Kingdom 3	1 318 666	1 142 923	0	0	0	0	0	0	10 527 643	10 736 967	0	0
United States	18 640 748	16 852 536	0	0	0	0	0	0	134 297 201	137 242 019	0	0

StatLink http://dx.doi.org/10.1787/888934273221

D Data not available

1. France: All returns that are filed electronically are included in category "Partially pre-filled" as it is not possible to distinguish between the different e-filing categories.
2. Poland: All returns that are filed electronically are included in category "Partially pre-filled" as it is not possible to distinguish between the different e-filing categories.
3. United Kingdom: All returns that are filed electronically are included in category "Not pre-filled" as it is not possible to distinguish between partially pre-filled and not pre-filled returns.

Table A.46. Tax return receipt channels: Value added tax

Jurisdiction	Number of returns received by tax type and channel											
	Value added tax											
			Electronic returns									
	Paper returns		Fully pre-filled, deemed acceptance		Fully pre-filled, confirmation required		Partially pre-filled with income and/or expense information		Not prefilled		Other	
	2018	2019	2018	2019	2018	2019	2018	2019	2018	2019	2018	2019
Argentina	0	0	0	0	0	33 092	0	0	13 432 257	13 181 319	0	0
Australia	D	D	D	D	D	D	D	D	D	D	D	D
Austria	53 149	55 665	0	0	0	0	0	0	648 960	664 113	0	0
Belgium	51 596	39 213	0	0	0	0	0	0	3 584 012	3 671 670	0	0
Brazil	0	0	0	0	0	0	0	0	12 523 352	12 408 838	0	0
Bulgaria	0	0	0	0	0	0	0	0	3 553 894	3 686 355	0	0
Canada	820 565	687 351	0	0	0	0	0	0	6 779 297	7 236 410	0	0
Chile	80 759	33 717	0	0	9 547 578	10 593 124	1 510 433	1 693 612	4 534 873	3 866 467	0	0
China (People's Republic of)	D	D	D	D	D	D	D	D	D	D	D	D
Colombia	549	98	0	0	0	0	0	0	1 407 836	1 451 116	0	0
Costa Rica	0	0	0	0	0	0	0	0	964 902	1 806 694	0	0
Croatia	7 412	5 149	0	0	0	0	0	0	1 516 126	1 583 566	0	0
Cyprus	18 894	13 939	0	0	0	0	0	0	309 724	322 420	0	0
Czech Republic	5 997	7 398	0	0	0	0	0	0	4 502 412	4 728 129	0	0
Denmark	0	0	0	0	0	0	0	0	1 582 150	1 605 347	0	0
Estonia	6 358	4 672	0	0	0	0	0	0	1 313 601	1 343 906	0	0
Finland	192 000	149 000	0	0	0	0	3 748 400	3 819 500	0	0	0	0
France	570 628	548 365	0	0	0	0	0	0	24 003 125	24 753 903	0	0
Georgia	0	0	0	0	0	0	0	0	684 491	736 326	0	0
Germany	498 000	434 000	0	0	0	0	5 407 000	5 459 000	0	0	0	0
Greece	17 626	17 628	0	0	0	0	0	0	4 606 335	4 689 371	0	0
Hong Kong (China)												
Hungary	2 119	1 483	0	0	0	0	0	0	4 098 978	4 239 269	0	0
Iceland	1 029	946	0	0	0	0	0	0	150 045	150 091	0	0
India												

Table A.46. **Tax return receipt channels: Value added tax** *(continued)*

Jurisdiction	Number of returns received by tax type and channel											
	Value added tax											
			Electronic returns									
	Paper returns		Fully pre-filled, deemed acceptance		Fully pre-filled, confirmation required		Partially pre-filled with income and/or expense information		Not prefilled		Other	
	2018	2019	2018	2019	2018	2019	2018	2019	2018	2019	2018	2019
Indonesia	D	D	D	D	D	D	D	D	D	D	D	D
Ireland	3 836	3 524	0	0	0	0	0	0	1 140 830	1 219 844	0	0
Israel	1 287 618	995 408	0	0	0	0	0	0	2 927 247	3 337 133	0	0
Italy	0	0	0	0	0	0	0	0	5 172 000	5 334 000	0	0
Japan	D	D	0	0	0	0	0	0	2 369 967	2 426 077	0	0
Kenya	0	0	0	0	0	0	0	0	1 888 780	2 071 280	0	0
Korea	D	D	D	D	D	D	D	D	D	D	D	D
Latvia	329	286	0	0	0	0	750 443	741 007	0	0	0	0
Lithuania	53	24	0	0	0	0	37 512	61 823	834 475	837 832	0	0
Luxembourg	17 488	6 619	0	0	0	0	0	0	336 146	329 592	0	0
Malaysia												
Malta	122 041	63 102	D	D	D	D	D	D	41 796	111 878	D	D
Mexico	D	D	D	D	D	D	D	D	D	D	D	D
Morocco	43 396	0	0	0	0	0	0	0	1 865 995	1 901 918	0	0
Netherlands	0	0	0	0	0	0	0	0	8 839 000	9 276 000	0	0
New Zealand	416 170	277 193	0	0	0	0	0	0	2 656 833	2 707 831	0	0
Norway	0	0	0	0	0	0	0	0	1 764 146	1 815 836	0	0
Peru	0	0	0	0	0	0	0	0	11 323 819	11 839 980	0	0
Poland[1]	423 323	107 204	0	0	0	0	25 171 838	26 503 378	0	0	0	0
Portugal	0	0	0	0	0	0	13 622	209 159	3 668 390	3 618 489	0	0
Romania	49 820	34 283	0	0	0	0	0	0	2 954 049	3 102 514	0	0
Russia	D	D	D	D	D	D	D	D	7 990 646	7 341 333	D	D
Saudi Arabia	0	0	0	0	0	0	0	0	515 841	673 173	0	0
Singapore	2 369	1 972	0	0	0	0	0	0	405 489	412 920	0	0

Table A.46. **Tax return receipt channels: Value added tax** *(continued)*

	Number of returns received by tax type and channel											
	Value added tax											
			Electronic returns									
	Paper returns		Fully pre-filled, deemed acceptance		Fully pre-filled, confirmation required		Partially pre-filled with income and/or expense information		Not prefilled		Other	
Jurisdiction	2018	2019	2018	2019	2018	2019	2018	2019	2018	2019	2018	2019
Slovak Republic	1 050	706	0	0	0	0	0	0	1 835 249	1 940 377	0	0
Slovenia	0	0	0	0	0	0	0	0	843 540	883 484	0	0
South Africa	393 119	525 454	0	0	0	0	3 047 528	3 234 849	0	0	0	0
Spain	0	0	0	0	0	0	0	0	14 215 612	14 473 327	0	0
Sweden	1 355 565	1 071 734	0	0	0	0	0	0	3 427 876	3 765 621	0	0
Switzerland	901 774	733 349	D	D	D	D	D	D	374 858	D	D	592 385
Thailand	3 402 077	3 211 451	0	0	0	0	0	0	3 963 455	4 458 973	0	0
Turkey	83 905	86 510	0	0	0	0	0	0	30 500 785	31 395 359	0	0
United Kingdom[2]	52 938	56 712	0	0	0	0	0	0	8 552 114	8 647 021	0	0
United States												

StatLink http://dx.doi.org/10.1787/888934273240

D Data not available

1. Poland: All returns that are filed electronically are included in category "Partially pre-filled" as it is not possible to distinguish between the different e-filing categories.
2. United Kingdom: All returns that are filed electronically are included in category "Not pre-filled" as it is not possible to distinguish between partially pre-filled and not pre-filled returns.

Table A.47. Electronic payments

Jurisdiction	Percentage of payments received electronically			
	By number of payments		By value of payments	
	2018	2019	2018	2019
Argentina	77.2	76.8	98.0	98.1
Australia	D	D	D	D
Austria	98.0	98.0	D	D
Belgium	100.0	100.0	100.0	100.0
Brazil	64.1	67.7	77.6	81.4
Bulgaria	100.0	100.0	100.0	100.0
Canada	82.1	83.8	89.1	89.5
Chile	D	D	D	D
China (People's Republic of)	84.0	88.0	79.0	81.0
Colombia	23.0	29.0	33.0	37.0
Costa Rica	99.5	99.6	99.5	99.6
Croatia	D	D	D	D
Cyprus	37.6	52.5	29.9	35.8
Czech Republic	87.1	87.9	99.6	99.6
Denmark	100.0	100.0	100.0	100.0
Estonia	98.1	98.1	100.0	100.0
Finland	100.0	100.0	100.0	100.0
France	D	D	90.3	92.8
Georgia	100.0	100.0	100.0	100.0
Germany	100.0	100.0	100.0	100.0
Greece	86.6	88.7	87.8	89.3
Hong Kong (China)	55.4	55.5	23.2	20.7
Hungary	86.5	86.6	99.3	99.3
Iceland	D	D	D	D
India	D	D	D	D
Indonesia	100.0	100.0	100.0	100.0
Ireland	94.6	96.9	93.9	94.4
Israel	34.0	41.0	36.0	42.0
Italy	66.0	67.0	96.0	96.0
Japan	23.2	25.6	D	D
Kenya	75.0	80.0	60.0	58.4
Korea	68.9	75.7	45.6	50.4
Latvia	100.0	100.0	100.0	100.0
Lithuania	100.0	100.0	100.0	100.0
Luxembourg	100.0	100.0	100.0	100.0
Malaysia	43.7	56.0	47.4	52.3
Malta	16.0	21.0	17.0	19.0
Mexico	34.0	35.0	94.0	93.0
Morocco	55.5	64.2	80.8	85.2
Netherlands	100.0	100.0	100.0	100.0

Table A.47. **Electronic payments** *(continued)*

	Percentage of payments received electronically			
	By number of payments		By value of payments	
Jurisdiction	**2018**	**2019**	**2018**	**2019**
New Zealand [1]	91.0	93.0	97.0	97.0
Norway	100.0	100.0	100.0	100.0
Peru	51.6	54.5	76.4	77.8
Poland	98.9	98.4	99.9	99.9
Portugal	84.0	86.0	89.0	91.0
Romania	47.2	53.9	84.0	86.3
Russia	D	D	D	D
Saudi Arabia	98.3	99.0	98.0	99.0
Singapore	97.1	97.7	83.5	86.1
Slovak Republic	100.0	100.0	100.0	100.0
Slovenia	100.0	100.0	100.0	100.0
South Africa	85.5	98.5	84.1	99.9
Spain	100.0	100.0	100.0	100.0
Sweden	100.0	100.0	100.0	100.0
Switzerland	D	D	D	D
Thailand	D	44.4	D	59.6
Turkey	62.5	63.1	81.3	80.5
United Kingdom	95.0	95.7	98.1	98.6
United States	D	D	D	D

StatLink http://dx.doi.org/10.1787/888934273259

D Data not available

1. New Zealand: Percentages refer to Goods and Services Tax only.

Table A.48. **Techniques and methodologies to improve compliance**

Jurisdiction	Administration uses behavioural insight methodologies or techniques		All or certain taxpayers are required to use an electronic invoice mechanism for tax purposes		Certain taxpayers are required to use electronic fiscal devices/ cash registers	
	2018	2019	2018	2019	2018	2019
Argentina	■	■	■	■	■	■
Australia	■	■	□	□	□	□
Austria	■	■	□	□	■	■
Belgium	■	■	□	□	■	■
Brazil	□	□	■	■	■	■
Bulgaria	□	□	□	□	■	■
Canada	■	■	□	□	□	□
Chile	■	■	■	■	□	□
China (People's Republic of)	□	□	□	□	■	■
Colombia	■	■	■	■	□	□
Costa Rica	□	□	■	■	□	□
Croatia	□	□	□	□	■	■
Cyprus	■	■	□	□	■	■
Czech Republic	□	□	■	■	■	■
Denmark	■	■	□	□	□	□
Estonia	■	■	□	□	□	□
Finland	□	□	□	□	■	■
France	■	■	□	□	■	■
Georgia	■	■	■	■	■	■
Germany	■	■	□	□	□	□
Greece	□	□	□	□	■	■
Hong Kong (China)	□	□	□	□	□	□
Hungary	■	■	■	■	■	■
Iceland	■	■	□	□	□	□
India	■	■	□	□	□	□
Indonesia	■	■	■	■	■	■
Ireland	■	■	□	□	□	□
Israel	■	■	□	□	□	□
Italy	■	■	■	■	■	■
Japan	■	■	□	□	□	□
Kenya	■	■	■	■	■	■
Korea	□	□	■	■	■	■
Latvia	■	■	□	□	■	■
Lithuania	■	■	■	■	■	■
Luxembourg	■	■	□	□	□	□
Malaysia	■	■	□	□	□	□
Malta	■	■	□	□	■	■
Mexico	□	□	■	■	■	■

Table A.48. **Techniques and methodologies to improve compliance** *(continued)*

Jurisdiction	Administration uses behavioural insight methodologies or techniques		All or certain taxpayers are required to use an electronic invoice mechanism for tax purposes		Certain taxpayers are required to use electronic fiscal devices/ cash registers	
	2018	2019	2018	2019	2018	2019
Morocco	■	■	□	□	□	□
Netherlands	■	■	□	□	□	□
New Zealand	■	■	■	■	□	□
Norway	■	■	□	□	■	■
Peru	■	■	■	■	□	□
Poland	□	□	■	■	■	■
Portugal	■	■	■	■	■	■
Romania	□	□	□	□	■	■
Russia	■	■	■	■	■	■
Saudi Arabia	□	□	□	□	□	□
Singapore	■	■	□	□	□	□
Slovak Republic	■	■	□	□	■	■
Slovenia	■	■	■	■	■	■
South Africa	□	□	□	□	□	□
Spain	□	□	■	■	□	□
Sweden	□	□	□	□	■	■
Switzerland	□	□	□	□	□	□
Thailand	□	□	□	□	□	□
Turkey	□	□	■	■	■	■
United Kingdom	■	■	□	□	□	□
United States	■	■	□	□	□	□

StatLink http://dx.doi.org/10.1787/888934273278

■ Yes

□ No

Table A.49. Co-operative compliance approches

	Co-operative compliance approach exists for ...					
	Large taxpayers		HNWI taxpayers		Other taxpayers	
Jurisdiction	2018	2019	2018	2019	2018	2019
Argentina	□	□	□	□	□	□
Australia	■	■	■	■	□	□
Austria	■	■	□	□	□	□
Belgium	■	■	□	□	□	□
Brazil	□	□	□	□	□	□
Bulgaria	■	■	□	□	□	□
Canada	□	□	□	□	□	□
Chile	■	■	■	■	■	■
China (People's Republic of)	■	■	□	□	□	□
Colombia	□	□	□	□	□	□
Costa Rica	□	□	□	□	□	□
Croatia	■	■	□	□	■	■
Cyprus	□	□	□	□	□	□
Czech Republic	□	□	□	□	□	□
Denmark	■	■	□	□	□	□
Estonia	□	□	□	□	□	□
Finland	■	■	□	□	□	□
France	■	■	□	□	□	□
Georgia	□	□	□	□	□	□
Germany	□	□	□	□	□	□
Greece	□	□	□	□	□	□
Hong Kong (China)	□	□	□	□	□	□
Hungary	■	■	■	■	■	■
Iceland	□	□	□	□	□	□
India	■	■	■	■	■	■
Indonesia	■	■	■	■	■	■
Ireland	■	■	□	□	□	□
Israel	■	■	□	□	■	■
Italy	■	■	□	□	□	□
Japan	■	■	□	□	□	□
Kenya	■	■	■	■	■	■
Korea	□	□	□	□	■	■
Latvia	■	■	□	□	■	■
Lithuania	■	■	□	□	■	■
Luxembourg	□	□	□	□	□	□
Malaysia	□	□	□	□	□	□
Malta	□	□	□	□	■	■
Mexico	■	■	■	■	■	■
Morocco	■	■	□	□	□	□

Table A.49. **Co-operative compliance approches** *(continued)*

	Co-operative compliance approach exists for ...					
	Large taxpayers		HNWI taxpayers		Other taxpayers	
Jurisdiction	**2018**	**2019**	**2018**	**2019**	**2018**	**2019**
Netherlands	■	■	■	■	■	■
New Zealand	■	■	■	■	■	■
Norway	■	■	□	■	□	□
Peru	■	■	□	□	□	□
Poland	□	□	□	□	□	□
Portugal	■	■	■	■	■	■
Romania	□	□	□	□	□	□
Russia	■	■	□	□	□	□
Saudi Arabia	■	■	□	□	□	□
Singapore	■	■	□	□	□	□
Slovak Republic	■	■	□	□	□	□
Slovenia	■	■	□	□	□	□
South Africa	□	□	□	□	□	□
Spain	■	■	■	■	■	■
Sweden	■	■	□	□	□	□
Switzerland	□	□	□	□	□	□
Thailand	□	□	□	□	□	□
Turkey	□	□	□	□	□	□
United Kingdom	■	■	■	■	■	■
United States	■	■	□	□	□	□

StatLink http://dx.doi.org/10.1787/888934273297

■ Yes

□ No

Table A.50. **Innovative technologies: Implementation and usage (Part 1)**

	Implementation and use of innovative technologies							
	Artificial intelligence (AI), including machine learning		Cloud computing		Data science/ analytics tools		Distributed ledger technology/ Blockchain	
Jurisdiction	2018	2019	2018	2019	2018	2019	2018	2019
Argentina	U	U	No	No	U	U	No	No
Australia	U	U	U	U	U	U	No	No
Austria	U	U	No	No	U	U	No	No
Belgium	No	IP	U	U	U	U	No	IP
Brazil	U	U	No	No	U	U	No	U
Bulgaria	IP	IP	No	No	IP	IP	No	No
Canada	U	U	U	U	U	U	No	No
Chile	No	IP	IP	IP	U	U	No	No
China (People's Republic of)	IP	IP	U	U	U	U	IP	IP
Colombia	IP	U	No	U	IP	U	No	No
Costa Rica	No	No	No	U	U	U	No	No
Croatia	No	No	No	No	No	No	No	No
Cyprus	No	No	No	No	IP	IP	No	No
Czech Republic	No	No	No	No	U	U	No	No
Denmark	U	U	U	U	U	U	No	No
Estonia	No	IP	U	U	U	U	No	No
Finland	No	IP	No	IP	U	U	No	No
France	U	U	No	No	U	U	No	No
Georgia	No	No	No	No	U	U	IP	IP
Germany								
Greece	No	No	No	IP	U	U	No	No
Hong Kong (China)	No	No	No	No	U	U	No	No
Hungary	No	IP	U	U	U	U	No	No
Iceland	U	U	IP	IP	U	U	No	No
India	IP	IP	U	U	IP	IP	No	No
Indonesia	No	No	IP	IP	IP	IP	No	No
Ireland	No	No	U	U	U	U	No	No
Israel	IP	IP	No	No	U	U	No	No
Italy	IP	IP	No	No	U	U	No	No
Japan	U	U	U	U	U	U	No	No
Kenya	IP	IP	U	U	IP	IP	U	U
Korea	No	U	No	No	No	U	No	No
Latvia	No	No	No	No	U	U	No	No
Lithuania	No	IP	U	U	U	U	No	No
Luxembourg	No	IP	No	No	U	U	No	No
Malaysia	U	U	U	U	U	U	No	No
Malta	No	IP	IP	U	No	IP	No	No
Mexico	No	No	U	U	No	U	No	No
Morocco	No	IP	No	No	IP	IP	No	No

Table A.50. **Innovative technologies: Implementation and usage (Part 1)** *(continued)*

	Implementation and use of innovative technologies							
	Artificial intelligence (AI), including machine learning		Cloud computing		Data science/ analytics tools		Distributed ledger technology/ Blockchain	
Jurisdiction	**2018**	**2019**	**2018**	**2019**	**2018**	**2019**	**2018**	**2019**
Netherlands	U	U	No	No	U	U	No	No
New Zealand	No	No	U	U	U	U	No	No
Norway	IP	IP	U	U	U	U	No	No
Peru	No	IP	IP	U	IP	U	No	IP
Poland	No	IP	U	U	U	U	No	No
Portugal	No	No	No	No	U	U	No	No
Romania	No	U	No	No	U	U	No	No
Russia	U	U	U	U	U	U	No	No
Saudi Arabia	No	No	U	U	U	U	No	No
Singapore	U	U	U	U	U	U	No	No
Slovak Republic	U	U	IP	IP	U	U	No	No
Slovenia	U	U	U	U	U	U	No	No
South Africa	No	IP	No	No	No	U	No	No
Spain	U	U	No	No	U	U	No	No
Sweden	U	U	No	No	U	U	No	No
Switzerland	No	No	No	IP	IP	U	No	No
Thailand	IP	IP	U	U	IP	IP	No	IP
Turkey	No	No	No	No	U	U	No	No
United Kingdom	U	U	U	U	U	U	No	No
United States	U	U	U	U	U	U	No	No

StatLink http://dx.doi.org/10.1787/888934273316

U Technology is implemented and used

IP Technology is in the implementation phase for future use

No Technology is not used, incl. situations where the implementation has not started

Table A.51. **Innovative technologies: Implementation and usage (Part 2)**

	Implementation and use of innovative technologies									
	Application programming interfaces (APIs)		Digital identification technology (e.g. biometrics, voice identification)		Robotics Process Automation (RPA)		Virtual assistants (e.g. chatbots)		Whole-of-government identification systems	
Jurisdiction	2018	2019	2018	2019	2018	2019	2018	2019	2018	2019
Argentina	No	No	No	No	No	No	No	No	No	No
Australia	U	U	U	U	IP	IP	U	U	IP	U
Austria	U	U	No	No	U	U	U	U	No	No
Belgium	U	U	No	No	No	No	No	IP	U	U
Brazil	U	U	U	U	No	No	No	No	No	No
Bulgaria	U	U	No	No	No	No	No	No	U	U
Canada	U	U	No	No	IP	IP	IP	U	No	No
Chile	U	U	No	No	No	No	No	No	No	No
China (People's Republic of)	U	U	U	U	No	No	U	U	No	No
Colombia	No	U	No	IP	No	IP	IP	U	No	IP
Costa Rica	No	U	No	U	No	No	No	U	U	U
Croatia	No	No	No	No	No	No	No	No	U	U
Cyprus	IP	IP	No	No	No	No	No	No	No	No
Czech Republic	U	U	U	U	No	No	No	No	U	U
Denmark	U	U	No	No	U	U	U	U	U	U
Estonia	U	U	No	No	No	No	No	IP	U	U
Finland	U	U	No	No	IP	U	IP	U	U	U
France	U	U	No	No	No	No	U	U	No	No
Georgia	U	U	U	U	U	U	No	No	No	No
Germany							U	U		
Greece	U	U	No	No	No	No	No	No	U	U
Hong Kong (China)	U	U	No	No	No	No	No	No	U	U
Hungary	U	U	No	IP	No	IP	No	IP	U	U
Iceland	U	U	No	No	IP	IP	No	No	No	No
India	U	U	No	No	U	U	U	U	No	No
Indonesia	IP	IP	No	No	No	No	No	No	No	No
Ireland	U	U	No	No	U	U	U	U	U	U
Israel	U	U	No	No	IP	IP	U	U	IP	IP
Italy	U	U	No	No	No	No	IP	IP	IP	IP
Japan	U	U	U	U	U	U	No	No	U	U
Kenya	U	U	U	U	No	No	U	U	U	U
Korea	No	No	No	No	No	No	No	U	No	No
Latvia	No	IP	U	U	U	U	No	IP	U	U
Lithuania	U	U	No	No	No	No	U	U	U	U
Luxembourg	U	U	No	No	No	No	No	No	U	U
Malaysia	U	U	No	No	No	No	IP	U	U	U
Malta	U	U	No	No	No	No	No	IP	U	U
Mexico	No	U	U	U	No	U	No	No	No	No

Table A.51. **Innovative technologies: Implementation and usage (Part 2)** *(continued)*

	Implementation and use of innovative technologies									
	Application programming interfaces (APIs)		Digital identification technology (e.g. biometrics, voice identification)		Robotics Process Automation (RPA)		Virtual assistants (e.g. chatbots)		Whole-of-government identification systems	
Jurisdiction	2018	2019	2018	2019	2018	2019	2018	2019	2018	2019
Morocco	U	U	No	No	No	No	No	IP	No	No
Netherlands	U	U	U	U	IP	IP	No	No	U	U
New Zealand	U	U	U	U	No	No	No	No	U	U
Norway	U	U	No	No	U	U	IP	U	U	U
Peru	No	IP	No	IP	No	No	IP	U	IP	IP
Poland	U	U	No	No	No	No	No	No	U	U
Portugal	U	U	No	No	No	No	U	U	U	U
Romania	U	U	No	No	No	No	No	No	No	No
Russia	U	U	No	U	No	No	No	IP	U	U
Saudi Arabia	U	U	U	U	No	No	No	No	No	No
Singapore	U	U	IP	U	U	U	U	U	U	U
Slovak Republic	IP	IP	No	No	No	No	U	U	No	No
Slovenia	U	U	No	No	U	U	No	No	IP	U
South Africa	U	U	U	U	No	No	U	U	No	No
Spain	U	U	No	No	U	U	U	U	U	U
Sweden	U	U	No	No	IP	U	U	U	No	No
Switzerland	U	U	No	No	No	No	No	IP	U	U
Thailand	IP	U	U	U	No	No	U	U	IP	IP
Turkey	U	U	No	No	U	U	No	No	No	No
United Kingdom	U	U	U	U	U	U	U	U	No	No
United States	U	U	IP	IP	IP	IP	IP	IP	No	No

StatLink http://dx.doi.org/10.1787/888934273335

U Technology is implemented and used

IP Technology is in the implementation phase for future use

No Technology is not used, incl. situations where the implementation has not started

Table E.1. **External variables**

Derived Indicators – External Variables								
	Total Population [1]		Labour Force [2]		Gross Domestic Product (in thousands in local currency) [3]		Total Government Revenue (in thousands in local currency) [4]	
Jurisdiction	2018	2019	2018	2019	2018	2019	2018	2019
Argentina	44 494 502	44 938 712	20 551 682	20 772 672	14 542 722 150	21 447 249 875	4 940 700 447	7 261 829 927
Australia	24 982 688	25 364 307	13 254 463	13 414 956	1 899 460 000	1 994 588 000	676 988 500	689 207 703
Austria	8 840 521	8 877 067	4 601 213	4 613 292	385 711 900	398 633 100	188 381 595	195 162 964
Belgium	11 427 054	11 484 055	5 089 752	5 101 824	459 531 000	473 085 000	236 500 500	238 598 700
Brazil	209 469 333	211 049 527	105 542 232	106 500 838	6 889 176 000	7 256 927 000	2 143 279 037	2 327 684 350
Bulgaria	7 025 037	6 975 761	3 327 614	3 295 081	109 694 800	118 668 800	37 865 354	42 014 100
Canada	37 057 765	37 589 262	20 344 918	20 583 847	2 223 856 000	2 303 878 000	917 946 000	958 823 000
Chile	18 729 160	18 952 038	9 391 133	9 557 893	191 214 437 897	198 495 061 227	45 693 478 256	46 054 762 407
China (People's Republic of)	1 392 730 000	1 397 715 000	783 424 134	781 074 570	91 577 425 509	99 492 740 000	25 890 901 000	27 519 459 000
Colombia	49 648 685	50 339 443	26 229 069	26 787 864	985 931 000 000	1 061 730 000 000	296 240 914 300	311 629 082 042
Costa Rica	4 999 441	5 047 561	2 445 858	2 473 778	34 937 936 000	36 295 619 700	4 766 509 419	5 675 661 012
Croatia	4 087 843	4 067 500	1 794 730	1 778 668	382 964 000	400 102 000	178 139 400	190 116 566
Cyprus [5]	875 899	888 005	437 495	448 181	21 432 400	22 286 900	8 471 600	9 256 000
Czech Republic	10 629 928	10 669 709	5 453 301	5 445 535	5 408 766 000	5 748 668 000	2 245 120 000	2 381 229 000
Denmark	5 793 636	5 818 553	3 014 756	3 026 441	2 245 954 000	2 314 507 000	1 154 679 000	1 238 147 000
Estonia	1 321 977	1 326 590	705 816	704 366	25 937 610	28 112 380	10 026 134	10 848 503
Finland	5 515 525	5 520 314	2 742 737	2 739 091	233 662 000	240 557 000	122 686 000	125 882 000
France	66 965 912	67 059 887	30 391 825	30 386 432	2 360 687 000	2 425 708 000	1 260 522 000	1 275 063 000
Georgia	3 726 549	3 720 382	2 040 890	2 032 911	44 599 343	50 002 147	11 760 969	13 349 759
Germany	82 905 782	83 132 799	43 560 137	43 577 709	3 356 410 000	3 449 050 000	1 553 846 000	1 610 560 000
Greece	10 732 882	10 716 322	4 804 346	4 776 602	184 714 000	187 456 000	88 279 000	87 661 000
Hong Kong (China)	7 451 000	7 507 400	3 964 816	3 953 996	2 835 161 000	2 865 679 000	599 773 679	567 299 410
Hungary	9 775 564	9 769 949	4 731 877	4 720 629	42 661 805 000	46 786 714 000	18 993 557 050	20 587 566 810
Iceland	352 721	361 313	212 899	217 840	2 787 574 000	2 970 076 000	1 275 334 000	1 276 399 000
India	1 352 617 328	1 366 417 754	487 622 021	494 261 426	189 712 400 000	203 398 500 000	38 395 871 530	39 404 582 083
Indonesia	267 663 435	270 625 568	132 737 405	134 776 525	14 838 311 500 000	15 833 943 400 000	2 208 112 528 847	2 240 904 412 722
Ireland	4 867 316	4 941 444	2 385 556	2 418 323	327 241 000	355 904 000	84 166 600	89 134 600

Table E.1. **External variables** *(continued)*

Derived Indicators – External Variables								
	Total Population[1]		Labour Force[2]		Gross Domestic Product (in thousands in local currency)[3]		Total Government Revenue (in thousands in local currency)[4]	
Jurisdiction	2018	2019	2018	2019	2018	2019	2018	2019
Israel	8 882 800	9 053 300	4 102 822	4 181 133	1 330 143 000	1 406 749 000	480 914 108	496 802 756
Italy	60 421 760	60 297 396	26 034 264	25 946 128	1 766 168 000	1 787 665 000	818 463 000	841 441 000
Japan	126 529 100	126 264 931	68 358 370	68 139 088	546 851 700 000	553 760 000 000	191 562 600 000	189 992 783 652
Kenya	51 393 010	52 573 973	23 057 935	23 879 160	8 892 110 800	9 740 359 900	1 620 413 773	1 722 105 327
Korea	51 606 633	51 709 098	28 272 711	28 410 822	1 898 192 600 000	1 919 039 800 000	435 558 000 000	441 148 000 000
Latvia	1 927 174	1 912 789	1 000 226	983 102	29 056 050	30 476 087	10 882 903	11 414 355
Lithuania	2 801 543	2 786 844	1 472 661	1 457 292	45 264 400	48 432 800	15 360 900	16 647 400
Luxembourg	607 950	619 896	302 721	310 000	60 053 100	63 516 300	27 248 600	28 441 400
Malaysia	31 528 585	31 949 777	15 381 536	15 673 198	1 447 452 000	1 510 693 000	281 034 000	304 818 015
Malta	484 630	502 653	235 579	243 422	12 490 969	13 390 045	4 771 900	5 045 200
Mexico	126 190 788	127 575 529	56 253 063	57 142 190	23 524 509 625	24 237 619 975	5 519 811 908	5 777 273 619
Morocco	36 029 138	36 471 769	11 918 297	12 067 484	1 106 821 937	1 140 271 551	289 763 740	295 218 921
Netherlands	17 231 624	17 332 850	9 227 941	9 275 661	773 987 000	810 247 000	331 134 000	354 351 000
New Zealand	4 841 000	4 917 000	2 721 966	2 764 798	297 790 000	311 272 000	112 977 500	116 535 500
Norway	5 311 916	5 347 896	2 799 958	2 818 011	3 530 860 000	3 549 360 000	1 993 522 000	2 079 279 889
Peru	31 989 256	32 510 453	18 346 713	18 864 899	740 420 000	769 963 000	143 784 863	153 458 392
Poland	37 974 750	37 970 874	18 391 322	18 260 472	2 120 479 500	2 273 556 000	875 423 000	938 668 000
Portugal	10 283 822	10 269 417	5 267 545	5 239 181	204 304 800	212 320 600	87 695 134	91 008 131
Romania	19 472 545	19 356 544	9 054 882	8 932 844	952 396 800	1 059 803 200	277 451 666	305 947 010
Russia	144 477 860	144 373 535	73 825 998	73 025 684	104 629 640 000	110 046 050 000	36 916 898 788	39 110 300 769
Saudi Arabia	33 699 947	34 268 528	14 019 589	14 387 604	2 949 456 868	2 973 625 643	905 600 000	926 600 000
Singapore	5 638 676	5 703 569	3 493 801	3 527 065	503 395 200	507 567 700	90 152 760	91 775 411
Slovak Republic	5 446 771	5 454 073	2 754 200	2 743 160	89 605 900	94 171 200	36 456 700	38 857 000
Slovenia	2 073 894	2 087 946	1 037 571	1 034 477	45 754 800	48 006 600	20 300 200	21 202 100
South Africa	57 779 622	58 558 270	22 947 458	23 300 226	4 873 899 000	5 077 625 000	1 415 555 766	1 475 838 298
Spain	46 797 754	47 076 781	23 065 037	23 120 097	1 202 193 000	1 245 331 000	471 730 000	487 804 000
Sweden	10 175 214	10 285 453	5 411 383	5 470 074	4 828 306 000	5 021 285 000	2 393 790 000	2 438 396 302

Table E.1. **External variables** *(continued)*

Derived Indicators – External Variables								
	Total Population [1]		Labour Force [2]		Gross Domestic Product (in thousands in local currency) [3]		Total Government Revenue (in thousands in local currency) [4]	
Jurisdiction	2018	2019	2018	2019	2018	2019	2018	2019
Switzerland	8 514 329	8 574 832	4 953 967	4 978 166	689 911 100	700 437 600	234 520 478	239 156 982
Thailand	69 428 524	69 625 582	38 907 795	38 989 896	16 365 572 000	16 875 891 000	3 462 565 912	3 530 927 000
Turkey	82 319 724	83 429 615	32 826 049	33 368 843	3 758 315 620	4 320 191 230	1 163 625 876	1 254 683 359
United Kingdom	66 460 344	66 834 405	34 329 233	34 530 463	2 144 304 000	2 216 452 000	787 183 000	810 844 000
United States	326 687 501	328 239 523	165 483 017	165 890 069	20 611 875 000	21 433 225 000	6 097 767 500	6 298 417 700

StatLink http://dx.doi.org/10.1787/888934273354

1. Population data source: World Bank, Indicator SP.POP.TOTL
2. Labour force data source: World Bank, Indicator SL.TLF.TOTL.IN
3. GDP data source: IMF, World Economic Outlook: Gross domestic product, current prices
4. Total government revenue data source: IMF, World Economic Outlook: General government revenue
5. Cyprus: Data provided by the Cyprus Statistical Service

Annex B

Participating tax administrations

Table A B.1. **Overview of tax administrations included in this report**

Country	Tax administration	Website address	Currency code
Argentina	Federal Administration of Public Revenues	www.afip.gob.ar	ARS
Australia	Australian Taxation Office	www.ato.gov.au	AUD
Austria	Federal Ministry of Finance	www.bmf.gv.at	EUR
Belgium	Federal Public Service Finance	https://finances.belgium.be	EUR
Brazil	Federal Revenue Service of Brazil	https://receita.economia.gov.br/	BRL
Bulgaria	National Revenue Agency	https://nap.bg/	BGN
Canada	Canada Revenue Agency	www.cra-arc.gc.ca	CAD
Chile	Servicio de Impuestos Internos	www.sii.cl	CLP
China	State Taxation Administration	www.chinatax.gov.cn	CNY
Colombia	National Tax and Customs Administration	www.dian.gov.co	COP
Costa Rica	Directorate of Taxation, Ministry of Finance	www.hacienda.go.cr	CRC
Croatia	Tax Administration, Ministry of Finance	www.porezna-uprava.hr	HRK
Cyprus	Cyprus Tax Department	www.mof.gov.cy/tax	EUR
Czech Republic	Financial Administration of the Czech Republic	www.financnisprava.cz	CZK
Denmark	Danish Tax Administration	www.skatteforvaltningen.dk	DKK
Estonia	Estonian Tax and Customs Board	www.emta.ee	EUR
Finland	Finnish Tax Administration	www.vero.fi	EUR
France	Direction Générale des Finances Publiques (General Directorate of Public Finances)	www.economie.gouv.fr/dgfip	EUR
Georgia	Georgia Revenue Service	www.rs.ge	GEL
Germany	Federal Ministry of Finance, Federal Central Tax Office and the State Tax Authorities	www.bundesfinanzministerium.de	EUR
Greece	Independent Authority for Public Revenue	www.aade.gr	EUR
Hong Kong (China)	Inland Revenue Department	www.ird.gov.hk	HKD
Hungary	National Tax and Customs Administration	https://nav.gov.hu	HUF
Iceland	Directorate of Internal Revenue	www.rsk.is	ISK
India	Income Tax Department	www.incometaxindia.gov.in	INR
Indonesia	Directorate General of Taxes	www.pajak.go.id	IDR
Ireland	Office of the Revenue Commissioners	www.revenue.ie	EUR
Israel	Israel Tax Authority	www.taxes.gov.il	ILS
Italy	Revenue Agency	www.agenziaentrate.gov.it	EUR

Country	Tax administration	Website address	Currency code
Japan	National Tax Agency	www.nta.go.jp	JPY
Kenya	Kenya Revenue Authority	www.kra.go.ke/en/	KES
Korea	National Tax Service	www.nts.go.kr	KRW
Latvia	State Revenue Service	www.vid.gov.lv	EUR
Lithuania	State Tax Inspectorate under the Ministry of Finance	www.vmi.lt	EUR
Luxembourg	Administration des contributions directes (Direct Tax Administration) Administration de l'enregistrement et des domaines (Indirect Tax Administration)	www.impotsdirects.public.lu www.aed.public.lu	EUR
Malaysia	Inland Revenue Board of Malaysia	www.hasil.gov.my	MYR
Malta	Office of the Commissioner for Revenue	https://cfr.gov.mt	EUR
Mexico	Tax Administration Service	www.sat.gob.mx	MXN
Morocco	General Administration of Taxes	www.tax.gov.ma	MAD
Netherlands	Netherlands Tax and Customs Administration	www.belastingdienst.nl	EUR
New Zealand	Inland Revenue Department – Te Tari Taake	www.ird.govt.nz	NZD
Norway	Norwegian Tax Administration	www.skatteetaten.no	NOK
Peru	Superintendencia Nacional de Administración Tributaria (SUNAT)	www.sunat.gob.pe	PEN
Poland	National Revenue Administration	www.finanse.mf.gov.pl	PLN
Portugal	Portuguese Tax and Customs Authority	www.portaldasfinancas.gov.pt	EUR
Romania	National Agency for Fiscal Administration	www.anaf.ro	RON
Russia	Federal Tax Service of Russia	www.nalog.gov.ru	RUB
Saudi Arabia	General Authority of Zakat and Tax	https://gazt.gov.sa/	SAR
Singapore	Inland Revenue Authority of Singapore	www.iras.gov.sg	SGD
Slovak Republic	Financial Administration of the Slovak Republic	www.financnasprava.sk	EUR
Slovenia	Financial Administration of the Republic of Slovenia	www.fu.gov.si	EUR
South Africa	South African Revenue Service	www.sars.gov.za	ZAR
Spain	Spanish Tax Agency (AEAT)	www.agenciatributaria.es	EUR
Sweden	Swedish Tax Agency	www.skatteverket.se	SEK
Switzerland	Federal Tax Administration	www.estv.admin.ch	CHF
Thailand	The Revenue Department	www.rd.go.th	THB
Turkey	Turkish Revenue Administration	www.gib.gov.tr	TRY
United Kingdom	Her Majesty's Revenue and Customs	www.hmrc.gov.uk	GBP
United States	Internal Revenue Service	www.irs.gov	USD

www.ingramcontent.com/pod-product-compliance
Ingram Content Group UK Ltd.
Pitfield, Milton Keynes, MK11 3LW, UK
UKHW051457290926
15471UKWH00008B/1248

9 789264 870765